ILL-GOTTEN GAINS

ILL-GOTTEN GAINS

Evasion, Blackmail, Fraud, and Kindred Puzzles of the Law

Leo Katz

THE UNIVERSITY OF CHICAGO PRESS • CHICAGO & LONDON

LEO KATZ is professor of law at the University of Pennsylvania. He is the author of *Bad Acts and Guilty Minds: Conundrums of the Criminal Law,* published by the University of Chicago Press in 1987.

Pages 24–59 of Part One, this volume, originally appeared as "Evading Responsibility: The Ethics of Ingenuity" (Leo Katz), in *Jahrbuch für Recht und Ethik: Annual Review of Law and Ethics,* 2:191–223 (Berlin: Duncker & Humblot, 1994). Reprinted with permission.

Pages 133–169 of Part Two, this volume, originally appeared as "Blackmail and Other Forms of Arm-Twisting" (Leo Katz), in the *University of Pennsylvania Law Review* 141 (1993): 1567. Reprinted with permission of the *University of Pennsylvania Law Review* and of Fred B. Rothman and Co., Littleton, Colorado.

Pages 171–173 and 178–195 of Part Two, this volume, originally appeared as "Crime, Consent, and Insider Trading" (Leo Katz), in the *Journal of Contemporary Legal Issues* 5 (Spring 1994): 212–235. Reprinted with permission.

The University of Chicago Press, Chicago 60637
The University of Chicago Press, Ltd., London
© 1996 by The University of Chicago
All rights reserved. Published 1996
Printed in the United States of America

05 04 03 02 01 00 99 98 97 96   1 2 3 4 5
ISBN: 0-226-42593-2 (cloth)
       0-226-42594-0 (paper)

Library of Congress Cataloging-in-Publication Data
Katz, Leo.
    Ill-gotten gains : evasion, blackmail, fraud, and kindred puzzles
of the law / Leo Katz.
        p.   cm.
    Includes bibliographical references and index.
    1. Commercial crimes—United States.   2. Fraud—United States.
3. Extortion—United States.   4. Tax evasion—United States.
5. Insider trading in securities—Law and legislation—United
States.   I. Title.
KF9350.K38   1996
364.1′63—dc20   95-32038
                                                          CIP

♾ The paper used in this publication meets the minimum requirements of the American National Standard for Information Sciences—Permanence of Paper for Printed Library Materials, ANSI Z39.48-1984.

For Debórah

Contents

CONTENTS

Unsolved Crimes: An Introduction

THIS BOOK AIMS to solve three related mysteries. They are not, I should warn you, of the "who-done-it" variety. They are rather "what's-wrong-with-it" kind of mysteries, but I have found them to be as alluring and perplexing as the best who-done-its.

What unites these three mysteries and leads me to treat them within one book is that they all involve legally and morally puzzling forms of theft. Or perhaps I should say "misappropriation," since theft tends to make people think of bank robbers, burglars, and pickpockets, and these are not the sorts of thieves I am concerned with here. It is blackmailers, tax evaders, insider traders, scheming lawyers, plagiarizers, unjust prize committees, cheaters, con men, and ruthless bargainers who are more within my target range; it is their activities that raise the legal and moral mysteries I propose to unravel. If that sounds like a somewhat specialized subject, or maybe just a hodgepodge, let me assure you it is not. But before explaining my subject's larger significance and how its various parts hang together, I will need to explain just what those mysteries are that I mean to solve.

The first of my what's-wrong-with-it mysteries involves the phenomenon of evasion. Tax evasion is the best known but by no means most important illustration of this phenomenon. Schemes reeking of evasion are ubiquitous throughout the law. Perhaps the most commonplace experience for a lawyer is for a client to say that there is something he would like to do that is ostensibly illegal, or at least subject to heavy taxes, fines, or other burdens and restrictions, and does the lawyer know some way of doing "the same thing" without running afoul of the law? Often the lawyer does. Indeed, lawyers have proved infinitely resourceful at coming up with such schemes. "You would like to change your visiting visa into a greencard, but seem to have no grounds for doing so? Well, why don't you make some statement that would cause you to be persecuted in your home country, and then ask for political asylum," the lawyer might say. Or: "You want to make a movie full of steamy sex but don't want to be subject to an obscenity suit? Well, why don't you load it up with some important social message and that way it no longer qualifies as obscene." Or: "You would like to disinherit your wife and leave your property to your children instead, but you realize that the law automatically awards a fixed percentage of your estate to her? Well, why don't you just give your property away to your children as you see death approaching? Or better yet, why don't you put it all in a joint bank account with your various children, and when you die it goes straight to them instead of your wife." Or: "You are self-employed and would like to qualify for unemployment insurance when you run out of work, even though the law does not make unemployment insurance available to the self-employed? Well, why don't you get together with a bunch of other self-employed workers, form a corporation and declare yourself its employees?" Of course the advice is rarely put this crassly, and the schemes are rarely so straightforward. But that aside, my examples are not unrepresentative. Are such schemes wrong? Legally? Morally? Courts have sometimes approved of them and sometimes not. Sometimes a judge will grudgingly compliment the lawyer on his clever maneuver, or even heartily congratulate him on his deft avoidance of a legal land mine; at other times the judge will denounce what was done as a farce, a sham, a fraud, an evasion of the law, a crime, and insist that it be undone; he might in an extreme case even call for the punishment of both lawyer and client. There is no body of law, indeed there is hardly a rule, that does not harbor the opportunity for such schemes. But are they really wrong? If not all of them, which? And why? Figuring out whether there is anything wrong with "avoision" (as such practices, hovering in the limbo between legitimate avoidance and illegitimate evasion, are sometimes called) makes up the first and longest of the three parts of this book.

The second of my what's-wrong-with-it mysteries is what is known as "the paradox of blackmail." A fellow with the conveniently descriptive name of Busybody approaches another fellow—let us call him Philanderer because that is what he is—and says to him with refreshing candor: "Pay me $10,000 or I'll reveal your infidelities to your wife." This being exactly what Philanderer dreads most, he pays up. Busybody, as everyone recognizes, is guilty of a crime—blackmail. What no one knows, or at least no one can agree on, is *why* blackmail is a crime. How is it different from an ordinary bargain? It happens all the time that one person is able to threaten to do something that would greatly displease another and in return for money desists. Most of the time we don't view that as blackmail. If a bank threatens to foreclose but is willing to desist if you repay your loan, or if a car dealer threatens to sell the car you have your eye on to another customer but is willing to desist if you top that other's offer, they are both threatening to do something that would displease you and offering to desist in return for money. Yet we wouldn't call that blackmail. What then is so terrible about what Busybody did? "Poetry is indispensable—if only I knew what for," Jean Cocteau once said. And that's how it seems to be with blackmail: everybody thinks blackmail is an indispensable part of a well-developed criminal code, but no one is sure what for. Figuring out what for is the primary focus of Part Two of this book.

Although the primary, it is not the only focus of Part Two. Once we have a solution to blackmail in hand, it will equip us to deal with some other long-standing puzzles, the puzzlingest of which is probably insider trading. Insider trading, like blackmail, is something everyone abhors and no one can say why. Economists have shown that under a variety of plausible circumstances insider trading is actually beneficial for all shareholders and investors, because, for instance, it can be used as a particularly efficient form of incentive compensation for corporate executives. For this reason many shareholders would be perfectly agreeable if their corporation would add a provision into its charter expressly authorizing its executives to engage in insider trading. Yet many people, even after they have grasped the economic case to be made for insider trading, continue to regard it as somehow immoral even if economically desirable. And the law certainly forbids companies to allow their executives to engage in insider trading, even if their shareholders should expressly authorize it. But no one to date has been able to explain why insider trading is immoral and why it continues to be immoral even if the shareholders unanimously authorize the management to engage in it. My account of blackmail will enable us to do so.

My third what's-wrong-with-it mystery concerns undeserved glory. Glory may not seem like something the law has much to say about. To be sure, there is the law of patents and copyright, but that's really about royalties, and there is the law of libel, but that's about reputation generally. The medals, prizes, and memorials by which glory is dispensed are largely out of the hands of the law. But they are well within the bounds of morality, and a morality whose principles seem rather similar to those employed in the law. They are also something about which we care as intensely as about those goods and interests the law expressly regulates. Glory can be stolen even if there is no criminal statute called "Theft of Glory"—and even if the theft is not carried out by its beneficiaries but by thoughtless historians or mapmakers who end up robbing Columbus to give to Amerigo.

Thinking about glory and who deserves it gives rise to a cluster of what's-wrong-with-it questions. A number of historians of science have pointed out that when Copernicus put forth the heliocentric idea, and when Alfred Wegener put forth his idea about Contintental Drift, they had no rational grounds for so fervently believing in the rightness of their ideas. In the end, lucky for them, they turned out to be right. But that still doesn't prove their rationality in the first place. This then raises the question: Is it wrong for us to honor, admire, celebrate, or glorify two scientists who were in essence lucky fools? Do they really have an honest claim to their fame? Some historians of science have attempted a similar debunking job on Alexander Fleming, the discoverer of penicillin. They have pointed out that however inestimable the practical value of penicillin, Fleming displayed no more than uncanny luck and the presence of mind to seize it. So are we wrong to honor, admire, celebrate, or glorify him as much as we do? Does he have an honest claim to his fame?

Others yet have suggested that there is something wrong in the honor usually bestowed on the discoverers of insulin—Frederick Banting and Charles Best—because they achieved their breakthrough in the course of a "wrongly conceived, wrongly conducted, and wrongly interpreted series of experiments." Their discovery, in the words of a marginally kinder critic, simply "proved to have resulted from a stumble into the right road where it crossed the course laid down by faulty conception."[1] Are we wrong, then, to glorify them? Was it wrong to give Banting the Nobel Prize in medicine? And speaking of the Nobel Prize: a recent book suggests that the German physicist Werner Heisenberg deliberately failed to develop the atom bomb for Hitler, although he could have, thus of course averting a calamity of unimaginable proportions. Would it be wrong, then, to give him a Nobel Peace Prize for that? Part Three will seek to figure out the rules that govern the proper allocation of glory.

Why bother with the particular kinds of ill-gotten gains with which this book concerns itself? Beyond the intrinsic intellectual interest they hold, they turn out to be among the most striking manifestations of a central feature of our legal and moral thinking, its nonutilitarian character. The general philosophical pros and cons of utilitarianism have been debated for more than a century, but the implications of a nonutilitarian perspective for law have only recently begun to be worked out. This book is an effort along those lines. Furthermore, I develop an approach in the course of thinking through evasion which will then lend itself to sorting out blackmail, insider trading, the misappropriation of glory, and a host of other topics touched on along the way.

The obvious candidates to read this book are of course lawyers and philosophers interested in ethics. I want to issue a special invitation, however, to economists. I believe that I am merely uttering a truism when I say that most economic thinking is a brand of utilitarianism. (More persnickety modern philosophers say consequentialism!) But when you scratch most economists, they turn out to be as non-utilitarian as the rest of us: they don't think that letting a stranger a continent away die unaided, for example by not contributing at least money to help him, is as bad as firing a bullet into a neighbor's neck, even if from a utilitarian point of view the two are hard to distinguish. Of course, most economists don't think there is anything very incompatible between this particular intuition and the way they ordinarily think. This book will attempt to show them that, by doing little more than conceding that the act of killing is worse than not contributing money to help save a life, they are committed to abandoning much of what they generally believe, and that once they do so they can understand much that ordinary economic analysis has real trouble explaining. Nothing in this book is hostile to economics, because it is not inherent in the subject that it be utilitarian, although that is the way it currently conducts most of its business. One of my grander hopes is to persuade the economists of the fruitfulness of departing from that paradigm, or at least to show them what happens if one does. It is only fair to admit that this is really less radical than it sounds. Amartya Sen, Robert Nozick, and others have with increasing force insisted over the last two decades on the incompatibility between being a utilitarian and a libertarian. Yet most economists continue to think that they can be both. They can't. That lesson and its ramifications is one of the things this book means especially to drive home.

In the hope of making you actually sit still for that lesson, I want to draw your attention to an observation by the philosopher of science Howard Margolis which has certainly made me more tolerant of things that at first glance seemed pure folly, especially when they concerned something "in my field." In the introduction to *Patterns, Thinking, and Cognition* Margolis writes:

> [A]n unconventional analysis is almost inevitably first seen (above all, first
> seen by some of its most expert first readers) in a way that lets each bit look
> familiar (look like something already known), or confused, or wrong.
> Hence the pervasiveness of the "where new, not true; where true, not new"
> response to novelty. Naturally, I cannot realistically feel sure that this study
> will be among the fortunate ones that survive that phase. But that it will
> have to go through that phase is probably the most reliable empirical regu-
> larity in the sociology of science.[2]

And who knows, maybe quoting Margolis will serve as the sort of inoculation that might actually shorten that phase.

I have mentioned lawyers, philosophers, and economists; but what about the general reader? Neither the subject matter nor the style of this book strikes me as esoteric. Indeed, being wrapped up in the subject matter as I am, I cannot think of a reader who would not want to read about it. I have tried to write it as though everyone would.

And, finally, a rhetorical point. There are more than a few things written here which at least on first encounter are going to strike nearly all readers as the height of absurdity: for example, that form should prevail over substance, that one cannot be a libertarian and believe in freedom of contract, that prizes and medals are not meant to encourage what they reward. Thus it was often tempting for me to hedge my bet and soften with qualifiers claims likely to elicit such a reaction, however true they appeared to me. But when so tempted I remembered the scornful way in which a reviewer once dismissed a book that was, he said, written as though the author had to defend every word in court. Seeking to avoid that reviewer's scorn, I have thrown to the winds much lawyerly caution and tried to forget whatever I knew about the drafting of a trust indenture. Instead, I have taken to heart one of the lesser-known pieces of advice in Strunk and White's *Elements of Style*. "When you don't know how to say a word, say it loud. . . . Why compound ignorance with inaudibility?"

Avoidance and Evasion

THE PROBLEM

I HAVE READ somewhere, and I do not remember where, a shrewd bit of marriage advice credited to F. Scott Fitzgerald: "Don't marry for money," he is supposed to have said, "go where the money is, then marry for love." What charmed
me about this statement when I first read it was the whiff of unabashed immorality
that surrounds it. What has come to fascinate me about it since then is that it seems
to epitomize much of the advice that good lawyers give their clients, advice that
consists of shrewd stratagems surrounded by the whiff of unabashed immorality.
The question one wants to ask about such advice is whether it only seems immoral,
or whether it really is. And if it is immoral, why isn't it illegal? Or *is it* illegal? But
then how can good lawyers give it?

What to make of such advice and such stratagems is one of the most enduring
puzzles of the law. Before I actually try to solve it, however, I will need to get it
properly stated, and the best way to do that is with an example. The example I am
about to offer may strike you at first as disconcertingly exotic, too unusual and
atypical to be illuminating; but I think you will quickly change your mind about
that. The lessons it teaches—better than a less-exotic hypothetical would—turn
out to be of the utmost generality.

The hypothetical is one with which I have been bugging various of my law
school colleagues for some time. Once upon a time there were two fiercely ambitious, aspiring actresses named Mildred and Abigail. They were of the same age,
looked vaguely alike, and often found themselves competing for the same part.
Alas, Abigail tended to be much the more successful of the two. Many a part that
was almost Mildred's ultimately eluded her when Abigail applied for it and was
found to be "just like Mildred, only better." As time passed, Mildred became increasingly jealous. One day, a truly attractive part was being offered up. Mildred
became convinced that that part would make her career if she could get it. She was
also convinced that she could get it only if Abigail stayed away from the audition,
but Abigail, of course, had no intention of doing that. Mildred, however, happened

to know that Abigail had been unfaithful to her husband on several occasions, and she decided to put that knowledge to good use.

What Mildred contemplated doing was to call up Abigail and tell her flat-out that, unless she stayed away from the audition that was to take place next Wednesday between nine and twelve in the morning, Mildred would tell her husband about those affairs. But then she had second thoughts. She worried that what she was about to do amounted to blackmail and that Abigail just might retaliate by reporting her threat to the police. She was correct, of course, in so thinking, for blackmail is what it would indisputably be. To be sure, the typical blackmailer seeks money, not a theatrical part, in return for not implementing his threat, but that's a difference without a distinction.

Having discarded her original plan, Mildred came up, however, with an alternative. She wrote out a detailed report of Abigail's infidelities, put it in an envelope addressed to Abigail's husband and mailed it off by next-day delivery the day before the audition. She then called up Abigail and told her the letter was in the mail, due to arrive the next day sometime between nine and twelve. "You can draw your own conclusions," she said. As expected, Abigail stayed home to intercept the letter before her husband could see it, and thus she was unable to make it to the audition.[1]

The question I then ask my colleagues is simply whether they think Mildred's stratagem works. Has she by this devious means succeeded in getting the benefits of blackmail without actually committing blackmail? Or, rather, should she be viewed as nothing more than an unusually devious blackmailer and be treated as such? Reactions have been as divided as they have been vehement. Most people tend to say, and they are rarely tentative about it, that Mildred is no better than a blackmailer. Their reaction is captured by the famous opening number in Bertolt Brecht's *Threepenny Opera*, the "Ballad of Mack the Knife":

> Oh the shark has pretty teeth, dear
> And he shows them pearly white
> Just a jackknife has Macheath, dear
> And he keeps it out of sight.[2]

All that Mildred's stratagem does, they are saying, is to keep the jackknife out of sight. Morally, Mildred is still a shark. What she has done may not technically amount to blackmail, but it is the functional equivalent of blackmail. She has committed blackmail in the thin disguise of a warning. And how can that make a moral difference? If we are concerned about blackmail, how can we not be concerned about Mildred's actions? To condemn blackmail but not condemn what Mildred did is like Yogi Berra telling the waitress to cut his pizza into four pieces rather than eight, because he wasn't hungry enough for eight. Nothing has changed but the way in which the crime is served up.

Worse yet (they say): to allow Mildred to get away with this is to eviscerate the law against blackmail. Soon every blackmailer will attain his evil ends by just being clever enough about the way in which he goes about it. Won't it nearly always be possible to rearrange a blackmail deal so as to turn it into a fait accompli followed by a warning—which is the essence of Mildred's trick?

So argues one side.

But my colleagues on the other side have been no less persuasive. There is a world of difference, they insist, between what Mildred considered doing and what she actually ended up doing. No doubt, they concede, whether Mildred threatens or warns, she is "trying to do the same thing," namely, keep Abigail away from the audition. But broadly speaking, a bank robber and a businessman are also "trying to do the same thing"—make money; nevertheless, we treat them differently. Indeed, tax lawyers make their living by exploiting such distinctions, by taking a deal their client is eager to enter into but for its unfortunate tax consequences and finding a way to restructure "the very same deal" so as to minimize the tax burden. Mildred was simply being a good tax lawyer.

What about the argument that it would eviscerate the law against blackmail to allow Mildred to use her stratagem? Never mind that, say Mildred's defenders, it would eviscerate personal liberty if we punished Mildred for blackmail every time she does something that is the functional equivalent of her original design. Suppose Mildred had decided to send her incriminating letter outright to Abigail's husband hoping that it would stir up enough of a marital spat to keep Abigail away from the audition. In doing so, Mildred would merely have found yet another way of using the nasty facts in her possession to achieve her original objective: she would have committed the "functional equivalent" of blackmail. Or suppose Mildred had decided to mail her incriminating letter to a *National Enquirer* columnist interested in juicy tidbits about up-and-coming starlets. This would be another "functional equivalent" of blackmail. Or suppose Mildred had merely turned some of the more spectacular episodes in Abigail's love life into a short story and published it without ever revealing Abigail's identity. Let us assume she didn't expect anyone but Abigail to recognize herself in the story, but she believed that just reading the story would be upsetting enough for Abigail to keep her away from the audition. That, too, would be a "functional equivalent" of her original blackmail scheme: Mildred is using the same incendiary information for the identical purpose as before. By now, however, the "functional equivalence" view is really starting to look absurd: we are now punishing Mildred for things most of us think she should be perfectly free to do.

So argue Mildred's defenders.

There is a certain pattern to the way opinion divides among my colleagues. Not surprisingly, I suppose, those who specialize in tax law or in civil and criminal procedure tend to side with Mildred. These are, after all, fields in which how you get someplace is at least as important as where you end up. By contrast, Mildred has her most intense foes among those who like to look at law through an economic lens, who tend to be found especially among specialists in fields like torts, contracts, antitrust, or corporations. Again, that seems only natural. The economically minded lawyer likes to cut through what he considers the layers of irrelevant legal formalism to the economic essence of things; and stripped to its economic essence, Mildred appears to be doing the same thing as long as she somehow manages to use her damaging information to keep Abigail from that audition.

THE PROBLEM MULTIPLIED

This then is the problem of avoidance and evasion: Should any of Mildred's various hypothetical strategies for keeping Abigail away from the audition—sending the letter and then issuing a warning, sending the letter and hoping for a spat, informing the *National Enquirer,* or publishing a short story *a clef*—should any of those, all of those, or some of those serve to get Mildred off the hook? If so, which ones, and why? Mildred's case has an infinite number of analogues. Just about every field of law—from Antitrust to Zoning—is replete with puzzling cases in which people routinely try to bypass, circumvent, plan around, duck, or slide past some legal provision or other, and we can't figure out whether to let them get away with it or not. When should we slap down what they did as sleazy evasion, when should we defer to it as circumspect avoidance? The problem of "avoision," as I will call it for short, is so commonplace lawyers practically don't notice it anymore, or at least don't notice just how problematic it is.

The problem has its natural habitat in the tax law. Restructuring transactions so as to minimize the tax burden is the tax lawyer's daily fare; and reviewing such transactions is the tax judge's daily nightmare. Indeed, it was the tax law that brought into being the avoidance-evasion terminology for distinguishing legitimate and illegitimate ways of getting around a law. Many of the most celebrated tax cases are chiefly about this problem.

One cannot properly think about (and hope to solve) the problem of evasion without figuring out the role it plays in the tax law. Unfortunately, most of the famous "avoision" cases of the tax law are bad vehicles for doing so, because they are weighed down by distracting side issues and convoluted facts. I suggest, therefore, that we limit our attention to my cleansed version of an uncommonly easy-to-explain "avoision" maneuver, which nevertheless manages to raise every important analytical problem found in the more arcane cases. The maneuver is known as the "gift-leaseback" strategy and traces its ancestry as far back as the Roman Empire:[3] There once was a very successful shoemaker who had a son whom he loved very dearly. The son was very lazy, so lazy that the shoemaker found himself supporting him well into adulthood with no end in sight. Year after year he paid his son some $1,000 to help him make ends meet. It occurred to the shoemaker that it would be nice if he were able to take a deduction on his $1,000, so that he would be taxed on $1,000 less than he ordinarily would be. Quite understandably, however, the law does not allow you to deduct gifts that you make to your children. The fact is that it was you who received those $1,000s in the first place. It was *your* income. Your spending it on the pleasure of helping out your son doesn't change the fact that it is income you earned, and it seems only fair to tax you on it.

But then the shoemaker had a clever idea. One year he gave his son a gift of $10,000. Of course that was a sizable outlay for him, which he couldn't easily afford. He needed the capital to run his business. Therefore, he asked his son for a loan of $10,000, for which he promised to pay the highly competitive interest rate of 10 percent, that is, $1,000. The son was perfectly agreeable. Thus, when all was said and done, the $10,000 were back in the hands of the father, and he continued to make annual payments of $1,000 to his son—by way of interest. The $1,000, of course, are now a business expense and can be deducted from his income. To be sure, they are now taxable to the son. But the son is in a much lower tax bracket—indeed, if his overall income is low enough, in a zero-percent tax bracket—and so the IRS gets a much smaller share of that $1,000 than before. Does this work? Should it?

The sides line up on this pretty much as they did on my Mildred-and-Abigail hypothetical. One side says: "Of course it works. Why shouldn't it work. The father pays $1,000 in interest which is a genuine business expense, and the son receives $1,000 in income on which he pays taxes." The other side says the whole thing is a transparent evasion of the tax law: "The father starts out by paying taxes on the $1,000 at the appropriate high rate at which a wealthy shoemaker is taxed. Then he engages in some hocus-pocus that leaves things exactly where they were before—with an annual payment of $1,000 going to his son—and suddenly his tax liabilities have changed? Ridiculous! Only a silly formalist would think so." "Formalist, maybe," retorts the other side, "but silly? Why?"

Although the problem of evasion is given most attention in tax law, it appears in just about every area of law. To get a sense of the full range of its manifestations, let me pluck several more random instances from the highways and byways of legal doctrine, all of which, I should add, are live and unresolved controversies. A few of them are elaborations of examples I already alluded to in the Introduction.

The Opportunistic Refugee

A woman from some Third World country is visiting in the United States and decides she would like to live here. That will require somehow changing her visitor's visa into a permanent residency in the United States. She knows that one way to obtain a permanent residency is to get political asylum. Unfortunately for her, she has absolutely no reason to fear persecution in her home country because she is a completely apolitical person who has never said anything critical of her government. So she quickly makes some highly provocative statements that render her persona non grata at home. Now she applies for political asylum. Is this sort of "bootstrapping" strategy, as the immigration lawyers call it, a fraud on the immigration law?[4] Is the law being avoided or evaded?

The Devious Decedent

The law in many states seeks to prevent husbands from disinheriting their wives. It does so by requiring that a fixed fraction of his estate go to the wife regardless of what the husband's will provides. Determined husbands have tried to circumvent these "forced share" statutes by a variety of means, the most straightforward being to give away their money before they die. Gifts, after all, are not regulated by the "forced share" statutes. Alternatively, if the husband wanted to make sure that he didn't lose control of his money while he was still alive, he might open a joint bank account with his favorite cousin, the person he really wanted to inherit it. Thus when he died, the money automatically belonged to the cousin. There are many more complicated variations on these themes, most of them involving the creation of trusts. The husband puts most of his assets into a trust, makes himself the trustee and his favorite cousin the beneficiary. That way he retains complete control of his assets until his death and has them pass to his cousin soon thereafter. The disappointed widow will, of course, claim this is a fraud on her rightful share. But is it? Has the husband avoided or evaded the "forced share" statute?[5]

The Socially Responsible Pornographer

First Amendment protection does not extend to obscene materials. What is obscene? Something that lacks a sufficient measure of "redeeming social value." A publisher eager to distribute some tantalizing pictures of a man and a woman in various positions of intercourse, but worried about the law, decides to make them part of a book he titles "Sex in Marriage." In addition to the pictures, the book is padded with sober discussions of sex education, overpopulation, birth control, venereal disease, frigidity, and the future of marriage. It also contains biblical passages, excerpts from the case law on obscenity, anatomical diagrams, a glossary, a bibliography, and an index. Throughout it all there are references to the pictures.[6] Is this an instance of avoidance or evasion?

The Prudent Spendthrift

Bankruptcy law provides that a debtor who has become overwhelmed with financial obligations, which he has no hope of being able to meet, can make a "fresh start" in life by declaring bankruptcy. What does that mean? It means that he is able to tell his creditors to come and take whatever assets he currently has, insufficient though they are, and in return never to bother him again. The idea is that the bankrupt is now able to go forth, seek out a new job, earn a salary, and not worry about creditors stripping him of every new penny he earns to pay off his old debts.

The critical prerequisite for getting this kind of "fresh start," free and clear of all of one's previous obligations, is that one actually give up all of one's current possessions. That critical prerequisite, however, has been softened in a variety of fairly predictable ways. You don't literally have to give up *everything* you own: you don't have to give up the shirt on your back. This idea is given a fairly natural extension in many states which provide that you also do not have to give up the house you live in, the furniture and various other stuff in it, your life insurance and certain kinds of pension plans, these being viewed as the figurative counterpart of the shirt on your back.

Imagine next the case of a doctor who has made some unlucky investments and incurred, let us say, about $20 million worth of debt which he doesn't have a prayer of paying off, since his current assets come to little more than $700,000. On the eve of declaring bankruptcy the doctor sells his crummy, old starter home and buys himself a villa, furnishes it extravagantly, covers the walls with some Old Masters, decks himself out with a fur-laden new wardrobe, and pours most of the remaining cash into life insurance and the exempt kinds of pension plans. That done, he tells his creditors to come and get what's left over and asks for a "fresh start." Can he do that? Is it all right to load up on exemptions? Is the exemption-planning debtor avoiding or evading his creditors?[7]

The Financial Aid Artist

Financial assistance for college students is based on the wealth of their parents. Leona, a successful real estate agent, takes a much lower-paying job as a high school music teacher, which she happens to enjoy more, but which she takes principally in the expectation that her son will now qualify for more financial aid when he goes to college. Avoidance or evasion?[8]

The Corporation's Ten-Foot Pole

The Grand Corporation wants to build a chemical plant but is worried that a mechanical mishap might cause calamitous injuries and result in ruinous tort liabilities. It decides to insulate against this contingency by incorporating a subsidiary which then goes ahead and builds the chemical plant. A calamity does happen. Thousands of people are severely injured. They sue Grand's subsidiary but discover that there isn't enough cash to compensate them all. They try to reach the assets of the parent corporation. Grand insists that as a mere shareholder in the subsidiary corporation it cannot be held liable. Incorporation, after all, means limited liability: a shareholder is never liable beyond the amount that he initially invested in his company. Does this work? By only touching its subsidiary with a shareholder's ten-foot pole, is Grand avoiding liability or evading it?

The Self-Employed Unemployed

Self-employed workers aren't entitled to unemployment compensation. A family of several self-employed workers, all of whom are in the wrecking business, get together to form a corporation, in which each of them receives some shares and of which each of them becomes an employee. Whenever the wrecking business slackens, which it does seasonally, a meeting of all shareholders is called, and it is then decided, by majority vote, which members shall be "laid off." The workers who have been laid off in this way apply for unemployment compensation, claiming that in forming this corporation they successfully turned themselves from a group of self-employeds into just regular employees. Should this be permitted? Are the workers avoiding or evading the restrictions the law puts on eligibility for unemployment compensation?[9]

A satisfying solution to the problem of evasion should tell us how to go about solving each of these controversial cases.

BOGUS SOLUTIONS

So how does the law cope with "avoision"? What have the courts actually done about the foregoing cases as they presented themselves?

A version of the Mildred-and-Abigail case involving a strikebreaker reached a German court in 1895. A manufacturer had asked an employee of his Cologne branch to replace striking workers in his Paris branch. A supporter of the Paris workers sent the Cologne man a letter telling him that he would earn the contempt of his Paris colleagues and that "other things too might happen, the comrades in Paris know what to do." He also mentioned to the Cologne man's wife that if her husband went to Paris he might end up with a knife between the ribs. The letter writer was prosecuted, among other things, for "coercion," the German designation for blackmail intended to procure a benefit other than property. He defended on the ground that, when he wrote his letter and spoke with the Cologne man's wife, he was not exerting any influence over the Paris workers' activities. He was merely communicating a *warning,* making a *forecast* of the insults and injuries that awaited the Cologne man, nothing more. The court said that as long as the defendant had a part in creating the menace he was now issuing warnings and forecasts about, this was good enough for a finding of coercion.[10]

But this has remained a minority view, both among courts and commentators. The prevailing approach has been to say: Once the threatening development has been launched on its course—once it has moved outside the defendant's control—anything the defendant says to the victim is purely informative, a mere warning, in no way different from a weather forecaster's announcement that a tornado is coming and that one would do best to get out of its way. Unfortunately, neither side makes much of a case for its view, and nothing that either side says gives us much of a clue as to what one should do about all those other cases of evasion I enumerated in the last section.[11]

Sometimes, however, courts try to be more systematic. Sometimes they have tried to devise more general approaches to the problem of avoision, each of which at first glance looks as though it might actually do the trick. There are about three such approaches. What are they? And how do they fare at second glance?

To begin with, there is the "form-versus-substance" approach. Consider how a number of courts have dealt with the case of the husband who tries to get around the law against disinheriting one's wife by giving his property to his favorite cousin on the eve of his death. It has seemed natural for courts to say here: in form, what the decedent did may look like a regular *inter vivos* gift. In truth, however, fundamentally, deep down, it is really a testamentary bequest dressed up to look like a gift. This is really no different than an employer who pays his employee for a service but tries to call it a gift so his employee doesn't have to pay income tax on it. As one scholar puts it: "When someone calls a dog a cow and then seeks a subsidy provided by statute for cows, the obvious response is that this is not what the statute means. . . . The principle of following 'substance' rather than 'form' has always meant sweeping aside pretenses of this sort."[12] In other words, to evade the law is to disguise what is in substance one thing in the form of something else. The court's job is to ignore the form and cut to the substance.

That works pretty well with some of those bequest cases, but it leaves us at bay with many others. For instance, it doesn't seem to help one bit with the many puzzling variations of the Mildred-and-Abigail case. When Mildred mails her letter and then calls Abigail to warn her of its impending arrival, is this in form a warning and in substance a blackmail threat? When Mildred sends the letter outright hoping for a marital spat, or when Mildred publishes her short story, should these "functional equivalents" of blackmail be viewed as blackmail in substance, though something else in form? The form-versus-substance approach doesn't tell us.

Worse yet, the answers it gives in cases where it speaks quite clearly leave one very uneasy. Consider how the approach would have us resolve the cases in the previous section. First, there is the shoemaker who gives his son $10,000 which he borrows back at a 10 percent interest rate so as to transform his annual $1,000 payment to his son from a gift into a business expense. Under the form-versus-substance approach, this maneuver works just fine because the father's annual payments are a business expense in both form and substance. To be sure, the father doesn't deny doing what he did to reduce taxes. He even admits feeling a bit silly about the whole procedure of first handing his son $10,000 as a gift and then immediately snatching it back as a loan, but that doesn't change the fact that it really is a business expense, both in form and in substance. For analogous reasons, the form-versus-substance approach would bless the maneuvers in each and every one of the other cases of the previous section. Why should that trouble us? It should trouble us because the answer is given by fiat and not by argument. There is nothing about the form-and-substance approach that serves to allay one's countervailing intuitions about those cases, nothing to instill confidence that the outcome it calls for is actually correct.

A second way in which the courts have tried to cope with the avoision problem has been the intent-to-evade approach. The way this approach works is again best illustrated by the case of the husband trying to disinherit his wife. Suppose the husband starts making gifts to his various cousins long before he dies, again because he wants to make sure that very little is left for his wife to inherit. Courts that were disturbed by how this frustrated the law against disinheritance saw themselves confronted with a formidable problem. It was very hard to characterize gifts made many years before the defendant died or expected to die as being "in substance" bequests and only in form gifts. So although these gifts reeked of evasion, the form-versus-substance approach was saying they were mere avoidance. The courts' response was to focus on the reason or motive behind these gifts. If it seemed that the gifts were made with the disinheritance law in mind, and would not have been made without such a law, then the judge was inclined to say that the gifts were motivated by an intent to evade the disinheritance laws and, therefore, invalid.

This approach has struck many as being just the right way to deal with cases like that of the shoemaker seeking to circumvent the income tax. He engaged in his complicated transaction with his son only because of the tax law; it was as the courts like to say a purely "tax-driven" transaction. It, therefore, seems natural to describe it as having been performed with an intent to evade and thus ineffective. This is, indeed, the chief ground on which the IRS has tried to challenge such maneuvers. In analogous fashion, the approach would condemn most of the other cases in the previous section as evasive: the tourist who makes some provocative political statements which she would not have made but for the immigration law, the producer who adds a frosting of "redeeming social content" to his pornographic movie which he would not have added but for the obscenity law, the debtor who converts most of his money into "exempt assets" which he would not have bought but for the bankruptcy law, the mother who takes a lower-paying job which she would not have taken but for the rules on college aid, the company that incorporates its subsidiary which it would not have incorporated but for the law of limited liability, the self-employed workers who form a corporation which they would not have formed but for the unemployment law, or for that matter Mildred who made sure to mail off her letter to Abigail's husband before calling her which she would not have done but for the law against blackmail—they all are doing something highly artificial, driven by legal doctrine, not by real-world concerns, devoid of what courts in a business context like to a call a "business purpose." In short, they all acted with an intent to evade.

But if the form-and-substance test's sweeping blessing of all of these maneuvers made us uneasy, the intent-to-evade test's equally sweeping condemnation should make us just as uneasy. Why exactly should we disapprove of someone for doing something *only* because of the law? Is the person who abstains from theft because of the law of theft to be punished as an evader? Isn't he in fact the archetypical example of an *avoider?* How can we blame Mildred for doing what she did *only* on account of the law against blackmail when the purpose of the blackmail law is to induce people not to commit blackmail?

A champion of the intent-to-evade test might try this reply: the test doesn't work for all laws, but it does for most. It doesn't work for laws that try to modify people's conduct, which the law of theft, and indeed all of criminal law, evidently tries to do. It wouldn't make sense to punish as an evader the person whose conduct is influenced by laws that are meant to influence his conduct. For that reason, the intent-to-evade approach might not be of much help in dealing with, say, the movie producer who adds a dollop of redeeming social value to his skin flick. Arguably that's what the obscenity law is meant to get him to do. Similarly, the approach might not be of much help with the tourist seeking political asylum. Arguably, the availability of political asylum is meant to encourage outspokenness. Finally, the approach might not be of much help with the company incorporating a subsidiary to insulate itself from liability. Arguably, the purpose of limited liability is to en-courage ventures someone otherwise might not undertake.

Nevertheless, says the defender of the "intent-to-evade" test, there are some cases where that test is just perfect, namely, cases involving laws that are not meant to influence conduct. Most tax cases are of this kind. To be sure, there are some taxes that are meant to influence conduct, most notably "sin" taxes and import tariffs. But the most pervasive taxes—like income, gift, or estate taxes—are not meant to do that. What the drafters of the income tax law, in particular, had in mind is for everyone to continue doing what they did before but to make sure that they turn over the requisite fraction of what they earn to the government. All of which makes it quite clear why the intent-to-evade approach works so well in the case of the shoemaker. The shoemaker modified his conduct in response to a law that wasn't supposed to influence conduct (except to make him pay taxes).

Persuaded? You shouldn't be. Just think about the taxpayer who decides to work less hard or who decides to take a lower-paying but more enjoyable job because the government is going to tax away a large chunk of his earnings anyway. Under the intent-to-evade approach, a judge would have to say to such taxpayers: "You only stopped working on account of the tax law," or "You only took the job you hold on account of the tax law," and find them both guilty of tax evasion. There are some who think that this would be just fine, or that the only reasons it wouldn't be fine are practical ones: that it's difficult to figure out how hard someone would have worked or what job he would have taken absent an income tax. Most of us, I suspect, feel deeper-seated reservations than that. It just doesn't seem fair, even if practical problems didn't stand in the way, to hold the potential neurosurgeon, who became a beach bum because taxes seemed too high, liable for tax evasion and to demand that he pay the IRS the sum he would be paying if he had actually become a neurosurgeon.[13]

The third approach to have found favor with the courts is the "spirit-versus-the-letter" test. Each law, the courts will frequently say, has a purpose, rationale, intention, policy, or spirit that animates it, which isn't always perfectly realized by its actual letter. The evader is someone who does what conforms to the letter but conflicts with the spirit of the law. A court applying this test to the case of the husband seeking to circumvent a "forced share" statute by giving away his money while he is still alive, might then say: "The purpose, the rationale, the intention, the policy, and the spirit behind the 'forced share' statute is to prevent the husband from leaving his wife destitute. Therefore gifts tending to do that, even if made long before one's death, are an evasion."

But wait a minute. Why is the court so sure that the purpose of the "forced share" is to prevent the husband from leaving his wife destitute? No doubt, the statute had something to do with that desire. It's quite clear, however, that the legislatures adopting such statutes were unwilling to do anything to restrict the husband's ability to freely dispose of his property during his lifetime, for instance, by specifying that he could not engage in transactions that made it likely that his wife would be left penniless. Their desire to protect the wife was quite clearly tempered by a competing desire not to meddle with *inter vivos* transactions. So here's the rub with the "spirit-versus-the-letter" approach: it tends to be vacuous.

It is vacuous even in cases where one would least expect it to be. Recall the example of the wreckers who wanted to get some unemployment compensation. They did so by founding a corporation of which they made themselves employees. Then whenever work ran out they could describe themselves as having been "laid off." Suppose we tried to analyze this case by asking why it is that the self-employed are excluded from unemployment benefits. Most likely because of so-called moral hazard problems: the fear that the self-employed will take vacations and describe themselves as "involuntarily unemployed" for that period. Of course, a regular employee might try the same ploy, but the ruse would be far more transparent and would require the employer's cooperation. If this is the rationale for the exclusion of the self-employed, one might be inclined to say: given that this corporation was formed by the members of a family who were previously self-employed, all the moral hazard problems of self-employment are still present, and "in truth" we are dealing with a situation of self-employment. Ergo this is a case of evasion.

But have we really analyzed the purpose of the statute correctly? Why not say: "The purpose of the statute is to help the genuinely unemployed. As long as these workers were genuinely out of work and not simply taking vacations at government expense, that purpose was not being frustrated." To be sure, someone might protest: "The purpose of general rules is to obviate the need to go into the particulars of every situation. The purpose of the self-employment exclusion was to dispose of a category of employment rife with the possibility of abuse without investigating every single instance for the presence of such abuse." To that argument, however, someone else might issue this rejoinder: "If we are not supposed to look at the particulars of a situation, why not stop as soon as we have determined that the workers are officially not self-employed?" And so it might go on for a while. What the exchange reveals is just how frustratingly indefinite the spirit-versus-the-letter approach can turn out to be. In cases like this one it offers no more guidance on the "avoision" problem than J. P. Morgan did on making money in the stock market when he said, "Buy cheap, sell dear."

There is a more general and profound difficulty with this approach than occasional indefiniteness. Sometimes the best way to hit a target is not to aim at it directly, just as the best way to fall asleep is not to focus on it too intently. Many laws turn out to be built around this principle, and, with regard to these, the spirit-versus-the-letter test proves to be downright incoherent. To see this clearly requires, appropriately enough, a slight detour.

In the spring of 1965, the political scientist Lloyd Jensen ran a study to determine how well various foreign policy specialists were able to predict impending developments. He interviewed some ninety policymakers in the State and Defense Departments, about forty foreign correspondents, and an equal number of academics. He asked them twenty-five yes-or-no questions about the future of international relations. Then he scored them as history unfolded. The result was interesting only in how disappointing it was: the experts barely outperformed chance. These are not unique results. In analogous studies, psychiatrists revealed themselves to be breathtakingly bad at predicting the course of mental illness, and doctors revealed themselves equally unable to predict the survival times of terminally ill patients.[14]

It is tempting to conclude that this just proves the worthlessness of expertise. But the source of the experts' failure turns out to be more interesting than that, as is shown by the results of another series of studies. Suppose we gave a college admissions officer a list of applicants and asked him to predict their relative class ranks by the time they graduate. In addition to asking him for an overall prediction, we also ask him for a list of the factors he takes into account in making such a prediction. The list would probably include such things as high school GPA, SAT scores, and imponderables like general maturity, motivation, self-discipline, emotional stability, and sense of humor. Finally, we ask him to grade the applicant on each of these attributes on a scale of 1–10. Eventually we aggregate the scores for each student and rank them by their total. What we would probably find when all is said and done is that the second procedure has generated far more accurate predictions of college success than the first procedure. In other words, the mechanical aggregation of scores along each of the dimensions will be a better predictor of success than the admissions officer's considered overall judgment. But how can that be? After all the formula reflects no more than the factors the admissions officer already knows to be relevant to college success, and it mixes them together in a much cruder fashion than the admissions officer does, who is able after all to consider the entire *gestalt* of the application before him and to exercise "judgment." Alas, mechanical formulas often turn out to be far superior to the exercise of judgment. The reason is that, while people are very good at noticing what factors about a situation are relevant to their decision (as the admissions officer was at noticing what factors make for college success), they are very poor, haphazard, even capricious at integrating that information. Thus, oftentimes even a crude mechanical rule (based not even on multiple regression!) is superior to the exercise of considered judgment in attaining the specified objective. When the above-mentioned psychiatrists and doctors, whose predictions of mental illness and survival times had previously been no better than chance, used this kind of method to predict, they proved to be uncannily on the mark.[15]

The moral for law is clear. Whatever one's particular objectives, there is much to be said for adopting mechanical rules to attain them and for applying them with mule-like consistency. That is, what is true for the admissions officer is likely to be true for the judge: if the judge is simply asked to unimaginatively and thoughtlessly apply the rule the legislator handed to him, he is more likely to produce the result the legislator aimed for than if he actively strives in every case to make the decision that seems most consistent with that aim. Imagine, for instance, that Congress has laid down a rule forbidding the armed forces to accept anyone who is in the bottom 10 percent of his high school class. Let us assume that this is just the sort of rule that works best when applied with a stubborn consistency, by which I mean, let us suppose that the quality of the armed forces is most likely to be promoted by a rigid application of this requirement. Imagine now a student who makes sure he meets these requirements by taking only the easiest courses, taught by the most lenient instructors, who immediately drops any course in which he seems not to be doing sufficiently well, who badgers teachers into improving bad grades into mediocre ones, in short, who uses gamesmanship to make sure his high school qualifications do not run afoul of army restrictions on recruitment. Has he evaded the army restrictions? If we tried to apply the spirit-versus-the-letter approach here, it would prove well-nigh incoherent. Is letting someone enlist who would not have succeeded without such gamesmanship consistent with the spirit of the rule? It seems not, since the animating spirit of the rule is to bring able recruits into the army. So is rejecting him consistent with the spirit of the rule? Again, it seems not, because the animating spirit of the rule is to eschew making individualized judgment calls. But then, which is it to be?

UNDERLYING ALL THREE of these approaches is a particular picture of how evasion comes about. The picture is that of a legislator who drafts a law to bring about a certain result but who bungles the job a little and, therefore, leaves behind loopholes, which it is then the judge's task, aided by an appropriate theory of evasion, to plug. Each of the three approaches just discussed aims to offer a way to plug such holes. This is most obviously the aim of the spirit-versus-the-letter approach, which tells us to forget about the faulty letter of the statute and just pay attention to its underlying spirit. The two other approaches try to accomplish the same thing by giving more specific guidance on how to recognize those who are trying to profit from the divergence between letter and spirit. "Watch for the fellow who has donned an unusual disguise, like the testator who is pretending to be a donor," the form-versus-substance approach tells us. "Watch for the fellow who is taking an unusual path to where he is going, like the shoemaker who makes a gift and takes it right back as a loan," the intent-to-evade approach tells us. "Who would be wearing such a disguise, who would be taking such a circuitous route if he weren't trying to slip past boundaries he wasn't meant to get past?" we are told. Loopholes, in this picture, are the inevitable byproducts of the principle of legality, which requires legislatures to announce in advance the rules by which the courts will then judge a citizen. Absent this requirement, there would be no misdrafted rules, no divergence of letter and spirit, no loopholes, no room for evasion, and no "avoision" problem.

However self-evidently right this picture will seem to most lawyers, I mean to show you that there is something seriously wrong with it.

LOOPHOLES WITHOUT LAWS

One thing that should give us pause about the conventional view of loopholes is that even the citizens of dictatorships have learned to play avoision games. Yet we know that dictators don't set much stock by the principle of legality. They have few compunctions about punishing their subjects, whether the dictatorial command they have run afoul of was well or poorly drafted. Thus, if there is avoision going on, if there are loopholes to be found, it can't be for the usual reason of bungled draftsmanship.

Here are some examples of avoision games played in dictatorships. In 1988 a group of East German high school students tried to find a way of protesting against East German militarism without incurring the usual penalties associated with such gestures. After a careful search through East Germany's official army newspaper, they found an embarrassingly bad poem titled "Lovesong to My Kalashnikov Machine Gun" and posted it on the school's bulletin board, adding the coy caption: "A poem which has impressed us deeply and given us much food for thought."[16] In the same spirit, East German dissidents in the early 1980s would gather in front of the Berlin Wall to sing officially approved songs, like the Communist "International," letting their voices soar when they got to words like "freedom" and "oppression." The authorities found themselves at a loss.

The technique used by certain Soviet history journals eager to publish articles critical of the regime was a bit crasser. They would quote long excerpts from writings by hostile Western Sovietologists but offer them up as examples of slanderous Western propaganda, carefully introducing them with expressions of apoplectic outrage at such capitalist villainy. "You write a dirty word on the fence and then invite everyone to come and read it, saying: 'Look, how disgusting!'" is how one historian described the technique.[17] Not that it always works. It didn't work for Galileo as he tried to circumvent the church's ban on the advocacy of Copernicanism. The cunning of his preface to the *Dialogue Concerning the Two World Systems* is altogether too obvious. The purpose of the *Dialogue,* he there insisted, was not to champion the Copernican view but, on the contrary, to defend the church against the charge that it had repudiated that view without really understanding it. He, Galileo, was going to demonstrate to the world that the Copernican doctrine was well understood in Italy and had only been repudiated after thorough reflection. "To this end," he wrote, "I have taken the Copernican side in the discourse . . . the celestial phenomena will be examined, strengthening the Copernican hypothesis until it might seem that it must triumph absolutely." Only thus would it become clear to everyone that "[i]t is not from failing to take account of what others have thought that we [the church and Galileo!] have yielded to asserting that the earth is motionless . . . , but for reasons of piety, religion, the knowledge of Divine Omnipotence and a consciousness of the limitations of the human mind."[18]

Yet a further instance of such avoision is described in Ernest Jones's biography of Freud. In the aftermath of the German annexation of Austria, life became unbearable for Freud and he decided to emigrate to London. He was permitted to leave Vienna, but only after negotiating an arduous bureaucratic obstacle course. Throughout it all, however,

> Freud retained his ironic attitude toward the complicated formalities that had to be gone through. One of the conditions for being granted an exit visa was that he sign a document that ran as follows: "I Prof. Freud, hereby confirm that after the Anschluss of Austria to the German Reich I have been treated by the German authorities and particularly by the Gestapo with all the respect and consideration due to my scientific reputation, that I could live and work in full freedom, that I could continue to pursue my activities in every way I desired, that I found full support from all concerned in this respect, and that I have not the slightest reason for any complaint." When the Nazi Commissar brought it along Freud had of course no compunction in signing it, but asked if he might be allowed to add a sentence, which was: "I can heartily recommend the Gestapo to anyone."

I should admit though that it is not entirely clear from Jones's account whether Freud was actually allowed to make the addition.[19]

Now perhaps the possibility of these kinds of maneuvers simply arises from a residual respect which even dictatorships pay the principle of legality. But then what about the fact that it is possible to play avoision games even with our own conscience? Many readers and moviegoers familiar with Woodward and Bernstein's Watergate saga, *All the President's Men*, remember one scene more distinctly than any other. The drama reached one of its early crescendos when the two reporters thought they had unearthed proof that Richard Nixon's chief-of-staff, H. R. Haldeman, was about to be indicted. But what proof they had wasn't enough to satisfy the *Washington Post*'s editor-in-chief, Ben Bradley. He insisted they get at least one more confirmation before he would run their story. In great desperation, Carl Bernstein called one of his secret contacts, a lawyer in the Justice Department, and pleaded with him to confirm the story. The lawyer refused, Bernstein persisted, and eventually they settled on a compromise. It came about like this:

> "I'd like to help you, I really would," said the lawyer. "But I just can't say anything."
> Bernstein thought for a moment and told the man they [meaning he and Woodward] understood why he couldn't say anything. So they would do it another way: Bernstein would count to 10. If there was any reason for the reporters to hold back on the story, the lawyer should hang up before 10. If he was on the line after 10, it would mean the story was ok.
> "Hang up, right?" the lawyer asked.
> That was right, Bernstein instructed, and started counting.
> "You've got it straight now?" the lawyer asked.
> Right. Bernstein thanked him again and hung up.
> He told the editors and Woodward that they now had a fourth confirmation, and thought himself quite clever.[20]

Why did the lawyer behave like this? My guess is that his grounds were as much moral as they were legal. He did not feel the same scruples about failing to deny a certain story as he did about confirming it, even though failing to deny here would have the same consequences as confirming. Whatever moral norm the lawyer thought prohibited him from talking out of school, he presumably did not think prohibited him from doing the functional equivalent of talking out of school by playing this little charade. If that is true, it reveals a serious problem with the customary picture of loopholes and avoision. What the lawyer did certainly reeks of avoision and of loopholes, but he didn't do it to comply with the law, he did it to assuage his conscience.

Although this is the most memorable, it is far from the only scene like that in *All the President's Men*. In fact, the entire account of how the two reporters tracked down the Watergate story is a string of minuets danced by the journalists and their sources in an effort to have the latter tell the former what they knew without actually seeming to tell them. Even their most uninhibited source, the as yet unidentified Deep Throat, insisted on such indirection.

> Though it wasn't true, Woodward told Deep Throat that he and Bernstein had a story for the following week saying that Haldeman was the fifth person in control of disbursements from the secret fund.
>
> "You'll have to do it on your own," Deep Throat said.
>
> Woodward tried another angle. He asked if Deep Throat would feel compelled to warn him if his information was wrong.
>
> Deep Throat said he would.
>
> Then you're confirming Haldeman on the fund? Woodward asked.
>
> "I'm not. You've got to do it on your own."
>
> [Deep Throat repeated that] he would try to keep the reporters out of trouble.
>
> Woodward asked if they were in trouble on Haldeman.
>
> "I'll keep you out" [meaning out of trouble] Deep Throat said.
>
> Since he had not cautioned them on Haldeman, he was effectively confirming the story. Woodward made it clear that he expected some sign from Deep Throat if there was any reason to hold back.
>
> Deep Throat replied that failing to warn Woodward off a bad story "would be a misconception of our friendship." He would not name Haldeman himself. He shook hands with Woodward and left.[21]

Occasionally Woodward would tire of Deep Throat's artifices and complain to him that "they were playing a chickenshit game—Deep Throat for pretending to himself that he never fed Woodward primary information, and Woodward for chewing up tidbits like a rat under a picnic table that didn't have the guts to go after the main dish." But that didn't sway Deep Throat.

These incidents, involving avoision but not any laws, are hard to reconcile with the idea that avoision is the product of a misdrafted law. But perhaps the interactions between a reporter and his source seem like a rather special case; so let me offer an illustration from a more commonplace setting. What does someone do who wants to break out of a relationship but lacks the gumption to tell her lover? Why, act real surly, provoke a fight, and make *him* do the breaking up. And if that person is as clever as Brenda Patimkin in Philip Roth's first novel, *Goodbye, Columbus,* she might give that old strategy a devious new spin. Brenda, a Radcliffe student and daughter of Patimkin, the king of kitchen and bathroom sinks, has been going out for one long summer with Neil Klugman, who, though bright and handsome, is two rungs below her on the social ladder: he works in a library and still lives with his Aunt Gladys and Uncle Max in Newark. At Brenda's invitation, he spends much of the summer in her parents' house. They secretly—this is the 1950s—sleep together, Brenda having managed to surreptitiously secure a diaphragm. Her parents would obviously not approve of the match; but Brenda herself has no intention of marrying Neil anyway. Still, she must find a graceful, ladylike way to end things. We learn just what that graceful, ladylike way is when Neil visits her in Boston for Rosh Hashana. Her parents, she explains to him with an air of panic, have just found her diaphragm and are in a frenzy. Neil is puzzled.

> "Why did you leave it home?"
> "Because I didn't plan on using it here, that's why."
> "Suppose I'd come up. I mean I have come up, what about that?"
> "I thought I'd come down first."
> "So then couldn't you have carried it down then? Like a toothbrush?"
> "Are you trying to be funny?"
> "No. I'm just asking you why you left it home."
> "I told you," Brenda said. "I thought I'd come home."
> "But, Brenda, that doesn't make any sense. Suppose you did come home, and then you came back again. Wouldn't you have taken it with you then?"
> "I don't know."[22]

What's to happen next, Neil eventually asks her. What will she do for Thanksgiving, whom will she bring home to her parents with her for Thanksgiving, her roommate Linda or him? Obviously, she can't take him, she explains, her parents would be too upset. So far, however, Brenda has said nothing about breaking up. It is Neil who pronounces the affair at an end. Outraged by her refusal to bring him home for Thanksgiving, and by her persistent you-just-don't-understands, he finally exclaims,

"Goddamit, I understand more than you think. I understand why the hell you left that thing lying around. Don't you? Can't you put two and two together?"

"Neil what are you talking about! You're the one who doesn't understand. You're the one who from the very beginning was accusing me of things? Remember? . . . You kept acting as if I was going to run away from you every minute. And now you're doing it again, telling me I planted that thing on purpose."

"I loved you Brenda, so I cared."

"I loved *you*. That's why I got that damn thing in the first place."

And then we heard the tense in which we'd spoken and we settled back into ourselves and silence.[23]

Why does Brenda choose this circuitous way of ending things? Why do people who cannot break off a relationship nevertheless find it possible to provoke the other party into doing it? The simple answer would be that they are trying to fool the other person, so they won't be blamed. But usually matters are as transparent as they are in *Goodbye, Columbus*: the other party isn't fooled, and the person who wants to break up knows it. I rather think that Brenda broke up in this way because she felt that was less immoral than to tell Neil that, although she was delighted to have him for a fling, she had no intention to marry beneath her station. Of course, that message was hardly lost on him, nor could she really hope that it would be lost on him. Nevertheless, she clearly felt she gained moral ground by having him call it quits rather than doing it herself. If Brenda is right, and the universality of the practice certainly supports her, that casts further doubt on the conventional theory of loopholes. What Brenda is doing very much smacks of avoision, except that she is not circumventing the law, she is circumventing a moral precept—the one that says you shouldn't throw your lover over just because he's your social inferior. But how can moral precepts have loopholes? They weren't drafted by anyone who might have bungled the job. If morality has loopholes, then the conventional theory of loopholes really can't be right.

Perhaps these examples from *All the President's Men* and *Goodbye, Columbus* illustrate merely that there is a loophole in human psychology. Perhaps all they show is that there is a way in which people can be convinced to do something they shouldn't do by deluding themselves into thinking that they are not "really" doing it. There certainly are plenty of examples of this kind of self-delusion. An amusing one is

22

told about the nineteenth-century historian William Prescott, renowned chiefly for his lively histories of the conquest of Mexico and Peru:

> [It] occurred at the time [Prescott] and [a friend] were travelling together in Europe. An oculist, or physician, whom he had consulted at Paris, had advised [Prescott], among other things, to live less freely, and when pushed by his patient, as was his wont, to fix a very precise limit to the quantity of wine he might take, his adviser told him that he ought never to exceed two glasses a day. This rule he forthwith announced his resolution to adhere to scrupulously. And he did. But his manner of observing it was peculiar. At every new house of entertainment they reached in their travels, one of the first things Prescott did was to require the waiter to show him specimens of all the wine-glasses the house afforded. He would then pick out from among them the largest; and this, though it might contain two or three times the quantity of a common wine-glass, he would have set by his plate as his measure at dinner to observe the rule in.[24]

An almost intolerably grim form of such self-delusion is described in Christopher Browning's *Ordinary Men,* the study of a special German police battalion in charge of massacring Polish Jews. The policemen not surprisingly came up with various rationalizations to justify to themselves what they were doing. "Perhaps the most astonishing" of these, writes Browning, "was that of a thirty-five year old metalworker from Bremerhaven" who only killed children. His neighbor would shoot the mother and he would shoot the mother's children. "It was supposed to be, so to speak, soothing to [his] conscience to release children unable to live without their mothers."[25]

Along the same lines is Charles Mackay's report in his famous nineteenth-century treatise *Extraordinary Popular Delusions and the Madness of Crowds:*

> It was once thought a venial offence, in very many countries of Europe, to destroy an enemy by slow poison. Persons who would have revolted at the idea of stabbing a man to the heart, drugged his potage without scruple. Ladies of gentle birth and manners caught the contagion of murder, until poisoning, under their auspices, became quite fashionable.[26]

Thus, it might be that Woodward and Bernstein's sources and Philip Roth's Brenda Patimkin were engaged in an analogous, albeit more benign, kind of self-delusion. But self-delusion should not be an explanation of first resort, and we shall discuss a more plausible one shortly. Before doing so, however, I will drive one more thorn into the side of the conventional view of loopholes. So far we have seen people employ avoision strategies with dictators and with their own conscience. We are about to see them do the same with God.

LOOPHOLES AND THE THEOLOGIANS

In his not-quite-memoirs *Surely You're Joking, Mr. Feynman,* the physicist Richard Feynman recounts the following experience:

> While I was at [a] conference, I stayed at the Jewish Theological Seminary. . . . one day—I guess it was a Saturday—I want to go up in the elevator. The elevator comes, I go in, and [a man] goes in with me. I say, "Which floor?" and my hand's ready to push one of the buttons.
>
> "No, no!" he says, "*I'm* supposed to push the buttons for *you.*"
>
> "*What?*"
>
> "Yes! The boys here can't push the buttons on Saturday, so I have to do it for them. You see, I'm not Jewish, so it's all right for *me* to push the buttons. I stand near the elevator, and they tell me what floor, and I push the button for them."[27]

What Feynman had with such naivete encountered was the institution of the "Shabbes Goy," the Sabbath gentile. Judaism forbids Jews, but not gentiles, to perform "creative work"—a broadly conceived category—on Sabbath. Over time the custom evolved for gentiles, not subject to the Shabbes restrictions, to do for Jews what they are forbidden from doing for themselves. Feynman was incensed by the practice. He explains:

> This really bothered me, so I decided to trap the students in a logical discussion. . . . My plan went like this: I'd start off by asking, "[I]s the Jewish viewpoint a viewpoint that *any* man can have? Because if it is not, then it's certainly not something that is truly valuable for humanity. . . . yak, yak, yak." And then they would have to say, "Yes, the Jewish viewpoint is good for any man." Then I would steer them around a little more by asking, "[I]s it ethical for a man to hire another man to do something which is unethical for him to do? Would you hire a man to rob for you, for instance?" And I keep working them into the channel, very slowly, and very carefully, until I've got them—trapped!
>
> And do you know what happened? They're rabbinical students, right?

They were ten times better than I was! As soon as they saw I could put them in a hole, they went twist, turn, twist—I can't remember how—and they were free! I thought I had come up with an original idea—phooey! It had been discussed in the Talmud for ages![28]

What here disturbs Feynman is the problem of corruption: How can a Jew ask somebody else to do something which he views as sinful to do. Actually, that particular problem has not troubled Judaism much, being disposed of relatively swiftly, if not altogether satisfactorily, with the observation that unlike the prohibition against stealing and killing, the commandments of the Sabbath are only meant for Jews, and a non-Jew does nothing sinful by breaking them. What has troubled Jewish theologians far more is the problem Feynman does not get into—evasion. If a Jew is not permitted to perform "creative labor" directly, how can he do so indirectly by hiring someone else to do it for him? A Jewish farmer might approach the rabbi and ask what he should do about fruit in his orchard that will spoil unless picked on the Sabbath. The rabinically approved solution was for the Jew to sell his un-picked fruit to a gentile on Friday and have him come on Sabbath to pick it for himself. What is a Jew to do about factories that need running, fields that need tilling, cows that need milking on the Sabbath? A blatant but grudgingly condoned way out was to sell them to a gentile on Friday and repurchase them on Sunday. Another way out was to take in a non-Jewish partner who would perform the appointed tasks on the Sabbath. (An employee would not do, because his work would redound to the benefit of the Jew, but a partner would be fine, because the profits would be divided up so as to allocate that day's share exclusively to the gentile.) So Feynman's elevator operator was merely continuing a long-standing, much controverted, but multiply blessed tradition of circumvention.[29]

In A SENSE, Feynman's encounter with the seminarians was but a farcical reen-actment of a confrontation that occurred several centuries earlier between another great scientist, Blaise Pascal, and another group of casuistical theologians, the seventeenth-century Jesuits. Reading through the Jesuits' moral treatises, Pascal was outraged by their relentless preoccupation with making it easy to be a good Christian by telling sinners how to circumvent their moral obligations. He collected what he considered the most offensive of such practices in a series of polemical pamphlets that has come to be known as The Provincial Letters, and it will be worth our while to look at these practices in some detail.

Pascal was annoyed, for instance, with various Jesuitical doctrines designed to subvert basic religious rituals—like hearing mass or fasting. On the hearing of mass, Pascal quotes some advice designed to considerably shorten the time required by this "chore":

> One can hear half of one priest's mass, and then the other half of another's, and one can also hear the end of one first and then the beginning of another. . . . *And I will also tell you that it has even been found lawful: to hear two halves of mass at the same time said by two different priests, when one begins the mass as the other comes to the Elevation; because it is possible to pay attention to both sides at the same time, and two halves of a mass make a whole one.* . . . From this I conclude that you can hear mass in a very short time, as when, for example, you find four masses going on at the same time, so arranged that one is beginning when the next has reached the Gospel, a third the Consecration, and the last the Communion. [Italics mine.][30]

If this were so, Pascal remarks to the priest who offered this advice, then "it would only take a minute to hear mass at Notre Dame." Quite so, agrees the priest: "You see then," he adds, "that [we] have done [our] very best to make it easy to hear mass."

More upsetting yet to Pascal were various Jesuitical teachings on basic questions of morality, most notably their treatment of dueling. The Jesuits agree that it is immoral to engage in a duel; but they suggest ways of getting around that prohibition:

> If a gentleman who is challenged to a duel is known not to be devout, and the sins which he is seen constantly committing without any scruples make it obvious that any refusal to duel will be motivated not by any fear of God but by cowardice; and so that it is said of him that he has the heart of a chicken and not of a man . . . [then] to preserve his honor he may be at the spot assigned, *not, it is true, with the express intention of fighting a duel, but merely with that of self-defence if his challenger comes there to attack him unjustly. And in itself his action will be quite indifferent, for what harm can there be in going to a field, walking about waiting for someone and defending oneself if attacked?* And so he is not sinning in any way, since it is by no means accepting a duel if the intention is directed to other circumstances. For acceptance of the duel consists in the express intention of fighting, which this man does not have. [Italics mine.][31]

The Jesuits readily concede that one may not aid another in the commission of a crime but, realizing that this is hard advice to take if one is a servant to a master bent on crime, they are quick to offer an expedient:

> We have considered how hard it is for [servants], when they are men of conscience, to serve dissolute masters. For if they do not perform all the commissions on which they are employed, they lose their livelihood, and if they do obey, they have scruples about it. It is in order to relieve these scruples that our . . . Fathers . . . have indicated the services which they can render with a safe conscience. Here are some of them: To carry letters and presents; to open doors and windows; to help their masters climb up to a window; to hold the ladder while he climbs; all that is permissible and morally indifferent. It is true that when it comes to holding the ladder they must be threatened more than usual in case of failure to do so. For it is an offence against the master of a house to enter through a window.
>
> [And we also] taught servants how to render such services to their masters innocently, by making them direct their intentions not towards the sins of which they are the accessories, but solely to the profit which accrues to them thereby. This is well explained in [the] *Compendium of Sins:* "Confessors should note" [it] says "that absolution cannot be given to servants who perform dishonest commissions, if they consent to their masters' sins; but we must say the opposite if they do it for their own temporal benefit." And that is easy enough; for why should they insist on consenting to sins which bring them nothing but trouble?[32]

The strategy they employ is a fairly general one, which they dub "directing one's intention." Pascal's interlocutor in *The Provincial Letters* refers to it as a "marvellous principle," "a great method," and has recourse to it repeatedly.

The Jesuits invoke this principle as well to defend the sale of church offices, that is, simony:

> Let us begin . . . with the holders of benefices. You know what traffic there is in benefices nowadays and that, if we had to go by what St. Thomas and the ancient authors have written, there would be plenty of simonists in the Church. And that is what made it so necessary that our Fathers should mitigate things with their prudence. . . . If anyone gives a temporal good for a spiritual good (that is, money for a benefice) and gives money as the price of a benefice, this is obviously simony. But if the money is given as a motive inducing the incumbent to resign the benefice . . . it is not simony, even if the

person resigning considers and expects the money as his main object. . . .
By this means we prevent countless acts of simony. For who in giving
money for a benefice would be so wicked as to refuse to form the intention
of giving it as a *motive* to induce the incumbent to resign, instead of giving it
as the *price* of the benefice? No one is abandoned by God to that extent.[33]

The Jesuits do not dispute that usury (here to be understood as the lending of
money for *any* amount of interest whatsoever) is bad, but they have some suggestions on how to get around that prohibition as well. One suggestion is for the
would-be lender to become a partner in the would-be borrower's business, and to
receive his interest in the form of partnership profits:

> Anyone who is asked for money shall answer in this way: I have no money to
> lend, but I do have some to put to honest and lawful profit. If you want the
> sum for which you ask in order to turn it to good account on a fifty-fifty ba-
> sis, I may agree. It is of course true that since it is difficult to agree about
> the profit, if you are willing to guarantee me a definite profit, together with
> security for my principal we shall reach agreement more quickly, and I will
> let you have the money forthwith. Is that not a very easy way to make
> money without sinning? . . . Here in my view is the means whereby numer-
> ous members of society, who through their usuries, extortions and unlawful
> contracts provoke God's righteous wrath, can save themselves while making
> handsome, honest and lawful profits.[34]

Another suggestion draws again on the principle of directing the intention. The
would-be lender should just make himself think of the interest as a token of gratitude.

> Usury, according to our Fathers, consists almost solely of the intention of
> taking this profit as usurious. And that is why our Father Escobar makes it
> possible to avoid usury by mere shift of intention. . . . It would be usury to
> make a profit from those to whom one lends if one demanded it as legally
> due; but if one demands it as due out of gratitude, it is not usury. . . . It is
> not lawful to have the intention of profiting directly from money lent; but
> appealing to the goodwill of the person to whom one has lent, *media benevo-
> lentia,* is not usury.[35]

A final suggestion for beating the usury ban is the so-called Mohatra contract. The
would-be borrower "sells" something to the would-be lender for the amount of the

loan, and by way of repayment with interest he may buy it back sometime later at a higher price.

> Its name is the only strange thing about it. . . . The Mohatra contract is that
> whereby one buys goods dear and for credit, and simultaneously sells them
> to the same person cheap and for cash. . . . [That is] the Mohatra is when
> someone who needs twenty *pistoles* buys goods from a merchant for thirty
> *pistoles,* payable in one year, and at once sells them back to him for twenty
> *pistoles* in cash.[36]

The Jesuits piously condemn lying but suggest a variety of alternative means for guiltlessly getting a falsehood cross:

> One of the most embarrassing problems is how to avoid lying, especially
> when one would like people to believe something untrue. This is where our
> doctrine of equivocation is marvellously helpful, for it allows one to use am-
> biguous terms, conveying a different meaning to the hearer from that in
> which one understands them himself. . . . and what to do when one cannot
> find equivocal terms? . . . [Use] the doctrine of mental restrictions. . . .
> One may swear . . . that one has not done something, though one really has
> done it, by inwardly understanding that one did not do it on a certain day,
> or before one was born, or by implying some other similar circumstance,
> but using words with no meaning capable of conveying this: this is very con-
> venient on many occasions, and is always quite legitimate when necessary,
> or useful, to health, honour or propriety. . . . [A]nother safer way of
> avoiding a lie; after saying aloud "I swear that I did not do that" you add un-
> der your breath "that I say" and then go on aloud that "I did not do that."
> You see that that is telling the truth.[37]

Related to that is the recommendation for circumventing the prohibition on idolatry:

> [I]n India and China, [we] have even allowed Christians to practice idolatry,
> by the ingenious idea of getting them to hide under their clothes an image
> of Christ, to which they are taught to apply mentally the worship paid pub-
> licly to the idol Chacim-Choan and their [Confucius].[38]

The Jesuits have no compunction about advertising the prospect of confession and repentance as a way of taking the risk out of sinning. To be sure, in the early days of Christianity there was the problem that the church still insisted on fairly painful forms of penance. But even then the forerunners of the Jesuits had a good way of easing that pain: "[T]o wait until the imminence of death. Arduous penitential exercises obviously could not be required of a dying man, and his exclusion from economic, military, and martial life would be similarly irrelevant. But formal reconciliation was still possible, and Pope Leo the Great [had] directed that dying Christians be reconciled without the imposition of pentitential exercises."[39]

Finally, when the Jesuits do not have a good substantive argument for circumventing a prohibition, they have a more general fall-back strategy—the doctrine of probabilism. A theological opinion is deemed probable if there is some substantial ground for holding it. Any opinion that is put forth by a Jesuitical scholar or equivalent authority, even if he be the only one to hold it, thereby automatically becomes probable: the fact that it is asserted by a respected authority is a sufficiently substantial reason for anyone who finds it convenient to follow it. When there is no other strategy available for circumventing a prohibition, this doctrine usually will yield one. All that needs to be done is to find some however questionable authority casting doubt on the validity of the prohibition, and one is entitled to disregard it. So, for instance, although the Jesuits do not by and large endorse killing an attacker in defense of mere property, they acknowledge that there is some biblical support for doing so and that slight support may be used as a bootstrap for making such killings perfectly legitimate.

COULD THE HAIRSPLITTERS BE RIGHT?

How outrageous are the practices advocated by the theologians in the last section? Were Pascal and Feynman right to denounce them as intolerable evasions? As we shall see, the maligned Jesuitic and Talmudic hairsplitters have the better of this argument. While they may not be right on the details of every one of their opinions, in general the advice they give is far from obviously unsound. And that is a fact of some significance for understanding the "avoision" problem. Let's take a second look at the advice they proffer.

Dueling

The Jesuits maintain that one can respect the prohibition against dueling and still proceed as follows: go to a place designated by one's challenger, hang around there weapon in hand until attacked, and then defend oneself when that becomes necessary. To see why this is not such an absurd suggestion, consider a modern-day analogue. A Hatfield wants to kill some McCoys. He knows that if he kills them outright he will be found guilty of murder. So he goes about the business of killing them somewhat more deviously. He goes to a gathering of McCoys and identifies himself as a Hatfield. The outraged McCoys immediately turn on him, but he is ready for them with his trusty machine gun and mows down several of them. To justify his actions before the law, he invokes self-defense. There is a lively controversy in the criminal law literature over whether he can do so.

The debate actually concerns a much larger genre of cases, of which the "contrived self-defense" scenario is only the most exemplary representative, namely, cases in which the defendant puts himself into a position where he gets to do what the law would ordinarily forbid by ensuring he has some kind of legal excuse or justification at his side. Think, for instance, of the newspaper heiress who hears rumors that there is a gang of terrorists out there planning to kidnap the children of prominent families and to humiliate their parents by forcing the children to perform criminal acts. Imagine that she happens to find the idea of participating in a bank heist alluring, although she would never, of course, venture to commit one on her own. Indeed, she entertains wishful daydreams about the possibility of being kidnapped by this gang, all of which she confesses in great detail to her diary. She grows so enchanted by the idea that she deliberately dissolves her private army of bodyguards hoping to make the gang's job easier. In due course she is kidnapped and compelled at gunpoint to carry out a bank robbery. If she were charged with bank robbery, could she defend on the grounds of necessity, saying that if she had not done what she was asked to do she would have been killed? Does the fact that she "welcomed" being thus forced and she actually made the task of the kidnappers easier—not that they had any idea of what was in her mind!—deprive her of the defense? This case, too, produces contradictory reactions among scholars.

Those who would deny a defense in such cases argue that the defendant is really no better than someone who kills both his parents and then asks the court for mercy because he is an orphan: it is only fair that someone who deliberately creates the conditions of his own excuse or justification thereby forfeits them. But others see the matter very differently. You have a right to visit any part of the city you choose, whether McCoys live there or not, and you have no obligation to keep your identity as a Hatfield a secret. If the others attack you, that's *their* choice, not something for which *you* can be blamed. So why should you lose your right of self-defense? Similarly, you have a right to live without bodyguards. If you are then kidnapped, again that's the kidnappers choice not something for which you can be blamed. So why should you lose your necessity defense? The German scholar Joachim Hruschka has found an especially felicitous way of making this point. He asks us to think about the person who passes by a gallery, sees a painting he doesn't like, goes in, buys it, and then destroys it. If we are going to say that someone who deliberately creates the condition of his own justification thereby forfeits it, it seems we would also have to say that he is guilty of destroying another person's property when he destroys that painting. Why? Because in buying the painting he created the condition of his own justification: the fact that the painting now belonged to him. You have a right to destroy your own paintings, and if you want to destroy another's painting you can bring about the destruction of the painting by making it your own first. And since you have a right to defend yourself by killing your attacker if necessary, asks Hruschka, how is making someone attack you so you can kill him different from making someone sell you his painting so you can destroy it? I don't mean to settle this controversy. I bring it up only to show that the position of the Jesuits is far from frivolous.[40]

The Shabbes Goy

It is all right to do indirectly what you cannot do directly—that's the principle that the Shabbes Goy practice seems to exploit so shamelessly. It is all right to bring about some forbidden result, the principle says, so long as you make sure the causal chain between you and the outcome has a sufficient number of distancing links. Can that be right? In a remarkable number of settings it is, and has proved to be of great practical significance.

1. Take the case of Angela who is standing at the end of a movie ticket line and who notices that X is about to fire a .22 automatic at her. She knows that a .22 bullet can kill one person but not two. So she seizes Brenda who is standing next to her and moves her in front as a shield. The bullet kills Brenda. Putting to the side a possible duress defense Angela might have (depending on the background circumstances), she is quite clearly guilty of murdering Brenda.

Suppose, however, that Angela had instead simply leaped aside, again with the result that the bullet kills Brenda rather than her. Now she is *not* guilty of murder. All she has done, of course, is to change the causal relationship between herself and Brenda's death from a direct to an indirect one. That alone serves to alter radically the moral character of her actions: to cause death by "ducking" is all right; to cause death by "shielding" is bad.[41]

A detective on my local public television station told his listeners that the key to protecting yourself against becoming a crime victim is to become a "tough target," which criminals will bypass for easier prey. He explained:

> Here we've got two people. Now these two people have two apartments, and these apartments are right across the back porch from each other. If you went up the back stairs, you will find that they have a common back porch. These two apartments are exactly the same. Except this woman, she went to the pet store and she bought a dog bowl. She bought a big dog bowl. She filled it with water, wrote the word "Killer" on it, and put it outside her door. Now, when Mickey the Moke comes up the back stairs to do one of these apartments, which one is he not going to pick? See how easy it is? Not being selected is the most important thing that you can do. Tough targets are not selected.[42]

Just to be sure his listeners got the point, he elaborated with a joke:

> Two guys are in a tent. They're sleeping in the middle of the woods, and a bear starts to claw his way through the back of the tent. The two guys tumble out of the tent, right in front. One guy jumps up and starts to run, the other guy jumps up and starts to put his gym shoes on. And the first guy says, "What are you putting your gym shoes on for, pal? You can't outrun that bear." And he said, "I don't have to outrun the bear. All I have to do is outrun you." Same lesson. You can't be the weakest one, the most vulnerable one there.[43]

2. Rella is suffering from a terminal illness and asks for Harry's help in ending her life. After making sure that Rella really means what she says, Harry wheels in a carbon monoxide delivery system, puts a face mask on Rella, and pulls the lever to start the gas flow. Notwithstanding Rella's consent, notwithstanding his humanitarian motives, in most states Harry will be found guilty of murder. Suppose, however, that at the last minute Harry had refused to pull the lever and instead asked Rella to do so herself. Now he is only guilty of assisting in a suicide, which is considerably less serious than murder. Rella's intervening voluntary action would be deemed to break the chain of proximate causation required to hold Harry guilty of her murder.

There is nothing, I should note, artificial or odd about the principle that says that certain voluntary actions break the chain of proximate causation. Imagine a wife about to leave her husband, who threatens to commit suicide if she goes

33

through with her intentions. As she is about to make her final exit from the apartment, her husband climbs to the edge of the windowsill and announces he will jump if she should take one further step. Although she may know with perfect certitude that he will make good on his threat, and perhaps even welcomes that outcome (the inheritance, the life insurance!), she still will not be held legally responsible for his death. His voluntary action breaks the chain of proximate causation. It is this very principle that allows someone to turn murder into assisted suicide.

3. Saul operates some complicated piece of machinery. He knows that if he is ever less than at least moderately attentive, this creates a significant risk of human injury. Whether or not such injury actually results, but especially if it does, we would blame Saul for his recklessness. Saul realizes that over the course of a lifetime of operating the machinery, on a few occasions he almost certainly will behave somewhat recklessly. All he can hope for is that on those occasions he will not cause harm.

Now imagine that Saul were to build a robot to take his place operating the machinery. The robot is as reliable as Saul, meaning its accident rate in operating the machinery is no higher, and no lower, than Saul's. After the robot has been operating in Saul's place for some time, an accident occurs, of precisely the kind that Saul's earlier recklessness might have brought about. Will Saul be blamable for this accident? Most certainly not. He constructed a state-of-the-art robot that was no less safe than anything else he could have used to run the machinery; and the accident was not caused through any recklessness on Saul's part. Again, simply by changing his causal relationship to the injury someone has managed to change greatly the moral character of the harm he triggers.

What Saul does is now commonplace. Companies routinely cope with the threat of tort liability by replacing human actors for whose predictable recklessness they would be held liable with machinery whose predictable failings are not evidence of recklessness on the part of anyone.[44]

4. Evelyn is pregnant. Nevertheless she continues to indulge freely in a recreational drug that is very likely to do significant damage to her unborn. To be precise, the effect of the drug is that a high percentage of fetuses exposed to it will be born without index fingers. We would surely be willing to seriously blame Evelyn for what she is doing and may well be willing to punish her criminally as well.

Suppose, instead, that Evelyn is not yet pregnant when she is indulging in the drug but that the drug causes genetic damage, and that children born to past consumers of the drug have the identically high likelihood of being born without index fingers as those exposed to it during pregnancy. While taking the drug, Evelyn is already planning to have children, but she is willing to reconsider the matter before making a final decision to make sure that she is doing the right thing. When the moment does come, she is perturbed by the possibility that her child will have no index fingers but decides that that is no reason not to conceive. How would we judge Evelyn's conduct under these altered circumstances? Much, much differently, I should think. Her initial decision to consume the drug is not blameworthy because she is only planning to have a child *if* when the time comes that is the morally right thing to do. Her subsequent decision to have the child is all right despite the genetic risk, because we do not think that people with genetic risks of such a relatively minor nature should abstain from procreating. So again, by just changing the causal chain around a bit we have dramatically altered the moral character of the actor's conduct.

Directing the Attention

The most common device that the Jesuits recommend for bypassing an unpleasant rule is to tinker with one's state of mind. So they tell the servants working for criminal masters to make sure they "direct their intentions not towards the sins of which they are the accessories, but solely to the profit which accrues to them thereby." And they tell the persons making a charitable contribution in hopes of getting a clerical post to be sure they "form the intention of giving it as a motive to induce the incumbent to resign, instead of giving it as the price of the benefice." Why is that not as silly as it sounds?

The Jesuits are on to a good point, but they make a hash of it as they try to apply it. The criminal law quite soundly distinguishes between several mental states with which a harm can be brought about. The defendant can do his killing, lying, stealing, and cheating with four fundamentally different attitudes: intentionally, knowingly, recklessly, or negligently. To kill intentionally, the Model Penal Code explains quite unsurprisingly, is to have someone's death as one's "conscious object." To kill knowingly is to be "aware that it is practically certain that [one's] conduct" will produce death. To kill recklessly is to "consciously disregard a substantial and unjustifiable risk" that death will occur. To kill negligently is to impose a "substantial and unjustifiable risk" of death which one *should* be aware of but may not actually be. Intentional acts are judged to be morally worse than knowing acts, which in turn are worse than reckless ones, which in turn are worse than negligent ones, which in turn are worse than accidental (and therefore not at all blamewor-thy) ones. Realizing all of this, the Jesuits recommend to a would-be criminal that he make sure he commits his bad act with a less rather than a more culpable mental state. Instead of killing intentionally, they recommend he try doing so only know-ingly, recklessly, negligently, or, better yet, altogether accidentally. But how is one supposed to do that? If I try to kill accidentally—or knowingly, recklessly, or negli-gently—well, then I have really killed intentionally! It's like trying to deliver a well-planned spontaneous repartee. The Jesuits' advice seems self-defeating.

But it can be done. In fact, it can be done in numerous ways. Let's begin by trying to turn an intentional killing into a knowing killing. That requires us to first understand clearly where exactly the difference between these two mental states lies. It is admittedly an elusive difference. Indeed, sometimes it seems as though it were impossible to do something knowingly but not intentionally, as illustrated by this English case: Smith was driving a car with a trunk full of sacks of stolen scaffolding clips. A constable noticed the sacks and ordered Smith to pull over to the curb. Smith began to do so, with the constable walking alongside. Then sud-denly he accelerated and tried to make a getaway. The constable clung to the side of the car, although it had no running board. He held on for some 130 yards, while Smith zigzagged down the street at a high speed in an effort to shake him off. He finally succeeded. The constable fell into the path of an oncoming car, which killed him. Let us assume (although that was a central issue in the case) that Smith had acted with virtual certainty that what he did would be the death of the constable. Yet he clearly would rather have made his getaway without injury to the constable. Had he intended the constable's death? If one intends something to which one knows something else to be inextricably tied, is one not also intending that some-thing else?[45] This case certainly makes it seem so.

But just because there are hard-to-classify cases doesn't mean that there isn't an important difference between acting knowingly and intentionally. First appear-ances notwithstanding, it really is possible to intend something to which one knows something else to be inextricably tied without also intending that other thing. Take the facts of *Serné,* a nineteenth-century English case, in which a father set fire to his house to collect the insurance and one of his sons died in the process.[46] Suppose the father knew in advance that someone was virtually certain to die in the fire and he greatly regretted that. We would, I think, describe that killing as knowing rather than intentional. Would we describe it so because Serné greatly regrets the death? Almost, but not quite. No one would say that the grandson who kills his grandmother for the inheritance has not killed her intentionally just because he regrets doing so and would rather have gotten the money without having to kill her. The difference between Serné and the grandson is not the regret but this: when Serné torches his house and kills his son, the death of the son is a mere *by-product* of his getting the insurance money he wants. When the grandson kills his grandmother, her death is his very *means* for getting the inheritance money he wants. (I take the difference between by-products and means to be a pretty clear one. Nevertheless, some readers might wonder: How *do* we decide whether the defendant who brings about a death in the course of pursuing some goal is bringing it about as a *by-product of* or a *means toward* reaching that goal? We do so by determining whether the defendant, if he had not thought the death to be tied to his goal, would have chosen a different course of action. If burning down her house would not result in the death of his grandmother, the grandson would not be doing it. If burning down his house would not result in killing his son, Serné would still be doing it. Hence the former death is a means and the latter death a by-product.)

You might wonder why it is worth trying to unravel the elusive distinction between intentional and knowing killings. Under current law—which I take to be a pretty accurate mirror of morality—the distinction between intentional and knowing killings matters only a little when it comes to a completed killing, since a knowing killing is only a little less blameworthy than an intentional one. The distinction matters more if the crime doesn't work out as contemplated. Suppose, for instance, that no one dies and that Serné's son makes a particularly narrow escape. Is the arsonist guilty of attempted murder? Only if he is deemed to have intended to kill someone, not if he is deemed merely to have foreseen such an outcome. The distinction also matters as to people who helped the arsonist. Suppose the person who sold Serné the kerosene and other wherewithal knew full well what he was up to. If we say that he intentionally helped torch the house, he is guilty as an accomplice. If we say that he did so only knowingly, he is not.

We now understand that there is a difference between knowing and intentional killings and that the distinction matters. What, then, of the Jesuits' suggestion that one can somehow turn one's intentional state into a knowing one? Their idea that one need only "redirect one's attention" to achieve that objective clearly will not work. The grandson who murders his grandmother to inherit her money will not transform his intentional killing into a knowing one by "directing his attention" at the gain that lies at the end of the road rather than the intermediate killing. But there is something else that will work.

Consider Serné once again. Suppose he had started out by taking out insurance on his son's life and had planned to kill him by burning down their house, figuring that this would be the only reliable way to do so without getting caught. If he went through with this plan, it would clearly be an intentional killing. Imagine now that just before putting his plan into practice, it occurs to him that he can get just as much money by insuring his house. Then he proceeds to torch it, realizing that there is a near certainty that his son will die in the process. Now he has killed his son only knowingly. And he has achieved that goal merely by changing the insurance policy—which is just the result the Jesuits were reaching for.

We can use the same technique to turn intentional killings into reckless killings, that is, murder into manslaughter. Suppose that Serné's initial plan of torching his house and collecting the life insurance on his son had only a 60 percent chance of working, because the only way he knew to do the job that would cover his tracks had only a 60 percent chance of resulting in a successful conflagration. If Serné's son died in the process, it would be an intentional killing. The fact that his death was not certain from the outset does not matter as long as it was the result Serné hoped to bring about. Next, imagine that Serné decided to change the insurance policy to cover his house rather than his son. Again, assume that torching the house only has a 60 percent chance of triggering a conflagration, in which case his son is certain to die. If, under this scenario, his son in fact dies, Serné will merely be guilty of a reckless killing, manslaughter, because the death was less than certain and Serné did not hope for it.

I suspect that a court would react to a defendant who tried to mitigate his guilt in this way with the same kind of perplexed uncertainty that the court would bring to a case of "contrived self-defense," which proves my point that the Jesuitic suggestion is not patently frivolous. But capitalizing on the distinction between means and by-products is just one way of implementing the Jesuits' suggestion. An alternative strategy, and one that has been tried by Jesuits and others alike, is "willful blindness": When a Jew is about to solicit rabbinical advice that he might might find too difficult to follow, it has not been uncommon for the rabbi to subtly discourage him from getting the advice, on the grounds that "it is better to err inadvertently than deliberately."[47] To put the matter more abstractly: to meet the criteria of any of the required mental states for a crime—intention, knowledge, recklessness, or negligence—requires awareness of certain facts. That's not true just of harm one knowingly commits but even of harm one negligently commits: here, of course, one need not actually be aware of the harm one is negligently inflicting, but one must be aware of facts that make it reasonable to infer that such harm is about to result from one's actions. What of the defendant who tries to act while keeping his eyes shut to facts, an awareness of which would render the actions criminal? Is that feasible? Is it ethical?

No case is better at bringing that issue to the fore than that of Albert Speer, Hitler's armaments minister and closest confidante, who in the aftermath of the war claimed to have remained willfully ignorant of the holocaust. This claim of ignorance is curious not so much for its wild implausibility as for the fact that Speer doesn't offer it as an excuse, at least not ostensibly. On several occasions in his memoirs, Speer goes to considerable pains to convince the reader of his genuine, if willful, ignorance, but he invariably conjoins it with the admission that, of course, that doesn't serve to exonerate him. "My decision to enter Hitler's party," he explains early in the memoirs, was made "frivolously:"

> For had I only wanted to, I could have found out even then that Hitler was
> proclaiming expansion of the Reich to the east; that he was a rank anti-
> Semite; that he was committed to a system of authoritarian rule; that after
> attaining power he intended to eliminate democratic procedures and would
> thereafter yield only to force. Not to have worked that out for myself . . .
> was already criminal. At this initial stage my guilt was as grave as . . . at the
> end, my work for Hitler. For being in a position to know and nevertheless
> shunning knowledge creates direct responsibility for the consequences—
> from the beginning.[48]

A bit later he continues along the same line:

> During the years after my release from Spandau I have been repeatedly
> asked what thoughts I had on this subject during my two decades alone in
> the cell with myself; what I actually knew of the persecution, the deporta-
> tion, and the annihilation of the Jews; what I should have known and what
> conclusions I ought to have drawn.
>
> I no longer give the answer with which I tried for so long to soothe the
> questioners, but chiefly myself: that in Hitler's system, as in every totalitar-
> ian regime, when a man's position rises, his isolation increases and he is
> therefore more sheltered from harsh reality; that with the application of
> technology to the process of murder the number of murderers is reduced
> and therefore the possibility of ignorance grows; that the craze for secrecy
> built into the system creates degrees of awareness, so it is easy to escape ob-
> serving human cruelties.

I no longer give any of these answers. For they are efforts at legalistic ex-
culpation. It is true that as a favorite and later as one of Hitler's most influ-
ential ministers I was isolated. It is also true that the habit of thinking within
the limits of my own field provided me, both as architect and as Armaments
Minister, with many opportunities for evasion. It is true that I did not know
what was really beginning on November 9, 1938 [that is, *Kristallnacht*] and
what ended in Auschwitz and Maidanek. But in the final analysis I myself determined the degree of my isolation, the extremity of my evasions, and the
extent of my ignorance.

I therefore know today that my agonized self-examinations posed the
question as wrongly as did the questioners whom I have met since my release [from the Spandau prison]. Whether I knew or did not know, or how
much or how little I knew, is totally unimportant when I consider what hor-
rors I ought to have known about and what conclusions would have been the
natural ones to draw from the little I did know. Those who ask me are fundamentally expecting me to offer justifications. But I have none. No apologies
are possible.[49]

He offers one very specific illustration of how he maintained his state of willful
ignorance:

[S]ome time in the summer of 1944, my friend Karl Hanke, the Gauleiter of
Lower Silesia, came to see me. . . . [S]itting in the green leather easy chair
in my office, he seemed confused and spoke falteringly, with many breaks.
He advised me never to accept an invitation to inspect a concentration camp
in Upper Silesia. Never under any circumstances. He had seen something
there which he was not permitted to describe and moreover could not describe. I did not query him, I did not query Himmler, I did not query Hitler,
I did not speak with personal friends. I did not investigate—for I did not
want to know what was happening there. Hanke must have been speaking of
Auschwitz. . . . From that moment on, I was inescapably contaminated morally; from fear of discovering something which might have made me turn
from my course, I had closed my eyes. . . . Because I failed at that time, I
still feel, to this day, responsibility for Auschwitz in a wholly personal
sense.[50]

Throughout the remaining years of his life, Speer tried hard to sustain this claim
of willful ignorance in the face of mounting evidence to the contrary. Critics
pointed out that for an extended period he was in charge of clearing out Jewish

apartments in Berlin and had to coordinate his efforts with those of authorities in charge of deportation. They also noted that as armaments minister he used a lot of slave labor and was responsible for allocating the materials from which the concentration camp barracks were built. Most important, they uncovered evidence that he actually attended a conference at which Himmler spoke very openly about the final solution and addressed Speer by name.

Speer went to great pains to rebut the charges, to insist, for instance, that he left the conference at which Himmler spoke before the latter began his address, but that Himmler was under the mistaken impression that he was still in the audience. So keen was Speer to maintain his claim of willful blindness that, when he was called on to testify in a trial of former SS guards at the Dora concentration camp, he refused credit for a good deed because accepting it would have betrayed too much guilty knowledge.[51]

It is clear then that Speer was being coy, was playing Marc Anthony by saying he was not seeking to excuse himself while going to such extraordinary pains to establish his willful ignorance. He really did think it mitigated his guilt. But did it? Indeed, is willful ignorance even a conceptually coherent state to be in? There is a paradox here. "[T]he root of the paradox," explains the political scientist Jon Elster,

> is the peculiar feature that the self-deceiver intentionally hides one of his beliefs from himself and professes the other as his official view. The idea of successful self-deception therefore raises two closely related questions: How does one manage to *forget intentionally* what one "really" (somehow, somewhere) believes? And having achieved this impossible feat, how does one achieve that of *believing at will* what one also believes that there are no adequate grounds for believing?[52]

In a book called *Did the Greeks Believe in Their Myths?* the French historian Paul Veyne expresses his wonderment at a certain Ethiopian tribe that views the leopard as a "Christian animal who respects the fasts of the Coptic church, the observance of which, in Ethiopia, is the principal test of religion. Nonetheless, [the Ethiopian] is no less careful to protect his livestock on Wednesdays and Fridays, the fast days, than on other days of the week. He holds it true that leopards fast and that they eat every day. Leopards are dangerous every day; this he knows by experience. They are Christian; tradition proves it."[53] How can they simultaneously believe both, Veyne asks?

As Elster goes on to very clearly explain, the paradox can be resolved. Willful ignorance is not a contradiction in terms.

> [C]onsider a man who wishes to be promoted and by his wish is led to believe that he is about to receive promotion. We might speak of self-deception here if the evidence available to him points in another direction and he somehow is aware of this, and yet manages to hide this knowledge from himself and believe that promotion is imminent. But it might also be the case that the man has very good grounds for believing himself about to be promoted, but that he arrived at the belief by wishful thinking rather than by a considered judgment on these grounds. Here . . . [t]here is no question of hiding from oneself an unpleasant truth or well-grounded belief, since the well-grounded belief is also the one that the believer wants to be true and indeed believes because he wants it to be true. He has good reasons for believing it, but it is not for those reasons that he believes it.
>
> This is not just an abstract possibility, but a configuration often met in everyday life. Surely we have all met persons basking in self-satisfaction that seems to be both justified and not justified: justified because they have good reasons for being satisfied with themselves, and not justified because we sense that they would be just as content were the reasons to disappear. Or, to take he opposite case, consider the congenital pessimist whose valuation of the situation is for once justified by the evidence: he is right and justified, and yet we hesitate to say that he is right and justified. . . . the criteria for rational belief involve looking at the actual *causal relation* between evidence and beliefs, the mere *comparison* between evidence and belief being insufficient.[54]

What this shows, he says is

> that in some cases at least wishful thinking does not involve self-deception, the cases, namely, in which the belief born of desire is also borne out by the evidence. But then, why should not the same argument apply to other cases? Why could it not be the case that the wishful believer goes directly for the pleasant belief, instead of going through the four-step process of (1) arriving at the well-grounded belief, (2) deciding that it is unpalatable, (3) suppressing it and only then (4) adhering to another more tolerable belief? Or again, why should the repellent force of an unpleasant belief have explanatory privilege over the attracting force of a pleasant belief?[55]

Willful blindness is no doubt a delicate state to maintain. In the case not just of Speer but of Germans more generally, it meant (as the historian Walter Lacqueur has pointed out) that while they "thought that the Jews were no longer alive, they did not necessarily believe that they were dead." If that still seems like an impossible mental feat, just think of the analogous feat we perform every time we watch a play. On seeing Othello express his sorrow over Desdemona's death we do not say to ourselves (the philosopher Kendall Walton notes), "How did Othello, a Moorish general and hardly an intellectual, manage to come up with such superb verse on the spur of the moment, and when immensely distraught? Apparently he is to be credited with an almost unbelievable natural literary flair. . . . And isn't it peculiarly inappropriate for Othello to make such a grandiloquent speech in such distressing circumstances? Why does he flaunt his literary skills so pompously? Why do other characters take no notice of his peculiar manner of discourse, or of his astounding literary talent?"[56]

But dodging such inferences is actually a tricky matter, because most of the time we need to be able to freely draw them for fiction to be intelligible to us. We need to be able to assume that the characters in a story have blood in their veins, that the couple described as "strolling in the park [also] eat and sleep and work and play; that they have friends and rivals, ambitions, satisfactions, and disappointments; that they live on a planet that spins on its axis and circles the sun, one with weather and seasons, mountains and oceans, peace and war, industry and agriculture, poverty and plenty; and so on and on and on."[57] We are supposed to arrange our fictional worlds to be just like the real one up to certain critical points, and at those points we are to artfully stop short of drawing an unwelcome inference. It is that skill that presumably goes into maintaining a state of willful ignorance.

We display the same skill in blocking natural inferences in the way we cope with the various indispensable forms of legal make-believe—the presumptions, presuppositions, fictions, demurrers, curative jury instructions, alternative holdings, and other artifices. "Everyone is presumed to know the law" is taken to imply that a thief won't be able to argue he didn't know theft was illegal, even if he could make a convincing case that he didn't. But it is not taken to imply that Miranda warnings are superfluous, that defendants don't need lawyers to represent them, that judicial mistakes must necessarily be willful—or that law students can be given their final exams on the first day of class. "Everyone is presumed innocent until proven guilty" works the same way. It is taken to imply that until proved guilty beyond a reasonable doubt you cannot be punished, stripped of your voting rights, or required to wear prison garb in court. It is not taken to imply that you cannot be searched, required to post bail, threatened with prosecution unless you plead guilty to a lesser crime, or found liable in tort for the wrongful death of the person you are "presumed" innocent of killing. We are quite willing to block natural inferences where it suits our purpose, whether that purpose be the preservation of the theatrical illusion or the wrongful death cause of action. It is this, I take it, that Holmes's famous salvo about the life of the law not being logic was meant to get at.

Shutting one's eyes to the logical consequences of something one already knows is only the most extreme kind of willful ignorance. A somewhat less extreme kind is often used in times of war, when the commanding officer is seeking to assemble a firing squad and is unable to find any volunteers. He might then put together an especially large group and randomly issue half of them blanks: No soldier can now easily tell whether his was the fatal shot.

Do these transparent ruses work? We know that they work at a psychological level: there *is* such a thing as willful ignorance. But does it mitigate guilt? Speer clearly is not the only one to think so. His critics who have tried to prove that he was not willfully ignorant but fully cognizant seem to think so too. Most of us often behave as though we thought so. Psychological experiments have shown that even people who feel morally obligated to help strangers in need will go out of their way to construe an ambiguous situation in such a way that no help on their part is required: Does it look like a man is bleeding on the sidewalk? If at all possible, passersby will try to construe him as a drunk in no need of assistance.

We also know that these ruses often work at a legal level. Lawyers are not allowed to *knowingly* help their clients commit perjury—but they can do so unknowingly. Lawyers routinely cope with this restriction by trying hard not to ask their clients questions the answers to which might be embarrassing and might bar them from putting that client on the stand. Defense lawyer Richard "Racehorse" Haynes flatly says: "I never [ask] the client what it is that he contends are the facts from his point of view in the initial interview. . . . in order to avoid being compromised in deciding whether to put him on the witness stand. The thing to do is to ask him what he suspects the other side might claim."[58] The law here as so often is a good gauge of our moral intuitions. So I rather think the ruses work at a moral level as well.

Forgiveness

"A person may be absolved who admits that the hope of being absolved encouraged him to sin more easily than he would have done without it," Pascal quotes one Father Bauny as saying. The question remains whether Pascal is right in thinking it intolerable to grant forgiveness when the sin was committed only because the sinner could count on forgiveness.

Like the other Jesuitical arguments to which Pascal so vehemently objected, this one also has its analogue in modern criminal law. It arises in connection with the criminal law's counterpart to the doctrine of forgiveness—the doctrine of abandonment, which the Model Penal Code states thus: "When the actor's conduct would otherwise constitute a [criminal] attempt . . . , it is an affirmative defense that he abandoned his effort to commit the crime or otherwise prevented its commission, under circumstances manifesting a complete and voluntary renunciation of his criminal purpose."[59] Imagine now a would-be assassin contemplating two ways of bringing his plan to fruition. First, he might fire at his target from a distant spot. Since he is not a terrific marksman, he rightly figures that he has only a two-in-three chance of killing his victim. In the alternative, he might ambush his victim from close-up and be sure to kill him. The only drawback is that he might have last-minute qualms about killing someone whose flesh and blood is in such immediate and palpable proximity. Because of the possibility of such last-minute qualms, he figures this undertaking too has only about a two-in-three chance of succeeding. It is at this point that the assassin remembers the doctrine of abandonment: if he tries to kill his victim from a distance and fails—because of his poor aim—he will be guilty of a criminal attempt. If, on the other hand, he tries to kill his victim from close-up and fails—because of his last-minute qualms—he will be able to avail himself of the abandonment defense and go free. Or so he thinks. I think he is right in thinking this, but no doubt some criminal law scholars would disagree. For now I mean to show only that the Jesuitic position is far from frivolous.

Lies and Idolatry

The Jesuits' approval of equivocation is really just an extreme application of the right to mislead by silence, which in turn is merely a straightforward application of the act-omission distinction, the rule that says that one is responsible solely for the consequences one causes by acting, not those one causes by failing to act. Killing is bad, letting die is all right. The distinction has come in for regular bursts of ridicule. Not surprisingly, critics have been able to concoct cases that are difficult to classify: a child is racing to escape a menacing dog and heads toward the open door of a neighbor's house. When the neighbor, who has always detested the child, sees him coming, he slams the door in the child's face—with the expected deadly consequences. Act or omission, ask the critics, killing or letting die? More pointedly, yet, the critics have very insistently wondered why we should care about the distinction at all. Why should it matter, morally speaking, whether I forcibly submerge my victim in the bathtub or whether I just fail to pull him up when he has fainted and thus submerged himself. If it doesn't make a difference to the victim, why should it matter to a judge of the case?

Such objections notwithstanding, the act-omission distinction has a lot of merit. It is built on some very powerful and deep-seated intuitions. The person who produces death by letting his victim die rather than killing him leaves the world no worse than he found it, no worse than it would be if he didn't exist at all. If we denied the distinction's moral significance, we would have to put on a par the person who drops a bomb on some Third World village and the person who simply lets its inhabitants go hungry, assuming the resulting death counts are equal.

Then, too, the act-omission distinction has a way of proving its sturdiness by appearing again and again in different contexts and guises. Actually, the very critics who belittle it have themselves been unable to do without it. Ask them what they do when they are uncertain about some issue. For that matter, ask yourself what you do if you cannot make up your mind whether to believe X or its opposite. Usually you will find it advisable to remain agnostic. What you will not do is to say: "I might as well believe both X and not-X. Although I am certain to be wrong about one of them, I am also certain to be right about the other. So it's a wash." Your not saying this indicates that errors of commission weigh more heavily than errors of omission. The philosopher Roy Sorensen puts the matter especially felicitously:

> The quick answer to why inconsistency is bad is that it inevitably saddles
> us with error. Those who like to accentuate the positive reply that . . .
> inconsistency—[believing X and believing non-X]—compensates for the
> inevitable error by inevitably providing a true belief. The rejoinder is that it
> is a lopsided exchange. The amount false beliefs harm us exceeds the
> amount true beliefs benefit us. Better therefore to abstain from belief than

to suffer the inevitable net loss. This double standard parallels those discussed in ethics. Just as letting evil happen is thought preferable to actively promoting it, omissive error is less bad than commissive error. Likewise the man who does nothing is better than the man who alternatively does good and evil.[60]

So the Jesuits are hardly being radical in attaching weight to this distinction. They are, admittedly, a bit aggressive in exploiting it in their doctrine of equivocation. It requires putting some pressure on the distinction to get it to support equivocation as opposed to mere silence. But not too much pressure. Consider the following case: defendant sees someone drowning in the middle of the lake. He jumps in to rescue him, takes hold of him and starts to swim back to shore. Suppose he now discovers that the victim is someone he has long regarded as his mortal enemy, and he decides to dump him. Would he not be within his rights? Would he not be guilty merely of failing to rescue rather than of killing? To be sure, if he discovers who the victim is only after having dragged him ashore, it would then be too late to put him back in the water, because that would require not just letting go but actually propelling the victim into the lake. What the Jesuits are, not unreasonably, suggesting is that making an equivocal statement without following it up with some clarification is the speech analogue to the uncompleted rescue.

Abraham Lincoln, for one, felt quite free to avail himself of this bit of Jesuitic wisdom. When he was running for Congress, his opponent suggested that Lincoln was not a very religious man, that he was something of a freethinker if not an actual atheist. Herndon's biography of Lincoln leaves little doubt that all this was essentially correct. Lincoln coped with these damaging charges by publishing a statement in a newspaper that satisfied most people that they were unfounded. Had Lincoln lied? Not quite. For in the statement, as later critics noted, he only said that he had "never denied the truth of the Scriptures." Alas, notes Edmund Wilson "he does not say that he affirms this truth." Lincoln wrote, "I have never spoken with intentional disrespect of religion in general, or of any denomination of Christians in particular," which as Wilson notes doesn't mean he is actually a Christian. Lincoln wrote that he would not support any man for office "whom I know to be an open enemy of and scoffer at, religion" because no man "has the right to insult the feelings, and injure the morals of the community in which he may live." Which again falls short of actually refuting the charges of his opponents. Nevertheless, it was clearly so taken by the public.[61]

We would probably even tolerate more active ways of misleading as still falling within the general category of harming-by-omission, like the case of the nineteenth-century financier Daniel Drew:

> [N]othing brought more glee to the Old Bear's craggy features, or made his gray eyes glint more merrily, than the knowledge that he was unloading [stock] on a dupe. Henry Clews tells how once on Wall Street, after being severely squeezed in the market, Drew was made the butt of much jesting, especially by a group of young operators who literally laughed in his face. One evening he appeared at a club that the young men frequented, where he seemed to be looking for someone whom he failed to find. Intensely preoccupied, time and again he drew forth from his pocket a big white hand-kerchief to wipe his brow. Just before he left, one last flurry of the hand-kerchief tossed out a small piece of paper that, apparently unseen by him, fluttered to the floor, where one of the young men covered it at once with his foot. After Drew had left, they examined it and found an order to his broker to buy all the Oshkosh stock he could get. The young men were elec-trified: here was advance warning of a big rise in Oshkosh! Immediately they formed a pool and bought 30,000 shares the next day, following which the stock plummeted, giving them a fearful loss. Of course the slip of paper had been planted and the stock had come from Drew.[62]

Although the Jesuits do not remark on it, one can sometimes go so far as to tell a substantial and effective lie without incurring much culpability. Consider the way lies figure in the law of rape. If a defendant disguises himself as the husband of his intended victim, enters her bedroom in the middle of the night and induces her to have intercourse, that will generally be considered rape. His pretense in this case negates the validity of her consent. But suppose that instead the defendant were to disguise himself as the wealthy CEO of a fictitious company and induce her to have intercourse, fully realizing that she would never have done so but for his pretense. That would *not* be rape; this pretense would not negate the validity of her con-sent.[63] You will have no problem surmising what lessons the Jesuits would draw from this.

What is one to make of the Jesuits' suggestion that it is all right to tell a lie so long as you accompany it by a mental reservation, that it is all right to "swear that one has not done something, though one really has done it, by inwardly under-standing that one did not do it on a certain day, or before one was born, or by implying some other similar circumstance." Taken literally, this seems bizarre; but here too lurks a defensible core behind the apparent absurdity. That defensible core starts to emerge once we look at the Jesuits' related acquiescence in idolatry in places where Christianity is forbidden. Remember that in such places the Jesuits approve of hiding the image of Christ under one's clothes, to which one is then asked "to apply mentally the worship paid publicly to the idol." In other words, what the Jesuits are really recommending is hypocrisy, which, unlike the doctrine of mental reservations, has a lot to be said for it.

Admittedly, the Jesuitic position here again is at variance with certain common-place sentiments, but it has a surprisingly sturdy foundation. The cases that have drawn most attention to the problem of hypocrisy over the last few years have been (1) the story of Dan Quayle's attempt to avoid active service in Vietnam while applauding our involvement there, and (2) the story of Jimmy Swaggart railing against pornography while being in the habit of consuming it. There is something extremely peculiar about the public outrage at someone who doesn't practice what he preaches, because the public isn't outraged by what is being preached or by what is being practiced; it is outraged by the dissonance between the two. The public wasn't outraged so much by the fact that Quayle was avoiding active service, or that he was applauding the war, but by the fact that he was doing both at the same time. It wasn't outraged so much by the fact that Swaggart was consuming pornography, or that he was railing against it, but that he was doing so at the same time. Why is that peculiar? Well, if you think the war was a good thing, then presumably you should think Quayle better for having at least applauded it than those who neither served nor applauded. If you think the war was a bad thing, then presumably you should think Quayle better for having at least avoided service than those who both served and applauded. Pari passu, for Jimmy Swaggart. What I am really asking is why we do not take this approach to hypocrisy: if the hypocrite preaches what we like but doesn't practice it, well then at least he is better than someone who neither preaches nor practices. If he preaches what we do not like but he doesn't practice it, well then at least he is better than someone who both preaches and practices. Or so one would argue in the Jesuits' behalf.

Usury

Most of the stratagems that the Jesuits advise for circumventing the prohibition on usury are alive and well in today's corporate law, even though the prohibition on usury itself is largely dead. Recall that one way in which the Jesuits suggested one might "lend without actually lending" is to become a partner in an enterprise and take one's return in the form of partnership profits. Under modern corporate income tax law, taxpayers are advised to use the very same stratagem—in reverse. The corporate income tax falls on all profits of a corporation that are left over once its various creditors, most especially its lenders, have been paid off. One way for an investor to escape the corporate income tax, therefore, is to dress up his investment as a mere loan.

Another way the Jesuits suggest for getting around the prohibition of usury is the Mohatra contract: the borrower sells something to the lender for the desired sum of money and promises to buy it back from the lender in due time for the original purchase price plus interest. The borrower, of course, is not called borrower in this transaction but buyer, the lender is not called lender but seller, and the interest is not called interest but resale profit. This is at present not an uncommon way for corporations to get around restrictions that corporate charters may place on their ability to borrow. The charter will rarely go so far as to restrict the corporation's ability to freely buy and sell, that being crucial to its mission. Many a corporation has thus succeeded in borrowing what funds its CEOs thought they needed by selling some of its assets for the desired amount of cash, with an accompanying promise to repurchase the assets in due time for the original price plus "interest."

Simony

What about the Jesuits' advice on how to circumvent the ban on simony, the purchase of church offices? The modern-day, secular analogue to the ban on simony is the law against bribery of public officials. Now suppose I give money to my senator because of his sympathy for a particular industry, section of the state, or economic class to which I belong, or because of his stand on a particular issue of uniquely strong concern to me personally. That's no bribe, that's a legitimate campaign contribution. If, on the other hand, I tell him that I will give him the money only if he expressly pledges to cast his vote in a particular way, that is a bribe. What the Jesuits would do is to point out to someone about to pay a bribe that he can accomplish the same thing by following the former strategy! This is the defensible core behind the Jesuit's advice on simony.

Probabilism

The doctrine that you can do anything for which you can find a Jesuitic treatise to support you, however outlandish and unpersuasive sounding, could not sound more familiar to a lawyer, as a quote from a statement of a former commissioner of the Internal Revenue Service nicely demonstrates:

> I'm sure that most of you have had the experience that I've had many times in practice in which a client would ask about the taxability of a particular transaction, and you would advise that in your view the matter was taxable, or was not deductible, or was ordinary income rather than a capital gain. The taxpayer would then ask, "Is there any argument at all to take the deduction?" You would say, "Yes, while there are three rulings against it, there is a District Court case in North Dakota that is not exactly on 'all fours' but from which one could draw a little solace." The taxpayer would remark, "What will happen to me if I claim it? Will it constitute fraud? Will I be penalized?" And the answer to that question in the best judgment of the adviser, would be "no." The taxpayer would then say, "Thank you, that's all I wanted to know."[64]

He would take the deduction (or whatever) and rely on the fact that the IRS doesn't have the resources to take a closer look at more than 2 percent of the returns submitted to it.

Defense of Property

The Jesuits thought that the way to sidestep the prohibition against defending your property with deadly force was to combine the doctrine of probabilism with the questionable pronouncements of those scholars who hold it acceptable to use deadly force in defense of property. Under modern criminal law, there is a better strategy. Cuthbert tries to steal Pemberton's car. Cuthbert has a gun and could stop Pemberton by shooting him; but he understands it would be illegal to do so. He knows, however, that Pemberton is carrying a knife and that if Pemberton were to threaten him with the knife he would then be entitled to make use of his gun. But all it takes to get Pemberton to use the knife is to interfere with his completion of the car theft: Cuthbert starts to run in the direction of the car, looking as though he is about to try to take hold of Pemberton with his bare hands. Pemberton takes out his knife to protect himself. And voila, now Cuthbert is free to pull out his gun and shoot him. So yes, indeed, if one is sufficiently roundabout, it is possible to protect one's property with deadly force.

THE HEART, THE LUNGS, AND THE KIDNEYS
OF THE MATTER

Where does all of this leave the problem of avoision? A bit of recapitulation is in order. We started out well aware that people "get around" rules in various ways, some legitimate, some not. The ways we consider legitimate we call avoidance; the others we call evasion. "Avoision" is how I referred to the panoply of questionable conduct about whose status as either avoidance or evasion we couldn't make up our minds. The avoision problem is to determine how and why to put which cases in either of those two slots.

At the outset we thought avoision had to do with loopholes in misdrafted laws. The approach most courts have taken to the various legal examples I presented first is certainly premised on this idea. But then it became clear to us that the avoision phenomenon transcends the law, that it arises even when the rules that are being circumvented are in no way the product of thoughtless draftsmanship: like the rules against lying, killing, or working on the Sabbath. We thought at first we could simply dismiss those cases as not really posing an avoision problem at all, as resting on mere self-deception: The various Jesuitic and Talmudic suggestions for getting around certain rules of religious and nonreligious morality seemed so patently silly—until we took a closer look and discovered that there was a good deal to be said in their behalf, not perhaps enough to prove them right but enough to move them back into the limbo of "avoision." Clearly there are cases of avoision even outside the law, and an account of avoision that views it as the product of misdrafted laws is bound to miss the essence of the phenomenon.

What these nonlegal instances of avoision strongly suggest is that it isn't merely the law that is formalistic but morality itself, and that the formalism of the law is merely a reflection of the formalism of morality. In other words, it may not be a failing of the law that a forbidden result is no longer forbidden if you will only pave a sufficiently circuitous path to it. It may actually be an ineradicable feature of morality. But how can that be? Can morality really be so ridiculously formalistic? Once when Samuel Johnson wanted to show his friend Mrs. Thrale the extent of his father Michael's madness, he told her how every night his father would painstakingly lock the door to his factory, even though the building was half-fallen-down and easily accessible from the back. If morality is susceptible to successful avoision, is it any saner than Samuel Johnson's father?

The question whether morality is at bottom formalistic, path-dependent, and

susceptible to successful avoision turns out to be equivalent to a longstanding philosophical problem. The debate surrounding that problem has, therefore, much light
to shed on the problem of avoision. The debate is one between two diametrically
opposing views of morality—the utilitarians, at the one end, and the deontologists
(or nonconsequentialists) at the other. For a full understanding and resolution of
the problem of avoision, a short exposition of that debate—more than a parenthet-
ical, less than a thumbnail sketch—is thus indispensable.

CONSIDER THE famous hypothetical case of the out-of-control trolley. The
trolley in question is heading down an incline when Edward, its driver, discovers
that the brakes aren't working. "On the track ahead of him are five people: the
banks are so steep that they will not be able to get off the track in time. The track
has a spur leading off to the right, and Edward can turn the trolley onto it. Unfortunately, there is one person on the right hand track. Edward can turn the trolley,
killing the one; or he can refrain from turning the trolley," which would mean the
death of the five.[65]

Nearly everyone here would say that it is all right for the driver to turn the
trolley, and many would go further and say that it is downright *obligatory* for him
to turn the trolley. I advisedly said "nearly everyone" and not everyone, because
there is at least one famous case, involving the British High Command during the
Second World War, in which important decision makers took a different view of
the matter. As Germany was raining its rocket attacks on London, someone in the
British High Command had an idea for reducing the number of casualties. He
pointed out that the Germans were relying on the reports of a London-based spy
ring to gauge how accurately they hit their targets. The British had infiltrated that
spy ring and headed it up with a double agent of their own. The proposed idea was
for the double agent to tell his German superiors that the rockets had fallen north
of London, though in fact they had not. That would lead the Germans to aim their
rockets farther south: on to Kent, Surrey, or Sussex and kill far fewer people than
if they fell on London. The proposal was rejected as it smacked of "playing God."
But in this I think the High Command was highly idiosyncratic.[66]

Why do the vast majority of people think it is all right to turn the trolley? The
obvious answer seems to be that that would minimize the number of lives lost. But
such reasoning immediately invites the challenge of another famous hypothetical,
the case of the "utilitarian surgeon" who has five patients, all of whom are at death's
door. They are destined to die unless they receive transplant organs. Two need

kidneys, two need lungs, one needs a heart. There is no donor to be found—
except for a perfectly healthy patient who walks into the surgeon's office for his
annual checkup. On seeing him, the surgeon realizes that he is a walking reservoir
of useful spare parts, which, if judiciously redeployed, could save five lives at the
cost of one. Suppose the surgeon were to quickly and painlessly kill his healthy
walk-in and use his organs to save the other five? If it is all right to minimize lives
lost by turning the trolley, why shouldn't it be all right to do the same here?

When confronted by this last hypothetical, many people try to think of reasons
why it might not actually minimize the total number of lives lost for the "utilitarian
surgeon" to kill his healthy patient. How else can they explain their instinctive
revulsion at allowing him to proceed but still defend their sense that it is all right
to turn the trolley because it achieves a net saving of lives? They will offer all kinds
of reasons why the "utilitarian surgeon," unlike the trolley driver, will *not* achieve
a net saving of lives: If organ harvesting becomes a common practice, sick people
will be afraid to go to doctors for fear that they will be turned into involuntary
donors, and many of them will die for lack of treatment. Besides, doctors might
make the wrong choices and harvest organs for patients who are too ill to benefit
from them. Furthermore . . . You can see how the list of indirect repercussions
could be extended indefinitely to show why allowing the utilitarian surgeon to
proceed would in the end cost more lives than it saves.

But none of those arguments deals adequately with the case of the utilitarian
surgeon as shown by a variation of the hypothetical invented by Michael Moore.
Suppose, he writes,

> [Ann] is a surgeon who performs transplant operations, harvesting organs
> from healthy victims whenever it is necessary to do so to effect a net saving
> of lives. [Ann] in the near future will harvest such organs from five healthy
> patients in order to save more than five dying patients. [Sue] is another sur-
> geon who knows this and knows that the only way to prevent this is to kill
> [Ann's] husband while he is on the operating table before her. ([Ann's] hus-
> band has just been rushed in to [Sue] for an emergency operation; [Ann] is
> so attached to her husband that she will not be able to carry on for some
> time after his death.) [Sue] also has several dying patients, and should she
> kill [Ann's] husband [Sue] would use the latter's organs to save as many pa-
> tients as possible. If killing a patient to harvest his organs is such a great evil,
> may [Sue] perpetrate that very evil in order to prevent even more of it from
> being done at the hands of someone else [i.e., Ann]?[67]

In other words, if you believed that in general allowing surgeons to engage in organ harvesting does more harm than good, because of its various indirect repercussions, then you should allow someone to engage in some organ harvesting here and now if by doing so you prevent many more such instances of organ harvesting in the future.

What all of this leads up to is this: if you really believe that the reason the trolley driver can turn his trolley is because that minimizes the number of lives lost, then you must, at least under some circumstances, also approve of what the utilitarian surgeon does, at least if the utilitarian surgeon engages in organ harvesting only to prevent many more such instances of organ harvesting in the future. If you are prepared to take that stand, then you are a utilitarian at heart. No need to apologize; you are in excellent company—but not in company that includes me. Actually, "utilitarian" has come to be considered a somewhat antiquated term; "consequentialist" is the more up-to-date one, and with good reason: minimizing lives lost does not necessarily mean maximizing utility.

Many committed consequentialists don't just bite this bullet, they bite it with relish. So, for instance, Bertolt Brecht who in his play *The Measure Taken* asks:

> What meanness would you not commit, to
> stamp out meanness?
>
> If, at last, you could change the world, what
> Would you think yourself too good for?[68]

SUPPOSE, HOWEVER, you are unwilling to bite the consequentialist bullet. Suppose you are unwilling to concede that it is all right for me to commit one great injustice now if by doing so I avert five equally great injustices in the future. You also are unwilling to allow me to engage in one instance of organ harvesting of a healthy patient, even if by doing so I avert five instances of organ harvesting by the patient's spouse. Similarly, you are unwilling to allow me to torture the innocent child of a terrorist kidnapper, even if by doing so I can get his accomplices to return (and stop the torture of) five other children (belonging to a prominent politician, let us say) they have kidnapped. And you are equally unwilling to allow me to execute an innocent defendant, even if by doing so I can appease a lynch mob that will otherwise kill at least five innocent bystanders in a riotous rampage. You do not, in other words, evaluate actions merely by whether they serve to maximize desirable (or minimize undesirable) outcomes but by whether they are *right*. That makes you, like me, a deontologist.

The tug-of-war between the consequentialist and the deontological view of such cases has endured and shows no signs of abating. That's because each side has some formidable intuitions backing it. What supports the consequentialist view is a simple canon of rationality: if one thinks that something is undesirable, then the best course of action would seem to be one that minimizes it, and if one thinks that something is desirable, then the best course of action would seem to be one that maximizes it. What supports the deontological view is the simple but profound horror we feel at soiling our hands with one horrible deed just to avert others committing a larger number of equally horrible deeds. I have no hope or intention of resolving that dispute here, although much of what I have to say should serve to throw light on it.

Let us assume that the deontologists are right and the consequentialists are wrong and see what implications this has for the problem of avoision. To unravel those implications, consider my own twisted version of the trolley problem. Imagine that Edward, the driver of the unstoppable trolley, cannot make up his mind about what to do and ends up running over the five instead of the one. Miraculously, he doesn't kill them but only hurts them badly. Nevertheless, they are certain to die from their injuries unless furnished with certain transplant organs, namely, two kidneys, two lungs, and one heart. Suppose now the driver deeply regrets not having turned the trolley and announces: "It would have been all right had I turned the trolley and thereby killed the one for the sake of the five. I hesitated because I wanted to give the matter more thought. Upon reflection, I have decided it would indeed have been better to have killed the one to save the five, and I want to make up for my earlier omission. The victim really isn't entitled to protest: he is giving up nothing other than what I would have been entitled to take from him anyway." Does this argument work? Of course not. There is no going back on the decision to run into the five instead of the one. The mere fact that by killing the one we would simply bring about a state of the world we were entitled to bring about minutes earlier does not entitle us to do so now.

What this twisted version of the trolley problem—this superimposition of the surgeon scenario on that of the trolley—serves to do is to highlight a feature of the deontological point of view that tends to go unnoticed—its inherent formalism, or as the economist would more illuminatingly call it, its *path-dependence*. The very same result, brought about by one path, is forbidden; brought about by another, however, it is acceptable. The death of one for the sake of many is all right if accomplished by the turning of the trolley, but not if accomplished by carving up the very same person only minutes later in a procedure that is arguably far less painful than being run over by a trolley. This feature of the deontological point of view casts a radically new light on avoision phenomena. To see this, just imagine that as the trolley is heading down the incline the driver is not initially thinking about turning the trolley at all. He only realizes with regret that he is about to run over five innocent people. Let us suppose, moreover, somewhat crazily, that he realizes that if he runs into them they will be injured in such a way that they can only be saved by getting some transplants, to wit, a heart, two lungs, and two kidneys. He thinks to himself that it would be nice if one could carve up the single bystander on the other spur and utilize his organs but notes with regret that this would not, of course, be morally permissible. Then finally inspiration strikes. He realizes that although he cannot sacrifice the single bystander by utilizing his organs to save the five, he can do so by running him over in the process of avoiding hitting the five, which is what he does. By turning the trolley and thus succeeding in carrying out the sacrifice he had previously believed to be off limits, he seems very much to be engaging in what we would ordinarily describe as avoision, except of course that in this case we are in no doubt as to the acceptability of what he is doing. It is perfectly all right to turn the trolley.

Precisely how does this help with the problem of avoision? It helps in that it suggests a hypothesis which, if true, would do much to clear up our puzzlement about avoision phenomena. The general hypothesis in all its generality is this:

Just as the trolley driver is exploiting the deontological features of his situation to get to a seemingly inaccessible outcome in a more roundabout way, so the parties in our various other avoision cases may simply be exploiting certain deontological features of THEIR situation to get to a seemingly inaccessible outcome in a more roundabout way.

It may sound extreme for me to suggest that there is an analogy between the planning carried out in the fairly concrete real-life situations with which this book opened and the planning carried out by the driver in the ridiculously contrived and far-fetched trolley scenario. To make that suggestion less implausible, let me point immediately to a very real-life counterpart of the trolley problem in which someone is engaged in planning which exactly mirrors that of the driver and which is very much of the sort we would expect from a Jesuit.

Think of a hypothetical hospital administrator who is constantly involved in allocation decisions about scarce life-support systems. It frequently will happen that he has put someone on life-support who after a few days have passed stands only a modest chance of really benefiting from it, that is, of making an eventual recovery. In that time other patients will have arrived at the hospital who stand a much better chance of benefiting from the very same system but who will have to be denied access, because a less promising patient is already hooked up to the equipment. The administrator is sorely tempted to unhook the unpromising patient and connect the equipment to the others, because he knows that this course will save several other lives while merely accelerating the death of the one already doomed patient. But he can't. To do that, he realizes, pretty clearly would be tantamount to organ harvesting, and although he feels bad he realizes there is nothing he can do.

Then inspiration strikes. He remembers that there are different life-support systems on the market. Some of them go on for a long time without needing much servicing or refilling. Others have to be rotated out every few days, replaced by other systems, while they are being serviced. In fact, the equipment that requires frequent rotation is a little better than the equipment that doesn't, but most hospitals find it too bothersome to use. (It is, let us say, like the difference between contact lenses that can be worn forever and those that have to be taken in and out frequently. The latter may be better but are more bother.) What occurs to the hospital administrator is that if he buys equipment that has to be disconnected regularly and replaced and serviced, he obtains a flexibility he didn't have before. Once a patient has been disconnected, and once the decision has to be made whether to hook him back up to the new machine or to use that machine for someone else who is more promising, it's a whole new ballgame. Surely we are entitled to ask, before we decide whom to hook up to some life-support system, who would most likely benefit from it, and that way we can pass up the unpromising patient and devote all of our attention to the more promising one.

To put the matter differently, with this new equipment the hospital administrator is in the position of the trolley driver rather than the organ-harvesting surgeon. Just as the trolley driver is entitled to turn his trolley in whatever direction will maximize the lives saved, or minimize the lives lost, so the hospital administrator is surely entitled to wheel his life-support system in whatever direction maximizes the lives saved, that is, minimizes the lives lost. The only difference between the hospital administrator and the trolley driver is that by turning the trolley in a certain direction the driver caused the death of the person in whose direction he turned the trolley, and he prevented the death of the person away from whom he turned the trolley. In the case of the life-support system, it's the other way around: the administrator causes the death of the person from whom he turns away the life-support system, and he prevents the death of the person in whose direction he turns the life-support system. But that is not an important difference. Ethically, the hospital administrator is now like the trolley driver and has the flexibility of the trolley driver as opposed to that of the surgeon.

Much of the Talmudic and Jesuitic advice is of precisely this kind. Just as the hospital administrator tinkers with the causal structure that connects his desire to transfer the life-support system to another patient and his achievement of that desire until it has attained a morally permissible shape, so does the observant Jew when he interposes a Shabbes Goy between his desire to ride the elevator and the actual operation of that elevator. Something like that is quite obviously going on with Serné, the arsonist, who changes his intentional killing of his son into a knowing killing by replacing the life insurance on his son with some building insurance. In doing so he reshapes the causal structure connecting him with his son's death in such a way as to turn the death into a by-product rather than a means of getting the insurance money. Looked at closely, all the other Jesuitic tricks involve similar attempts at causal restructuring; indeed, it is my claim that just about all other instances of avoision do this. This claim, however, is so far only a hypothesis. To substantiate it requires me to investigate two further questions: (1) Is the deontological point of view on which this solution to the avoision problem is premised really valid? I have merely assumed it to be valid so far, but that needs some argument to back it up. (2) Does the analogy to the hospital administrator and the combined trolley case that I have argued for really hold up when applied specifically to the various instances of avoision with which I began? It is these two questions to which the next few sections will address themselves.

Let me backtrack on point (1) immediately. I do not actually expect to end the debate between the consequentialists and the deontologists, but something more modest will meet our needs here. I will show just how deeply the deontological point of view is woven into the structure of the law, so that, whether right or not in some larger sense, certainly the implications that flow from embracing the deontological position are remarkably in sync with the deep structure of law as we know it. And in fact I will venture quite a bit further than that. I will actually suggest several lines of argument to help make the case for the deontological position more generally plausible.[69]

AN ANALOGY: LEGISLATION

Although (as I have noted) the inherently formalistic, path-dependent character of the deontological point of view is rarely made explicit, it is what most people find to be its most bothersome, counterintuitive aspect. It is not usually expressed this way, but what bothers most people about taking something like the act-omission distinction too seriously is the possibility that we might then have to say it's all right to kill a terminally ill patient by *not reactivating* his life-support system, even though it's not all right to kill him by *deactivating* his life-support system.

To make such path-dependence seem less counterintuitive, I will draw your attention to two legal contexts in which we have, after some initial resistance, come to find path-dependence fairly natural, acceptable, unavoidable, even if still somewhat counterintuitive and bothersome. Put differently, I will try to show why, despite occasional misgivings, the legal mind is right to find formalism and path-dependence so congenial. The first analogy, the subject of this section, is the process of legislation. The second analogy, the process of litigation, will be taken up in the next section.

The process of legislation is instructive because the kind of formalism, path-dependence, and Jesuitic gamesmanship that seem so disturbing about the deonto-logical view of morality are an intrinsic part of that process. A rather ancient ex-ample of democratic decision making will help to introduce the point. Circa 100 A.D., the Roman senate confronted the question of what to do with the servants of a recently deceased consul, one Afranius Dexter. It was unclear whether Afranius Dexter had died by his own hand, had been killed by his servants, or perhaps a little of both, in that his servants had helped him commit suicide, which was illegal under Roman law. The senate had to decide first on the servants' guilt and, if guilty, on the appropriate punishment, either banishment or death. One senator, Pliny, very much wanted to see the servants acquitted. He realized that a majority of his colleagues wanted to convict and that among those some only wanted to banish the convicted servants, others to execute them. He proposed that the senate vote on the matter as follows: all senators favoring acquittal were to seat themselves in one part of the chamber. All senators favoring conviction with banishment were to seat themselves in another part of the chamber. All senators favoring conviction and execution were to seat themselves in a third location. The verdict supported by the largest group would win. What Pliny was doing was, of course, merely an early version of what is now a fairly commonplace electoral strategy: if you encourage more than one Liberal to run in a heavily Liberal district, that will split the vote and allow the Conservative candidate to win with a plurality. Naturally, the strategy will fail if enough Liberals decide to respond with a counterstrategy and concentrate their votes on just one of the Liberal candidates, even though he may not be their absolute favorite. And this is why Pliny's strategy failed in the end. The supporters of execution frustrated Pliny's plan by seating themselves with the supporters of banishment, and thus the servants were convicted after all.

Pliny's strategy, as well as the counterstrategy of his opponents, are examples of something the political scientist William Riker has called "heresthetics," the art of political manipulation, or "agenda-rigging," as others have called it. Just as the Jesuits restructure a moral transaction until they can get to the goal they desire by moral means, so the heresthetically astute parliamentarian will restructure the agenda, the order in which issues are considered and votes taken, until he can get to the goal he desires by perfectly democratic means. [70]

A few more examples are in order to show that there is nothing isolated or extreme about the story of Pliny. A particularly common strategy for playing Jesuit with the voting agenda is to capitalize on the so-called voting paradox, first noticed two centuries ago by the Marquis de Condorcet. What he noticed was that sometimes in a popular vote a majority of the voters will prefer candidate A to candidate B; a majority will prefer candidate B to candidate C; and a majority will prefer, not as one would expect candidate A to candidate C but candidate C to candidate A. How can this happen? Simple: suppose a third of all voters prefer Wallace to Nixon and Nixon to Humphrey. A third prefer Nixon to Humphrey and Humphrey to Wallace. A third prefer Humphrey to Wallace and Wallace to Nixon. The result is that a two-thirds majority prefers Nixon to Humphrey, a two-thirds majority prefers Humphrey to Wallace, and a two-thirds majority prefers Wallace to Nixon. Now, if one could only get the vote to be conducted seriatim, one could get one's chosen candidate to win. If, say, you want Wallace to win, you first run Nixon against Humphrey, and the victor of that contest, Nixon, against Wallace. Wallace would emerge victorious. If you want Nixon to win, you proceed analogously: first run Humphrey against Wallace, which will cause Humphrey to win, and then run Nixon against Humphrey, and Nixon will be the eventual victor. If your candidate is Humphrey, run Wallace against Humphrey. Of course, you can employ this strategy only if the voters' preferences have this curious structure. But that is not at all uncommon, and indeed it is not even beyond your control: you can try to support those candidates for office who are most likely to create this kind of curious preference pattern.

A spectacular historical example of how this happened in real life is the fate of the so-called Depew Amendment. In 1902 a precursor of the later Seventeenth Amendment was proposed which for the first time would have permitted senators to be popularly elected. A majority of the senators favored such an amendment. Senator Depew, who opposed the idea, devised a way to kill it. He understood that among those supporting the popular election of senators were many Southerners who would resent federal meddling in local elections—as well as many Northerners who would think it a splendid idea. Federal regulation of local elections would mean reenfranchising blacks and hence produce more Republican senators. He, therefore, proposed an amendment to the proposed bill that called for federal regulation of the popular election of senators. What Depew saw was that now the senators' votes would divide the way they did in the above example involving Nixon, Humphrey, and Wallace: a large group favored popular elections over the customary method but also favored the customary method over federal regulation of elections. Another large group favored the customary method over popular elections with federal regulation but favored that over a popular election without federal regulation. Finally, a third group favored popular elections with federal regulation over popular elections without federal regulation and favored that over the customary method. By first proposing to amend the bill with the federal regulation provision, Depew got a majority to sign off on that. But then there was no longer a majority to support the resulting, amended bill. For the time being, then, the popular election of senators was rejected.[71]

The same trick is described as being used in a slightly different setting in Sun Tzu's *Art of War*:

> T'ien Chi frequently gambled on horse races with the Princes of Ch'i. Sun Pin noticed that the teams of horses did not differ greatly. The horses were of three classes, first, second, and third. Observing this, Sun Pin said to T'ien Chi, "You place a bet on this contest; your servant can make you win."
>
> T'ien Chi believed him and agreed with the King and the Princes on a wager of one thousand pieces of gold on the races. As he was about to put up his money, Sun Pin said, "Match your third string against his first, your best against his second, and your second best against his weakest." The three competitions were completed, and while T'ien Chi did not win the first, he won the last two, and a thousand pieces of gold from the King. Thereupon

T'ien Chi introduced Sun Pin to King Wei, who discussed military matters
with him and made him a staff officer.[72]

This sort of strategizing was carried to perfection by two social scientists belonging to a flying club which had to choose a new fleet of airplanes. They had
pretty good guesses about what each member of the club wanted. They imagined
the outcomes of various plausible, fair-sounding voting schemes, found a few that
generated the outcome they liked, and proposed one of them to the club. It
sounded fine to everyone around. The votes were taken and the desired result
came about.[73]

Now you might try to object to this sort of gamesmanship the way you were at
first inclined to object to Jesuitic gamesmanship. But you would be singularly hard-
pressed to make the objection stick. To find these games objectionable you would
have to believe that there is such a thing as the "public will," which the right kind
of voting procedure could tease out. Alas, there is not. There are simply an infinity
of appealing voting procedures, each of which yields a different outcome. To be
sure, we might try to make a list of the basic attributes we want a fair voting procedure to have and see if we can't narrow the field that way. Unfortunately, as Kenneth
Arrow has famously shown, even the most elementary demands of fairness we
might make turn out to be inconsistent with each other. Condorcet's voting paradox is just a special illustration of this. It reveals the inconsistency of two appealing
prerequisites of a fair voting mechanism: the principle of majority rule and the
principle of transitivity, the latter of which says that if whatever voting system is
used ranks A above B and B above C, it should rank A above C. But majority voting,
as we have seen, might well give A a majority over B, give B a majority over C,
and—in blatant violation of transitivity—give C a majority over A. Which is what
allows the astute parliamentarian to have his field day.

But although the absence of a coherent notion of a "collective will"—the non-
existence of a voting system that could be said to really express society's preferences—makes it hard to object to parliamentary maneuvering, people admittedly
often do. Often, of course, no more than ignorance of the foregoing facts is involved. But maybe not always. When Woodward and Armstrong published *The
Brethren,* their 1979 expose of the Supreme Court, they caused then Chief Justice
Warren Burger great embarrassment by showing him to engage in quite a bit of
quasi-parliamentary maneuvering. For instance, finding himself in the minority in
a given case, he would frequently change his vote to the majority when all other

votes had been cast, so as to be able to control the assignment of the majority opinion, or indeed to draft it himself. His aim was to exercise damage control, making it harder for the majority to get an opinion that was fully to its liking. He wanted "to make sure that important cases in criminal law, racial discrimination, and free speech were kept away from Douglas, Brennan and Marshall, his ideological 'enemies,' as he called them. If necessary, the Chief would switch his own vote to retain the assignment power, and thus prevent them from writing ground-breaking decisions that expanded the Court's power or extended the application of liberal Warren Court decisions. Instead, he assigned them innocuous cases where their opinions couldn't have much impact." He is said to have wielded the assignment power with special force in *Roe v. Wade*. According to *The Brethren*, he assigned the first draft to Justice Blackmun, because he calculated

> as a judicial craftsman, [Blackmun's] work was crude. A poor draft would scare off [Justice] Stewart, who was already queasy, and leave only four votes. Or if Blackmun himself were to desert the position—a distinct possibility—precious time would be lost. Either defection would leave only a four-man majority. It would be difficult to argue that such a major decision should be handed down on a 4-to-3 vote. There would be increasing pressure to put the case over for rehearing with the two new Nixon [-appointed] Justices. This was no doubt exactly the sort of case that Nixon had in mind when he chose Powell and Rehnquist [to fill the existing vacancies].[74]

Even less crass forms of judicial heresthetics raise eyebrows, are registered with discomfort, and are admitted to only reluctantly. So, for instance, the practice of "defensive denials" of cert petitions: "There are areas of law generally, and cases specifically, where a justice believes that if a case is reviewed, he will not like the outcome on the merits. Therefore, even if he believes the case is certworthy, and perhaps he believes that the ruling below is a horrible injustice, he still will vote to deny the case. The reasoning is, why make a bad situation worse? . . . [A] denial of cert has no precedential value, and refusal to take a case in no way signifies that the Supreme Court agrees with the ruling below. Difficult as it may be for a justice to let a ruling stand, by doing so he has let the precedent remain only for its immediate jurisdiction—for example, only the second circuit—rather than for the entire country."[75] Still, the justices do this with a notably bad conscience. ("I see the

Court as a tribunal and our case selection process should be less result oriented," says a former clerk about his justice.)[76] So uncomfortable does heresthetic manipulation make the justices that when an interviewer asked one of them a most inoffensive-sounding question about how they went about negotiating the language in an opinion among each other, he was immediately interrupted with the comment: "We don't negotiate, we accommodate."

I don't know whether the judges are right in thinking of heresthetics as inconsistent with their role, especially since their prudishness does not extend to the judicial appointments process: No one, it seems, was much offended by the sort of strategizing that prompted Earl Warren to resign well in advance of the 1968 election to enable Lyndon Johnson to pick his successor. I will concede, though, that there may be special contexts, like the judicial one, in which for reasons yet to be uncovered the use of heresthetics is unethical. In most instances of collective decision making, however, I believe it will be impossible to show heresthetics to be morally objectionable.

But is there more than just a loose analogy between heresthetics and the advice the Jesuits are peddling? I believe the connection to be quite intimate. One gets some sense of the intimacy of the connection from the fact that occasionally agenda manipulation is directly recommended as a way of dealing with certain moral dilemmas. The philosopher Adam Morton, for instance, has suggested that agenda manipulation is one way of alleviating certain of the moral difficulties surrounding affirmative action:

> You are on a committee which is making an appointment to a job. It is
> important to you to get the best person for the job. The job is open to both
> men and women but there are disproportionately many men in that department and, if only for the sake of the company's public image, you would like
> to appoint a woman. But you cannot say how much weight the need to appoint a woman has compared to the need to appoint the otherwise best candidate. If the best candidate is a woman you will have no problem, and if
> there is a tie between a man and a woman you will appoint the woman, but
> you know that things rarely work out so nicely.
>
> Here is one way in which the committee can deal with its problem. Suppose that appointments are made in the standard way: the job is advertised
> and then the committee goes through the applications of people who have
> responded to the advertisement and selects a shortlist of people to be given

intense scrutiny. Then the people on the shortlist are interviewed and the most impressive of them is offered the job. Often it is decided in advance how large the shortlist is to be. In many cases the basis for the decision is something pretty superficial, like the amount of time it would be convenient to spend interviewing. Now suppose that you determine in advance the maximum and minimum size of the shortlist, for example that it will contain at most six and at least three people, and that at least three of them will be women. Then you follow the standard procedure, except that when you draw up the shortlist you are constrained to have three women on it, even at the expense of having a longer list than usual.

If you can persuade your colleagues to adopt this procedure, you will have increased the likelihood that the job will go to a woman, without compromising the principle that the committee should choose the best person or forcing you to balance qualifications against gender. [That is in part because] the apparent suitability of candidates usually changes a lot from the rough scrutiny that gets them on to a shortlist to the more intense consideration before and during the interview. So one thing that manipulating the shortlist does is to increase the chances that one of the people whose rough acceptability turned on closer examination into real suitability will be a woman.

The general trick here is to avoid having to balance gender and qualifications by instead balancing gender and administrative effort. . . . *Sometimes a value that cannot easily be balanced against another can more easily be balanced against some other aspect of the decision-making process. In that case a suitable procedure for finding options to decide between may remove the need to compare the two hard-to-compare values.* [Italics added.][77]

The connection between Jesuitical and parliamentary gamesmanship is even closer than the above suggests. What gives rise to agenda manipulation, what renders it so relatively inoffensive, is that we no longer believe there is much coherence to the notion of a collective will. Thus it becomes hard to argue that agenda manipulation frustrates the expression of such a collective will. To be sure, we are able to say about some outcomes that they are less faithful to the collective will than others: if everybody prefers outcome *A* to outcome *B*, then we certainly can say that outcome *A* would be more faithful to the collective will than *B*. But for most outcomes we are not able to make such a comparative assessment. Arguably, the same is true of morality. We cannot say that a world in which a trolley turns and runs over one is better than a world in which it continues and runs over five, which is why we allow the driver to do either. We cannot say whether it is better if a hospital has life-support systems that require little servicing and that cause unpromising patients who have been hooked up to them to block access to more promising patients, or whether it is better if a hospital has life-support systems that require regular replacement and that allow unpromising patients who have been hooked up to them to lose their turn to patients who have a better chance. Or at least one can plausibly argue that we cannot really call one outcome better, which is why the doctor is allowed to bring about either. Our inability to rank final outcomes renders Jesuitic gamesmanship as inoffensive as parliamentary gamesmanship. It is, in a sense, because neither morality nor parliamentary decision making seek to *maximize* anything that gamesmanship has a legitimate place.

A FURTHER ANALOGY: LITIGATION

The rules of litigation, the process of trying cases, is a second context in which we have come to find path-dependence and the formalism it entails relatively natural. Those rules, most people realize, aren't designed solely to get at the truth but to do so by *fair* means, subject of course to considerable uncertainty as to what means are fair. A few people occasionally also understand that this requirement to uncover the truth through fair means makes for considerable, but unavoidable, formalism. The following four paradoxical-seeming features of the litigation process will illuminate the nonconsequentialist character of the rules of litigation particularly clearly.

The Twin Paradox

An undisguised man robs a bank in New York. A camera records the entire episode, wanted-posters with his likeness are plastered across the country and someone is soon arrested. At the very time that the bank robbery occurred in New York, another man, also undisguised, commits a murder in Los Angeles. As luck will have it, his actions too are recorded by a camera, wanted-posters with his likeness are plastered everywhere, and someone is soon arrested. But then there is a snag: the two arrested men, it turns out, are identical twins; thus, despite the wonderfully clear-cut photographic evidence available, it is impossible to decide which of them committed the bank robbery and which committed the murder. The defendants deny all guilt.

The two cases are joined and tried before a judge, who disposes of the case by declaring both defendants guilty of bank robbery and imposing commensurate sentences. His reasoning is simple: we know beyond a reasonable doubt that one of the defendants is guilty of bank robbery and one of them is guilty of murder, but we don't know who committed which crime. Whatever the truth, no defendant will end up with less than a sentence for bank robbery; therefore, it is fair to sentence them for that offense.

How will the judge's verdict fare on appeal? Very poorly. Any appellate court following the common understanding of the proof-beyond-a-reasonable-doubt requirement will insist that the crime of which the defendant is convicted (in this case bank robbery) be proved beyond a reasonable doubt. This has not been done. Therefore, the verdict cannot stand.

Although the appellate court's approach might seem like a very technical, legalistic one, it doesn't depart from what we do in nonlegal contexts. Suppose a wife has evidence entitling her to conclude that one of two things must be true: (a) her husband has been unfaithful, or (b) her husband has been grossly remiss in doing some of his daily chores. How might this happen? Just imagine that in examining a recent American Express bill she finds a charge for expensive jewelry, which allows only one of two conclusions: (a) he bought the jewelry for someone else, or (b) he failed to notice a costly mistake by the credit card company. In other words, she knows that her husband is guilty either of infidelity or of gross slothfulness, but she doesn't know which. How will she cope with this uncertainty? If she were like the trial judge in the twin case, she would say: "At the very least my husband deserves the degree of resentment that goes with extreme slothfulness, and quite possibly he deserves worse. Hence I will, pending further evidence, resent him for his slothfulness." That seems like an unlikely reaction. It would probably seem silly to the woman to treat her husband as though he were guilty of extreme slothfulness in billing when she knows that there is at least as large a probability that he is guilty of infidelity.

One could conceive of another reaction. She might say: "At the very least, he deserves a degree of resentment corresponding to a weighted average of the resentment he would deserve were he guilty of infidelity and the resentment he would deserve were he guilty of extreme slothfulness." That too seems unlikely. The wife probably would feel uncomfortable holding her husband even partially liable for the infidelity unless she has at the very least proof thereof by a preponderance of the evidence, and she would probably insist on quite a bit more. Her most likely (and, I believe, most rational) reaction will be to hold her resentment in abeyance pending further evidence—which may never be forthcoming. In short, she would behave exactly like the appellate court.

My twin example is, of course, thoroughly zany, but the problem it exemplifies is not at all uncommon. Perhaps its most typical manifestation is the defendant found in possession of stolen goods. There is evidence that he bought them from the thief, and there is evidence that he stole them himself. Perhaps there is even evidence that they are not stolen at all but were obtained through some other kind of illegal transaction, like smuggling, bribery, or blackmail. One of these, but not all of them, we are certain occurred. Jurisdictions differ widely as to how they would handle such a case. But all would have some difficulty with it. None would view it as a straightforward matter where at a minimum the defendant should be found guilty of the least serious of those offenses if one cannot in fact determine beyond a reasonable doubt which offense he committed.

If the rules of litigation were designed simply to achieve some overall conse-quentialist objective, such as making sure that as many criminals as possible receive their just deserts, this treatment of the twin paradox would make absolutely no sense. After all, we are absolutely sure that both defendants in the twin case de-serve at the very least to be punished as severely as a bank robber. If we refuse to mete out that punishment, it is because we believe that just deserts may only be passed out by a certain route, along a certain path, in a certain form, which includes proof beyond a reasonable doubt that the defendant has committed a particular identifiable bad act.

The Insanity Paradox

If a perfectly sane person commits a crime and goes mad before he is tried, he cannot be tried so long as he remains mad. And if he goes mad after being tried, he cannot be punished so long as he remains mad. That applies even if the punish-ment is the death penalty: someone who goes mad on death row cannot be exe-cuted.[78]

These prohibitions are very hard to explain in a consequentialist vein. Whether one believes the purpose of punishment to be deterrence or retribution, it is very hard to see how such indulgence for the insane furthers either. It has occasionally been argued in behalf of requiring competency at trial that, if we try a mad defen-dant, he cannot properly assist in his defense, and thus we will be denied important evidence to determine the truth. Undoubtedly, this will be true sometimes. Very often, however, it will not. Why not proceed at least in those cases? Indeed, we generally have a perfectly straightforward way of dealing with a lack of desirable evidence. We present the case to the jury, permit each side to draw attention to missing evidence it considers crucial, and let the members of the jury decide whether they can confidently convict beyond a reasonable doubt. And just in case the jury errs egregiously, the judge has it in his power to reverse a guilty verdict.

In an even feebler attempt to rationalize not punishing the insane, it is argued sometimes that insanity itself is punishment enough. But we don't take the general position that natural misfortunes should be offset against the punishment someone deserves for a crime. Nor is there any reason to think that madness is punishment enough for all crimes. The fact is that deterrence is certainly furthered by punishing the insane (assuming they were sane when committing the crime), and the punishment becomes no less deserved just because the defendant is insane. He still has done terrible things, and he still is capable—and deserving—of suffering for them.

That is not to say that it would, therefore, be appropriate to make the insane undergo trial and punishment. Rather it shows that whatever inhibits us from doing so has nothing to do with an overall objective that the criminal trial is meant to attain. It has to do with a deontological, that is, nonconsequentialist, constraint imposed by the trial itself: a guilty verdict is permitted to result only from a process that does not involve trying or punishing the insane. Rather, it must involve a process in which the defendant understands every step of the way what he is being tried and punished for—even at the point of execution.

Imagine now this case: the most dangerous evidence facing the defendant is the eyewitness testimony of a frail, terminally ill woman. His best chance for acquittal is to wait for her to die. The prosecution, however, is not about to give him that opportunity. So he injects himself with a drug designed to put him into a deranged state for about six months, by which point he hopes the witness will have died. Does this work? It is tempting to say "no." It is tempting to say that the rule against trying the incompetent is not meant to permit defendants to tamper with the evidence against them. It is tempting to say that a defendant who tries to strategically exploit rules intended to protect the fairness of the trial forfeits the protection of those rules. But if you yield to that temptation, what will you do about the defendant who tries to achieve the same end by fleeing the jurisdiction or going into hiding until the critical witness has died? Are you going to tolerate trials in absentia on the grounds that the rule requiring the presence of the accused at his trial was not meant to permit a defendant to tamper with the evidence against him, that a defendant who strategically exploits rules intended to protect the fairness of the trial forfeits the protection of those rules?

And if despite initial hesitations you are willing to go this far, let me try to press you against the wall with one further, even more extreme example. The government is about to install Pershing missiles in a military base. Some protesters are desperate to frustrate this undertaking. They lie down in front of the tanks carrying the missiles as those are about to roll into the base. Of course, the tanks cannot keep rolling. The rule (roughly) is that we cannot take a life to further an end less weighty than the direct protection of life. It is clearly not the aim of this rule to enable protesters to exploit it in the manner in which they are doing here. Nevertheless, it applies and prevents the tanks from rolling on. It would seem that, analogously, the rules prohibiting trying someone incompetent or in absentia continue to apply even where the defendant has deliberately rendered himself incompetent or absent.

I should note that this is close to one of the problem cases I posed in an earlier section, in which the defendant bypassed the immigration laws by making statements that rendered him a political refugee. We can see now that this form of avoision might quite sensibly be permitted to work, even though the purpose of political asylum laws is obviously not to induce this kind of conduct. The analogy between the defendant who lies down in front of tanks and the defendant who makes politically dangerous statements could be made even closer. Imagine that the protester has positioned himself on the edge of a precipice along which the tanks will have to roll to get to their destination. If they continue rolling, they will not actually run him over but will push him into the abyss. Can they continue rolling? Of course not. That's not to say that we cannot punish the protester for interfering. Similarly, we might be free to punish the "strategic" political refugee, but what we cannot do is to say that he has forfeited the protection of the rules he is trying to exploit and that we may, therefore, throw him out of the country and into the offended dictator's jaws.

The Exclusionary Rule Paradox

The exclusionary rule excludes evidence gathered in the process of an illegal search and seizure. The chief rationale offered for the exclusionary rule is that what it costs in valuable evidence it more than makes up in the amount of illegal searching-

and-seizing that it deters. But looked at closely, it turns out to have no such consequentialist purpose.

Imagine, for instance, that the Internal Affairs Division of a municipal police department is investigating allegations of systematic illegal searches, which occurred notwithstanding the exclusionary rule. Suppose that a successful investigation by Internal Affairs would very likely put an end to such searches. Suppose further that a successful investigation could be conducted only if the Internal Affairs Division itself could engage in some searches which by traditional standards would be considered illegal. Would we now allow such actions, because on balance they diminish rather than increase the total amount of illegal searching? I think not. But that shows the deontological, as opposed to consequentialist, character of the exclusionary rule. We decline to use illegally seized evidence not to deter future illegal searches but because an illegal search is an impermissible path to a conviction.

The Statistical Evidence Paradox

Mrs. Smith is run over by a cab, and that is all she remembers about it. The town in which she lives has two cab companies. Sixty percent of the cabs belong to the Yellow Cab Company. Forty percent belong to the Green Cab Company. She sues the Yellow Cab Company and argues that the mere fact that sixty percent of all cabs are owned by them proves by a preponderance of the evidence that they are guilty. The courts will react very negatively to naked statistical evidence of this sort. They will dismiss the case.

Here is a criminal law version of the same problem. Defendants are both hunters. They recklessly fire bullets in a direction where they heard a rustle even though they have good grounds for fearing that the rustle might have been caused by a person rather than an animal. Defendant One fires 95 shots; Defendant Two fires 5. In the end, it cannot be determined whose bullet killed the victim. Defendant One is prosecuted for manslaughter. The argument is made that the mere fact that he fired 95 of the 100 bullets that rained down in the vicinity of the victim proves by a preponderance of the evidence that he is the killer. Again, courts would refuse to so interpret the evidence. But why?

The best explanation I have read is that of the philosopher Judith Jarvis Thomson.[79] She concedes that the court would have excellent grounds for believing that a yellow cab ran over Mrs. Smith and that Defendant One killed the victim. But she draws an interesting analogy to a problem of epistemology to explain why we nonetheless refuse to convict. A central issue in epistemology is the question of when we are entitled to say that a belief someone holds amounts to knowledge. It is clear that what he believes must be true, else it clearly cannot be knowledge. However, that is not enough: I may truthfully believe that on December 4, 2005, there will be an earthquake in Los Angeles, and the earthquake may in fact come to pass on that date. Does that mean I "knew" that the earthquake would happen? Most certainly not: I had no justification for believing there would be an earthquake on that particular day. In other words, for a true belief to amount to knowledge it must also be justified. Is that enough? Well, suppose I look at my watch, and it so happens that it stopped working exactly twelve hours ago. Right now it is nine o'clock, and since the watch got stuck twelve hours ago, without my noticing it, I happen to form a correct belief about the current time by glancing at it. Moreover, as my watch has never malfunctioned in the past, the belief is a justified one. Do I therefore "know" that it is nine o'clock? Again, I think not. Because there is an insufficient causal connection between my true, justified belief that it is nine o'clock and the fact that it is nine o'clock. The connection is one of pure coincidence.

Something analogous, Thomson points out, can be said about the court's belief that a yellow cab ran over Mrs. Smith or that the ninety-five-bullet man killed the victim. Even if the belief is true, and even though it would be justified by the statistical evidence, it would not be connected with the actual facts in the right kind of way to permit one to say that the court actually "knew" a yellow cab ran over Mrs. Smith or that it "knew" that the ninety-five-bullet man killed the victim. The connection here too has the look of coincidence. Thus although a conviction in each case would tend on average very much toward the truth, we refuse to accept it because the court is not able to say that it actually "knows" that to be so. Mind you, the defect is not that the court cannot be confident beyond a reasonable doubt that the defendants are guilty. It is rather that even if they are in fact guilty, it does not "know" them to be so, given the kind of coincidental connection the statistical evidence creates between the truth of the matter and the court's assessment thereof. Again, it seems we are pursuing highly nonconsequentialist procedural aims.

THE IMPORTANCE OF PEDIGREE

Although the two legal contexts we have just examined go a long way toward making path-dependence plausible, I want to draw your attention to a few nonlegal contexts in which we find this phenomenon acceptable, indeed natural and inevitable, even if puzzling.

In *Anarchy, State and Utopia,* the philosopher Robert Nozick asks us to perform the following thought experiment:

> Suppose there were an experience machine that would give you any experience you desired. Superduper neuropsychologists could stimulate your brain so that you would think and feel you were writing a great novel, or making a friend, or reading an interesting book. All the time you would be floating in a tank, with electrodes attached to your brain. Should you plug into this machine for life, preprogramming your life's experience?[80]

Nozick's answer to what he takes to be a rhetorical question is "No." More matters to us, he concludes, than how our lives "feel from the inside." We want to *do* certain things and *be* certain things, in addition to having the experience of doing and being. The Oxford philosopher James Griffin elaborates:

> I prefer, in important matters of my life, bitter truth to comfortable illusion. Even if I were surrounded by consummate actors able to give me sweet simulacra of love and affection, I should prefer the relatively bitter diet of their authentic reactions. And I should prefer it not because it would be morally better, or aesthetically better, or more noble, but because it would make for a better life for me to live.[81]

What this means, for instance, is that as between person *A* who mistakenly thinks that his home team won the championship this year and person *B* who correctly believes that *his* home team won the championship, *B* enjoys the higher state of well-being, *even though there is no difference in their subjective degrees of happiness.* Happiness, at least if it is understood to correspond to well-being, turns out not to be all in the head.

I am sure that some of you will balk at that. You might *insist* that having happy experiences is really all that counts, at least all that counts for you, regardless of their causal origin. You might *insist* that you would be perfectly happy to enter an experience machine, that you prefer comfortable illusion to bitter truth. You might *insist* that although you really value writing a great novel, making a friend, or reading an interesting book, you do so only on account of the pleasures that these things bring and that if a machine could bring you these pleasures more directly without your having to bother to actually write the novel, make the friend, or read the book, that would be just as good. You might insist that although you rejoice when your home team wins, you do so only for the sake of the pleasure that affords, and if someone could convince you that it won, even though in fact it did not, that would be just as good.

You might *insist* on all of those things, but I venture to say you wouldn't mean it, as a thought experiment suggested by the philosopher Peter Unger of New York University will demonstrate. Ask yourself, says Unger, why you buy life insurance for your family. The insurance is paid out only after you are dead and, therefore, will not generate any pleasurable experiences for you. Now, you might object that it does generate pleasurable experiences for you because it gives your family peace of mind and thus makes them more pleasant to be with now. But suppose someone offered you for a small sum (much smaller than the insurance premium required by a real policy) impressive papers that look like a policy and give your family the completely impenetrable illusion that they are cared for in the event of your death. You would, I suspect, be unwilling to do this. (And the reason for that, Unger emphatically notes, is *not* that we abhor lying so much.) It is very hard to square this fact with the assertion that illusory experiences are as good as real ones.[82]

Of course, there is a bit of a mystery about how far one should take the aversion to experience machines. A controversy has recently erupted over the use of mood-brightening drugs. Is it all right to prescribe them as a way of dealing with the travails of everyday living? Some psychiatrists insist it is unethical to give such a drug to those not suffering from a pathological depression, because by doing so "you bring about a break, however small, between the individual and either his external reality or his humanity, by which I mean his tendency to react 'humanly' to external circumstances. Either you have reduced his awareness of what is going on around him or you have reduced his capacity to care about it in the ways that human beings have historically cared as far back as myths and legends take us."[83]

The pedigree of an experience matters—that's the lesson the science fiction experience machine is meant to teach. To clinch that lesson, let us consider some other areas in which it operates, such as the problem of forgeries. What makes the forgery of a painting, which to the naked eye is indistinguishable from the original, less valuable than the original? A not inconsiderable number of critics have reluctantly reached the conclusion that there is no difference, that sheer foolishness is displayed by our behaving as if there were such a difference. As far as they can see, claiming that the original is more valuable than a perfect fake is much like George Bernard Shaw's joke that Wagner's music is better than it sounds.

Two philosophers, Francis Sparshot and Peter Unger, have rather conclusively blown that argument to smithereens by constructing an ingenious variation to the Nozick experience machine. They ask us to think about human instead of artistic forgeries. Specifically, Francis Sparshot asks us to consider situations in which someone manages to deceive us by substituting "in conditions of desperation or poor visibility . . . an alternative sex object for the loved one." He has in mind situations like that depicted in Yeats's poem cycle "The Three Bushes," in which a woman who has promised to visit her lover in the dark sends him her chambermaid instead. He dies without ever learning what has been done to him, but we think he has been badly cheated all the same. When Yeats writes that "maybe we are all the same / Where no candles are," he says it with irony, sarcasm, or some such mood of double entendre, but certainly not with sincerity.[84]

Peter Unger makes the same point with an even more fanciful and perhaps even more compelling hypothetical. Imagine, Unger says, that someone has invented a machine capable of cloning adult human beings to create perfect duplicates, not just physically but psychologically, which possess not only all of the original's psychological traits but his memories as well. The machine "record[s] the exact nature of, and the precise relative arrangement of, all of the person's atoms and molecules. Using this information and using a different batch of matter . . . the device arranges, over there [that is, in some other place] exactly as many molecules, of just those sorts, in precisely that same arrangement." Now, imagine that someone has cloned an exact duplicate of your daughter and confronts you with a choice between two options: "On the first option, your daughter will live and will continue to occupy the same place in your family, while the duplicate is destroyed. Further, on this option, after the duplicate is killed, you will suffer some considerable painful experience, produced by some electric shocks and, except for the stipulated fact regarding your daughter, you will get no reward. On the second option, the duplicate lives and occupies that role, while your daughter is destroyed. Further, after the switch you will suffer no painful electric shocks and you will get a large reward. For example, in some apparently plausible way, such as the inheritance from your cousin of a patent that becomes very valuable only later, you will acquire a hundred million dollars."[85] In other words, you can trade in your daughter for a perfect duplicate and in return save yourself a lot of physical pain and make a lot of money to boot. Would you do it? The answer is, of course, no. Not because the clone is lacking in any attribute that your original daughter possesses but just because it isn't your original daughter. It lacks the right pedigree. The same goes for works of art.

Let me now turn to another area that serves to underscore the importance of pedigree. Occasionally a nonfiction book is published—somebody's memoirs, a history, an insider's account, a diary—whose dramatic structure, surprising twists of fate, allegorical cast of characters, and symbolic significance rival that of a well-crafted novel. The book is eagerly read and greatly admired. As time passes, we learn that if the book resembles a novel that's probably because it really is. It may have some slender link with real events but not much more than most fiction has with its authors' lives. When this comes out, we often feel cheated. But why? Few of us will have bought the book because we had to make some decision that hinged on its truthfulness. Most of us bought it to be entertained, and we were entertained. So why do we feel cheated when what we took to be truth turns out not to be? Let's take a look at two examples of this problem.

In his book *The Train Robbers,* Piers Paul Read tells the true story of a spectacular heist in which 15 of London's most ambitious—or shall we just say greedy—thieves managed to steal the unprecedented sum of £2½ million (worth today perhaps $25 million) from a mail train in 1963. The characters making up the gang were a dramatist's dream. There was, for one, a gentleman bandit named Bruce Reynolds who "drove an Aston Martin, dressed elegantly, ate at the best restaurants, took holidays in the South of France," and claimed to have been the youngest major in the British army. Then there was a brash gangster named Gordon Goody who liked to walk up to the prosecutor in a case in which he had just been acquitted and point out the evidence that would have gotten him convicted if only the prosecutor had been more attentive. There was also an owlish-looking florist named Roger Cowdray who had a passion for trains and a special talent for tinkering with traffic signals (for which he insisted his fellow bandits compensate him with a separate "expert's fee" of £10,000 in addition to his regular cut of the booty). The book recounts the meticulous planning that went into the robbery, its remarkably smooth execution (which required hijacking the train engine and the two train cars carrying the loot), and the botch-up that proved their eventual undoing: the bandits had bought a farm near their intended place of attack, to be used as a hideout and base of operations. Once the heist was over and the bandits had dispersed, a clean-up man was supposed to purge the farm of all incriminating evidence. He never came. The farm was found by the police with all the equipment that had been used in the robbery and made it easy to identify most of the gang. The book goes on to tell how much of the stolen money was in turn stolen from the thieves by those purporting to help them hide it, how the few robbers who managed to find a safe haven in Mexico were so bored by the "good life" that they accepted long prison sentences just to get back to England, how the one bandit who fled to Brazil avoided extradition by impregnating a Brazilian dancer and taking refuge under a bizarre Brazilian law prohibiting the extradition of the fathers of Brazilian children. Finally, it tells of the long period that nearly all participants ended up spending in British jails (initially set at thirty years for most of them) and of their daredevil but generally unsuccessful attempts to escape.

All of this makes for a grand yarn. But the reason I had picked up Read's book in the first place was a promise held out in the book's blurb that it would reveal a "titillating" connection between the Great Train Robbery and "one of the darkest chapters in world history." Indeed, in the introduction to the book Read himself explains that he was unsure whether to undertake to write the train robbers' story given that other accounts had already been published, and that he was worried about the train robbers' ability and willingness to be forthcoming with details they had not already told to others. What changed his mind, Read says, is that he learned that there was in fact something crucial about the train robbery that no one had uncovered yet:

> There was a Mr. Big behind the crime—a man who had financed it and had received in return a million pounds of the stolen money. He was Otto Skorzeny, the officer in the Waffen SS who had commanded the German commandos during the war and had rescued Mussolini from the Gran Sasso, where he had been imprisoned by the government of Marshal Badoglio. Skorzeny had put up 80,000 pounds; one of his men had been at their hideout, Leatherslade Farm; others had abducted Charlie Wilson [one of the robbers] from Windson Green prison. They had arranged for Buster Edwards [another of the robbers] to leave the country and have his appearance changed by plastic surgery.[86]

Read admits to having been wary at first of this extraordinary claim. What convinced him in due course of the robbers' sincerity was the amount of prodding required to get them to tell this story, their evident fear of offending their German sponsors, and what appeared to be an independent corroboration of an account of a meeting with Skorzeny. Thus satisfied, Read undertook to tell their story.

I read their tale with proverbially bated breath until I got to the final chapter, "Corroboration," in which Read explains that he sought further confirmation for the Nazi connection once he had completed his manuscript, and that he found the whole story to be a lie. Beyond a rather tangential involvement that one of the thieves had with Skorzeny long after the train robbery, on which Read based the various confidence-inspiring aspects of the story, the whole thing was fiction. Confronted with this fact by Read, several of the robbers admitted to their fabrication; the others sullenly and half-heartedly insisted on its truth. What then was Read to do with his manuscript in the face of all this? He tells us in the final sentence of his book: "[E]ven though I was satisfied now that I was near to the truth, I could never be certain and thought it best to leave the story as they had told it to me and let each reader decide upon its veracity himself."[87]

I for one felt cheated. But why? The book had given me a great thrill. I had read it the way one reads a novel, not for information but as entertainment. So why should I be bothered to learn that much of the spice of the story was just fiction? To the thrill I felt on reading it my belief in its truth made a substantial difference. Had it been identified as fiction beforehand I would not have enjoyed it in the same way. The thrill certainly was not undone by the later revelation. It was quite genuinely felt. So why do I mind? Presumably because I felt that I had just been yanked out of an experience machine; I had just been told that what I thrilled to as reality was mere illusion. That doesn't undo the thrill, but it does change the value I attach to it!

What I have just said allows us to understand more clearly a debate that has been raging for nearly a decade about another work of alleged nonfiction, the three volumes of Lillian Hellman's reminiscences. Lillian Hellman first gained fame as a playwright, most notably as the author of *The Children's Hour, The Little Foxes,* and *Watch on the Rhine,* all of which reaped numerous awards and after impressive Broadway runs were turned into equally successful movies. Her star faded a bit thereafter, but she leaped back into prominence with a series of memoirs which she wrote in the 1960s and 1970s: *An Unfinished Woman, Pentimento,* and *Scoundrel Time,* the first of which won the National Book Award, and each of which earned sustained acclaim. They were not memoirs in the usual sense but rather the artful, novelistic reconstruction of emotionally salient episodes and friendships in Hellman's life. Written in a style that is at once lyrical and pithy, loose in word choice and punctuation, tight in syntax and description, they drew the portrait of an enchantingly gutsy, brainy, sensual, no-nonsense woman, who is by appropriate turns self-effacing and assertive, fearful and valorous, a cheering blend of Katherine Hepburn, Lauren Bacall, and Barbra Streisand. A chapter of *Pentimento*, "Julia," was turned into a successful movie casting Jane Fonda (as Hellman), Vanessa Redgrave (as Julia), and Jason Robards (as Hellman's long-time lover Dashiell Hammett, the mystery writer). The chapter is about Hellman's intense involvement with the rebellious childhood friend for whom it is named, the daughter of a wealthy New York family, who went to Vienna to study with Freud, there did heroic battle against Nazis and kindred folk on the eve of the Second World War, and later persuaded Hellman—in the climactic moments of the chapter—to go on a mission smuggling money into Germany to buy the freedom of political prisoners.

Although enormously successful when first published, the memoirs over time fell into curious disrepute. First, there was some predictable grumbling by her political adversaries about her very partial (in both senses of the word) account of the McCarthy era in *Scoundrel Time:* particularly her insinuation that she had been the first to offer serious resistance to the Committee for Un-American Activities and her silence about the warm support she had paid Stalin at the height of his purges. Then there were the acerbic comments of those who knew and detested Hellman and who were infuriated by the flattering self-portrait. "Goodness to Betsey, . . . what an *important* lady," exclaimed the sardonic review by the novelist Martha Gellhorn, sometime acquaintance of Hellman and sometime wife of Ernest Hemingway, "How marvelous for Miss Hellman to be Miss Hellman." More serious for Hellman, however, was what happened thereafter. Participants in numerous of the episodes she recounted denied not only that they had happened as she remembered them but denied that they had happened at all. Martha Gellhorn made a long list of such incidents, concluding that as an "apocryphiar . . . Miss Hellman ranks sublime."[88] Others began to note the inherent implausibility of some of the most striking anecdotes she told: one concerns her black wet-nurse Sophronia whom she describes as claiming a seat in the whites-only section of a New Orleans bus several decades before Rosa Parks launched the Montgomery bus boycott with the same act. Another involves Hellman's trip to Moscow in 1944 at which time Stalin supposedly offered to meet with her, and she coyly declined on the grounds that since she had nothing important to tell him she did not want to take up the great man's time. Most damaging of all, however, was that the story about "Julia" turned out to be an utter fabrication. In the early 1980s a woman fitting Hellman's description of Julia actually wrote her own memoirs, made it quite clear that she was the only woman alive who possibly could fit Hellman's description—and said she had never met Hellman in her life. She had, however, employed and shared her story with a lawyer who happened to be one of Hellman's friends and most likely relayed it to her. Indeed, when Hellman first heard about the woman in the late 1930s, she made use of it in her anti-Nazi play *Watch on the Rhine*. Much later, writing her memoirs, she dreamed into her life a relationship with this fascinating creature and the dramatic episode of smuggling that forms the centerpiece of her "Julia" chapter. With these revelations, distrust of Hellman's memoirs reached such a pitch that Mary McCarthy during an interview with Dick Cavett said she believed that "every word [Hellman] writes is a lie, including 'the' and 'and.'" Hellman's subsequent $2-million lawsuit against McCarthy did not help. (The lawsuit died when Hellman did.) Others began to speculate that Hellman had in fact been the model for the consummately mendacious females at the center of several of Dashiell Hammett's mysteries.

Why should a reader of Hellman's memoirs feel cheated on learning all this? Does it affect the literary, as opposed to documentary or historical, value of her work? Her style is just as pleasing to the ear as it was before. Many of the stories are just as entertaining as they were before; like the one she tells about Dorothy Parker: Dorothy's husband had just been quarreling with his mother before he joined his wife and Lillian sitting by the fireside in the living-room. "It's hot as hell in here," he complained. "Not for orphans," Dorothy replied.

If these stories are invented, one might say, that only does Hellman greater credit. One of her chief unmaskers, the biographer William Wright, goes so far as to insist that the revelations of fabrication only enhance the literary value of the memoirs:

> For all of her prodigious impact on the world—plays, books, loves, friends, politics, social criticism—there seems little doubt that her greatest contribution was the character that she created in the memoirs. So much attention has been given to the truth or falsity of the portrait that the creative feat has been overlooked. In order to be able to get such a character down on paper, a writer must have a profound knowledge of the world, of human nature and of the particular psychology being created. It requires much torturous life experience and an ensuing catharsis. It requires a rare sensitivity to what delights or repels others, an original flair to set the character apart, a strong moral sense (to be projected into the character) and a facility with words that precisely complements the personality being presented. In fact, it requires many of the skills and sensibilities that make up a great fiction

writer or dramatist. The achievement in such a creation is major and renders all but irrelevant the question of whether or not such a character actually existed. For the author to stand up at the end and say, "This Lillian Hellman you've been reading about, this is me," is of course, a lie. And the fraudulence must alter the perception of her integrity. But it doesn't diminish Hellman's creative achievement.[89]

Ah, but it does. Wright himself offers a telling reason:

> [Once] Hellman's memoirs are reread with a degree of skepticism, [o]dd
> happenings and coincidences that seemed delightfully serendipitous on first
> reading now become jejune plotting and clumsy manipulation. One of the
> most memorable moments in the three memoirs occurs in *Scoundrel Time*
> when Hellman and Hammett are preparing to leave the farm they have been
> forced to give up. They look up from their work inside the house to see
> forty or fifty deer emerge from the woods to nibble, idly and without fear,
> leaves and buds around the house. The deer remain in plain view near the
> house for over two hours while Hellman and Hammett sit silently watching
> the animals' moving farewell. The story, which is told with considerable art-
> istry, is beautiful and mystical. So much of its beauty, however, depends on
> the unearthliness of an actual happening. If it was a product of imagination,
> any six-year-old child could have done as well.[90]

Wright overlooks, however, just how many passages in the book are vulnerable to this kind of criticism. Consider one episode in which Hellman describes herself as quarreling with Dashiell Hammet, in the middle of which, she says, he began "grinding a burning cigarette into his cheek." She asked him what he was doing. "Keeping myself from doing it to you," he supposedly replied. If this is invented—big deal. If it really happened—wow! Or consider her account of getting a gift from her uncle when she was still a child:

> I had only one real contact with my Uncle Jake: when I graduated from
> school at fifteen, he gave me a ring that I took to a 59th Street hock shop,
> got twenty-five dollars, and bought books. I went immediately to tell him
> what I'd done, deciding, I think, that day that the break had to come. He
> stared at me for a long time, and then he laughed and said the words I later
> used in *The Little Foxes:* "So you've got spirit after all. Most of the rest of
> them are made of sugar water."[91]

Again this is interesting only if it really is the story behind those well-known lines. The same goes for her alleged refusal to meet with Stalin and for innumerable other anecdotes.

An analogy will help clarify the esthetic problem with Hellman's memoirs. Imagine someone were to put on the radio a fictitious baseball game: a reporter weaves together a plausible narrative of a fairly exciting game, modeled in part on real games that have been played, and he records it against the background noise of a real baseball game. Better yet, he pretends the game is being played by two very real teams, which are in fact about to confront each other in the next few days. He is not the least bit deceptive about what he is doing. He tells you in advance that his is just a "baseball fiction." Would you care to listen? I should think not. You wouldn't enjoy it. To be sure, if he fooled you into thinking it is the real thing, you would listen intently, and you would enjoy it. But you would feel cheated once told that it was all made up. Now why should that be so? Why should you not be able to enjoy a baseball fiction? Why should you feel cheated rather than pleased with the entertaining illusion once its illusory nature has been revealed? Why do you feel as though you wasted your time? Getting the true facts about baseball has no practical significance for your career, your finances, your family, your life. You listen to it so as to be entertained by images of baseball, and you really have been entertained by images of baseball. So why do you mind? You mind because you value the *reality connection,* the authenticity, for its own sweet sake. You do not merely value the thrill engendered by baseball. You value the thrill plus the fact that that thrill is triggered by a very real contest. So when the thrill turns out to have been provided by the wrong kind of trigger, you feel cheated. There is some baseball fiction, of course, we do enjoy as such. There are made-up games in movies and books that we follow with enormous solicitude, but those offer much more than just a suspenseful baseball game. They are embedded in a dramatic story, and we judge them as part of that story, which has to be very good to make up for the lack of a reality-connection. In this regard its relation is emblematic of the relationship between novels and memoirs generally. We demand more of our fiction than of our memoirs, because memoirs do offer the reality connection. Shorn of that connection, memoirs inevitably depreciate. Authenticity excuses bad plotting and implausible, out-of-character behavior by its protagonists. All of which makes it very tempting to falsely claim authenticity for a work of mere fiction. It's a bit like the advice someone once gave me for dealing with a boorish party guest: "Tell the other guests he is your cousin, that way they can't blame you for inviting him."

Implications and Applications: Tax Law and Related Problems

Having made a plausible case for the deontological point of view, we need to trace out its implications by solving the problems posed in the early sections of this book. So far I have suggested a solution to only one of those problems, the one involving political asylum, and I will now take up those of the others which in one way or another, either on the face of it or on deeper analysis, have to do with tax law.

In what way do I expect what I have said so far to imply an answer to these problems? The question as to each of them will be: Are there deontological rules we truly believe in that inevitably create room for the kind of strategizing and manipulation that so worries us in these examples, and are we really sufficiently committed to these deontological rules to accept those features as part of the bargain?

Let me try to clarify a bit further what I mean by "solving" these problems. Suppose that, at the outset of this book, I had used as one of my problem cases the example of the hospital administrator who switches life-support systems so as to maximize the number of patients saved. Suppose, that is, I had asked whether his switching from life-support systems that need servicing every few days to life-support systems that need replacement every day is a permissible way of getting around the general prohibition against killing one to save several others. I would then have solved that problem by bringing up the trolley problem and showing that we are quite strongly committed to the view that the trolley may be turned but that the utilitarian surgeon may not carve up one of his patients to obtain organs for five others, and that the life-support system "trick" is a hidden implication of that commitment. I will try to solve the remaining problems in analogous fashion.

The Generous Shoemaker

Recall: the shoemaker had been paying his son an annual stipend of $1,000. In order to make these annual payments tax deductible, he decided one year to give his son $10,000 instead, then asked his son for a $10,000 loan and proceeded to pay him $1,000 (that is, 10 percent) annually by way of interest. Since the purpose of the loan was to run his business, he now claimed the $1,000 annual payment as a business expense.

Skeptical commentators, and for a while the IRS was among the skeptics, have viewed this as the quintessential instance of tax evasion. Others have thought it a perfectly fine form of tax planning, that is, avoidance. To challenge the skeptics, they often ask us to imagine the shoemaker had been just a bit more roundabout in his strategy. Suppose that after he had given his son the $10,000, he had gone to his neighborhood bank and borrowed $10,000 from *them* at roughly the going 10 percent interest rate. Suppose, further, that his son had deposited his $10,000 in that or another bank and received interest at roughly the same rate. Since the end result is virtually the same as before, it now is hard to insist that the interest payments are not a legitimate business deduction for the shoemaker. This sort of argument does not solve the problem. What it does do is heighten the dilemma by showing each side in this dispute to be backed by equally formidable intuitions.

To solve the problem we need to lay bare the basic feature of our tax system that gives rise to this sort of tax-planning opportunity. That feature is the way in which we decide to whom to attribute a stream of income. If you receive wages for some work you perform, quite clearly that is income that is attributable to you. If you receive dividends on some stocks or bonds you own, that too is quite clearly income that is attributable to you. But what if you decide to give some part or all of your wages or dividends to your wife or your son? Now are they still "your" income, or are they the income of the person to whom you have given them? In the early days of the income tax many people were sorely tempted to try this, since by doing so a family could neatly divide all of the husband's income across the various family members and put themselves in a much lower tax bracket. But the courts did not accept this stratagem. They insisted that even if you give some of your income to someone else, it still is your income and taxable to you: after all, spending money on your son is not that different from spending money on yourself. It's just another way of using your income to give yourself pleasure.

But suppose that instead of assigning part of his income stream to his son the taxpayer just hands his son some stock. Over time that stock produces dividends which now flow into the son's pockets. Whose income is that? Quite clearly the son's, he owns the stock. It's hard to see how it could be attributed to anyone other than the current owner. By saying this, however, we have created a gigantic opportunity for cutting one's taxes. Although you will derive no benefit from assigning your income, you will derive great benefit if you can find a way to give away an asset that generates income, because that income is now taxable to the recipient of the asset. It is this fact which the shoemaker so cleverly exploited. He realized that he could not just assign $1,000 a month to his son and have that considered his son's as opposed to his own salary. But he also realized that a lump sum of money, like $10,000, is an asset generating a stream of income, and he simply could give his son that sum and achieve the same end as if he had assigned his income.

Although we now can see how this tax-planning opportunity arose, we still are not sure whether a sensible tax system ought to permit it to arise. Can our tax system really be said to rest on any kind of moral footing if this sort of thing can happen? If we believe that people of certain wealth have an ethical obligation to pay a certain amount of taxes, how can that obligation be abrogated by this sort of game? What kind of sensible moral principle would allow that?

An elaborate analogy should help. The saga of the *Nibelungen* has it that when King Gunther of Burgundy embarked to woo the Valkyrie Brunhild, he was required to defeat her in a duel first. As the duel proceeded, it became increasingly clear that Gunther might not be up to the task:

> Brunhild's strength was clearly tremendous, for they brought a heavy boulder to the ring for her, round, and of monstrous size—twelve lusty warriours could barely carry it!—and this she would always hurl after throwing her javelin. The Burgundians' fears rose high at the sight of it. "Mercy on us!" said Hagen [one of Gunther's vassals]. "What sort of a lover has the King got here? Rather should she be the Devil's drab in Hell!" She furled her sleeves over her dazzling white arms, took a grip on her shield, snatched her spear aloft, and the contest was on![92]

Indeed, we are told "she would have taken the king's life" had not then and there the king's good friend, the ferocious Siegfried, intervened, by making use of his magical cap which had the convenient property of rendering him invisible. As Gunther was struggling,

> Siegfried went up to him unseen and touched his hand, startling him with his magic powers. "What was it that touched me?" the brave man wondered, looking all around him, yet finding no one there. "It is I, your dear friend Siegfried," said the other. "You must not fear the Queen. Give me your shield, and let me bear it, and take careful note of what I say to you. Now, you go through the motions, and I shall do the deeds."[93]

With Siegfried's help, Gunther won his contest with Brunhild and her hand in marriage. In return, he rewarded Siegfried with countless royal favors, including the hand of his very own sister, the beautiful Kriemhild.

This episode has had some historical counterparts. In 1692, the marquis de l'Hospital, a French mathematician of more wealth than talent, hired another mathematician, Johann Bernoulli, to teach him calculus and to share with him exclusively some of his more recent discoveries in that field—which de l'Hospital then planned to publish under his own name. As a result, de l'Hospital went on to win much renown as the author of the first calculus textbook.[94] According to persistent rumors, something analogous happened when John F. Kennedy supposedly arranged for Theodore Sorensen and Arthur Schlesinger to ghostwrite *Profiles in Courage* for him, which then won the Pulitzer Prize.

What makes these episodes interesting to me is that they dramatize a somewhat peculiar feature of fame. They are quite unlike ordinary cases of misappropriated fame, because the person claiming credit for another's accomplishment does so with the complete consent of that other person. Nevertheless, we think it is wrong. Although what exactly the two mathematicians had agreed on, and whether de l'Hospital took credit in his book for any of Bernoulli's work, is subject to some dispute; what has not been subject to dispute is that if de l'Hospital really did so, he acted wrongly. *Even if Bernoulli was perfectly delighted and munificently compensated for his sacrifice.* Although what exactly Sorensen and Schlesinger contributed to Kennedy's book is much debated, what no one debates is that if they really did write Kennedy's book for him, he acted wrongly in publishing it under his own name and collecting the resulting kudos for it. *Even if Sorensen and Schlesinger were perfectly delighted and munificently compensated for their sacrifice.*

More broadly speaking, what these examples teach us is this: Although copyrights and patents, the law's formal rewards for intellectual achievement, are traded, donated, bequeathed, mortgaged, and rented out all the time, the less formal rewards of intellectual achievement—the honors, the prizes, the trophies, the laurels, the tokens of glory—these are not, or at least are not supposed to be, alienable. Fortunes may be given away, fame may not. A wag writing for the op-ed page of the *Wall Street Journal* once speculated that the reason academics are so free and easy about advocating redistribution of wealth is that the good they care most about—prestige—cannot be redistributed. Of course, that's not a hard and fast rule. We tolerate a certain amount of prestige-trading; a little bit of imposture is acceptable. Winning an election with a ghostwritten speech is all right, winning the Pulitzer with a ghostwritten book is not. The Italian poet Eugenio Montale's practice of having his friend Henry Furst, an accomplished literary critic, ghostwrite some of his book reviews seems perched at the outer edges of what is tolerable, and quite possibly tolerable only because of Montale's diffident marching orders to Furst: "You shouldn't write with a wealth of erudition regarding English and American literary matters; you ought to display a kind of medium competence that may be attributed to me."[95]

Now, back to the income tax. There is a noteworthy parallel between the attribution of fame and the attribution of income. Neither can be reassigned by the recipient. But there is another equally important parallel. Just as it is possible to get around the prohibition on assigning income by assigning the underlying asset generating the income, it is possible to get around the prohibition on assigning fame by doing something quite analogous.

Antony Leeuwenhoek is commonly designated the first of the microbe hunters. He was the first to peer through a microscope—one of his own making—and see the swarming microbes. He reported his findings to the Royal Society of London. Since he was a much better lens maker than observer, it was thought that others might use his lenses more fruitfully than he. The Royal Society sent a representative, a Dr. Molyneux, to acquire some lenses. Leeuwenhoek replied that he was

> sorry, but that was impossible to do, while he lived. . . . Molyneux offered Leeuwenhoek a fine price for one of his microscopes—surely he could spare one?—for there were hundreds of them in cabinets that lined his study. But no! . . .
>
> "But your instruments are marvelous!" cried Molyneux. "A thousand times more clear they show things than any lens we have in England!"
>
> "How I wish, Sir," said Leeuwenhoek, "that I could show you my best lens, with my special way of observing, but I keep that only for myself and do not show it to any one—not even to my own family."[96]

Leeuwenhoek was not acting differently from most modern researchers.

Imagine, however, that Leeuwenhoek had had a son with whom he wanted to share some of his new-won scientific fame. Suppose he proposed to do so by telling the Royal Society what a smart fellow his son was, that given the opportunity he would have made the identical observations, and that Leeuwenhoek would like some of the prestige bestowed on him to be bestowed instead on his son—most especially the recognition embodied by admission to the society itself. It's clear that wouldn't work. But a more roundabout version of the same strategy would work: Leeuwenhoek might give his son the unique access to his microscopes he had denied everyone else. Now his son would make discoveries no one else had been able to make, and in due course would come to be recognized as a major discoverer, in the same way many physicists are who happen to be lucky enough to have access to some critical piece of equipment, which in the hands of many (though of course not in the hands of just any fool) would have yielded such discoveries.

Here then we have a moral rule, in many ways like the rule against assigning income, that nevertheless can be circumvented. If Leeuwenhoek plans things right we believe he can insure that some of the fame he would otherwise receive is given instead to his son. It should thus not really offend our moral sensibilities when the shoemaker accomplishes the same thing by making his son a gift of $10,000.

The Financial Aid Artist, the Prudent Spendthrift, and the Socially Responsible Pornographer

Leona, the financial aid artist, had given up a successful real estate career in favor of a lower-paying but more enjoyable job as high school music teacher, in order to help her son qualify for more college financial aid.

The doctor in my bankruptcy hypothetical had debts of $20 million and assets of about $700,000. To qualify for various bankruptcy exemptions, he sold his modest house and bought a villa instead, furnished it extravagantly, decked himself out with a fur-laden wardrobe, and put his remaining cash into exempt kinds of pension and life insurance.

The socially responsible pornographer had embedded his sexually explicit materials amidst layers of medical commentary, biblical excerpts, Japanese poetry, and scholarly discussion of sex-related topics.

Let's try to unravel first what bothers us about what Leona did. We think that in granting financial aid, as in choosing our tax rates, we are aiming to achieve some measure of equality between rich and poor—not actually to achieve equality but to move in that direction. We have the sense that when Leona took that lower-paying job as music teacher, she was transforming some of her monetary income into psychic income, as though she had switched to a company with lower pay but higher fringe benefits. By increasing her family's financial aid we seem to be doing more than just putting her on a par with higher-paid people, her former colleagues in the real estate business, for instance; we are in fact boosting her beyond that level. There seems to be something wrong with a system that doesn't aim merely to equalize rich and poor but actually to make the poor better off than the rich. By allowing Leona to engage in this maneuver, we seem to be doing exactly that.

This objection rests crucially on the presupposition that what we aim to do in granting financial aid and setting the tax rate is to achieve equality of *happiness*. For it is not the case that Leona ends up with more monetary income than her former colleagues in the real estate business; she ends up only with greater happiness, and that is what is bothersome. But do you really want a tax or financial aid system that aims to equalize happiness? Are you willing to tax Mother Theresa, Richard Feynman, or Robert Penn Warren as heavily as some much-better-heeled but much-less-happy corporate executive on the grounds that they are happier? In general, do you think happy-go-lucky people deserve to be taxed more heavily on the same monetary income?

It seems then that what we aim to equalize in taxing and subsidizing is not happiness but material well-being. In fact, if you are honest with yourself, are you not more likely to envy someone his wealth, brains, good looks, and fame than his happiness (even though it seems you only want those so as to achieve happiness)? I know I am.

Our mistake here lies in thinking that just because we generally desire wealth, brains, and good looks for the sake of the happiness they allow us to achieve, it follows that it is happiness we are really trying to equalize when we try to equalize income. But one only *seems* to imply the other. It is a perfectly coherent aim to want to equalize people's means and opportunities for achieving happiness rather than happiness itself.

But as soon as we say that it is something other than raw happiness that we seek to equalize we have opened the door to maneuvers like that by Leona. The only way to nail that door shut is to pursue the ethically unattractive alternative of equalizing happiness.

The problem of the prudent spendthrift who so aggressively exploits the bankruptcy exemptions is analogous but not identical. The rationale behind the exemption is that we want every bankrupt debtor to be left the same basic minimum, the proverbial shirt on his back. But if we define that minimum in terms of specific assets, we then create the opportunity for the kind of maneuvers the shrewd doctor engaged in.

Admittedly, we could prevent such maneuvers by defining the minimum in monetary terms. In other words, we could decree that every bankrupt is entitled to retain the equivalent of, say, $5,000. But that would not be an ethically attractive thing to do. To see why, imagine that a friend were to call you up to tell you of a painful, but not especially disabling, ailment that might be much alleviated by a fairly expensive experimental medical procedure not covered by her insurance. She doesn't have much money; she isn't sure yet just how much it will cost; she wants to know if you would be willing to help her out. You tell her that, within certain limits, you are. She calls you back to let you know that it would cost about $3,000—which she does not have. That's steep, you say, but certainly well within the bounds of friendship. She gratefully accepts. A short while later she calls you back again, thanks you for the offer, and says that she would really rather just put the money in the bank or use it for a vacation, and go on living with her pain. You ask her whether that means the pain isn't so bad, but she assures you that it certainly is. It's just that she *really* likes the idea of having some money in the bank, and she *really* likes the idea of a cruise, and while she values the relief of her ailment greatly she doesn't value it as highly as either of the others. Will you still give her the money? I suspect not. But why not? You don't doubt that the pain is severe enough to be worth spending $3,000 to alleviate. You don't doubt that she will get more pleasure out of putting the money in the bank or spending it on a cruise. She is your friend and you want to see her happy. Nevertheless, you will think her claim upon you much greater when it involves her health than when it involves financing a nest egg or a vacation. The point most worth noting, however, is this: you do not express the scope of your obligations as a friend in a fixed sum. If you are called upon to help finance a vacation, you will feel obliged to pitch in only in a small amount. If you are called upon to help finance a medical procedure, you feel obliged to contribute a much larger sum. For various other desires of your friend, you would feel obligations intermediate between those two. Is this because you are being paternalistic, because you think she is making a mistake in preferring to spend the money on things other than the medical treatment? Not at all! It is only that you don't believe that being a friend requires you to be quite so solicitous in attending to certain of her desires than in attending to others.

But note some of the more peculiar consequences this aspect of your friendship obligations has: if your friend wants to get as much help from you as she possibly can, she simply will make sure that she spends her money on the things you will not provide for her and turns to you for those "basics" she knows you are willing to pay for. She also will cast about among the "basics" for things that happen to be near-equivalents of the extravagances you refuse to pay for. If she would like a vacation but knows you won't spring for a cruise, she might ask you to pay for a sanatorium instead.

This example pretty much captures our attitude toward bankrupt debtors.

Creditors owe obligations to debtors analogous to those of the friend, obligations whose scope is expressed not by some monetary amount but depends rather on the form which the assets have that they are asking the debtor to give up.

THAT LEAVES the problem of the socially responsible pornographer. On the surface it seems to have little relation to the two cases we just discussed, but it will prove to be the same. The Supreme Court's obscenity test seems to rest on the idea that we should accept pornographic content in a movie to the extent that it is the necessary by-product of the movie's "socially redeeming values." What initially disturbs us about the movie producer who strategically injects enough "socially redeeming value" into his movies to immunize his pornography is that the pornography doesn't seem a necessary by-product. We have the impression that the same amount of "socially redeeming value" could have been poured into some other movie with much less pornographic content. But that's rather like telling a taxpayer who seeks to deduct certain expenditures from his revenues that the expenditures are not deductible as necessary business expenses if he could have gone into some other business that would involve higher revenues and lower expenditures. Then again, what exactly would be wrong with that?

Compare two taxpayers, both of whom could enter profession A, and one of whom could also enter profession B which would produce higher revenues and entail lower expenditures. Both much prefer A to B, which is why they both go into A. Should the second taxpayer be taxed at a higher rate, just because he could have gone into B? That's what denying him his expenditures as unnecessary would amount to. We can pose an analogous example in the movie context. Compare two movie producers, both of whom could produce a commercially very successful movie of type A (lots of sex, some socially redeeming content), and one of whom could also produce a commercially moderately successful movie of type B (less sex, more socially redeeming content). Should the second producer not be permitted to make the more profitable movie? That's what denying his pornographic ingredients as unnecessary would amount to.

The Devious Decedent

The devious decedent is the husband who tries to circumvent the law that automatically awards his widow a fixed fraction of his estate. He does so by giving the property away before he dies.

To get a grip on this case, imagine you are about to marry someone of whom your father would strongly disapprove. If he is still alive, it might give you serious second thoughts about the marriage. If he is dead, it still might mildly disturb you that he would disapprove if he were around, but it will matter rather less. The desires of the living matter to you more than the desires of the dead. That is, I think, a perfectly sensible principle to embrace. Realizing that you will feel free to disregard his wishes once he is gone, he tries to make sure you get hitched up in some difficult-to-untangle way before he dies, say, by not only getting you to marry but also getting you to produce some children. In doing so, is he unfairly "circumventing" the principle which says that his desires get much less weight once he is dead than while he is alive? I should think not. He is simply making a permissible adjustment to it.

Arguably the husband who gives his property away in light of a forced share statute is behaving in exactly the same way. The reason we feel free to override his testamentary wishes with a forced share statute but not to override his gifts in the same way is that the plight of the surviving spouse is strong enough to override the relatively unimportant desires of the deceased husband but not the far weightier desires of the living husband. The husband who adjusts to this by giving away a lot of his property before he dies is not unfairly circumventing that principle but simply making a permissible adjustment to it.

IMPLICATIONS AND APPLICATIONS:
CORPORATE LAW AND RELATED PROBLEMS

At the outset of Part I, I presented a long-standing, unresolved problem of corporate law, which the analysis of the intervening pages should help us bring to its knees. Since it is more technical than the others, I had better just quote it in full:

> *The corporation's ten-foot pole.* The Grand Corporation wants to build a chemical plant but is worried that a mechanical mishap might cause calamitous injuries and result in ruinous tort liabilities. It decides to insulate against this contingency by incorporating a subsidiary which then goes ahead and builds the chemical plant. A calamity does happen. Thousands of people are severely injured. They sue Grand's subsidiary, but discover that there isn't enough cash to compensate them all. They try to reach the assets of the parent corporation. Grand insists that as a mere shareholder in the subsidiary corporation it cannot be held liable. Incorporation, after all, means limited liability: A shareholder is never liable beyond the amount that he initially in-

vested in his company. Does this work? By only touching its subsidiary with a shareholder's ten-foot pole, is Grand avoiding liability or evading it?

Most courts have tended to uphold limited liability in such cases as long as the parent corporation punctiliously observed all the formalities that go with treating its subsidiary as a corporation rather than a mere unincorporated division of the parent corporation. The purpose of limited liability, they sometimes add, is to encourage industrial development by relieving corporations of the threat of ruinous tort liability, and here it is serving this very purpose.

Outrageous nonsense, say the critics, who have been vociferous and who have gradually grown to include not just academics but some courts as well. It is unconscionable, they say, to allow corporations to prosper by simply relieving them of the obligation to compensate decently the victims of tortious misdeeds. Not only is it unconscionable, they note, it is also inefficient, because it encourages corporations to pursue all sorts of activities whose benefits to society are outweighed by their costs, but whose costs the corporation simply loses sight of because it doesn't have to pay its tort victims. Limited liability only makes sense, they contend, as to parties who have entered into a contractual relationship with the corporation, because they know as soon as they start doing business with the enterprise that their recourse is going to be limited to its assets.

The defenders of limited liability vis-à-vis tort victims have issued several rejoinders. All of these, however, have to do with the issue of efficiency. On the issue of fairness—the claimed unconscionability of letting shareholders relieve themselves of their just tort liabilities by filing a piece of paper declaring the entity in which they have invested to be a corporation—on that issue they have had little to say. Yet it is on that issue on which I suspect the debate over limited liability in cases like the above will ultimately be decided.

Our discussion of the Shabbes Goy puts us in a position to resolve that issue decisively. We have determined that running an elevator, a farm, or a factory through the use of an intermediary is ethically different from doing so directly. Similarly, killing someone by ducking is ethically different from killing him by using him as a shield. Operating a train through the use of a computer is ethically different from doing so through a human driver. Although they may produce identical accidents with an identical frequency, in the first case the "causer" of the accident, the manufacturer of the computer, is beyond reproach. He has assembled a product which like all products will sometimes fail, and there is no negligence in that, so long as the failure rate isn't greater than that of alternative arrangements. The driver, on the other hand, has been negligent and ought in fairness to be held liable for that. (It doesn't matter that everyone can expect to be negligent sometimes in the course of a lifetime and to produce injuries if he is unlucky enough. Everyone can expect to yield to the temptation to embezzle, if the temptation is great enough and the odds of being caught low enough, as Abraham Lincoln so aptly made clear when he virtually pushed a lobbyist out of the Oval Office: not because he was above being bribed, he explained, but because he was not!) The reason for treating the "causer" of the accident differently in these two cases is that causal chains run differently in the two cases. And we now understand the nature of the causal chain to be crucial in determining the fairness of blaming someone. Similarly, injuring someone via the intermediary tool of a corporation over whom one only has the sort of indirect control that shareholders have over a business is different from doing so as a partner directly involved in the day-to-day operation of his business.[97]

To the critics who ask how we can allow investors simply to, as it were, opt out of the tort system by filing a statement of incorporation, we can reply that they already are in a position to opt out of the tort system (and amply avail themselves of it) when they replace what the tort scholar Mark Grady has called "nondurable" with "durable precautions," which is the generalized version of deciding to run your train through a computer rather than a human driver. We might also point out to such critics that opting out of the tort system in this way is no different than opting out of the tax system by transferring income-generating property to one's son rather than transferring the income itself. The latter has no effect on taxes, but the former, though it comes to the same thing, does.

M ANY OTHER PROBLEMS of corporate law take on a different appearance when looked at in analogous fashion. For now I will offer just one more example, the puzzle surrounding the so-called de facto merger doctrine.

Megga Inc. wants to own Minni Corp. There are several ways this can be done. It could merge Minni into Megga, or Megga into Minni. It could also consolidate the two into Meggaminni Inc. Or Megga could buy all of Minni's assets. Or Megga could buy the stock of all of Minni's stockholders. The end result is the same, but the route chosen makes a difference. Perhaps it shouldn't make any difference, but it does; each route demands different legal procedures. And given those different procedures, not all routes are equally attractive.

If Minni and Megga merge or consolidate, both companies must obtain the approval of their shareholders. If Megga buys a chunk of Minni's assets instead of merging, only Minni will have to ask its stockholders for approval, and even it might not have to if the sale is "in the regular course of business," that is, if the proceeds will be reinvested in Minni's business. (A real estate company might well sell all of its assets in the regular course of business.) Finally, if Megga buys Minni's stock, no one's vote is required. Megga only has to make its tender offer and wait.

It may seem silly that the law should impose such very different consent requirements depending on how the property is acquired. The reason seems to be that the statutes were drafted with certain paradigmatic cases in mind. The typical merger the drafters envisioned is the joining of two equally large companies, in which the stockholders of both companies would continue to invest and in which the managers of both companies would continue to have a part. The typical sale they envisioned is the absorption of a small company by a much larger one. It now becomes clear why they wanted the consent of both sets of stockholders for a merger but not for a sale.

Problems arise when two companies structure what seems fundamentally like the merger of two companies, as if it were a sale of assets to escape the requirement to let one or another group of shareholders vote on it. Courts have sometimes, but inconsistently, responded to such efforts by invoking the de facto merger doctrine, declaring that "really" this is a merger and, therefore, everyone should get to vote on it. Is the courts' distrust of the formalistic circumvention of merger rules justified?

Two somewhat extravagant science fiction scenarios concocted by Peter Unger prove to be oddly relevant here. They both involve brain transplants. Case I goes like this: imagine two people, let us say "you" and "me." They remove my brain from my skull and your brain from your skull and switch them around. Your body ends up with my brain. My body ends up with your brain. Now, which of the two of us is Leo Katz? Surely the person with your body and my brain. How do I know this? Well, if somebody had told me in advance of going through this procedure that he was going to subject one of the two bodies to some excruciating pain and that I could tell him in advance which body it should be, I most certainly would have selected my own body which I knew would be occupied by your brain rather than mine. Clearly then I expect my identity to follow my brain rather than my body. And I am pretty sure you feel the same way.

Next consider Unger's Case II, and let's start over again. Again the case will involve two people, "you" and "me," with a brain exchange much like Case I but with a major new wrinkle. Rather than taking out my brain and your brain and trading places *in one fell swoop,* this is going to be done in a piecemeal fashion. A sliver of your brain is removed, and a sliver of my brain is removed, and the two are switched. Then we are each asked who we think is who. My answer will be that the person with my original brain, my original body, and a sliver of your brain is still me. And you will reply symmetrically. Now suppose that this process is carried out over and over again, and after each sliver switch we are each asked who we think is who. The answer I believe will always be: I will think the person in the Leo Katz body is Leo Katz and you will think the person with your body is you. But when it's all over, the person I continue to think of as "me," as "Leo Katz," is the person whose entire brain consists of slivers from what used to be your brain, and vice versa for you. What this shows is that when we make judgments of identity, it isn't just the end result that matters but the path by which that end result is reached. In Case I and Case II, we end up with the same end results but with different identities. In Case I, identity follows the brain. In Case II, identity follows the body.

Nothing in this example turns on my having focused on people. The very same point could have been made more realistically, but less dramatically and less convincingly, by talking about organizations. In lieu of Case I, I could have asked you to think about two organizations swapping buildings and asked you whether the people in the original A-building or the people in the original B-building are the A-organization (and whether the others, therefore, are the B-organization). You would have said that organizational identity follows people, not buildings, and, therefore, the people in the B-building are the A-organization (and the people in the A-building are the B-organization). In lieu of Case II, I could then have asked you to think about two organizations that gradually, one-by-one, over some extended period traded personnel. After each personnel switch, I would then ask you which is the A-organization and which the B-organization, and you would continue to assert that the A-organization is in the A-building and the B-organization in the B-building. You would continue to say that even after all of the personnel has been switched. Which would show us that organizational identity is highly path-dependent.[98]

The lawyer "manipulating" the rules of corporate combination—the rules of merger, consolidation, asset sales, etc.—is simply exploiting these facts about identity. He is taking advantage of the fact that the identity of the organization one ends up with is not just dependent on what the eventual organization looks like but how it gets there. It is only natural that if organization B disappears in the process, but organization A survives, its shareholders have more of a claim to vote than if organization A disappears in the process and organization B survives. And this remains true regardless of whether the end product looks mostly like A or mostly like B or like something else altogether.

But won't shareholders feel fooled, or worse yet, refuse to be fooled and claim to have been cheated? Won't shareholders insist that it is the end result that matters to them, not the path of getting there? Even if they do, they are not entitled to do so. If my brain-exchange cases weren't enough to clinch the case for you, just think about how path-dependent the loyalties of alumni to their alma mater are. In the decades between the time someone attends a university and the moment he is rich enough to make a substantial donation, the faculty and students will have turned over completely, the physical plant might have been replaced, the location shifted, the name changed (from Trinity to Duke or from the College of New Jersey to Princeton). Nonetheless, so long as there is the right kind of continuous spatiotemporal path connecting his alma mater with the current university laying claim to his loyalty, that's the institution he will feel beholden to. What's more, he would feel offended if before "his" university were to merge into some other institution he had not been asked, but he would not feel so offended if another university had merged into "his" university and he had not been asked. Never mind that the look of the end result would be the same. That doesn't mean he is a fool. It only means that identity and all the emotions tied in with it are path-dependent.

You still may be left with this objection: corporate combinations and rearrangements happen overnight. In all of my examples, in which I managed to influence identities by the path chosen, the process took some time. It may be true that if one were to turn a merger into an asset sale by gradually selling the assets of corporation A to corporation B, one can get to the same end-result by an asset sale as by a merger, but where a lawyer restructures a merger as an asset sale, things happen instantaneously. Doesn't that put my explanation in serious jeopardy?

Not at all, because the instantaneousness of corporate combinations is an illusion. A deal does not happen instantaneously; only its closing date does. There is a tortuous lawyer-intensive process that goes into carrying out the entire transaction, which looks different depending on what kind of combination, merger, or asset sale is being executed. To be sure, it mostly looks different with respect to the paper work that goes into it. But paper is where legal transactions happen.

FURTHER IMPLICATIONS AND APPLICATIONS:
CRACKING THE TEST, BEATING THE SYSTEM,
AVOIDING THE TICKET,
AND OTHER DEONTOLOGICAL TRICKS OF EVERYDAY LIFE

In the course of daily life, we often engage in strategic conduct that we believe to be perfectly legal, quite moral, or at least not terribly immoral, but which nevertheless leaves us with surprisingly intense pangs of conscience. Presumably, many of Woodward and Bernstein's sources felt bad just after making one of their sleight-of-hand leaks. The lover who has provoked a breakup, the politician who (in LBJ fashion) has talked himself into believing what political expediency calls for him to say—they too will often feel far more uncomfortable than they think they should. The reason is that they have engaged in a game of deontological avoision and that unless one has thought the matter through with some care—or read Part I of this book—one is left with a residual suspicion that the game accomplishes nothing of real moral consequence. The same kind of unease I believe accounts for our ambivalence about many other practices of daily life in which we engage aplenty but with an ever-nagging bad conscience.

Heeding the advice of a test-coaching service is one such instance. The Princeton Review may be the most infamous of these services currently around. It boldly promises to raise the SAT scores of its students by an average of 150 points. *Cracking The System* is the paperback summary of the program. Its preface states emphatically: "We're not going to teach you math. We're not going to teach you English. We're going to teach you the SAT."[99] Many of the test-cracking strategies the Princeton Review propounds seem innocuous enough—like the advice not to scrutinize the reading comprehension passages too carefully on first reading—and in particular don't seem very likely to subvert the purpose of the test. But some of the strategies certainly do appear to have that potential. Standardized tests like the SAT are constructed according to certain statistical and pedagogical constraints. By drawing attention to these constraints, the Princeton Review makes the test-taker's task considerably easier. There is, for instance, what the Princeton Review calls the Joe Bloggs principle:

> Joe Bloggs is the average student. He earns an average score on the SAT. On easy SAT questions, the answers that *seem* correct to him are always correct. On medium questions, they're sometimes correct. On hard questions,

they're always wrong. The correct answer on a hard question could never *seem right* to *most people*. If it did, the question would be easy, not hard.[100]

Combine this with the further observation that questions in each subsection of the test have to be presented in order of difficulty (if they weren't, Joe Bloggs would give up too soon), and you have a potent tool for guessing the right answer with a minimum of actual knowledge.

Another constraint to which the Princeton Review draws attention is the testers' preference for indisputably right answers. This means that on reading comprehension questions specific answers are more likely to be right than general ones. Answers with categorical terms, like "each," "all," "will," "totally," "must," "always," are more likely to be right than answers with "may," "can," "most," "sometimes," "might," or "suggest."

The Princeton Review also advises against picking as an answer to a reading comprehension question a response that reproduces verbatim some portion of the reading passage. That's because, as they explain, the testers assume that Joe Bloggs will tend to pick anything that sounds familiar as his answer. Thus to prevent Joe Bloggs from "inadvertently" getting the right answer, the correct response cannot contain familiar-sounding language.

The Princeton Review advises keeping in mind that the tester has some fairly predictable attitudes:

> One of them is admiration for doctors, lawyers, scientists, writers, and
> artists. SAT reading passages treat such people with dignity and respect.
> You would be exceedingly unlikely to find an SAT reading passage about un-
> caring doctors, ruthless lawyers, or unscrupulous scientists. Nor would you
> be likely to find a passage about a bad writer or an untalented artist. . . .
> [The tester] avoids strong, unqualified emotions on the SAT. The author of a
> reading passage may be "admiring," or "somewhat skeptical," but would
> never be "irrational" or "wildly enthusiastic." On reading comprehension
> questions about the attitude, style, or tone of a passage or its author, you
> can simply eliminate answer choices containing emotions that are too posi-
> tive or too negative.[101]

The Princeton Review also tells you that when you run out of time at the end of a section and have to guess, you should pick either *A* or *E*. That's because when Joe Bloggs runs out of time, he tends to pick *B, C,* or *D*. Therefore, the tester will make the right answer an *A* or an *E*.

What the Princeton Review does for getting into college, a book called *How to Beat the System* does for surviving college once you are in. Its authors, Kathy Crafts and Brenda Hauther, offer anxious college students advice about getting through college with a maximum grade point average and a minimum of effort.

The book's epitaph is a verse from Alan Price's song *O Lucky Man!*

> So, smile while you're makin' it
> Laugh while you're takin' it,
> Even though you're fakin' it,
> Nobody's gonna know . . .

The book suggests doing well in certain courses by auditing them before taking them, explains how to take exams on books you never read, and how to display more erudition in your papers than you really possess. Here is a sample piece of advice about how to do well on an essay exam:

> The essay exam is the one type that you are going to meet over and over again. It begs for bullshit. . . . Most of the questions that you are going to be asked to answer in the essay form could be answered in a sentence or two, but they want an essay. Give it to them. Write, write, write. Write until the hand begins to cramp and shake. Then write some more.
>
> What you write is important, but to take an essay exam you do not have to have actually read everything you mention in the essay. Just mention the books you have not read in a vague way, and concentrate on the ones that you did read. This can be done easily by writing, "Of course one can see this theme in so-and-so's (author) BLAH-BLAH (title) and in what's-his-name's (author) SUCH-AND-SUCH (title), but for the sake of brevity, it is most clearly illustrated in THE ONE BOOK I DID READ by THE AUTHOR. . . . Now as far as writing about the theme of any book, one should forget fact and concentrate on TRUTH. In essence, one must deal with general profundities, and universal TRUTHS. For the sake of brevity, we will list them.
>
> THE TRUTHS
> Man struggles against: MAN (history, poli.sci.)
> FATE (history, literature)
> NATURE (geology, literature)
> HIMSELF (psychology, literature)
> TECHNOLOGY (urban studies, lit)
> And there is always LOVE: of anything, anybody, and everybody.[102]

And if somehow you manage to flunk an exam despite this sound advice, they tell you how to manipulate the professor into giving you a passing grade anyway—by begging:

> [B]egging is an art. (Ask any professional beggar in the world.) For your pur-
> poses, begging is centered around learning how to give the impression of
> deep psychological problems. You never have to nor should you go into the
> specifics. (The unknown is far more powerful than the known.) Allude, in-
> sinuate anything but the fact that you just were not prepared for the exam
> or that you could not be bothered to do the paper. The vaguer the prob-
> lems, the better. The best ploy today is the overpowering mental anguish
> you are suffering because of the way your personal life is going. It is so in-
> sufferable that it renders you incapable of thinking, working etc. You are
> simply too upset to think straight. Do not worry—after flunking you will
> be in the proper frame of mind to pull this off. And do not be afraid to let
> the tears flow. For the men, the breaking voice is an excellent technique be-
> cause it will seem as if you are going to plunge over the edge any moment.
> Do not go in like this; build to it slowly during the course of your private
> chat with the professor. Do not fall apart visibly. You should hold it just un-
> der the surface. (The tension the professor will feel will be enormous; he
> will be on edge waiting for the explosion.)[103]

The literary genre of which these two books are such outstanding examples does not cover educational advice alone. The bookstore's business and self-help sections are studded with manuals ranging from the trite to the diabolically clever on how to beat one or another system: how to win at office politics, how to dress up your resumé, how to "handle" the press, how to seduce the recalcitrant customer, or how to marry rich. An especially noteworthy recent entry in the genre is a book by Sergeant James Eagan, retired New York state trooper, called *A Speeder's Guide to Avoiding Tickets*. Among its choicer morsels is the suggestion that if the speeding driver should suddenly sight a police car heading his way in the opposite lane, he should look straight at the officer and give him a perceptible nod. Such display of *sangfroid* will lead the cop to think you are yourself an off-duty cop and not ticket you. Alternatively, consider wearing a priest's garb or putting a bump-ersticker on your car that reads "My other car is a firetruck" or "Nurses Save Lives"—all of which will cause the policeman to put you in a professional category he doesn't like to ticket. Eagan urges women to tell the officer their boyfriend will beat them up if they get a ticket. He tells you to be extracareful near the end of a month when police are likely to have a monthly ticket quota to fill. And he includes a questionnaire you can send to your local traffic judge, made out to look like part of a social science survey, to find out what the de facto speed limit in your area is.[104]

The people who buy such advice do so with appreciable discomfort, and the people who sell such advice at least pretend to share some of that discomfort. How else explain the pains to which all three books go to justify their enterprise! The Princeton Review flatly assures its readers that the SAT is a totally invalid test and thus there is nothing wrong with trying to "crack" it. Sergeant James Eagan devotes an entire introductory chapter to bemoaning the hypocrisy of speed enforcement (the selectivity with which it is enforced, that is, that certain classes of people, such as off-duty policemen, tend to be spared, the fact that cars are permitted to be built with the capacity to exceed the speed limit, the revenue-raising function of speeding tickets—you get the idea). Perhaps most forthright are the authors of the guide to surviving in college: they go little beyond the jocular suggestion that even if as a result of their book you don't learn the things your teachers think you have learned, you have learned "something that will be a hell of a lot more important in the long run: how to use a system to your advantage. 'So what,' you say. Good Lord! Listen, government is a system. Corporations are systems. Medicine is a system. Life is a system. Now are you properly in awe of what you have mastered?"[105]

None of those apologetics is too convincing, which leaves us with the question: Is there something unethical about proffering or availing yourself of such advice, advice which we may confidently assume—at least for the purposes of discussion—subverts the purposes of the institution it helps you to negotiate, advice which makes the SAT a less accurate measure of aptitude, college grades less accurate reflections of achievement, and speeding tickets a less reliable means of punishment?

The drift of the argument so far should suggest that there is in fact nothing wrong with such advice, even if it does subvert institutions we view as highly ethical: advice that subverts highly ethical institutions is not necessarily unethical. We have a sense of what the argument is going to be, because the sort of advice the Princeton Review, *How to Beat the System,* and *The Speeder's Guide to Avoiding Tickets* give smacks of tax avoision. And we know tax avoision to have this character: it subverts an ethical institution but is not itself unethical!

Let us make that argument more precise. Suppose a student falls ill on the eve of his SAT test. It is important that he take it on this particular date or various bad consequences will follow. He realizes that if he takes it while he is ill he is going to do much worse than he otherwise would and will end up with an undeservedly low score. He persuades a friend to take the test for him, a friend who, if anything, is less able than he, but who in this case will do better because he is not sick. (We might even be more fanciful and have his twin brother take the test for him!) Has he committed a serious dishonesty? If found out, should he be severely sanctioned? I think everyone's answer to that is "yes," even though he has rendered the test more rather than less accurate, even though he has furthered rather than subverted the purposes of the test. This shows that we decide if something is a breach of the ethics of test taking not by looking to whether it increases or decreases the accuracy of the test. We look to the way in which the score is achieved. In other words, the ethics of test taking have a deontological component to them. As soon as this is recognized, as soon as we decide it matters how a score is achieved regardless of how it affects the accuracy of the test, there is room for deontological strategizing of the sort that is the bread and butter of the tax advisor—and that has become the bread and butter of the Princeton Review and of the authors of books about doing college the easy way and cruising the highways without traffic tickets.

Let me put the matter in another way. Imagine that a driver is erroneously stopped for speeding. The police officer's radar is malfunctioning, but the driver cannot persuade the cop of that. He has two ways of getting out of his predicament: (1) blackmail the officer into not issuing the ticket (e.g., by threatening to reveal something embarrassing he happens to know about this particular person); (2) charm the officer into not issuing the ticket. Neither strategy impairs the accuracy of the punishment system, but since we are deontologists we nevertheless distinguish between them. It is that fact on which Eagan's book capitalizes.*

The alleged dishonesties of a zealous salesman or fund raiser are of the same kind. Psychologists, who have repeatedly decried these "compliance strategies" as

---

*Some readers might find the following consideration particularly persuasive. As is well-known, the test makers occasionally goof and give the wrong answer to their own questions. When a test taker manages to catch them at it and to point out that a different alternative than the approved one is correct, they usually feel compelled to revise the scores. What is noteworthy, however, is that the approved wrong alternative may be statistically a very good discriminator between the able and the less able student. The complaining student thus lowers the accuracy of the test. Nonetheless, we think his complaint perfectly legitimate.

being just a more devious form of fraud, have overlooked this fact. In a truly wonderful book called *Influence: The New Psychology of Persuasion*, Robert Cialdini describes the most effective of the "compliance strategies," and I find little to quarrel with in his analysis of how they work.[106] By contrast, I find much to quarrel with in his moral evaluation of them. The opening chapter, for instance, is devoted to demonstrating the uncanny strength of our impulse to reciprocate for favors someone has done us, even if they are entirely uninvited and unwelcome—the crassest example being the Hare Krishna technique of urging a "free" flower on you and then soliciting a "donation." But there are plenty of others: the offer of free samples at the grocery counter to entice you to buy the product, or all those free greeting cards from charities intended not to be paid for but "to encourage your kindness." Cialdini judges these practices to be deeply unethical, because they appeal to a hard-to-control, innate form of irrationality within us. In responding to them, he believes, we are behaving like the baby turkeys in a notorious zoological experiment, who would treat anything as their mother that made the appropriate cheep-cheep sound, even if it was just a stuffed polecat. What Cialdini overlooks is that obedience to any deontological rule will resemble the behavior of those baby turkeys. To decry our obedience to them as irrational (and others' exploitation of them as dishonest) leaves you with no choice but to declare yourself an out-and-out utilitarian. And that we now know has other implications which Cialdini would surely decry even more vehemently.

The bottom line of everything that I have said so far is remarkably simple: avoision games can be played with anyone or anything that embraces at least some deontological principles. That includes the law as well as the morality of everyday life. It even includes gangsters, tyrants, and terrorists. However wicked they may be, it is very likely that they too embrace certain deontological principles that make them vulnerable to avoision games. Even the wicked man finds it impossible to judge his enemies without making use of deontological distinctions. He will find it difficult not to hate those among his enemies who hurt him intentionally more than those who hurt him inadvertently or recklessly, or those who hurt him by an act more than those who do it by a mere omission to help, or those who hurt him directly more than those who hurt him indirectly, or those who lead the charge more than those who merely aid, or those who try and fail more than those who try and voluntarily desist. A clever enemy thus might be able to play Jesuit with the devil himself.

FROM RESTRUCTURING TO REFRAMING

The problem of avoision has a twin—not an identical twin, just a fraternal one. It is this related problem I propose to take up next. I know of no better way to state it than in the form of a joke I learned many years ago from Gerhard Caspar, then a law professor at the University of Chicago. Two monks, Theophilus and Gottlieb, are quarreling over whether one may engage in smoking and praying at the same time. Theophilus, an unbending ascetic, says no. Gottlieb, an easy-going smoker, says why not. They meet again some weeks later. Theophilus gloats: "I took the issue to the pope. I asked him point blank, 'Is it permissible to smoke during prayer?' and he said absolutely not." Gottlieb protests: "That's not what he said when I asked him." He smiles sheepishly. "Of course I did phrase the question in a more illuminating way. I asked him whether it is permissible to pray while I smoke and he naturally said yes." If you see an attorney as you are planning a questionable transaction, which you fear poses great risks of tax or civil or even criminal liability, he will as we have seen try to restructure it until it passes legal muster. Whether and when this kind of restructuring works is the issue we have just gotten through examining. If by contrast you see an attorney after you have already carried out the questionable transaction, as you are about to have to defend it in court, he will do something different but analogous and far more familiar. He will do what Gottlieb did with the smoking issue. He will try to reframe, recast, repaint, and relabel— in short, do everything other than recreate the transaction, until the questions imperiling it have been made to go away. The problem this raises for the judge is how to decide whether the reframing works—whether to accept the reframed characterization as the right one and decide for the reframer, or whether to reject it as too clever by half, as ingenious but misleading.

Some examples are needed to flesh out this problem.

1. *The foreseeability doctrine.* A negligent driver hits a pedestrian. An ambulance picks up the injured pedestrian, but on the way to the hospital it collides with a truck whose poorly maintained brakes have just failed. In the course of this collision the pedestrian dies. Can the negligent driver be held liable for the death of the pedestrian, that is, can he be forced to pay damages to the pedestrian's estate? That question in many jurisdictions is to be answered by determining whether the death was a foreseeable consequence of the driver's negligence. Well, was it? Theophilus might say: Of course it was. Death is a foreseeable result of negligent driving. Gottlieb, however, would reframe the matter thus: It is hardly foreseeable, indeed

it is a near-miraculous coincidence that the ambulance picking up the injured victim of a negligent driver should in turn have a collision with a truck that has gone out of control because its poorly maintained brakes just then decide to go into total failure. Does this reframing work? Or is the original characterization closer to the truth?

2. *The tax expenditure debate.* One day Rudolfini, the symphony conductor, takes a spill on the ice and badly breaks both his arms. Many thousands of dollars of orthopedic surgery later, he is at last back to being his usual arm-waving self and able to resume conducting. He would like to deduct his tremendous medical expenses from his annual income taxes. Should that be allowed?

There is a very plausible, fairly obvious (or should we say Theophilus-like) way of looking at the matter that makes one want to answer Yes to that question. Income, one is inclined to think, is something that increases your wealth, either in the form of consumption or saving. That portion of his salary which Rudolfini had to spend merely returning his body to its original state is not really spent on either consumption or saving: it does not enhance his overall position. Hence it should not be considered income, should not be taxed. In other words, it should be deductible. The same point could be put slightly differently: Rudolfini's colleague Lamborghini does not have an accident that same year and has the same salary as Rudolfini. As a result, he has $50,000 more than Rudolfini to spend on things he enjoys or to put in the bank. It seems that during this particular year Lamborghini really had $50,000 more in income than Rudolfini. This is in fact how our tax law has tended to view the matter. Rudolfini would probably get his deduction.

But there is another plausible, albeit less obvious (or shall we say Gottlieb-like) way of looking at the matter that leads to diametrically opposite results. Everytime the government grants a deduction for something it is giving up some cash it would otherwise be able to collect. That of course is no different from actually granting a subsidy to someone. So it seems we can say that granting a deduction is tantamount to granting a subsidy or, as some have expressed it, making a "tax expenditure," since the subsidy is granted via the tax system. Now, the idea of granting a subsidy to someone like Rudolfini who has suffered a serious reversal does not by any means seem repugnant. But what does seem repugnant is that when we grant a subsidy in the form of a deduction, the wealthy stand to benefit from it far more than the poor. If you tell someone in the 20 percent bracket that he can deduct $1,000, you are subsidizing him to the tune of $200; but if you tell someone in the 50 percent bracket he can deduct $1,000, you are subsidizing him to the tune of

$500. Is it fair to subsidize wealthy people with medical problems more than poor people with medical problems? Suddenly the deduction seems like a terrible idea.

This sort of analytical game can be played, and has been played, with lots of tax-deductible items (most notably the charitable deduction).[107] If we think about the question, in Theophilus fashion, as being about whether we should grant a deduction for a certain item, the case for doing so seems reasonably strong. But if we think about the question, in Gottlieb fashion, as being about whether we should grant a subsidy for that item, the case for doing so seems incredibly weak. Which way of framing the issue is the right one?

3. *The evil deity.* In his book *Ideals, Beliefs, Attitudes and the Law,* Guido Calabresi reports a puzzle he regularly presents to his students at the Yale Law School:

> After about a month of studying cases, I put to my first term torts students a couple of hypothetical questions. The first concerns an "evil deity." "Suppose," I ask my students, "such a deity were to appear to you, as president of this country or as controller of our legal system, and offer a gift, a boon, which would make life more pleasant, more enjoyable than it is today. The gift can be anything you want—be as idealistic, or as obscene, or as greedy as you wish—except that it cannot save lives." Later I will drop even that requirement. "The evil deity suggests that he can deliver this gift in exchange for one thing . . . the lives of one thousand young men and women picked by him at random who will each year die horrible deaths."
>
> When I ask "Would you accept?" my students almost uniformly answer, "No." Indeed, they are shocked that one could even ask the question. I then ask, quietly, what the difference is between this gift and the automobile, which takes fifty-five thousand lives each year.[108]

Which of these two ways of thinking about the automobile is the right one? Are we correct in framing the question in the traditional Theophilus-like way, or is Calabresi's Gottlieb-like framing of it really the right one?

4. *Theft. United States v. Girard* is a case about a corrupt agent of the Drug Enforcement Agency who decided to sell the identities of some undercover agents to drug smugglers. He was arrested and charged under a federal theft statute covering the unauthorized sale of any "record . . . or thing of value" belonging to the United States. He argued that what he had done could not really be properly characterized as the theft of either a "record . . . or a thing of value." He was simply passing on some names, not *things,* and not *records* either.[109]

A similar problem arose in *United States v. Bottone,* a case about the agents of a foreign corporation seeking to acquire some trade secrets of their American competitors. They paid employees of some American corporations to make copies for them of certain secret documents detailing important industrial processes. When caught, they were charged under a receipt-of-stolen-goods statute covering the purchase of "any goods, wares, merchandise, securities, or money, of the value of $5,000 or more, knowing the same to have been stolen, converted or taken by fraud." The defendants argued that they could not properly be described as having purchased stolen goods since they didn't purchase the original documents but only copies of those documents, and those copies were not the property of the American corporation. To be sure, the intellectual content of those documents belonged to the American corporation, but that intellectual content was not a "good," and the documents containing them, therefore, not a stolen good.[110]

Finally, to round out the picture, there is the case of *McNally v. United States* about some employees of the Kentucky state government who gave out some government contracts in return for kickbacks. They were charged under the federal mail fraud statute, covering "schemes or artifices to defraud." Their fraud was said to consist in depriving the citizens of Kentucky of their "right to honest and impartial government." They defended on the grounds that the "right to honest and impartial government" wasn't property that one could defraud someone out of.[111]

Which of those characterizations applies? Are the names of DEA agents stealable *things of value*? Is the intellectual content of a document a stealable *good*? Is the "right to honest and impartial government" stealable *property*? If you are inclined to say Yes to all of these questions, if you think we should not be too persnickety about the notion of a *thing of value* or a *good* or *property* in deciding whether a certain violation constitutes a theft, would you be prepared to treat rape as the theft of sexual services, kidnapping as the theft of someone's time, mayhem as the theft of someone's health, murder as the theft of someone's life? Perhaps you'll say they clearly are theft but they are much more than that, and thus to call them theft does not punish the defendant harshly enough. Well, then what about treating a contract breach as the theft of someone's expectation, trespass as the theft of someone's exclusive control over his premises, negligent driving as the theft of someone's security, sloppy service in a restaurant as the theft of someone's comfort, boisterous noise on the street as the theft of someone's right to peace and quiet? These we ordinarily think of as offenses much less significant than theft (and indeed not rising to the level of a crime at all, but rather only a violation of the civil law). Why? Because they do not involve tangible things, goods, property? But you just declined to treat those notions with persnickety literalness. Why then can't we characterize these and all other violations of someone's rights as species of theft?

5. *The per diem method.* Personal injury lawyers seeking compensation for their client's pain and suffering are not content just to tell the jury to pick an appropriate amount. Melvin Belli explains:

> You must break up the 30-year life expectancy into *finite* detailed periods of time. You must take these small periods of time, seconds and minutes, and determine in dollars and cents what each period is worth. You must start with the seconds and minutes rather than the other end of thirty years. You cannot stand in front of a jury and say, "Here is a man horribly injured, permanently disabled, who will suffer excruciating pain for the rest of his life, he is entitled to a verdict of $225,000." . . . Pain and suffering is a continuous thing. With a life expectancy of thirty years, it is 15,768,000 minutes! How much for each minute pain and suffering? The fact of the pain and suffering has been proved, the fact of 60 seconds in a minute is within judicial knowledge, all that remains is the computation in general damages once time has been reduced to the finite.[112]

Inevitably a much larger award results. Plaintiffs of course hate this method for the very same reason and claim it is grossly misleading. What about this kind of reframing? Does it lead us toward or away from the right verdict?

The characterization problem is not a peculiarly legal one although it assumes peculiar importance in the legal context. The problem is posed whenever a seller decides to price his product at "299 plus tax" and you decide to mentally relabel it as "300 plus." The problem is also posed when your daughter writes you a letter conveying some upsetting news and goes about it in the following way:

> Dear Mother and Dad:
>
> Since I left for College I have been remiss in writing and I am sorry for my thoughtlessness in not having written before. I will bring you up to date now, but before you read on, please sit down. You are not to read any further unless you are sitting down, okay?
>
> Well, then, I am getting along pretty well now. The skull fracture and the concussion I got when I jumped out of the window of my dormitory when it caught on fire shortly after my arrival here is pretty well healed now. I only spent two weeks in the hospital and now I can see almost normally and only get those sick headaches once a day. Fortunately, the fire in the dormitory, and my jump, was witnessed by an attendant at the gas sta-

tion near the dorm, and he was the one who called the Fire Department and the ambulance. He also visited me in the hospital and since I had nowhere to live because of the burntout dormitory, he was kind enough to invite me to share his apartment with him. It's really a basement room, but it's kind of cute. He is a very fine boy and we have fallen deeply in love and are planning to get married. We haven't got the exact date yet, but it will be before my pregnancy begins to show.

Yes, Mother and Dad, I am pregnant. I know how much you are looking forward to being grandparents and I know you will welcome the baby and give it the same love and devotion and tender care you gave me when I was a child. The reason for the delay in our marriage is that my boyfriend has a minor infection which prevents us from passing our pre-marital blood tests and I carelessly caught it from him. I know that you will welcome him into our family with open arms. He is kind and, although not well educated, he is ambitious. Although he is of a different race and religion than ours, I know your often expressed tolerance will not permit you to be bothered by that.

Now that I have brought you up to date, I want to tell you that there was no dormitory fire, I did not have a concussion or skull fracture, I was not in the hospital, I am not pregnant, I am not engaged, I am not infected and there is no boyfriend. However, I am getting a "D" in American History, and an "F" in Chemistry and I want you to see those marks in their proper perspective.

Your loving daughter,
Sharon[113]

The characterization problem assumes a particularly acute form in a famous experiment conducted by Amos Tversky and Daniel Kahneman. They asked doctors attending a medical convention how they would cope with an impending hypothetical epidemic, "an unusual Asian disease, which is expected to kill 600 people. Two alternative programs to combat the disease have been proposed. . . . If program A is adopted, 200 people will be saved. If program B is adopted, there is a $\frac{1}{3}$ probability that 600 people will be saved, and $\frac{2}{3}$ probability that no people will be saved. Which of the two programs would you favor?" Most doctors preferred the program where they would be sure to save 200. Then the psychologists posed the same hypothetical to another group of doctors but slightly altered the wording of the alternatives. Rather than describing the choice as one between saving 200 people for sure and saving 600 with only a $\frac{1}{3}$ probability, they described the alternatives thus: "If program A is adopted, 400 people will die." (Of course, if 200 are saved, 400 will die!) "If program B is adopted, there is a ⅓ probability that nobody will die, and ⅔ probability that 600 people will die." (Of course, if no one dies, 600 are saved, and if 600 die, no one is saved.) Most doctors opted for the second alternative. In short, if the choice was between saving a few people for sure and saving everyone possibly, they opted for the sure thing. But if the same choice was redescribed as being between letting some people die for sure and possibly not letting anyone die, they opted for the risky thing. In the end, the psychologists alerted their subjects to this inconsistency and asked them what choice they would make. The doctors were at a loss. They acknowledged that when they looked at the issue in the first way, they tended toward one answer; when they looked at it in the second way, they tended toward the other answer; but that they really could not tell which way of looking at it was the correct one.[114]

It would seem that whatever the answer to the recharacterization problem it should hold equally for legal and nonlegal contexts.

Maybe some of these cases don't seem like problems at all, because one way of looking at them seems so obviously superior to the suggested alternative. Maybe you think, for instance, that the right way to think about a $299 price tag is clearly to think of it as $300. Or that the proper way to think about Sharon's letter is clearly to just excise from one's mind all of her introductory fabrications and to focus squarely on the one true statement that she makes regarding her academic mishaps. Or that the accident in example 1 is clearly unforeseeable . . . or clearly foreseeable. Or that a medical deduction is clearly a deduction and not a subsidy. But stare at it for a little while and your certitude is sure to vanish.

There is an episode in Thomas Mann's novel *Confessions of Felix Krull, Confidence Man,* a novel whose central preoccupation is the relationship of appearance and reality, that captures rather nicely one's reaction to many of these cases. When Felix Krull is just a boy, his father takes him to a play in a Vienna theater, where he is transfixed by the Maurice Chevalier–like leading man—with his flawlessly fitted suit, his silvery voice, his graceful pirouettes, his milky-white hands, his rosy, immaculate face, almond-shaped eyes, well-sculpted coral-red mouth, and the picture-perfect black mustache that sits atop it. But when Krull's father brings the boy backstage to meet the actor, Felix is in for a shock: the man he finds backstage is sweaty, vulgar, vain, obnoxious, and—worst of all—covered throughout with "red-rimmed, suppurating, bleeding" pustules which only thick makeup and skillful lighting had managed to disguise. As the boy starts to reflect more deeply on the episode later on, however, as he tries to make sense of the odd and disconcerting fact that "this grease-smeared and pimply individual is the charmer at whom the twilight crowd [had been] gazing so soulfully," that "[t]his repulsive worm is the reality of the glorious butterfly in whom those deluded spectators believed they were beholding the realization of all their own secret dreams of beauty, grace and perfection," as he keeps turning these facts over in his mind, his disappointment gradually vanishes. For he hits upon a useful analogy. "[W]hen you come to think of it, which is the real shape of the glowworm: the insignificant little creature crawling about on the palm of your hand, or the poetic spark that swims through the summer night."[115] Why treat the actor's on-stage displays of debonair charm and dashing good looks as the illusion and his repulsive backstage appearance as the reality? After all, it is his on-stage appearance that the actor probably considers the substance of his life, and the exigencies of everyday living that he considers banal formalities.

What makes us so sure that her parents aren't really only seeing Sharon's academic mishaps in their proper light once they have been made to contemplate how much worse things could be? What makes us so sure that the reaction we have when we see the $299 price tag isn't more reflective of our true desires than the reaction we have when we see the $300 label? What makes us so sure that . . . well, you get the idea.

THE CONSEQUENTIALIST FRAME-UP

From the perspective of the preceding sections, many of the cases posing recharacterization problems should cease pretty quickly to be puzzling. Take Calabresi's recharacterization of cars as an invention by an evil deity who wants a certain number of human sacrifices per year. To a deontologist the differences between the two cases are vast. Only to the consequentialist would it be puzzling, given that the human toll has been kept constant. After all, we are willing to distinguish between the case in which the trolley is turned to run over the one (in order to save the five) and the case in which the trolley is allowed to run over the five and *then* the one is killed so that his organs may be used to save the five. It's hardly surprising then that cases as disparate as that of letting cars operate and run over their annual toll and *killing* the same number as a sacrifice to the evil deity should warrant different evaluation. One cannot legitimately reframe the automobile case by introducing the evil deity *if one believes that deontological differences matter.*

More challenging, but eminently tractable now, is the problem of tax expenditures. Consider an analogy. An elderly widow, as she is about to run out of funds to support herself, turns to her three adult daughters for help. They are perfectly agreeable, recognize this immediately as their solemn duty, and come up with an estimate of how much money their mother will need for financial security and independence, to wit $300,000. All that remains is for them to decide how much each daughter is to contribute. They consider having each contribute exactly a third, that is, $100,000. They also consider keying everyone's contribution to her income, since one of them is a millionaire and another just two steps up from subsistence. They end up arranging it so that each pays an equal percentage of her net wealth, namely, 20 percent. The first daughter will contribute $200,000, the second $80,000, the third $20,000.

Suppose the widow contracts a terminal disease, and it is clear that she will die before all of the $300,000 have been exhausted. To be exact, $60,000 will be left over by the time she dies, and she is trying to decide how to divide them up among her three daughters. Several possibilities occur to her: first, she could just divide the sum in three, giving $20,000 to each. Second, she could adjust the amount she left to their financial need, leaving a bit more than a third to her poorest daughter, less than a third to her richest, something in between to the middle one. Third, she thinks about what her daughters would have done if they had known in advance that she would only need $240,000. Under the approach they were using, the richest daughter would then have had to contribute $40,000 less than she did, the middle daughter would have had to contribute $16,000 less than she did, the poorest daughter would have had to contribute $4,000 less than she did. So one final possibility she contemplates is simply remitting to each daughter the "excess" she contributed, namely, $40,000 to her richest daughter, $16,000 to the middle one, and $4,000 to the poorest one. She likes the first and simplest option best. It seems fairest to her. She asks her daughters what they think, and they agree with her. So this is what she does.

All of this has only been by way of setting the stage for the analogy I am about to develop between this situation and the tax-expenditure controversy. Let's switch back to the time at which the three daughters are deciding how much to set aside for their mother and how much each daughter should contribute to that sum. They have just, let us imagine, decided that each will contribute in proportion to her wealth, that the sum total required is about $300,000 and that that means that each will have to contribute about 20 percent of her wealth. Then they learn of their mother's illness and revise the sum they expect she will need until her death down to $240,000. That means, the richest daughter explains, that each now only needs to contribute one-fifth less than expected.

At this point, however, the poorest daughter protests and advances the following devious argument: "The way I see it, you agreed just a minute ago, when we all thought that $300,000 would be required to carry Mama through, that in fairness I only needed to contribute $20,000. Now I think you also would agree that if Mama had found out about her illness a few years from now, and she had realized that she was going to leave behind $60,000 she should and would in fairness divide that money equally among us, giving us $20,000 apiece. Well, that's in effect what has happened now. We gave her $60,000 too much and the $60,000 presumably should be redistributed among us as it would be if it were being bequeathed by her. That means that I really owe nothing whatsoever, and you two should just divide the burden amongst yourselves!"

"Now wait a minute," protests the millionaire daughter. "The fact is that the money is not being bequeathed by her. We are just revising downward our estimate of how much money she will be needing."

"That's true," concedes the poorest daughter, "but every time you agree for her to leave me a dollar you are really lowering my burden of contribution to this thing by a dollar. And let's just forget about the interest rate just now; I'm sure you'll agree that that little complication really wouldn't affect our argument."

Replies the millionaire: "I agree we should just forget about the interest rate. But here's the mistake you are making. You are saying that it would be fair for Mama to leave you $20,000 if there's an excess. You are also saying that every time I agree to have her leave you a dollar I am effectively lightening your burden of contribution by one dollar. And that is true as well. But although these two ways of lightening your burden are monetarily equivalent, that does not mean they are ethically equivalent. While I see a lot of reasons to have Mama divide whatever property she happens to possess at her death in equal parts, I see no reason to divide a sum of money into equal parts that we were about to give her but have not yet given her. To insist that the two have to be treated equally is like arguing that if I am entitled not to rescue a drowning person I am entitled to throw him back into the sea once I have rescued him, because the end result is the same."

Counters the poor daughter: "Gee, your way of looking really doesn't make sense to me. It has some really funny consequences. What would you do if we had already allocated the money to Mama, and perhaps even put the money in a special bank account we had set up but not yet given her the means of accessing that bank account. Would you say the allocation should be in equal parts or according to the formula we worked out? It seems awfully peculiar to me that anything of significance should hinge on whether we have merely put the money into the account, or whether we have already given her access, or whether we have merely telephonically let her know that we are about to give her access. Those just seem like ethically insignificant facts."

Rejoins the millionaire daughter: "But we run into the same problem when we have to decide whether in causing the drowning person to die you are merely letting him die or actually killing him. It's clear that if you haven't gone out yet, or if you have gone out already but not yet shouldered him when you turn back, you are merely letting him die. It's also clear that if you kick him back into the sea after pulling him ashore you are killing him. It's less clear what you are doing if you actively remove him from your back as you swim back to shore."

How does this help with tax expenditures? Well, it helps us with a special kind of tax-expenditure case. Imagine that the country faces an impending emergency requiring extensive additional expenditures. To meet those, the government raises a special tax, again imposing more heavily on the rich than the poor, not even necessarily a progressive tax—for our purposes a simple proportionate tax will do. The emergency passes without consuming all or even most of the funds specially raised to deal with it. The government now has to decide what to do with the excess funds. Should it simply remit to each taxpayer the extra amount he was taxed for the emergency? It might, I would say, but it doesn't have to. There are, I would argue, good grounds for remitting the funds in a way that helps the poor more than the rich. It is at this point that the advocate of the tax-expenditure perspective says I am being inconsistent. *If I really believe that the poor have a greater claim to the funds I just extracted from the pockets of the rich than the rich, then why did I not insist that the rich contribute that very amount to the poor in the first place, regardless of the emergency?* If I really believe that the poor deserve a special subsidy and the rich do not, then why have I instead been giving subsidies to the rich up until now by not taxing them the very amount that ought to go to the poor? Our previous examples tell us why. Just because I am willing for Mother to divide her excess funds equally among her offspring does not mean I am willing to transfer an equivalent amount to my sibling if the excess funds haven't already accumulated. Just because I am willing to have her give a dollar to you rather than to me, if she happens to have the money, does not mean that I should be willing to give you a dollar rather than to keep it myself, if she does not happen to have the money. A dollar we do not tax away from the rich is not ethically the same thing as a dollar we pay them by way of subsidy! Not imposing a special burden on someone to help a suffering person is not ethically the same thing as giving preferential support to someone who is not suffering over someone who is.

W E   A R E   N O W approaching a solution of the tax expenditure problem, but we are not quite there yet. That's because the typical context in which the tax-expenditure controversy arises is not one in which a certain sum has inadvertently been accumulated—the way it happened in my two examples—but rather is one in which taxes are collected and disbursed on an ongoing basis. The approach we have taken to the foregoing problems, however, can be extended quite easily. To see this clearly let us modify the example with which we started.

Imagine that at the beginning of every year the three daughters get together to set aside an amount for their mother's needs. Generally each makes a contribution that is proportionate to her income during the past year. One year the eldest daughter has to undergo some expensive medical treatments. Quite independently of their usual negotiations over their mother's annual budget, she asks her two sisters if they might be willing to help *her* out with some money, given the financial strains she has just experienced. The two sisters then point out to her that even with her heavy expenditures she still is earning vastly more than they and that it, therefore, seems inappropriate for them to transfer some of their income to her. She is persuaded by that. Shortly thereafter, the three of them get together to set their mother's budget and determine each other's contribution to that budget. In the course of these negotiations, the eldest daughter again points to her heavy medical expenses and asks that they be subtracted from her annual income before her obligatory annual contribution is determined. "After all," she explains, "money that I have to expend on just restoring my body to the state in which you were lucky to be already is not really income that I get to enjoy." Her two sisters are perfectly agreeable to that. Shortly after they have agreed, the eldest daughter starts looking puzzled and turns to the others: "There is something I don't understand. When I asked you for some money on account of the heavy medical expenses I had this year you said it was unseemly for me to expect you to help me financially since I was already earning so much more than either of you. But when I asked you to subtract my medical expenses from my annual income before setting my annual contribution to Mother's fund you had no problem with that. Isn't that a little inconsistent? If you think I am so rich that I shouldn't get any support from you when I have extra medical expenses, then why do you in effect grant me that kind of support as we negotiate over Mother's budget?"

To this the middle daughter replies: "It's not at all inconsistent. When you ask me to assist you in shouldering a burden your claim on me is much weaker than when you ask me to forbear from imposing a further burden on you. It's just a special case of the distinction between harming someone by acting and "harming" someone by omitting to prevent some harm from befalling him.

"But it comes to the same thing."

"Yes and no. The outcome is the same, the means are not. This is how it always is with acts and omissions."

"But I don't understand how you decide whether I am asking for you to help me carry a burden or to forbear from imposing a burden. When I ask for a tax break it seems to me you could describe it as either."

"Not really. Perhaps one could have described it as either if we had just settled on some suitable sum without taking into account your medical expenditures and then you had asked for an adjustment. It's hard to decide here whether you are asking for help or forbearance. And, admittedly, there are many cases like that. If you ask me to desist from polluting a river because you live downstream from me, are you asking for my assistance or my forbearance? If you ask me to desist from building a house that will block your view, are you asking for my assistance or my forbearance? Those are hard cases, indeed they may even be indeterminate cases. They do raise the question of what to do with cases that we cannot at present figure out or whose answer is indeterminate, but it doesn't disturb the general proposition that different norms attach to demands for forbearance and demands for assistance."

We are now able to resolve the tax-expenditure controversy. Citizens have a stronger claim when they ask the government to forbear from taking a dollar from them than when they ask the government to assist them with a dollar. In many cases it will not be difficult to decide whether the citizen is asking for the one or the other. But there are situations where something is hard to classify—all those cases in which Republicans and Democrats quarreled over whether something amounted to an expenditure increase or a tax cut. Some of those cases we will with time and ingenuity figure out, others are probably inherently indeterminate. They do pose the question as to how we should decide how strong a weight to accord to a claim when we cannot decide whether it is a claim for assistance or forbearance. That is really a more general question: What ought we, as judges and legislators, to do in cases of moral and legal uncertainty? I shall take that question up shortly. But answering it has no special bearing on the tax-expenditure controversy. The thesis of those who maintain that our answer to budgetary questions ought to be the same whether we think of them as concerning expenditures or taxes is wrong. They either don't understand or don't accept the ethical difference between acts and omissions. They are fundamentally out-and-out consequentialists, the kind of people who, if they were consistent, would have to punish innocents if that would lower the crime rate, torture children if that would prevent many more children from being tortured, and harvest organs from healthy people if many more deaths could be averted thereby.

T HE THEFT PROBLEM can be similarly disposed of. The uniqueness of theft when compared to other kinds of violations lies in the physical misappropriation of a particular thing of value, good, or piece of property. From a consequentialist point of view it is hard to understand what should be so special about that kind of violation. Why should the manner in which a right is violated matter so much?

Blow fumes into your neighbor's yard or shine a light into his window and you may be found guilty of creating a nuisance. But suppose you build a house that prevents pleasant sea breezes from reaching his house or blocks out the sunlight, and you have no legal problem. Why? Because in one case you are guilty of physical intrusions and in the other you are not. That's not to say that your neighbor much cares about the distinction. In either case he loses something of value and you gain something of value. But the route by which the redistribution takes place is a different one, and, therefore, he has nothing to complain about.

It has struck some people as downright idiotic that someone would want to find significance in that kind of distinction. Could this possibly be what an important ethical principle comes down to? Could there really be an ethically relevant distinction between shining a light into someone's window and blocking the sunlight he so values? Absolutely! Explanations that seek to show you the component parts that a whole is made up of almost necessarily look that way.[116] Certainly the act-omission distinction, the ducking-shielding distinction, etc., once explicated in detail will consist of nitty-gritty rules that have that kind of appearance. But of course many people are skeptical of those kinds of distinctions on precisely that ground.

W ILL ALL characterization questions yield to this kind of analysis? I doubt it. Specifically, I am not sure whether all of the characterization questions I presented in the previous section can be resolved in this way. But rather than continue my efforts to tackle them, I will take our very uncertainty about what to do with them as the occasion to address a broader question: If we cannot figure out what the appropriate characterization is, what are we to do? If because of ignorance or perhaps even inherent indeterminacy we cannot find out whether a certain mishap is foreseeable, whether the monetary value of an injury is misrepresented by the per diem method, or whether a certain policy decision is best thought of as a choice between uncertain prospects of gain or as a choice between uncertain prospects of loss, what are we to do? For that matter, even if we think we know what the appropriate way of characterizing a case is, but aren't totally sure that we have gotten it right, what are we to do? How sure must we be that a certain tax deduction is not really a subsidy, or that a certain violation is not really a form of theft, or that a certain accident-producing policy is not really tantamount to making a sacrifice at the altar of an evil deity, before we are permitted to act on those judgments?

INDETERMINACY AND DOUBT

Giovanni Boccaccio's fourteenth-century classic *The Decameron* is a collection of wise and bawdy tales with which some exiled Florentines passed the time until the plague had left their city. One of these stories happens to speak directly to the issue I just raised: If we don't know the answer to a characterization question, what should we do? More generally, if we don't know the answer to a legal or moral question, what ought we to do? The story goes as follows.

When the Sultan Saladin ran out of money he decided to turn to a Jewish moneylender named Melchizedek for help. Realizing that Melchizedek was not especially eager to lend to him, but also being disinclined to just take the money by force, the sultan resorted to a more indirect strategy:

> [H]e sent for the Jew, gave him a cordial reception, invited him to sit down beside him, and said:
>
> "O man of excellent worth, many men have told me of your great wis-

dom and your superior knowledge of the ways of God. Hence I would be glad if you would tell me which of the three laws, whether the Jewish, the Saracen, or the Christian, you deem to be truly authentic."

The Jew, who was indeed a wise man, realized all too well that Saladin was aiming to trip him up with the intention of picking a quarrel with him, and that if he were to praise any of the three more than the others, the Sultan would achieve his object. He therefore had need of a reply that would save him from falling into the trap, and having sharpened his wits, in no time at all he was ready with his answer.

"My lord," he said, "your question is a very good one, and in order to explain my views on the subject, I must ask you to listen to the following little story:

"Unless I am mistaken, I recall having frequently heard that there was once a great and wealthy man who, apart from the other fine jewels contained in his treasury, possessed a most precious and beautiful ring. Because of its value and beauty, he wanted to do it the honour of leaving it in perpetuity to his descendants, and so he announced that he would bequeath the ring to one of his sons, and that whichever of them should be found to have it in his keeping, this man was to be looked upon as his heir, and the others were to honour and respect him as the head of the family.

"The man to whom he left the ring, having made a similar provision regarding his own descendants, followed the example set by his predecessor. To cut a long story short, the ring was handed down through many generations till it finally came to rest in the hands of a man who had three most splendid and virtuous sons who were very obedient to their father, and he loved all three of them equally. Each of the three young men, being aware of the tradition concerning the ring, was eager to take precedence over the others, and they all did their utmost to persuade the father, who was now an old man, to leave them the ring when he died.

"The good man, who loved all three and was unable to decide which of them should inherit the ring, resolved, having promised it to each, to try and please them all. So he secretly commissioned a master-craftsman to make two more rings, which were so like the first that even the man who had made them could barely distinguish them from the original. And when he was dying, he took each of his sons aside in turn, and gave one ring to each.

"After their father's death, they all desired to succeed to his title and estate, and each man denied the claims of the others, producing his ring to prove his case. But finding that the rings were so alike that it was impossible to tell them apart, the question of which of the sons was the true and rightful heir remained in abeyance, and has never been settled.

"And I say to you, my lord, that the same applies to the three laws which God the Father granted to His three peoples, and which formed the subject of your inquiry. Each of them considers itself the legitimate heir to His estate, each believes it possesses His one true law and observes His commandments. But as with the rings, the question as to which of them is right remains in abeyance."

Saladin perceived that the fellow had ingeniously sidestepped the trap he had set before him, and therefore decided to make a clean breast of his needs, and see if the Jew would come to his assistance. This he did, freely admitting what he had intended to do, but for the fact that the Jew had answered him so discreetly.

Melchizedek gladly provided the Sultan with the money he required. The Sultan later paid him back in full, in addition to which he showered magnificent gifts upon him, made him his lifelong friend, and maintained him at his court in a state of importance and honour.[117]

This parable so enchanted the eighteenth-century German playwright Gotthold Ephraim Lessing that he decided to build an entire play, *Nathan the Wise,* around it and to make the parable of the rings the linchpin of his argument for religious tolerance. To be sure, in having the Jew, here called Nathan, tell the sultan the parable, Lessing embellishes and refines it in various artful ways, not the least of which is shaping it into pentameter:

> In days of yore, there dwelt in eastern lands
> A man who had a ring of priceless worth
> Received from hands beloved. The stone it held,
> An opal, shed a hundred colors fair,
> And had the magic power that he who wore it,
> Trusting its strength, was loved by God and men.[118]

From here on out the story pretty much proceeds as in the original version. Unlike the original, however, Lessing's version quite explicitly culminates in a judicial proceeding. For when the father died,

> the sons preferred complaint;
> And each swore to the judge, he had received

The ring directly from his father's hand.—
As was the truth!—And long before had had
His father's promise, one day to enjoy
The privilege of the ring.—No less than truth!—
His father, each asserted, could not have
Been false to him; and sooner than suspect
This thing of him, of such a loving father:
He must accuse his brothers—howsoever
Inclined in other things to think the best
Of them—of some false play; and he the traitors
Would promptly ferret out; would take revenge.

What does the judge do? He pleads agnosticism.

> Instead of verdict, go! My counsel is:
> Accept the matter wholly as it stands.
> If each one from his father has his ring,
> Then let each one believe his ring to be
> The true one.—Possibly the father wished
> To tolerate no longer in his house
> The tyranny of just one ring!—And know:
> That you, all three, he loved; and loved alike;
> Since two of you he'd not humiliate
> To favor one.—Well then! Let each aspire
> To emulate his father's unbeguiled,
> Unprejudiced affection! Let each strive
> To match the rest in bringing to the fore
> The magic of the opal in his ring!
> Assist that power with all humility,
> With benefaction, hearty peacefulness,
> And with profound submission to God's will!
> And when the magic powers of the stones
> Reveal themselves in children's children's children:
> I bid you, in a thousand thousand years,
> To stand again before this seat. For then
> A wiser man than I will sit as judge
> Upon this bench, and speak. Depart!—So said
> The modest judge.

The cleverness of Melchizedek/Nathan's reply to the sultan lies in this: we are generally content to accept and live with factual doubt. If we cannot decide who committed a killing, sired a child, robbed a bank, torched a building, invented a gadget, we can pretty well tolerate that uncertainty. Indeed, even if we have a good idea who did, but we are not sure about that beyond a reasonable doubt (if it's a criminal case) or by a preponderance of the evidence (if it's a civil case), we'll let him go unscathed. Ordinarily, however, our attitude is different vis-à-vis nonfactual matters, namely, theological, moral, and legal matters. Here we are inclined to reach for an answer by a leap of faith and defend it with a zeal and intransigence seemingly unwarranted by the evidence we have in its favor. By metaphorically reducing the sultan's question of doctrine to one of fact—which *is* the real ring?— the parable of the rings makes us approach doctrinal uncertainty as deliberately as we approach factual uncertainty. Apply Melchizedek/Nathan's approach to the question of which is the proper way to characterize certain transactions, and we would be led to say: As long as we are not sure beyond a reasonable doubt that the injury the defendant caused was foreseeable or that the violation he committed was mail fraud, acquit. As for the questions about the evil deity and tax expenditures, which tend to arise not during a judicial proceeding but while putting together legislation, it suggests we do something analogous—choose some standard of proof that strikes us as plausible and take no action unless that standard has been met.

However obviously sound, straightforward, and, in several senses of the word "enlightened" such an approach may seem, it is not the one the law has taken to such issues (although it is the approach that one boldly iconoclastic legal scholar, Gary Lawson, has indeed advocated).[119] As a judge is about to make a doctrinal decision that will result in someone's criminal conviction, he ordinarily will not ask himself whether he is sure of himself beyond a reasonable doubt. And when a judge is about to make a doctrinal decision that will result in imposing back-breaking liability on a civil defendant, he ordinarily will not ask himself whether he is sure of himself by a preponderance of the arguments: if there are four possible doctrinal resolutions, each with a probability of somewhere around 25 percent, three of which would result in an acquittal, he will feel free to adopt the fourth one that results in a conviction, although it has a probability only slightly over 25 percent of being the right one—which is exactly the opposite of what Melchizedek's theory would imply.

But is the law right to do this? Doesn't Melchizedek's theory make more sense?

To evaluate it, one must first get a sense of just how radically the law would change if we were to put Melchizedek's theory into operation.

—To begin with, Melchizedek's theory would wipe out the doctrine of vagueness. In a criminal case, vague-looking statutes would be applied only to those whom they covered beyond a reasonable doubt and no one else; in a civil case to those whom they covered by a preponderance of the arguments.

—Melchizedek's theory would also give a jolt to *stare decicis,* the rule of precedent. Take the typical antitrust statute prohibiting "unreasonable restraints on trade," that is, anticompetitive behavior. When such statutes were first passed, in the early part of the century, some forms of behavior clearly qualified as anticompetitive beyond a reasonable doubt; we weren't so sure of others. Under Melchizedek's approach, all who engaged in practices not anticompetitive beyond a reasonable doubt would have been acquitted. As economic science progressed we would have come to recognize that certain conduct that used to lie in the statute's vague penumbra really is anticompetitive beyond a reasonable doubt. If the conduct were to become an issue in a new case, judges should treat these economic discoveries as additional evidence and declare such conduct illegal. In doing so, they are throwing *stare decisis* to the winds.

—Melchizedek's theory would wreak havoc with the rules that govern the reopening of completed criminal proceedings. Ordinarily, new exculpatory evidence of a convicted defendant will almost automatically result in his exoneration, but not exculpatory revisions in the doctrine under which he was convicted, or only rarely. Under Melchizedek's theory, new doctrinal developments would require reversal of guilty verdicts just as much as new evidentiary discoveries.

—Melchizedek's theory would change appreciably the behavior of prosecutors. At present, a prosecutor who has a certain not-too-low level of confidence that the evidence supports a conviction of the defendant is permitted to press charges and to negotiate for a plea bargain. But suppose he is very confident of the evidence in the case but not at all confident that the law supports a conviction. He nevertheless will be permitted to press charges and to negotiate for a plea bargain. His confidence that the evidence supports him is required to be much higher than his confidence that the law supports him before he is allowed to forge ahead. Melchizedek's theory would make that difference disappear.

—Melchizedek's theory would greatly affect the process of legislation. A notorious form of doctrinal uncertainty is whether a crime that lies at the borderline between one kind of theft (say, larceny) and another kind (say, embezzlement) qualifies as one or the other: if Bridget's boyfriend asks her to let him count the money she has just been paid by her employer and then refuses to give it back, is he guilty of larceny or embezzlement? If charged with larceny, the defendant would sometimes be able to successfully defend on the ground that he was really guilty of embezzlement, which he hadn't been charged with, and should thus be acquitted. And if charged with embezzlement, he would argue that he was really guilty of larceny—and should thus be acquitted. To avoid acquittal on such technicalities, many of these theft offenses were consolidated into one large theft statute. Now juries were allowed to convict as long as they determined that the defendant had committed some kind of theft, even if they differed among themselves as to what kind of theft it was. Once doctrinal and evidentiary uncertainty are viewed as being on a par, this consolidation procedure will avail the legislature nothing. Disagreement over the nature of the theft committed would now be viewed as equivalent to disagreement about the specific circumstances of the theft (Did the defendant steal a car from *X* or a truck from *Y*?) and thus would still result in acquittal.

—Melchizedek's theory would significantly modify the process of sentencing. Under a traditional indeterminate sentencing scheme, a judge is called upon to choose among a large number of possible sentences the one the defendant deserves. If we insist that he be sure beyond a reasonable doubt that the sentence is one the defendant deserves, the judge will almost invariably award one that is not much more severe than the mandated minimum.

But is Melchizedek/Nathan right? Is doctrinal uncertainty really the same as factual uncertainty, and should doctrines of doubt that were invented to cope with factual uncertainty really just be applied pari passu to cope with doctrinal uncertainty? At least when it is legal doctrine that is at issue, many people will insist that there is one crucial difference between the two kinds of uncertainties that (rightly) causes us to rarely think of them in the same breath: as to factual questions, we generally think they have an answer and we just don't know it. As to legal questions, we often feel they don't really have an answer, they are indeterminate. If we fail to find it it's not for lack of ingenuity but because it doesn't exist. Often the question whether a certain transaction counts as mail fraud is like the question whether a five-foot-five man is "short." The answer seems indeterminate. It seems as though there is no evidence out there we could search for to settle the question conclusively. And since these kinds of indeterminacies are rampant, the law would be inviting anarchy if it refused to resolve all conflicts in which such indeterminacies cropped up.

This, however, is not a very convincing reply.

Suppose we had a large number of sticks, ranging from a little under a meter in length to a little over. The sticks themselves differ among each other by only the most marginal amounts, differences that are way beyond the capacity of the naked eye to make out. Suppose, further, that you are called upon to classify each stick as being either shorter-than-a-meter or at-least-a-meter-long, the former to be called "short sticks," the latter to be called "long sticks." You are permitted to use certain measuring instruments. There is nothing vague about the terms "short stick" or "long stick." They could not be defined more precisely. Nevertheless, in a very fundamental way, they will turn out to behave just like vague predicates. For as you try to classify various sticks as being either short or long, you will find that some classifications are very easy to make out and some much harder. In fact, all sticks exactly a meter long or very close to it will be very hard to classify, the degree of difficulty forming a bell-shaped curve around the one-meter mark. They will be hard to classify because any measurement technique has error built into it, and that error mounts as we approach the precise one-meter stick. This sort of classificatory difficulty is exactly what we expect of a vague predicate, except that the band of difficulty here is considerably slimmer.[120]

But it need not be. Let us modify our example somewhat. Imagine that some federal regulation defines a very technical term, a "house," in a very precise way. What the regulation contemplates is actually an ordinary house; but for regulatory purposes a very precise definition is provided. A "house," as defined, is a building with various specified components no longer and no shorter than certain specified width, height, and depth requirements, and bearing certain specified numerical relationships to each other. A house that comfortably fits within these specifications would look to us like an ordinary, archtypical, one-family, two-story dwelling. Consider now the process of deciding whether a given house is a "house," whether it lives up to specs. Houses that are comfortably within specifications we would find easy to classify (at least if we are given suitable tools with which to measure compliance). Houses that are comfortably outside specifications we would also find easy to classify. Houses, some or many of whose measurements are either barely within or barely outside the specifications, would represent considerable problems. There would be a lot of error and a lot of uncertainty. Moreover, the degree of uncertainty would cluster in the usual bell-like curve around the houses that comply "exactly" with the outer limits of the house definition. The cluster would be a very sizable one—unlike our previous example about the sticks—because of the number of measurements involved and the manifold opportunities for error. If the number of measurements that needed to be carried out were sufficiently numerous and difficult, the vagueness of the technical term "house" would easily approximate that of the undefined everyday term "one-family house."

This strategy could be pursued more generally. One could take a vague-looking term, define an archetypical version thereof in very precise and rigid ways, and one would find that the gray zone of cases of potential measurement error surrounding the defining numerical boundary values would be indistinguishable from the gray zone of vagueness that surrounded the original, undefined, everyday term. Vagueness thus seems truly equivalent to evidentiary uncertainty. Doctrines that treat it as something different seem hard to justify.

So why do we do it? What could account for our not insisting on proof beyond a reasonable doubt when it comes to doctrinal as opposed to factual questions? The key, I believe, is to be found in the familiar precept that ignorance of law is no defense. Although a well-worn phrase, most people find it on closer scrutiny to be a very odd one. Why exactly is it fair to punish someone for wrongdoing when he had no idea he was doing wrong? Is it fair to punish an off-duty federal prison guard in New York for carrying a weapon because he doesn't realize that the New York statute permitting prison guards to do this only applies to guards working in state prisons, not those working in federal prisons? (Which is what happened in the 1987 New York case of *People v. Marrero*.)[121] Is it fair to punish an ex-convict who has just moved to Los Angeles from out of state for failing to register with the Los Angeles authorities because he doesn't realize that there is an unusual Los Angeles ordinance requiring this of ex-convicts? (Which is what nearly happened in the 1957 Supreme Court case of *Lambert v. California*.)[122] After thinking about such cases, many are inclined to conclude that the ignorance-of-law-is-no-defense precept really has no moral basis, only a practical one. If we didn't have it, some people would make it a point to deliberately remain ignorant of the law, and of course would abuse the defense by invoking that lack even when they did know the law. But those are not very powerful arguments, they are unfair and inconsistent with what we do elsewhere in the criminal law: we don't punish a driver who accidentally runs over a pedestrian on the grounds that doing so will cause other drivers to be more vigilant, or that it will prevent intentional killers from pretending to have killed their victims accidentally.

In truth, the ignorance-of-law-is-no-defense precept does have a moral basis. What it says is that at least some immoral conduct we are willing to condemn whether or not the perpetrator realizes that he is doing something immoral. And when you think about it, that makes a lot of sense. We frequently are willing to both praise and blame people for their actions regardless of whether they themselves think those actions praiseworthy or blameworthy.

There are people who think they have accomplished something of great note if they break the Guinness record for the highest number of uninterrupted hula hoop gyrations, or the longest period of continuous ironing, or the largest weather balloon blown up by mouth. Three-year-old Hannah Marek has been known to drop toys on the floor and, as she bends down to retrieve them, announce this accomplishment with all the pride of an arctic explorer: "Look Mom, I found them. Aren't you amazed?" On completing her first session on the potty, she declared with a sense of achievement we expect from someone who has just swum the English channel: "I did it! I did it! All by myself!" George Bernard Shaw insisted that although "people think of me as a theatrical man," what he was most proud of was "having served six years as a municipal councillor."[123] Lyndon Johnson, whose active service in World War II consisted of riding along—and getting shot at—on exactly one bomb run in the Pacific as a visiting congressman, for which a politically shrewd General McArthur decided to award him the Silver Star, came to believe he had performed a genuinely heroic feat.[124] In all of these cases we are willing to rate the moral status of the actor's performance much lower than he does himself—which is exactly what the ignorance-of-law-is-no-defense precept calls for.

Conversely, of course, we are frequently willing to rate the moral status of the actor's performance much higher than he does himself. John F. Kennedy was occasionally given to brushing aside his impressive performance in the PT 109 incident with comments such as: "The whole story was more fucked up than Cuba."[125] Even if he really mistakenly thought this, it won't deprive him of the glory. Kurt Goedel near the end of his life was periodically depressed by the thought, writes a colleague, Stanislaw Ulam, that "maybe all he had discovered was another paradox a la Burali Forte or Russel." Goedel was simply deluded. Goedel's theorem, adds Ulam, is of course "much, much more. It is a revolutionary discovery which changed both the philosophical and the technical aspects of mathematics." Goedel's delusion won't lower the status of his discovery. The mathematician G. H. Hardy is thought to have viewed his contribution to the so-called Hardy-Weinberg law of genetics as trivial. Again, his thinking so has no bearing on our assessment of his accomplishment.

Finally, consider the numerous examples of people we have no moral qualms condemning despite their unquestionably sincere belief in their own rectitude. Hitler and Stalin no doubt thought they were good men. Eichmann was probably not lying (just ignorant) when he insisted that he was only following Kantian ethics. The slaveholders and inquisitorial torturers of ancient times, although oftentimes morally scrupulous men, enjoyed an untroubled conscience. Stanley Milgram's obedient subjects did not like to inflict pain on their partners, but thought that's what "doing the right thing" required. In all of these cases we are perfectly comfortable saying that moral or legal ignorance does not excuse.

Let us return then to the original question that prompted this little excursion into the moral justification of the ignorance-of-law precept. Why does the law treat factual and doctrinal uncertainty so differently, and should it? It should do so because it treats mistakes about matters of fact differently from mistakes about matters of law and morality. If someone commits a factual mistake but has been behaving with the requisite care, prudence, and circumspection, he is morally beyond reproach, even if his mistake precipitates some terrible calamity. For a judge to behave with care, prudence, and circumspection means, among other things, applying a suitably high standard of proof to any factual issues that he needs to resolve. It means not convicting a defendant in a criminal case unless he is sure of his guilt beyond a reasonable doubt. And as long as he does this, he is morally beyond reproach even if he has mistakenly convicted an innocent.

If someone commits a moral, rather than a factual, mistake, things are quite different. Then, however much care, prudence, and circumspection preceded his decision, he still acted immorally, because as we now know, *ignorance of morality is no defense.* Thus for a judge to behave with great care, prudence, and circumspection, for him to only convict a defendant if he is sure of the right answer to a moral conundrum beyond a reasonable doubt, will do him no good if in the end he turns out to have been wrong. If he made a mistake, then however reasonable his ignorance he still acted immorally. As far as doctrinal questions go, the notion of a standard of proof is thus a chimera. It makes no sense to recommend a standard of proof to a judge, because it will give him no solace if his decision in the end turns out to have been wrong. If he made the right decision, then regardless of how foolish he seemed to the keenest legal scholars and moral philosophers of his day, he acted morally. And if he made the wrong decision, then regardless of how sensible he seemed to every legal scholar and moral philosopher he consulted, he acted immorally. Unhampered and unaided by a standard of proof, a judge is, morally speaking, "free" to decide a doctrinal question any which way he likes just as long as he gets it right.

THE SHORT ANSWER

Recently lawyers have come to be referred to as "transactional engineers." Their essential role is said to be that of making certain useful transactions happen that might not without their help. The classic example of the kind of productive assistance lawyers are supposedly meant to provide is a negotiation over the sale of a company. The seller is asking a price far in excess of what the buyer is willing to pay. That's because the seller is convinced the company will generate a large income over the next few years, and the buyer is convinced it will not. The two parties seem at an impasse. Enter the lawyer. He proposes to put a so-called earnout provision into the sales contract: while some of the price of the company is to be paid outright, a significant part is to be paid only as the company earns what the seller is projecting it will earn over the next five years. That's the kind of contract both parties are happy to sign: the buyer is happy because he is now assured he won't have to overpay if the company turns out to perform as poorly as he fears it will. The seller is happy because he is now assured he will receive adequate compensation for his company if it turns out to perform as grandly as he believes it will. The lawyer-as-engineer has kept a deal from collapsing.

I won't deny that oftentimes this is exactly the kind of role the lawyer plays. But I claim that this does not go to the essence of what the lawyer does. At heart, I believe the lawyer is the latter-day incarnation of the Jesuit or the Talmudist. His specialty is the ability to generate strategies for capitalizing on the deontological properties of legal rules.

This assertion has left many of my colleagues exceedingly uneasy. "You are saying," they say, "that avoision is a perfectly moral thing to do, and not only that, but that it is what lawyers were put into this world to do. Well, if it is, then why does it make us feel so bad to do it? Why do so many people think such strategies are outrageous?" My troubled colleagues are particularly troubled that I endorse such a seemingly ruthless approach to morality in the name not of consequentialism, which is often associated with ruthlessness, but deontology, usually associated with holier-than-thou scrupulousness. ("You're making Kant look like Machiavelli," quipped my colleague Michael Moore.) There is something to their point, but only just something.

Compare our reactions to the following two misdeeds: *A* steals your wallet. *B* (a perfect stranger) lets you drown in a lake when he could easily throw you a life vest. Who is worse? In a sense *B* of course is far more outrageous than *A*. What he did was more callous and damaging. But in another sense, *A* is really more outrageous than *B*. We have no trouble punishing *A* for what he did, clearly a violation of your rights; whereas we have far more trouble punishing *B* for what he did. In fact, we are generally disinclined to punish *B* at all, because it was not a violation of your rights. It was mean and outrageous, but mean and outrageous in a different way than stealing your cash. It is *A*'s brand of outrageous conduct that we generally believe the law is entitled to act on. What the lawyer engaged in avoision games generally accomplishes is to find a way for us to get to our goal while not committing an outrage of the *A*-variety. Frequently we will still be committing outrages of the *B*-variety. In fact, frequently he will increase the number of outrages of the *B*-variety he has us commit in an effort to eliminate outrages of the *A*-variety. Not surprisingly, we still feel queasy when we follow his recommendations, because it still means being outrageous in a sense. But it is a far different, far more benign kind of outrageousness than the sort he helps us avoid.

Blackmail and Other Criminal Bargains

THE PROBLEM

LET ME REMIND YOU what constitutes the paradox of blackmail by recalling for you the canonical blackmail scenario: Busybody says to Philanderer, "Pay me $10,000 or I'll reveal your affairs to your wife." Busybody is guilty of blackmail. What is strange, however, is that if Busybody had actually revealed Philanderer's affairs, or if he had threatened Philanderer with doing so but not mentioned the money, or if he had asked for the money but not mentioned what he was going to do if he didn't get it—if he had done any one of these things, he would not be guilty of any crime whatsoever. Yet when he combines these various innocent actions, paradoxically a crime results—blackmail. How odd; how mysterious; how come?

To put the matter slightly differently, Busybody has a perfect right to tell Philanderer's wife about the latter's infidelities. He just can't agree not to exercise that right in return for money. That's strange, because generally when I have a right to do or not do something it means I am free to agree not to use that right in return for some remuneration. Suppose I own some undeveloped land on which I want to put up an office building, but someone else would rather have it left as is so that in time he can put a country club there. He offers me some money in return for a long-term lease, or maybe even an outright sale, of the land (which he is planning to recover in admission fees). I am of course free to desist from my initial plans: I am free not to exercise my right to use the land as I wanted to in return for the offered remuneration. Why is what Busybody is doing any different? Why isn't his right to tell Philanderer's wife about his infidelities exactly like my right to build an office building on land I own, and why, therefore, doesn't his right to tell her entail the right not to tell her in return for a fee, just as my right to build entails the right not to build in return for a fee? That is the paradox of blackmail.

It is tempting to think that this is an interesting, exotic, but not very important problem. The error here is in keeping one's gaze too narrowly focused on the canonical case—the use of embarrassing information to extract money. Although blackmail is usually thought of as a "crime of information," the threat involved can consist of lots of things other than an embarrassing disclosure. "Pay me $10,000, or I'll call on my men to strike"; "Pay me $10,000, or I'll flunk you on this exam," "Pay me $10,000, or I'll cause some really bad blood at the next faculty meeting"—all of these pretty easily qualify as blackmail, though none of them involves the threatened disclosure of embarrassing facts. Quite possibly (though more controversially) blackmail even includes cases like the following: "Pay me $10,000, or I will seduce your fiance"; "Pay me $10,000, or I will persuade your son that it is his patriotic duty to volunteer for combat in Korea"; "Pay me $10,000, or I will give your high-spirited, risk-addicted nineteen-year-old daughter a motorcycle for a Christmas present"; "Pay me $10,000, or I will hasten our ailing father's death by leaving the Catholic church." Again, none of these involves the threatened disclosure of embarrassing facts. Yet all of the foregoing cases raise the blackmail paradox as squarely as the more typical, informational kind of case: it is perfectly legal for me to call a strike, to flunk you on your exam, to cause bad blood at the next faculty meeting, to seduce your fiance, to give a motorcycle to your daughter, to talk your son into enlisting, or to abandon the Catholic church. It is also legal for me to threaten any of these things (so long as I don't ask for, or insinuate I want, money). And it is legal for me to ask you for money, so long as I don't tell you what unpleasant things I plan to do to you unless you oblige me. Yet it isn't legal for me to ask you for money in exchange for not doing those unpleasant things to you. In short, whether the blackmailer's threat is one of disclosure or of something more extravagant, the puzzle remains the same.

The significance of the blackmail problem becomes even clearer once one realizes that, although blackmail is often referred to as a crime of property, and although the canonical case involves a request for money, this need not be the case. "Let me sleep with you or I will reveal your affairs to your wife," "Don't testify against me or I will reveal your affairs to your wife," "Don't accept this job with my competitor or I will reveal your affairs to your wife"—these all seem pretty clear instances of blackmail, just as though Busybody had asked for $10,000. The sought-after benefit need not be money or even property.

I should immediately point out, however, that we often do not call it blackmail, although it is blackmail, when the threat is something other than a disclosure or when the benefit is something other than money—in other words, when the case deviates in some inessential way from the canonical example. We still condemn it, prohibit it, punish it, but usually do so under some other heading than blackmail. That doesn't change the fact that fundamentally what bothers us is the blackmail character of the transaction. Once we are willing to recognize the blackmail problem as it appears under different headings and guises, we will see how ubiquitous it is.

My examples of the "sleep-with-me-or-else" variety point toward one such alternative heading under which the blackmail paradox has made an incognito appearance: rape and related sexual offenses. Rape is intercourse without consent. If the defendant holds a gun to the victim's head as he insists on intercourse, we have no trouble describing this as intercourse without consent. But what if the threat is less crass, like the various examples given above? (Sleep with me or I'll flunk you on this exam, or call a strike, or cause bad blood at the next faculty meeting, or whatever.) Is this still rape, or is it just a plain bargain? Since the threatened behavior is perfectly legal, is this any different from "sleep with me or I won't see you again," which clearly is not rape? Yielding to *that* threat would just be a bargain: sex for the chance at another date. Many statutes have taken the position that there is something special about the former kinds of threats that makes them different from "sleep with me or I won't see you again."

The statutes often do not go so far as to call it outright rape to obtain sex by use of such threats, instead they have grouped it under a more genteel heading called "gross sexual imposition" (carrying with it correspondingly lighter punishments), which is defined as "compelling [someone] to submit [to intercourse] by any threat that would prevent resistance by a woman of ordinary resolution." Commentators have acknowledged that distinguishing "gross sexual imposition" from plain bargains is a "task of surpassing subtlety." That's because it causes us to run right smack into the paradox of blackmail: although flunking someone on an exam, calling a strike, causing bad blood at a faculty meeting (even in retaliation for not sleeping with you) is no more than a minor form of misconduct, and certainly not a criminal offense, not to engage in this minor misconduct in return for sex is treated as a major offense—gross sexual imposition, a variant of rape. To put the matter differently, if a man threatens to stop seeing you unless you sleep with him on the first date, he is at worst guilty of unseemly impatience. But when a professor threatens to flunk you unless you sleep with him, he is not merely guilty of abuse of professorial authority (which at worst means getting disciplined or fired); he is guilty of a species of rape. Similarly, when the union leader threatens to call a strike unless you sleep with him, he is not merely guilty of a breach of fiduciary duty toward his members; and when your colleague threatens to cause bad blood at the next faculty meeting unless you sleep with him, he is not merely guilty of bad faith toward the rest of the faculty. Why, in all of these cases, is obtaining sex by use of these threats worse than actually making good on them? Again, we have the paradox of blackmail.

Another heading under which the blackmail problem surfaces in slight disguise is the doctrine of unconstitutional conditions. In the wake of World War II, the state of California offered a special tax benefit to veterans, *but only* if they were willing to swear a loyalty oath. The Supreme Court declared this to be an "unconstitutional condition," one that infringed on veterans' First Amendment rights. The Court required the state to make the benefit available, oath or no oath. In a similar vein, the federal government some years ago offered unemployment benefits, *but only* if the applicant was willing to work all days of the week other than Sunday. A Seventh-Day Adventist took exception to this requirement on the grounds that her religion forbade her to work on Saturday. The Supreme Court agreed and declared the government's requirement to be an unconstitutional condition, one that infringed on applicants' religious freedom. The Supreme Court did not deny that the state of California was free to grant a tax break to veterans or not, just as it liked, or that the federal government was free to make available unemployment benefits or not, just as it liked. But what it did deny was that the government could exchange its tax or unemployment benefits for a loyalty oath or a commitment to accept Saturday work. And that, as a dissenting justice in the taxbreak-for-loyalty-oath case explained, is very strange:

> So far as [the state of California] is concerned, [the veterans] are free to speak as they wish, to advocate what they will. If they advocate the violent and forceful overthrow of the California government, California will take no action against them under the tax provisions here in question. But it will refuse to take any action *for them,* in the sense of extending to them the legislative largesse that is inherent in the granting of any tax exemption or deduction.[1]

This problem, which keeps arising whenever the government tries to impose a requirement as a precondition for receiving some subsidy, job, contract, or tax-break, has the exact structure of the blackmail paradox: although the government is entitled to do X or not do it, entitled to ask for Y or not ask for it, it is not entitled to ask for Y in exchange for doing $X,$ even though the citizen would be perfectly happy to agree to this. Courts have been as puzzled by the doctrine of unconstitutional conditions as by blackmail, and on some rare occasions have even glimpsed the near-identity of the two problems.

Yet a further heading under which blackmail sometimes flashes its Cheshire Cat's grin is "passive resistance." A jailed terrorist goes on a hunger strike demanding the government improve prison conditions for him and his cohorts. A protester sits down in front of a tank to block the installation of Pershing missiles. An aggressive city dweller tries to save a parking spot for a friend, who has not yet arrived, by standing in the middle of the vacant space and telling other would-be parkers "Over my dead body." A desperate daughter tells her parents she will kill herself unless they pay off her boyfriend's gambling debts. A jealous husband threatens to leap out the window if his wife makes good her intention to leave him. In all of these cases the defendant threatens a self-sacrifice that qualifies at worst as a mild offense, and maybe not even that. But courts have been led to wonder whether the whole setup doesn't amount to the very serious crime of "criminal coercion," usually applied to uncomplicated threats to blow someone's head off unless he does what you want him to do (like staying out of a parking spot or not divorcing you). Which returns us to the blackmail issue: How can threatening to do what is at worst a minor offense (self-injury) and trading it in for some benefit amount to a serious crime?

The fact is that, just about wherever bargains are struck, blackmail sooner or later enters the picture. Whatever class of bargains we examine, we will find instances in which one side is offering something to the other which it is entitled to trade, and yet somehow the terms of exchange strike us as "extortionate," that is, blackmail. That's most transparent when borrowers denounce interest rates as extortionate. It is equally transparent when corporate managers complain that the money they had to pay a corporate raider, to keep him from taking control of their company, amounts to greenmail. It is only slightly less transparent when corporate managers refer to a hostile tender offer as coercion, or to a frivolous lawsuit as pure harassment. And it lurks behind people's objections to a whole range of controversial consensual transactions, like insider trading, plea bargains, the assumption of risk, and so-called unconscionable contracts.

BLACKMAIL IN RELATION TO "PLAIN VANILLA" COERCION

To fully understand the nature of the blackmail paradox one must see it against the background of more common kinds of coercion.

The easiest kind is exemplified by "Your money or your life"—the coercion exerted in a straightforward robbery. For the sake of clarity, it is worth asking even of this trivial kind of coercion why we call it that. Why do we not view the transaction between robber and victim as just another bargain, one in which the chance to continue living is exchanged for cash? In other words, what is the difference between a threat—which is deemed coercive—and an offer—which is not? The answer is that a threat shrinks your opportunity set and an offer enlarges it. A threat permits you to choose which of many things you are entitled to you will give up. The offer permits you to choose which of many things you are entitled to you will, if you want to, exchange for something else you are not entitled to. The robber coerces because he offers to sell you back what he has first unlawfully taken from you, the chance to go on living.[2]

As the political scientist Alan Wertheimer has shown with great clarity in his book *Coercion,* many seemingly harder cases are really just the robbery case in disguise.[3] Ask yourself whether (and why) we should reject the assumption of risk defense in this tort case:

> A illegally blocks the public sidewalk, so that pedestrians can pass only by walking in the street. In order to pass, B walks in the street, knowing that there is substantial danger of being struck by passing traffic. He is struck and injured by a negligently driven automobile.[4]

Did B assume the risk of injury and is he, therefore, barred from recovering from A? Keeping in mind the robbery analogy, one soon sees why the answer should be No. A illegally narrowed B's choices, much as the robber narrowed those of his victim. A forced B to buy back—by exposing himself to the risk of being hit by a car—something that was already his, namely, the right to walk down the street.

Ask yourself whether (and why) we should accept a duress defense in the following contracts case: plaintiff contracts to cater defendant's party. An hour before the guests are to arrive, defendant raises his price by 50 percent and refuses to start preparing until the plaintiff consents. Defendant reluctantly agrees. Thereafter he refuses to pay, arguing the contract modification was coerced. Again, keeping in mind the robbery analogy, the answer quickly comes to hand. The contractor forced the defendant to buy back what was already his: the right to have the party catered at the original price.[5]

Ask yourself next whether the following case involves an illegal search and seizure: the police stop a traveler at an airport because he resembles the Drug Enforcement Agency's courier profile. Stops on the basis of such profiles have been ruled unconstitutional. Notwithstanding this ruling, the police tell the traveler that unless he consents to be searched they will detain him until they have obtained a search warrant. The traveler consents. The robbery analogy makes clear why his consent will be found coerced and hence invalid. The traveler was being asked to buy back (through his consent to the search) what was already his: the right not to be detained.

Finally, ask yourself whether the following plea bargain is valid or coerced: the prosecutor has inadmissible but conclusive evidence demonstrating that the defendant is guilty of murder. He also has admissible but flimsy evidence implicating him in a rape. The prosecutor does not believe the defendant committed the rape. Nonetheless, desperate to put in jail someone he knows to be a murderer, he threatens the defendant with a rape prosecution unless he pleads guilty to some lesser charge (let's say, the aggravated battery of the fellow he murdered). The fearful defendant consents. But his consent is no more valid than that of the robbery victim. The defendant is being asked to buy back (by pleading guilty to aggravated battery) relief from a trial, which the prosecutor is not entitled to launch anyway (given the frivolousness of the rape charge).

Fundamentally, then, the foregoing cases of coercion are quite straightforward. To be sure, they can give rise to greater conceptual difficulties than I have let on so far: not everyone who is pressured into accepting a contract modification can claim duress—we don't always find the robbery analogy compelling—but it's not quite clear who can and who cannot. Generally speaking, though, there is little doubt about what is coercive and immoral in the standard cases of coercion. The standard cases all involve impermissible boundary crossings. They involve easily discernible invasions of that line surrounding each individual—Nozick calls it a hyperplane—which harbors his possessions, entitlements, and rights. Blackmail isn't like that.[6]

Admittedly, blackmail superficially resembles robbery, but only superficially. For the robber's wrong—his boundary crossing—is easy to pinpoint. He sells back what he doesn't own, the victim's life and limb. Not so the blackmailer threatening to disclose the victim's infidelity. The victim doesn't own the right to control the blackmailer's communications with his wife; the blackmailer does. The blackmailer, unlike the robber, is selling something he owns. Or so it seems.[7]

But if blackmail isn't like standard cases of coercion, if it doesn't involve boundary crossings, what's wrong with it?

OTHER PEOPLE'S THOUGHTS

Scholars have advanced a number of ingenious suggestions seeking to supply the missing link between standard cases of coercion and blackmail. I will take a look at a small sample of those just to give a sense of the sort of difficulties such approaches run into.[8] Each of these approaches tries to uncover some kind of significant indirect relationship with coercion.

In an essay called "Blackmail, Inc.," Richard Epstein suggests that what is wrong with blackmail is that although it is not actually coercive, it foments conduct that is as bad as coercion, like fraud, embezzlement, and theft. If blackmail were legal, he points out,

> there would then be an open and public market for a new set of social institutions to exploit the gains from this new form of legal activity. Blackmail, Inc. could with impunity place advertisements in the newspapers offering to acquire for top dollar any information with the capacity to degrade or humiliate persons or business associates. Thereafter, Blackmail, Inc. as a commercial organization, could negotiate contracts with its sources to suppress the information acquired.[9]

And that would only be the first step.

> [The victim] may not have the money to satisfy [Blackmail, Inc.'s monetary demands.] What is to prevent Blackmail, Inc. from hinting, ever so slightly, that it thinks strenuous efforts to obtain the necessary cash should be undertaken? Do we believe that [the victim] would never resort to fraud or theft given this kind of pressure, when the very nature of the transaction cuts off his access to the usual financial sources, such as banks or friends, who would want to know the purpose of the loan. ("To pay Blackmail, Inc.," he would say in a burst of candor.) Moreover, suppose Blackmail, Inc. recognizes that its ability to extract future payments from [the victim] depends upon [third parties, namely, the wife or business associates] being kept in the dark. As it is a full-service firm, it can do more than collect moneys from [the victim]. It can instruct him in the proper way to arrange his affairs in order to keep the disclosures from being made, as there are mutual gains from trade—greater wealth for Blackmail, Inc. . . . and greater serenity and peace of mind for [the victim]. What Blackmail, Inc. can do is to participate in the very fraud that [the victim] is engaged in against [a third party].[10]

In short, blackmail is wrong, first, because it facilitates fraud against the person from whom the blackmail victim is trying to keep his embarrassing secret; and second, because like drug addiction it induces the crimes necessary to support the "fraud habit," the crimes the blackmail victim commits to pay his blackmailer.

In his prediction that legalizing blackmail would usher forth organizations like Blackmail, Inc., Epstein has clearly proved right. When the blackmail prohibition is only laxly enforced, organizations like this have indeed made their appearance. In fin de siècle Paris, someone formed a limited-subscription newspaper called *The Independent* whose exclusive purpose was to sniff out scandalous facts about wealthy targets and make them buy the newspaper's silence.[11]

But Epstein's analysis nonetheless has serious problems. One such problem is that the analysis is so specifically tailored to informational blackmail and cannot easily be extended to the noninformational examples cited in the last section: the threat to call a strike, to cause bad blood at the faculty meeting, to give the blackmail victim's daughter a motorcycle, or to persuade his son to enlist.

A second problem with Epstein's account is its assumption that anytime a victim tries to hide an embarrassing fact about himself, this amounts to a form of fraud and should be prevented. Is the reason we are so upset with the blackmailer who promises not to reveal a fellow employee's homosexuality (for a fee) that we would in fact like him to tell the employer what he knows?

A third problem is that Epstein's account makes the blackmail prohibition dependent on certain (admittedly very plausible) empirical assumptions about blackmail's second-order effects on the crime rate: more people will embezzle their employers, defraud their customers, cheat the IRS, in order to pay off Blackmail, Inc. But those effects seem to have nothing to do with our instinctive revulsion at the practice: even if we imagine that those second-order effects are going to be trivial-to-nil, our aversion to blackmail doesn't seem to wane one bit.

In *Anarchy, State and Utopia*, Robert Nozick finds a different kind of link between blackmail and the standard forms of coercion. "If I buy a good or service from you, I benefit from your activity; I am better off due to it, better off than if your activity wasn't done or you didn't exist at all." On the other hand, "[I]f I pay you for not harming me, I gain nothing from you that I wouldn't possess if either you didn't exist at all or existed without having anything to do with me."[12] Roughly speaking, then, Nozick sees the critical line between ordinary bargains and coercive kinds of bargains (that is, your-money-or-your-life kinds of bargains) as lying in the answer to the question whether the alleged victim would be better off if the defendant weren't around. By that test, blackmail starts to look like standard forms of coercion. Like victims of your-money-or-your-life transactions, and unlike a party to a regular contract, the blackmail victim, it seems, would be better off if the defendant didn't exist.[13]

Nozick's theory of blackmail, however, is both over- and underinclusive. It sweeps a lot of perfectly innocent contracts into the blackmail category: GM might be better off if Ford didn't exist. But is a contract between them, therefore, blackmail? A more serious shortcoming is his theory's underinclusiveness. It covers only the kind of blackmail in which the blackmailer promises to *omit* an act in return for a payoff; it does not cover the kind of blackmail in which the blackmailer promises to *perform* some beneficial act in return for the payoff. (Only in promised-omission cases will it be true that the victim would be better off if the blackmailer didn't exist.) Although the most commonly thought of kinds of blackmail cases do involve omissions, this, as I will show later on, does not hold for *all* blackmail cases.

In the course of his magisterial, four-volume exploration of *The Moral Limits of the Criminal Law,* Joel Feinberg tries to forge yet a different sort of link between blackmail and standard forms of coercion. All cases of blackmail, he basically claims, fall into one of two categories: first, cases in which the blackmailer *threatens* to do something only an immoral, even if not criminal, person would do ("Pay me $10,000, or I will let everyone know about your homosexuality"); second, cases in which he *offers* to do something only an immoral, even if not criminal, person would do ("Pay me $10,000, and I won't tell the police that you are the one who has been sending arson threats to the new neighbor on the block"). On Feinberg's account, blackmailers, therefore, come in two versions, each of which is objectionable for a slightly different reason. The first version, the blackmailer who threatens, is a more genteel species of robber: like a robber, he is asking his victim to buy back a right which the latter, morally even if not legally, already owns, for example, the right to keep his homosexuality a secret. The second version, the blackmailer who *offers,* is a more genteel species of criminal accomplice: he is willing to assist the victim in keeping secret something the latter, morally even if not legally, ought to disclose.[14]

Like Nozick's, Feinberg's account seems both over- and underinclusive. Overinclusive: take the case of a contract killer. He has promised to do something immoral in return for a fee. Feinberg's account would brand him a blackmailer. But that hardly seems the right label. Underinclusive: one only needs to consider the canonical case—"Pay me $10,000 or I'll reveal your affairs to your wife." Feinberg's account suggests that this isn't a case of blackmail at all, because the threatened conduct—warning a wife about her husband's infidelities—isn't obviously a wrong thing to do. But how can we accept an account that implies that what we hitherto viewed as the canonical blackmail case quite simply isn't?[15]

The most intriguing approach, however, is offered in an essay by James Lindgren, "Unraveling the Paradox of Blackmail." The feature of blackmail that most impresses Lindgren is that the blackmailer who exploits the victim's concern about what a third party might think is in a sense "playing with someone else's bargaining chips":

> [T]he blackmailer threatens to tell others damaging information about the blackmail victim unless the victim heeds the blackmailer's request, usually a request for money. The blackmailer obtains what he wants by using extra leverage. But that leverage belongs more to a third person than to the blackmailer. The blackmail victim pays the blackmailer to avoid involving third parties: he pays to avoid being harmed by *persons other than the blackmailer*. When the reputation of a person is damaged, he is punished by all those who change their opinion of him. They may "punish" him by treating him differently or he may be punished merely by the knowledge that others no longer respect him.
>
> Thus when a blackmailer threatens to turn in a criminal unless paid money, the blackmailer is bargaining with the state's chip. The blackmail victim pays to avoid the harm that the state would inflict; he pays because he believes that he can thereby suppress the state's potential criminal claim. . . . Likewise, when a blackmailer threatens to expose damaging noncriminal behavior unless paid money, he is also turning third-party leverage to his own benefit. What makes his conduct blackmail is that he interposes himself parasitically in an actual or potential dispute in which he lacks a sufficiently direct interest. What right has he to make money by settling other people's claims?
>
> At the heart of blackmail, then, is the triangular nature of the transaction, and particularly this disjunction between the blackmailer's personal benefit and the interests of the third parties whose leverage he uses. In effect, the blackmailer attempts to gain an advantage in return for suppressing someone else's actual or potential interest. The blackmailer is negotiating for his own gain with someone else's leverage or bargaining chips.[16]

Lindgren's theory pretty closely matches our intuitions at the descriptive level, although it seems perhaps a bit underinclusive. It does not for instance account for several cases many would agree clearly reek of blackmail: pay me $10,000—or I will cause bad blood at our club, seduce your fiance, persuade your son to enlist, give your daughter a motorcycle, or leave the Catholic church. In none of these cases is it easy to see in what sense the perpetrator is playing with somebody else's bargaining chips. Even if it is plausible to say that the blackmailer who threatens to reveal the victim's infidelities is somehow misappropriating compensation that is really due the injured wife, it is not plausible to say about my other cases that the blackmailer is misappropriating compensation that is really due the annoyed club members, the jilted fiancé, the patriotic son, the risk-loving daughter, or the sick father.

A more bothersome aspect of Lindgren's theory is its lack of normative moorings. The bargaining chips he finds the blackmailer guilty of misappropriating seem like a very unreal sort of commodity, made of the most diaphanous of tissues. It is hard to see the principle that elevates this very metaphorical kind of misappropriation to the level of a robbery.

I don't want to make too much of these criticisms. Above all, I don't want to make too much of the counterexamples. Counterexamples generally sound worse than they are. Just about every important mathematical theorem when first set forth is vulnerable to them, because it is too general or too simple in its initial formulation. In time, it is revised, honed, hedged, and qualified in a process the philosopher Imre Lakatos has aptly named "monster-barring."

Eventually the initial theorem is revealed to have been all wrong but basically sound. (Littlewood once defined the great mathematician as the creator of defective theorems.) Indeed I believe none of the above theories to be just plain wrong. There is much that is right about every single one of them. Despite the problems that afflict them, they cater to some very strong intuitions, and they retain that intuitive appeal, even after the problems have been pointed out. Most likely, each captures some important aspect, some special case, of *the* solution to the blackmail puzzle, and it would be a distinct virtue of any new account if it managed to reveal that to be so: it is pretty clear that a good theory of blackmail should explain why the typical blackmail case involves information and promises of omission, why either the behavior that is threatened or the behavior that is promised will typically be immoral, and why the typical blackmailer appears to be playing with somebody else's bargaining chips. In what follows I will try to provide such an account.

My solution strategy will be to introduce and solve a seemingly unrelated and simpler puzzle first and then to show that the blackmail problem is but a variant of that puzzle and responds to a variant of its solution.

A Puzzle about Punishment

One night, Smithy, the burglar, breaks into the house of Bartleby. He finds very little of value, but as he is about to leave he discovers a safe. He is, however, unable to open it. Wielding a club, he awakens Bartleby and demands the combination. Bartleby refuses to tell him. "Look here," says the exasperated Smithy, "unless you tell me the combination, I am going to beat you to pulp." But Bartleby is adamant: "What's in that safe really isn't very valuable. Just some cheap family jewelry. But it has enormous sentimental value for me, having been passed through the generations for ages. I simply cannot give it up." But Smithy persists: "Tell me the combination, or I'll make you regret it." Bartleby quite sincerely replies: "Much as I fear physical violence, I'd rather you give me a savage beating than give up what's inside that safe." "As you wish," says Smithy, and proceeds to administer a fairly severe pummeling.

Another night, another burglar, let's call him Louie, breaks into Bartleby's house. Like Smithy, he finds very little of value. As he is about to leave, he too discovers Bartleby's safe, which he is as unable to open as Smithy was. Wielding a club, he wakes up Bartleby and asks him for the combination, but Bartleby refuses to tell him. "Look here," says the exasperated Louie, "unless you tell me the combination, I am going to beat you to pulp." But again Bartleby is adamant. "What's in that safe really isn't very valuable. Just some cheap family jewelry. But it has enormous sentimental value for me, having been passed through the generations for ages. I simply cannot give it up." Louie persists: "Tell me the combination. Or I swear I'll make you regret it." Bartleby replies as before: "Much as I fear physical violence, I'd rather you give me a savage beating than give up what's inside that safe." "As you wish," says Louie, and is about to launch into the beating when his eyes fall on a slip of paper lying at Bartleby's bedside. He takes a closer look and realizes that this is the combination to the safe. As he is about to open the safe, Bartleby implores him: "Please. It's just like I said. I am really attached to those trinkets inside the safe. I really would rather you beat me to pulp than strip me of those trinkets." Louie remains unmoved, opens the safe, takes what he finds inside, and makes off.

Both Smithy and Louie are caught. You are the judge. Which of them should you punish more harshly?

What the law would do is reasonably clear: punish Smithy, the batterer, worse than Louie, the thief. The batterer would probably be found guilty of aggravated robbery, the thief of simple robbery. But that could vary. What is unlikely to vary is the significantly graver treatment of batterers than thieves. But does that make sense?

Informal polling among my law school colleagues, as well as at a party of economists, suggests that it does not. What strikes most as the most plausible solution is the following: ordinarily, someone who commits a serious battery is worse than someone who commits a theft, especially a relatively modest one. But that's because most victims prefer being stolen from to being battered. Not so in this bizarre case. Here the victim, for very idiosyncratic reasons, preferred being battered to being stolen from. Smithy did what the victim preferred; Louie did not. Hence Louie, the thief, is worse than Smithy, the batterer.

There's a lot that could be said to fortify this argument. For instance, one could point to tort law and note that in a perfectly run tort system, one that tried to obtain the most accurate possible measure of someone's loss, Bartleby would be entitled to more compensation from Louie than from Smithy, since he considered what Louie did to him worse than what Smithy did to him. Although the tort system is a little wary of recognizing excessively idiosyncratic tastes, by and large it tries to avoid discriminating against the eccentric, the thin skull, or—as Calabresi shows in his essay on the "reasonable" tort victim—the devoutly religious: a Christian Scientist woman whose pelvis has been shattered in an auto accident delays seeking medical care and renders her injury irreparable; a Catholic woman refuses to use contraception after a similarly serious injury to her pelvis and enters into a life-threatening pregnancy; a Jewish woman is stalled on a ski lift, sitting next to a man, on Sabbath, and seeks to escape her predicament by taking a disastrous leap to the ground. We deem all of these victims entitled to a full tort recovery, even though their idiosyncratic beliefs greatly exacerbated their injuries. Given all that, it would seem churlish to treat Bartleby's strong attachment to his heirlooms any differently.[17]

The recent tendency to consult victim impact statements when deciding on the death penalty further supports this conclusion.[18] Granted, victim impact statements are controversial inasmuch as they arguably ignore the most important victim, the deceased, and give a disproportionate role to collateral victims, the family. But the basic idea that victims need to be consulted in assessing harm and meting out suitable punishment seems intuitively sound—as well as consistent with the decision to punish the thief more harshly than the batterer, because that's how the victim perceived the acts.

But the most important point in favor of the preference-based view is probably this one: harm is in the eye of the victim. The very conduct that is a crime or tort, if done against the victim's wishes, is neither if it has his consent. If consented-to, the taking isn't theft, the intercourse isn't rape, the tackling isn't battery, even the killing may not be murder. The absence of consent seems like a crucial, a defining, attribute of harm. Excepting odd cases, like prostitution and drugs, what a victim wants cannot count as an injury. It seems to follow almost inexorably that even among bona fide harms, those the victim likes least are most harmful, and those the victim can tolerate most are least harmful. At least it *seems* that way.

But consider some of the more oddball consequences of the preference-based view:

1. A man is about to rape a woman. As he holds the knife to her throat, the woman declares: "I would rather die than be violated." Thereupon the man kills her. Or: the defendant kidnaps the victim, intending to hold him for ransom. The victim insists: "I would rather die than be used for ransom against my family." Whereupon the defendant, obligingly, kills the victim. At the trial the attorneys of the rapist and the kidnapper argue: "Ordinarily murder is a more heinous offense than rape or kidnapping, indeed it is the only one that qualifies for the death penalty. In these cases, however, the victims preferred murder to rape or kidnapping. The defendants, heinous though their conduct was, did their victims a favor inasmuch as they killed them rather than raping or holding them for ransom. Therefore, their penalty should be no more severe than would have been the case had they committed a rape or a kidnapping." I take it the argument would not persuade.

It might be objected, though, that this example proves very little. We simply do not ordinarily take people's preferences for death into account. But my hunch is that it is not *this* circumstance that makes us resistant to the defense attorney's argument. Even if death cannot ordinarily be consented to, consent does tend to diminish the guilt of the killer—assisting suicide or committing euthanasia seem less heinous to us than outright murder.

2. Assume the same facts as above, but suppose that the rapist and the kidnapper, instead of killing their victims, proceed with the rape and the kidnapping. At trial, the prosecutor argues: "Ordinarily, the death penalty cannot be imposed in cases of rape or kidnapping. But *this* rape and *this* kidnapping, as far as *these* victims are concerned, were *worse than murder,* and the defendant knew this. Therefore,

they should be treated with the same severity as a murder." I take it, this argument would not persuade either.

3. Suppose Louie had broken not into the house of Bartleby but that of Bartholemea. All other facts remain the same. Bartholomea, like Bartleby, declares she would rather be beaten than give up the family heirlooms inside her safe. Louie, seeing the combination to the safe on her night table, manages to open the safe and to make off with the jewelry without ever laying a hand on Bartholomea. Louie presumably should be treated just as he would be if he had broken into Bartleby's house. Yet by punishing Louie more severely than Smithy we are now asserting that the theft from Bartholomea was worse than the battery of Bartleby. But the only thing of which we can be at all confident is that both Bartleby and Bartholomea judge thefts of family jewelry to be worse than batteries. We have no basis for thinking that the battery of Bartleby is less painful to him than the theft from Bartholomea is painful to her. For that sort of interpersonal comparison we have been given absolutely no data.

4. Suppose Smithy had never been given a choice between battery and theft. Upon not finding any valuables in Bartleby's house, he simply bursts into his bedroom and administers the beating. It is clear, however, that if he had noticed the safe, Bartleby would have pleaded with him to beat him rather than steal the contents of the safe. If this comes out during the trial, the preference-based view suggests that we let the defense attorney argue that since the victim in fact preferred what the defendant did to something we would count as a lesser crime, the defendant should only be punished at the level of that lesser crime. Indeed, it doesn't really seem to matter whether Bartleby's house actually has such a safe in it. The mere fact that the defense attorney is able to point out that he could envision circumstances under which the victim would have preferred what the defendant did, to something else which would have rated a lesser penalty, should entitle the defendant to be punished no more harshly than for that lesser crime. All this is suggested by the preference-based view, and it seems absurd.

If the preference-based approach generates such absurd-sounding consequences, it must contain some logical flaw. But what is that flaw? Before proceeding to lay bare the source of the problem, I need to clear a preliminary difficulty out of the way.

From the very outset of this section, I have been pressing the question "Who deserves to be punished more harshly?" and at more than one point readers might have been inclined to say: How should I know unless you first tell me how one makes judgments about deserts, whether one follows a retributivist, a utilitarian, or a mixed agenda, or something else altogether? I have implicitly assumed retributivism to be the key objective of punishment, but this is probably only a helpful, not a crucial assumption. Does it make sense to seek such help? Does retributivism have any plausibility? Yes, and a great deal of it; more, in fact, than any of its best-known alternatives. It is, most familiarly, superior to a simple utilitarian account of punishment, which would permit the punishment of mere innocents for the sake of some utilitarian goal. But it is also superior to the so-called mixed account favored by H. L. A. Hart, which permits punishment only when both retributivist and utilitarian goals are furthered thereby.[19] Michael Moore offers a simple but compelling hypothetical to show the inadequacy of the mixed account. He asks us to imagine a robber-rapist who has inherited a fortune and had an accident that makes it impossible for him ever again to feel any sexual impulse. Put differently, Moore creates a situation involving a heinous criminal whose punishment would serve none of the usual (or even the not-so-usual) utilitarian purposes: deterrence, rehabilitation, incapacitation, and the like. (He deals with the problem of general deterrence by arranging for a ruse by which the judge would only pretend to punish.) Agreement here is well-nigh universal that the defendant should be punished nonetheless, revealing us all to be what Moore calls "closet retributivists."[20]

Even if Moore's hypothetical has convinced you of retributivism's attractions, you may wonder how much solid content the theory really has. Does it mean anything to say that a criminal should receive the punishment he deserves, if we can't tell how much he deserves? Sure, we know that one week, two weeks, or even three weeks isn't enough for the robber-rapist, but whether two-and-a-half years is required, or five, or maybe seven-and-a-half, we have a hard time telling. Where should we look to find out what's deserved? (By contrast, utilitarianism superficially looks like it offers an easy recipe for figuring out the right measure of punishment: choose the punishment that maximizes whatever the utilitarian happens to value, whether it be deterrence, or rehabilitation, or maybe something else altogether. Why that's just superficial is nicely explained by Robert Nozick).[21] Admittedly, the executioners of past centuries had a pretty clear-cut sense of what punishment each crime deserved: an execution that imitated the crime. The robber who killed his victim by hitting him twice with an iron spade was himself hit twice with that very spade before being garroted. The servant girl who torched her victim's house had her face scorched. The woman who cut her victim to pieces was liquidated in similarly piecemeal fashion: first her throat was cut, then her head lopped off, then her limbs wrenched out. The aptly named Grimm fairy tales teem with such punishments. But is this the only way to give concrete content to retributivism?[22]

Psychologists have shown in an elegant series of experiments, initiated by Thorsten Sellin and Marvin Wolfgang's landmark study *The Measurement of Delinquency*, that our intuitions about penal desert are a lot more precise than our intuitions about those intuitions suggest. We know more than we think we know.[23] Wolfgang, Sellin, and those who came after them asked their subjects to rate the seriousness of various offenses by a variety of means. Sometimes they just asked them to rate the offenses on a scale of 1 to 11. Sometimes they asked them to compare every offense to some standard offense and state whether it was twice, ten times, or perhaps only half or one-tenth as serious as that standard. Sometimes they asked them to press a "dynamometer" with the degree of intensity that best expressed how strongly they felt. The initial results were reassuring although not completely surprising: subjects almost invariably rated as more serious those offenses we in fact punish more severely. But there was a fly in the ointment. If subjects deemed one offense two-and-a-half times as serious as another, the sentence the law gave out for the one would rarely turn out to be exactly two-and-a-half times as long as what it gave out for the other. Some psychologists worried: "Does the systematic deviation from a linear relationship imply that, in our judicial system, punishments do not fit the crime?" Having asked this question, they began to realize that the analysis so far was missing a step.[24] We have been comparing the seriousness of crimes with the length of the sentence meted out. We should instead be comparing the seriousness of the crime with the *seriousness* of the sentence meted out. We should use the very techniques we used to rate the seriousness of punishment to then rate the seriousness of crimes and see what we get. We should ask subjects how they would score a three-year sentence on a scale of 1 to 11, and we should again have them press the dynamometer with the appropriate level of intensity. All this was done and with great success. It turns out that if one offense is judged two-and-a-half times as serious as another, then it will generally carry a penalty that has been rated two-and-a-half times as serious as the penalty of the other.[25] Punishments fit their crime like a glove—admittedly, though, a store-bought glove, not a tailor-made one.[26]

THE PUNISHMENT PUZZLE RESOLVED

So who should be punished more harshly, the batterer or the thief? I have already made it pretty clear that I think the preference-based approach is wrong, that the batterer is indeed worse than the thief, notwithstanding Bartleby's weird preferences. But why?

Suppose you had the choice of living in either of two towns. Town *A* harbors exactly one negligent person who happens to be running a chemical factory. Given his habits and the consequent odds of an accident, twenty people are expected to die as a result of his negligence over the next decade. Town *B* harbors exactly one vicious torturer-murderer. Over the next decade he will kidnap, torture, and kill exactly one person—someone he comes to consider his mortal enemy. Which of the two towns would you rather live in? If you're at all like me, you prefer town *B*—the chances of dying seem substantially slimmer there. Which of the two criminals—the highly negligent chemical plant operator, or the vicious torturer-murderer—deserves the more severe punishment? Presumably, the vicious torturer-murderer. (Indeed the parallel to the case of Bartleby can be made even greater. Just imagine a defendant who puts his victim to the choice: "I can either act the part of the negligent chemical plant operator and thus cause some calamity over the next few years, or I can act the part of a vicious torturer-murderer and kill exactly one person. Which would you rather have?")

This example makes clear a good part of what is amiss with the preference-based approach: the victim's decision as to whom he would rather be victimized by need bear absolutely no relationship to the culpability of the perpetrator. The victim cares only about one dimension of the perpetrator's activities—the expected harm. The judge—the criminal law—cares about harm only as one among several criteria of culpability. Let me spell that out just a bit more. An omission may produce as much harm as an act. The victim certainly doesn't care much whether he was done in by an act or an omission. The judge, by contrast, must: he will generally deem the omission innocent and the act culpable. An intentional, a knowing, a reckless, a negligent act—they all can result in the identical injury; indeed, they may result in the same probability of injury. (Remember that in my two-town example a negligently inflicted injury is more probable than an intentional injury.) Again, the victim couldn't care less how it's done. The judge, however, must: he will punish the former more harshly than the latter. A remotely caused injury can be just as severe as a proximately caused one. The victim won't care about anything other than severity. The judge, nevertheless, must: only if the injury is proximately caused can he convict. The participation of an accomplice in a group crime may make no difference to the outcome, because the group was already formidable enough to accomplish the task on its own. The victim won't care whether the defendant added his mite to the effort. Yet again, the judge must: he will punish the defendant's complicity even if his efforts were perfectly redundant (and known by the defendant to be redundant!).

Oddly enough, this feature of the criminal law, that a judge must punish a defendant in accordance with his *culpability* rather than merely the *harm* he caused (although of course harm is one crucial factor that goes into culpability) is often overlooked. It is overlooked for instance when scholars try to explain the difference between criminal law and tort law. Criminal and tort law cover largely identical kinds of undesirable conduct, and it appears that both seek to discourage it—the one through a jail term, the other through a damage award. Which raises the question: Why have both? One answer that is sometimes given is that the criminal law is a tort law for the poor defendant, a means of controlling the conduct of the judgment-proof sinner. What this overlooks is the very different role that culpability plays in criminal and tort law. Our analysis of the preference-based fallacy rivets our attention on that difference: although both tort and criminal law care about culpability, tort law only uses it to determine whether the defendant is liable, not how heavy that liability should be. The heaviness of tort liability is governed by just one criterion, the seriousness of the harm, the damage done. Criminal law, by contrast, uses culpability not merely to determine *whether,* but also to determine *how severely,* to punish. Harm still plays a role, but it has to share the limelight with fault.[27]

A RE WE NOW in a position to solve the punishment puzzle? Not quite yet. We may be confident that by and large—regardless of the victim's preferences—intentional wrongs are worse than negligent ones, act-produced wrongs are worse than omission-produced wrongs, proximately caused wrongs worse than remotely caused wrongs, but do we have grounds for equal confidence that battery-inflicted wrongs are worse than theft-inflicted wrongs? In my two-town example it seems perfectly clear why the victim's attitudes are not to be trusted: he takes no account of dimensions of wrongdoing other than harm. But where in the comparison of a battery and a theft are there dimensions of wrongdoing that a judge should take into account but a victim might not? What about the case is analogous to the act/ omission distinction or the proximate causation/remote causation distinction?

A somewhat farfetched example will help to find the analogy. I have a diseased kidney and would like it replaced with a healthy one. I am thinking about "stealing" one of two kidneys that have recently become available for transplantation. I learn that the first of those kidneys has just been implanted in a healthy recipient who only had one kidney and wanted a full complement just to be on the safe side. (Let's assume my own needs weren't known yet when the kidney was given to him!) The second kidney has not been implanted yet but has been committed to another recipient with at least as great a need for it as I have. I am contemplating two courses of action:

1. Stealing the "redundant" kidney that has already been implanted in the first recipient. Let's assume that removing the kidney could be accomplished through a completely risk- and painfree procedure.

2. Stealing the yet-to-be-implanted kidney out of the refrigerator in which it is being stored.

Which course of action would be worse? Quite clearly, I think, the first. It's worse *even though* the victim of my action in (1) suffers far fewer ill effects than the victim in (2). It is worse because it is more invasive! But not because being more invasive means greater risk or greater pain. What makes the difference, rather, is that the rightful owner's claim on the kidney in (1) is far stronger than the rightful owner's claim in (2). The claim is stronger simply because the kidney has passed into the owner's body.

Not everyone may be convinced yet. How do I know that one's claim to things inside one's body (even recently implanted things) is stronger than one's claim to things outside one's body, assuming they are both important to one's well-being? Well, for one there is the law of self-defense. You are entitled to defend your body in ways you are not entitled to defend your property—even if the attack on your property will affect your well-being far more than the attack on your body. Note that this has nothing to do with paternalism. It is not that we believe that you are silly to value something outside your body more than your body itself.

The prohibition of torture as a means of punishment bears me out further. What exactly is wrong with torture as a means of punishment? There is no doubt that prisoners would often prefer or deem equivalent many forms of torture to moderately lengthy jail terms. After all, many us would submit to a fairly painful medical procedure just to avoid being bedridden for an extended portion of our lives. If torture is wrong, it must have to do with the high degree of invasiveness associated with it. We all—criminals included—have such an extraordinary claim to the integrity of our bodies that it cannot generally be invaded (except, say, for medical treatment) even where other, more painful means of punishment are appropriate.

The law of search and seizure is a natural extension of these ideas. You have more of a claim to the things in your immediate vicinity than to those further away, and thus are more entitled to keep them immune from frivolous rifling. That's not because you in fact would mind it more if things in your immediate vicinity were rifled through. It might very well be the reverse: you might mind it far more if things outside your domain of privacy are being touched. Nor is it the case that we respect your private things more out of convenience, say, because it would be too hard to learn what you most feared having idly rifled through and it is easiest to just have a flat rule. After all, even if you told us what your preferences were, we wouldn't abide by them. What counts is that your claim to noninterference is far greater as to things immediately around you than as to other things, *regardless of your preferences.*

There is a further consideration that may help to convince you that your claim to things inside your body is automatically greater than your claim to things outside it, *regardless* of how much more important things outside your body actually are to you. Consider the various stages through which a kidney recipient's relationship with his donated kidney passes before it reaches the inside of his body: first, the recipient's doctors make contact with the doctors of the donor's hospital; then they may actually enter into some sort of contract with that other hospital; after which the recipient's doctors will actually take delivery of the kidney and store it in their own facilities; and finally they will implant the kidney. The importance of the kidney to the recipient does not change at any of these stages, but his claim to it does. If I were to interfere with the transplant, the intervention would be more serious the later it occurs. Using my personal contacts to dissuade the doctors of the donor hospital to offer the kidney to that other recipient (because I want it) is less serious than actually getting them to break their contract with the recipient's hospital. Getting them to break their contract is less serious than stealing the kidney from the recipient hospital's premises. Stealing it from the premises is less serious than removing it from the other recipient's body—which is what I asserted above but now made more plausible by showing it to be part of a continuum.

My point is worth making in yet a different way. Recall the example I offered in Part I concerning the friend who asks you for financial assistance so she can deal with a bothersome medical problem. After you have agreed to help, she calls you back, thanks you for the offer, and says she would rather just put the money in the bank or use it for a vacation, and go on living with her problem. Not because the problem isn't genuinely bothersome. It's just that she *really* likes money, or that she *really* likes cruises. Much as she hates her problem, she hates even more having no money in the bank or never going on vacation. We noted that you wouldn't give her the money even though you do not doubt that the problem is severe enough to be worth spending substantial sums to alleviate. You do not doubt that she gets more utility out of putting the money in the bank or spending it on a vacation. Although she is your friend and you want to see her happy, nevertheless you will think her claim upon you much greater when it comes to health than wealth or vacation.

This example has a straightforward analogy in governmental assistance for the poor. Many of us would rather grant aid-in-kind than in cash. Not because we don't believe that the poor would be happier with money, which they could, after all, spend on the very things that aid-in-kind would otherwise provide. Not because we are necessarily paternalistic and think we know better what is good for the poor than do they. But rather because we believe that they only have a claim on our providing them the particular things usually granted as part of aid-in-kind: medical care, foodstamps, and the like.[28]

This fits well with a point I made about our tax system in Part I. Although the progressive tax aims at equality (not to create it, just to further it!), it does not aim at equality of happiness, only equality of income. We are not willing to tax Mother Teresa, Richard Feynman, or Robert Penn Warren as heavily as some much-better-heeled but much-less-happy corporate executive. The claim each of us has is to an equality of *things*, not an equality of happiness. Individual preferences are not the determinants of the tax burden we inflict on someone.

Our approach to sentencing criminals offers a final analogy. It is often said that justice requires us to equalize the punishment of those who are equally culpable. But that could mean either of two slightly different things: it could mean equalizing their actual sentences (jail time served), or equalizing their suffering. Since the purpose of punishment is to inflict suffering, it may seem as though equality of suffering is what ultimately we must be aiming for. But if we were, presumably we would want to punish more harshly the happy-go-lucky person who tends to make his peace with his surroundings, and who finds happiness wherever he is, than the melancholic person who is miserable no matter where he is. Again, individual preferences are not the determinants of the punishment burden we inflict on someone.

Let me remind you what these examples are meant to corroborate: certain kinds of harms are to be objectively rather than subjectively judged. Economists will find this very alien, although a few philosophers and an occasional economist have made some quite related points. Their focus, however, has usually been the objectivity of benefits rather than harms. "The fact that someone would be willing to forgo a decent diet in order to build a monument to his god does not mean that his claim on others for aid in his project has the same strength as a claim for aid in obtaining enough to eat," writes Thomas Scanlon.[29] And Ronald Dworkin argues in a classic essay on equality that it is resources and not welfare that the egalitarian should seek to equalize.[30]

Even if you are by now fully persuaded of the fallacy of the preference-based view, you may be troubled by examples like these: Smithy breaks into Bartleby's house and finds two vases. He cannot carry both of them off and, therefore, plans to steal only one. He is about to choose the vase he finds more attractive when Bartleby, who has been witnessing the entire break-in, starts to plead with him: "Please do not take *that* vase. It's far less expensive than the other one, but I happen to be much more attached to it."

Consider again two possible sequels to my story.

Variation I: Smithy says, "I don't care. I don't really want to sell the vase, and I happen to like this one better. So, whether or not it is the cheaper one, that's the one I'm going to take."

Variation II: Smithy says, "Fine. Although I would much prefer to take this one, and exhibit it in my living room, as a small concession to you I will take the other one and sell it."

Suppose that there are two theft statutes. One covering thefts of small value, the other covering thefts of greater value. Should the Smithy in Variation I really be punished less harshly than the Smithy in Variation II? Our previous analysis with its objective assessment of harm suggests as much. But can that really be?

I do indeed think it is so. The way to convince oneself is to imagine that a week earlier Smithy broke into Bartholemea's house and stole an expensive vase from her. Presumably he should be punished as severely for the theft of her expensive vase as for the theft of Bartleby's expensive vase, since we have no reason for thinking that she values her expensive vase any less than Bartleby values his. It is true that Bartleby values his cheap vase more than his expensive vase, but that doesn't mean that he values his expensive vase any less than Bartholomea values hers. To put the same point more broadly: if we took the position that what we are really after in assessing the wickedness of the theft is the victim's subjective sense of loss, then presumably the theft of $1,000 from a millionaire is a less serious affair than the theft of the same amount from someone less wealthy. And that would certainly seem odd. Or rather: my theory is no more absurd than the proposition that the theft of $1,000 from a millionaire ought to be deemed as serious, or at least nearly as serious, a crime as the theft of the same sum from a poorer man.

Blackmail Proper

How does any of this help us with blackmail? At first glance little. The punishment puzzle appears to be quite different from the blackmail puzzle. The burglar puts his victim to the choice of tolerating either one of two criminal wrongs. By contrast, the blackmailer puts his victim to a choice of tolerating either one of two things, neither of which appears to be a wrong: the payment of some money, or the occurrence of something unpleasant but perfectly legal. Nevertheless, the punishment puzzle and the blackmail puzzle share this crucial attribute: in both puzzles does the defendant's accommodation of the victim's preferences aggravate rather than improve his moral position. In both puzzles is the defendant considered worse, not better, for having gone along with the victim's choice. We now have a pretty complete explanation of why that occurs in the case of the punishment puzzle: culpability, and therefore deserved punishment, is only in small part a function of harm, whereas the victim's choice between two modes of defendant misconduct is exclusively a function of harm and, therefore, often at variance with deserved punishment. But can that explanation somehow be generalized so as to account for blackmail as well?

I think it can, and a small step is all that it takes. Consider side by side the following six attempts to extract money:

1. "Pay me $10,000, or I'll shoot you."
2. "Pay me $10,000, or I'll punch you in the stomach."
3. "Pay me $10,000, or I'll drive by your house at a negligent speed twenty times whenever I see your children out there playing."

    4. "Pay me $10,000, or I'll steal the heart of your bride."

    5. "Pay me $10,000, or I'll tell your bride some things about your past love life I'm sure she doesn't know."

    6. "Pay me $10,000, or I will no longer be your friend."

That (1) is a serious crime we can take as given. Most people would not think that there is anything puzzling about (2) either, because, after all, what the defendant is threatening, a battery, is criminal as well. But actually there is something puzzling about (2) which it is important to clarify. One might wonder whether it would be fair to punish the defendant more harshly for his robbery of $10,000 than for the assault. After all, the defendant gave the victim the option of being assaulted, and then he proceeded to take the $10,000 instead because that is what the victim preferred. *If the assault would be rated only a moderate wrong, then how can the taking of money—which the victim prefers to that moderate immorality—itself be anything more than a moderate immorality?*

    This is where our solution to the punishment puzzle comes in. The lesson of the punishment puzzle was that *when the defendant has the victim choose between either of two immoralities which he must endure, the gravity of the defendant's wrongdoing is to be judged by what he actually did (or sought to achieve), not by what he threatened to do.*[31]

    What about the defendant who uses (3) to get his money? The analysis is the same. He is threatening to do something wrongful—speeding by the victim's house twenty times while his children are playing—but the wrong he is threatening is not a crime, it is merely a tort (and will result in liability only if he ever actually runs one over). Again one might be led to wonder: "Would it be fair to punish the defendant more harshly for taking $10,000 than he would be for the tort of negligent driving, namely, not at all? After all, the defendant gave the victim the option of enduring the negligent driving in front of his house, and only proceeded to take the $10,000 instead because that is what the victim preferred. *If the negligent driving would be rated a mere tort, then how can the taking of money which the victim prefers to the commission of that tort itself be anything more than a tort?*"

    From our analysis of the punishment puzzle we know that *when the defendant has the victim choose between either of two immoralities which he must endure, the gravity of the defendant's wrongdoing is to be judged by what he actually did (or sought to achieve), not by what he threatened to do.* Nothing in our analysis of the punishment puzzle depended on the fact that the alternatives the victim was given to choose between were both crimes. All it really required was that the threatened action constituted a wrong, so that any advantage obtained on the basis of it constituted a wrong as well. The lesson of the punishment puzzle then tells us that the relatively minor wrongfulness of the threatened wrong does not prevent the leveraging of it into a major advantage from being a major wrong.

For the defendant who uses (4) to get his money the analysis is the same. Again he is threatening to do something wrongful—alienating the affections of the victim's bride—but the wrong he is threatening is not a crime. In fact, it is (probably) not even a tort. But it is certainly a moral wrong. That, however, does not seem to change any important part of the analysis. It is true that one might object as before: "Would it be fair to punish the defendant more harshly for taking the $10,000 than he would be for alienating the affections of the bride, namely, not at all? It's the kind of act that merits strong disapproval, shrill castigation, undying hatred, but not criminal punishment. Given that the defendant gave the victim the option of enduring the alienation of his bride's affection, and then proceeded to take the $10,000 instead because that is what the victim preferred, how can the taking of the money deserve more than strong disapproval, shrill castigation, and undying hatred?"

From our analysis of the punishment puzzle we know that *when the defendant has the victim choose between either of two immoralities which he must endure, the gravity of the defendant's wrongdoing is to be judged by what he actually did (or sought to achieve), not by what he threatened to do.* Nothing in our analysis of the punishment puzzle depended on the fact that the alternatives the victim was given to choose between were both crimes. All it really required was that the threatened action constituted a wrong, so that any advantage obtained on the basis of it constituted a wrong as well. The lesson of the punishment puzzle then tells us that the relatively minor wrongfulness of the threatened wrong does not prevent the leveraging of it into a major advantage from being a major wrong. (Do I seem to be repeating myself?)

The canonical blackmail case is seen in (5). The defendant threatens to reveal the victim's infidelities to his bride unless he gets paid. The wrong he is threatening is not a crime, it is almost certainly not a tort, it is quite simply a wrong. Again one might be led to wonder: "Would it be fair to punish the defendant more harshly for his taking of $10,000 than he would be for the wrong of revealing the victim's infidelities, namely, not at all? After all, the defendant gave the victim the option of enduring the revelation of the infidelities, and then proceeded to take the $10,000 instead because that is what the victim preferred."

Once again: From our analysis of the punishment puzzle we know that *when the defendant has the victim choose between either of two immoralities which he must endure, the gravity of the defendant's wrongdoing is to be judged by what he actually did (or sought to achieve), not by what he threatened to do.* Nothing in our analysis of the punishment puzzle depended on the fact that the alternatives the victim was given to choose between were both crimes. All it really required was that the threatened action constituted a wrong, so that any advantage obtained on the basis of it constituted a wrong as well. The lesson of the punishment puzzle then tells us that the relatively minor wrongfulness of the threatened wrong does not prevent the leveraging of it into a major advantage from being a major wrong.

I CONFIDENTLY asserted that for the defendant to reveal the victim's infidelities to his bride was a wrong. I was not claiming that it was a very major wrong, only a simple piece of "swinishness." But you might very well take issue with that. If for instance the defendant reveals the infidelities out of friendship for the bride, then one would certainly not want to regard it as a wrong. The typical blackmailer, however, is not threatening to act out of friendship for the bride but threatening to act by way of retaliation for not having been paid. And it's not really blackmail if something like retaliation isn't his motive.[32]

We are left then with the final of the six threats: "Pay me $10,000, or I will no longer be your friend." I do not believe this to be blackmail, but my reasons require explanation as to why the analysis would not be exactly the same as before. Sure, the victim is here confronted with a choice between two wrongs just as in the punishment puzzle, namely, taking the $10,000 or the cancellation of a friendship for purely mean-spirited, retaliatory reasons. The right way to think about (6), however, is to analogize it to the typical panhandler's threat. "Give me money, or I'll mutter some mean insults under my breath." Even if we regard the panhandler's muttered insults as wrong, we would view them as such minor wrongs that they do not invalidate the consent of the passerby who hands him some money. For the punishment puzzle's analysis to apply, it seems that the threatened wrong must exceed some de minimis threshhold: the retaliatory cancellation of a friendship does not seem to rise to that level.

I AM NOT SURE I have managed to convince you yet that the solution to the punishment puzzle offers the key to solving the blackmail paradox. If the above analysis did not persuade you, perhaps the following alternative route will.

Consider this hypothetical, based on an actual case: Anatole steals a Rembrandt from the Metropolitan Museum. He sends a letter to the museum which reads: "Pay me $10,000, or you will never see that Rembrandt again." The museum buys back its painting for $10,000. Anatole clearly is guilty of theft for taking the Rembrandt. But what about the second transaction? Is it a simple sale (as one German court held), or blackmail? ("Pay me $10,000 or else . . ." certainly sounds like blackmail.) Morally and legally, has the defendant made things better or worse, or has he pretty much left them the same by selling back the painting? The German court before whom this case arose decided on the last option, to view the transaction as just a sale that pretty much left the defendant's level of culpability where it was originally. Many people's intuition, however, is likely to be that the defendant improved things at least a little, because the victim (the museum) was certainly made happier being offered the painting for a buyback than having it remain in permanent possession of the defendant.

The punishment puzzle suggests another way of looking at the buyback. Anatole is basically in the position of Smithy, the burglar. He is putting the victim in the position of Bartleby, the homeowner. That is, he is asking the victim to tolerate one of two immoral courses of action: Anatole's continued possession of the stolen paintings, or his appropriation of the money the museum is being asked to pay for the buyback. The museum prefers the appropriation. The punishment puzzle taught us that this does not settle the question of moral culpability. Just because the museum prefers the second course does not mean the second course is less worthy of condemnation and punishment than the first course. Indeed, we usually treat continuing possession of a stolen good as not much of an aggravation of the original offense; and we don't even give all that much credit for the thief's return of the goods he stole. The continuing possession seems to lack the moral culpability of a theft. But an additional theft is what Anatole is in fact committing when he makes the museum choose between giving up one of two things it already owns, its money or its painting. Thus Anatole's sale makes things morally worse for him (much like the burglar's decision to batter rather than steal). The treatment he merits, having completed the buyback deal, is that of a two-time thief, the first theft being that of the painting, the second being that of the money he got in exchange for it.

Looking at the matter a bit differently, it seems at first that the buyback problem and the punishment puzzle are worlds apart. Unlike the burglar, Anatole is putting the museum to the choice between accepting Anatole's continuing noncriminal possession of the painting or paying him $10,000. But with only a little effort one can make that choice sound like the punishment puzzle. In essence, Anatole is saying to the museum: "Allow me to commit a further theft of $10,000 from the museum's treasury, or else accept the noncriminal wrong of my sitting forever on that Rembrandt." The only detail that distinguishes Anatole's offer from that of the burglar is that one of the threatened wrongs, the continued possession of the stolen painting, is not, or may not be, criminal. But since it still is a wrong, albeit a noncriminal one, the conclusion derived from the punishment puzzle seems to still apply: when a wrongdoer puts his victim to the choice between two wrongs, then the degree of blameworthiness is not much affected by the preferences of the victim. Hence even though the threatened wrong is noncriminal, the level of blameworthiness is no less than it would be if the threatened wrong were a criminal one—the level of blameworthiness is determined by the wrong committed, not the wrong threatened. Nothing about the fact that the threatened wrong is not criminal seems to affect the logic of my argument!

What this means more generally is that when a wrongdoer threatens a victim with two wrongs and then carries out the greater wrong, the degree of blameworthiness will not diminish as the wrongdoer starts to diminish the threat. To be sure, there comes a point when the wrong threatened is so minor that it no longer counts. At that point the balance tips and the transaction between wrongdoer and victim turns into a regular bargain with a level of blameworthiness of zero. If, for instance, Anatole's threat to the museum had not been to sit on the Rembrandt forever but merely to be surly with the museum director, that threat too would involve a wrong, but altogether too minor a one to turn the transaction into blackmail. (Even if we assumed the museum director to be so supersensitive that he might actually pay $10,000 to avoid being insulted by Anatole!)

We can now see the central problem with blackmail in a different light: the blackmailer puts the victim to a choice between a theft (or some other criminal encroachment) and some other, minor wrong. The execution of the theft then carries with it the level of blameworthiness of a theft. To be sure, the wrong must not be *too* minor. The mere threat to be nasty or unpleasant won't suffice; the immorality has to be more substantial than that. But it need not—and this is the crucial point—be an immorality that comes anywhere close to being criminal.

MY ANALYSIS WILL ALLOW us to gain a clearer understanding of the exact relationship between blackmail and more ordinary, "plain vanilla" forms of coercion. Blackmail is a form of robbery in which the threatened action is itself noncriminal—indeed, it is often perfectly legal—but still immoral. Because we tend to think—prior to thinking through the punishment puzzle—that the unconsented-to taking of another's property can morally be no worse than the threatened action would have been, we think that blackmail is unlike a straight robbery. Now that we know that the defendant's moral status is determined not by what he threatened to do but by what he actually did or sought to achieve (that is, take money without the owner's consent), we know that he is as bad as a robber.[33]

My analysis will also allow us to gain a clearer understanding of another puzzling feature of blackmail. In the archetypical case, the blackmailer threatens an unpleasant act unless paid off. What of the atypical case in which a person threatens an unpleasant *omission* unless paid off? That begins to sound very much like an ordinary bargain and, therefore, seems outside the ambit of blackmail. This happens in every contract negotiation—one party threatens to omit performing some beneficial deed unless suitably "paid off." To avoid collapsing all bargains into the blackmail category, we must insist that blackmail only include threatened acts, not threatened omissions. Or must we? For instance, what about the stranger who sees me drown at sea, who could easily throw a life vest my way, but who first makes me promise to pay him $10,000 for this easy favor? Isn't this blackmail?

Blackmail will generally but not invariably involve the threat of an act, because in my analysis it requires the threat of at least mildly wrongful conduct, and most even mildly wrongful conduct entails an act. Nevertheless, there are omissions that are at least mildly immoral: not throwing the drowning stranger a life vest, for instance. Hence, not surprisingly, it sounds like blackmail for the defendant to say to the drowning victim: "Pay me $10,000, or I won't throw you that life vest." In at least some jurisdictions, such requests have actually been criminalized—under statutory provisions that the drafters usually recognize to be variations of blackmail. An example is the German criminal code's provision on "usurious conduct" (*Wucher*), which is directed at defendants who "exploit the dire straits of another" for material advantage.[34]

AN OBJECTION: THE KREPLACH PROBLEM

One aspect of my account of blackmail is bound to seem very disturbing. As I describe it, the blackmailer puts his victim to a choice between a taking and some other minor wrong. The taking is then considered unconsented and carries a corresponding level of blameworthiness: that of a theft—if what was taken involves property; that of a rape—if what was taken involves sex; that of a kidnapping—if what was taken was the freedom to move about. The threatened wrong, I kept emphasizing, need not itself be a crime (hence the paradox of blackmail!), need not even be a tort, indeed need not be anything more than a sufficiently grave piece of obnoxiousness which all by itself would not merit legal intervention. To be sure, I also kept emphasizing that this does not endow blackmail with as sweeping a scope as first appears, because threats of nothing more than garden-variety mean-ness wouldn't qualify. On the other hand, although the threat has to be of something more serious than just everyday meanness, it does not have to be that much more serious. (I said it has to rise to the level of swinishness.) And that makes for a very odd-looking kind of offense: as the defendant's threat edges up on, but stays shy of, some ill-specified magical threshold (swinishness), he is merely considered a crafty, nasty, unsavory, slightly immoral negotiator. Once he has passed that thresh-old, his blameworthiness suddenly soars into the stratosphere—soars, that is, to the level of a regular blackmailer. That sort of radical discontinuity must seem both alarming and implausible.

We expect the path between moral and immoral conduct to be a pretty contin-uous one: as the defendant's conduct slightly changes, we expect his moral status to do the same. We don't expect a slight modification in someone's behavior to result in a radical shift in his moral status.

The problem with sharp boundaries in ethics is well captured by the joke about the Jewish boy who had a pathological fear of a dish called *kreplach,* an envelope made of dough with meat inside. To cure him of his fear, his mother had him watch her prepare one. After she had flattened a slab of dough and shaped it into a square, she asked him whether he was afraid. He said no. After she had inserted the meat and folded over one of the four corners of the *kreplach*-to-be, she again asked him whether he was afraid. He said no. After she had folded over the second and third corner of the nearly done *kreplach,* she asked him yet again if he was afraid. Still "no." But when she folded over the last corner, the peaceable expression on the boy's face suddenly gave way. "*Kreplach!*" he shrieked, and ran off panic-stricken. My theory of blackmail seems to put us in a similar position vis-à-vis the tough negotiator. As he gradually increases the immorality of the threats by which he seeks to pressure the other side, we keep telling him that his moral status is only getting marginally worse. Then, as he passes some boundary, we yell "Black-mailer!" By a single step, we seem to be saying, the person has turned from a cad into a thug. And that seems perverse.[35]

To be sure, the law exhibits such patterns not infrequently: one step shy of some critical line and you're safe; one step over that line and you're jailbait. But we don't think that this mirrors the underlying moral reality. We think it simply results from the need to have clear rules. Indeed, the long-standing debate about the relative advantages of rules and standards is built on the premise that the moral ideas and policies that motivate certain rules have tapered boundaries, and that the needs of fair notice cause these tapered boundaries to be transmuted into sharp edges when laws get formulated. My theory of blackmail, however, is itself a moral theory. If it gives the prohibition against blackmail sharp edges, that has nothing to do with considerations of clarity or fair notice. In fact, since I have not been able to spell out exactly where that sharp edge is located, the definition of blackmail that results from my theory manages to be sharp-edged without being clear. Hardly a virtue.

We are right to be surprised when we find discontinuity in the world around us, whether that be the moral, the social, or the natural world; but we are not right to be astonished. We are entitled to expect small causes to have small effects. But we are not entitled to invariably count on it. The philosopher Roy Sorensen aptly made this point about the natural world:

> An extremely tiny change in the velocity of an object can make the crucial difference as to whether it achieves escape velocity and travels far out into space, or fails to escape and crashes to earth. . . . A difference of one proton, one neutron, and one electron is responsible for the dramatic difference in the chemical properties of fluorine and neon. The question of whether the universe will expand endlessly or contract in on itself turns on the issue of whether the neutrino has appreciable mass. . . . A banana peel can elicit spectacular acrobatics from a lumbering pedestrian, and one vote amongst millions can determine the outcome of a presidential election.[36]

In the same spirit, the physicist Emilio Segre is quoted in the epigraph to Richard Rhodes's *The Making of the Atomic Bomb* as saying: "All the committees, the politicking and the plans would have come to naught if a few unpredictable nuclear cross sections had been different from what they are by a factor of two."[37]

At least one kind of natural phenomenon is notorious for such discontinuities—human perception. Think of those legendary experiments in gestalt psychology in which subjects swing from seeing something as a duck to seeing it as a rabbit, from seeing someone as a young woman to seeing her as an old hag, from seeing the Necker cube bulge in to seeing it bulge out, from seeing two dark faces against a white background to seeing a white wine glass against a dark background, from hearing only one strain in a musical canon to hearing only another, or (to quote a quip of Richard Posner's) from thinking law and economics obviously false to thinking it obvious.

Social scientists have started to accumulate examples of such discontinuities in the social world. The anthropologist Michael Thompson offers an especially striking one: the process by which one generation's rubbish becomes another generation's valued antique. Commodities will gradually obsolesce into a state of rubbishhood, where most of them in fact remain. But a few formerly discarded items will suddenly regain value. They won't do so gradually. Rather after a brief period of hovering in a limbo of indeterminate value they positively soar out of the junk heap, their price leaping from less than zero (because it costs something to dispose of them) to Sotheby levels.[38]

I am inclined to offer the iterated prisoners dilemma paradox as another illustration. We know that although it is rational to defect in a regular prisoners' dilemma, it will frequently no longer be rational to defect if the game is meant to be iterated an indefinite number of times: now there are future gains to be had from cooperating. The paradox arises because it seems that if the game is slated to be played an exact number of times, say 1,000, it again becomes rational to defect. (It will be rational to defect on the last game. Hence it will be rational to defect on the next-to-last game; hence it will be rational to defect on the next-to-the-next-to-last game, and so on to the very first game.) That makes for a striking discontinuity between long-lasting games of indefinite and definite length. Game theory is said to be full of such discontinuities. If it captures even a fraction of the amount of social reality game theorists claim it does, discontinuity is really the order of the day.

My most potent argument, however, against those who are skeptical about such discontinuities in the moral world is to point out that we already know it to exist at the moral heart of the criminal law, the doctrines of mens rea. Take a look at the notion of negligence. The most natural interpretation of negligence is the "Learned Hand" formula: one is acting negligently if the costs of one's actions discounted by their probability exceed the benefits discounted by probability. But if one does behave negligently, blameworthiness will be measured by either the expected or the actual harm, not by the difference between the expected harm and the expected benefit. In other words, if a speeding driver runs over someone, and he is just one scintilla short of being negligent (because the expected costs of his speeding are exactly one scintilla short of the expected benefits), his conduct is morally beyond reproach. But if the speeding driver is just one scintilla past the point of negligence (because the expected costs of his speeding are exactly one scintilla greater than the expected benefits), he is guilty of manslaughter. So the definition of negligence has a very sharp edge indeed.

Consider next the mens rea of knowledge. To harm knowingly is deemed appreciably worse than to harm recklessly or negligently. Yet the transition between recklessly and knowingly bringing about harm lies at some fairly precise point somewhere on top of 90 percent, dubbed "virtual certainty." So again there is no gradual shading of bad into worse but a rather sudden jump from bad to terrible.

There is a second kind of discontinuity involving the mens rea of knowledge. Suppose someone falls well short of recklessness because the appreciable harm he risks is outweighed by the appreciable benefits he can expect. As the probability of the harm rises past the threshhold of virtual certainty the benefits suddenly cease to count and blameworthiness soars from zero to a level measured by the harm knowingly brought about. That is, the defendant who takes a 45 percent chance of losing a life in exchange for the certain rescue of two other lives has not killed recklessly if someone should die. But the defendant who takes a 90 percent (that is, two times 45 percent) chance of losing a life in exchange for the certain rescue of four (that is, two times two) other lives has committed a murder for the sake of saving four other lives, something which we usually do not permit.

Consider, finally, intention. If the defendant intends to kill someone by an act that has an extremely small probability of succeeding (such as giving his victim an airplane ticket in the hope that the plane he takes will crash), he is not guilty of murder even if his victim dies.[39] But as the probability rises, while still staying well short of the substantial level required for negligence (not to mention recklessness or knowledge), it will reach a point where, combined with the hope of death, it makes for an intentional killing. Thus the defendant's culpability rather suddenly jumps from zero to murder, without ever traversing the intermediate levels of a negligent or reckless killing.

Once one starts looking for them, the moral world seems to abound with such discontinuities. Our attitudes toward death seem to display them. We know the passage into death to be a fairly continuous process involving a gradual cessation of a variety of life-sustaining functions. The dying person becomes increasingly less life-like and increasingly more corpse-like. But the dying person's rights do not change so continuously. Very little in the way of bodily invasion can be committed against someone just at death's door; nearly everything can be done to him just past that point.

Our attitudes toward voting in a national election display a similar discontinuity. When I ask students whether they feel a moral obligation to vote, they generally say yes, while fully acknowledging that the chances are one in a gazillion that their vote is going to make a difference to the outcome. Voting, they often add, has a symbolic importance for them. I then proceed to ask them to imagine themselves to be traveling abroad while a presidential election is being held. "You do not have an absentee ballot," I add, "but the local American embassy has organized a 'symbolic' voting booth, in which visiting Americans can cast their presidential vote. To be sure, the vote won't count for anything; the ballots will be thrown away; but you will have an opportunity to cast your vote. Would you seize that opportunity?" Everyone I have ever asked has said no. I then continue to press them: "What if the embassy told you that the votes will be counted just in case the election turns out to be in the balance, the chance of which is of course one in a gazillion?" Now most respondents say they would vote. That shows the morality of voting to have an incredible discontinuity built into it: with a zero chance of making a difference, people will not vote. With a one-in-a-gazillion chance, they will.

One final example of radical moral discontinuity. Think about the sort of loyalty alumni feel vis-à-vis their alma mater. Imagine that a part of the University of Pennsylvania were to break off, migrate to Valley Forge, and call itself Valley Forge University. Valley Forge University would command next to none of the old Penn's alumni loyalty and financial support. But suppose we gradually increase the number of faculty who migrate from the University of Pennsylvania to Valley Forge University and actually start to move some crucial parts of the physical plant—the Ben Franklin sculpture, the portal to the law school, the Palestra—as well. There surely would come a *point* where Valley Forge University would come to be viewed as the proper continuation of the University of Pennsylvania. I underscore point, because it would be a point, not an interval. Relatively suddenly nearly all alumni would shift their allegiances from the place in Philadelphia to the place in Valley Forge. It would not be the case that as the place in Philadelphia started to look less and less like the old Penn, and the place in Valley Forge started to look more and more like the old Penn, allegiances would gradually drift. The change would be a discontinuous one.[40]

What this survey is meant to show is that discontinuities of the kind exhibited by my account of blackmail are unusual enough to be interesting but not so unusual as to be incredible.

ANOTHER BLACKMAIL PARADOX

Imagine the following: someone has found out about your affairs and is determined to reveal them to your spouse, not out of friendship for your spouse, just out of hatred of you. He has no intention of blackmailing you, all he is aiming for is your exposure and embarrassment. Having somehow learned of his plans, you seek him out and offer him a substantial sum of money for his silence. He accepts. Is he guilty of blackmail? Absolutely not. He never threatened you. He merely let himself be bribed by you. But isn't that strange, that a mere change in who takes the initiative, should turn what would otherwise be blackmail into legal conduct? Strange though it is, it certainly is the case. The law and our moral intuitions are quite firm on this. The legal scholar Sidney DeLong has called this "the second paradox of blackmail: it is not unlawful for one who knows another's secret to *accept* an offer of payment by the unthreatened victim in return for a potential blackmailer's promise not to disclose the secret. What would otherwise be an unlawful blackmail exchange is a lawful sale of secrecy if it takes the form of a 'bribe.'"[41] How odd; how mysterious; how come?[42]

It will help to dissolve the "second paradox of blackmail" to think about a simple robbery. Here too something like the "second paradox" arises, only it is no longer paradoxical. As I walk down the street, I am approached by a dangerous-looking individual carrying a baseball bat and staring at me menacingly. "Mister, can you help me . . ." he begins. I quickly reach into my pocket, pull out a wad of $10 bills, and hand them to him. He beams, looks downright friendly now, thanks me profusely, and moves on. I did what I did because I was sure he was about to rob me. Let us suppose I was right and that I simply succeeded in "bribing" him into not robbing me. What's more, let us suppose that he actually played on my fears and hoped that I might try to "bribe" him with a preemptive gift without his ever having to utter an explicit threat. (He has done it to many others, and we can pin down his motives conclusively from a very self-revelatory diary he keeps.) Is he guilty of robbery? I should think not. And any robber who consistently manages to thus "restructure" his robberies into such "voluntary donations" is well within his rights.

The "second paradox of blackmail" simply forces us to relearn the chief lesson of Part I of this book in the context of blackmail, that form matters crucially to the morality of one's conduct, and that it is, therefore, often moral to achieve indirectly what would be immoral if achieved directly. Remember, I actually used a blackmail example to first suggest as much: Mildred's transmutation of a threat into a warning.[43] It is useful to be reminded of this lesson, because there are numerous other paradoxical-looking aspects of blackmail that dissolve in the light of it. They all arise out of cases in which a blackmailer seems to be committing blackmail "by other means." Until we forcibly remind ourselves of the moral significance of form, it seems paradoxical that he should be able to get away with it.

To fully appreciate this point, think back to the buyback problem, the story of Anatole who stole a painting and sold it back to the museum for $10,000, a fraction of its true worth. Exchanging the painting for $10,000, I argued, constituted blackmail even though it made things better for the museum than if he had not engaged in the transaction. Anatole, I argued, is guilty of two separate offenses: stealing the painting to begin with, and then blackmailing the museum by threatening not to return it unless he was paid $10,000. Some of my colleagues were very uncomfortable with my view of this case because they noted that if we change the nature of the stolen object from a painting to money, something very odd seems to happen. Imagine, asked Anthony D'Amato of Northwestern University, that instead of breaking into a museum and stealing a painting, Anatole had broken into a bank and stolen a sack of money containing, say, $100,000. Suppose further that as in the original case he developed second thoughts after sitting on the money for a while, and he decided to send the bank a note: "Promise to pay me a reward of 10 percent for the money I shall be returning, or else you will see none of it ever again." Assume the bank was only too happy to acquiesce: Anatole turned the bag of money over to them, and they in turn gave him a bag with $10,000. Under my analysis, he would now be guilty of the blackmail of $10,000, in addition to the theft of the $100,000. The reason this struck D'Amato as strange was this: suppose that rather than asking for a 10 percent commission Anatole had simply removed $10,000 from the bag and returned the $90,000 to the bank. Now he would be guilty only of the original theft, and quite possibly he would have his guilt mitigated by the partial return of the money. The fact that he got $10,000 out of it would not be considered to aggravate his guilt. How can the result be different if he returns the money in exchange for $10,000, when in the end it really comes to the same thing? A penny saved is a penny earned. Right? Wrong! Ethically speaking, a penny saved is not a penny earned. Turning-the-trolley is different from not-turning-the-trolley-and-carving-someone-up-for-his-organs, even though the end result is the same. Marrying for money is different from going where the money is and then marrying for love.

THE INSIDER TRADING PUZZLE

My account of blackmail gives us the tools, I believe, for solving another long-standing puzzle—insider trading. What is puzzling about insider trading is that, as with blackmail, most people think it is wrong but cannot say why. Unlike blackmail, however, insider trading does not wear its puzzling nature on its face. Figuring out why it is so puzzling will take some paragraphs of explaining.

The canonical case of insider trading is this: the CEO of a company learns from his engineers that they have struck an oil field. Before the news becomes public, he buys up a lot of stock in his company. When the news is finally announced, the stock price shoots through the roof; the CEO resells the stock and makes a bundle. Most of us will, at least initially, feel great outrage at the CEO's conduct. Our first difficulty in justifying that outrage will be that the CEO didn't actually tell anyone a lie. So this is not a straightforward case of fraud. But that thought needn't detain us long. Sometimes it amounts to fraud for a buyer to withhold some crucial piece of information from the seller, namely, where there is a special fiduciary relationship between buyer and seller. Just as we would think it unseemly for someone to sell his friend a car without telling him that a car with lower mileage and in better condition can be had from a used car dealer in the neighboring town for a few thousand dollars less, so the law requires that those who are our "professional friends"—trustees, brokers, agents of various sorts—make extensive disclosures to us before transacting business with us. Thus the fact that the CEO defrauded his shareholders by withholding information rather than by lying is probably no compelling reason not to call what he did fraud.

To see what's puzzling about insider trading we will need to ask ourselves who has been hurt by the insider's trading: Who is the victim of his alleged wrongdoing? Why, the seller of the soon-to-be-valuable stock, of course. Or so we are tempted to reply. The stockholder who gave up his stock to the insider looks like the person with the grievance. *But only at first glance.* Think more closely about the situation of the seller. He owns some stock which for one reason or another he thinks he wants to sell, either because he needs money or because some other investment has started to look good to him. He, therefore, offers it up on the open market where it is snapped up by the insider. What would have happened if the insider had not been there to buy it? *Someone else would have bought it and would probably have bought it at the very same price.* Later on, as the newly discovered oil field is announced, the seller would of course be kicking himself for selling prematurely. But he would be kicking himself whether the insider was buying up shares or not, because he would have sold his stock no matter what. So in fact the seller of the stock has not been hurt by what the insider did. What is objectionable, then, about the insider's activity?

If the sellers of the stock aren't the victims of insider trading, who is? Could it be that no one is? Not likely. After all, the insider did get richer. That money must have come out of somebody's pocket. But whose pocket? Which victim? Well, if not the person who sold the stock, then the person who would have bought the stock if the insider had not bought it. It is of course nearly impossible to tell who those persons would have been, but there clearly would have been such people. They are the victims. The problem is that, although they would in fact have been better off if the insider had not engaged in trading, they do not at all look like the typical fraud victim. Their relationship to the insider is a very indirect one.

What makes the problem even harder is that there is a strong argument that, once we take the proper view of the matter, even these potential purchasers have not really been hurt by the insider's activity. Economists have pointed out that there are many economic benefits associated with insider trading. Allowing insiders to trade on their special knowledge can function as an effective form of incentive compensation. If insiders can trade on special knowledge they have concerning recently discovered oil fields, that might act as an extra spur to discover such oil fields. That's only the most obvious benefit. Another one arises from the fact that once insiders start to trade on their special information, they will gradually cause the stock price to rise, and thus can subtly let the market know about economically significant developments without actually having to announce what they are. This is important if making an outright announcement of the discovery would spoil its value to the company, as would happen if the company announced its finding of oil before it had actually been able to buy up all the land on which the oil field is located. To be sure, there are economic costs to allowing insider trading as well: for instance, insiders may delay the release of important information until they have had a chance to trade on it. Whether the economic benefits outweigh the economic costs of insider trading is quite uncertain. But if they do, then all shareholders, including those who do not get to buy some stock because the insiders buy it up instead, reap the benefits. That's because stock values in general will be higher as a result, and that increase more than makes up for what is lost when a stockholder does not get to buy some stock because an insider bought it instead.

The puzzle arises because we abhor insider trading regardless of these arguments. We not only abhor it if we are convinced that on balance it is economically harmful. We continue to abhor it, or many of us do, even if we conclude that it is economically beneficial. Why, then, does it feel unfair?

The puzzle is further heightened if we imagine that the company, recognizing the economic benefits of insider trading, expressly authorizes it, that in all of its advertising literature, it prominently displays a statement that "This company believes in letting its insiders trade. If you don't like it, don't buy our stock." Under these circumstances, the question then presents itself with special force: What could possibly be unfair about insider trading? Stockholders have been fully forewarned—and are benefited to boot. They have assumed the risk, and on balance they come out ahead as a result.

Many economists, foremost among them the lawyer-economist Henry Manne, who was the first to understand and make everyone else understand the puzzling nature of insider trading, have concluded that in the end there is nothing really objectionable about insider trading under the above circumstances. They say that it is just lack of understanding that makes us react with such visceral outrage. This is of course an avenue that has tempted some, though fewer, in connection with blackmail. Is Manne right? How could he possibly fail to be? *How can we justify not letting stockholders, who ardently want to, assume the risks associated with investing in companies whose insiders engage in insider trading?*

A RED (BUT NOT UNSAVORY) HERRING: IGNORANCE AND INCOMMENSURABILITY (STRICTLY OPTIONAL, TO BE SKIPPED BY THOSE WHO HATE DETOURS)

One reason an assumption of risk argument is said to fail occasionally is that it is too uninformed. For instance, the Securities and Exchange Commission has rejected an attempt by a company to absolve itself of liability by issuing stock with this accompanying prospectus:

> (i) The present directors do not foresee the possibility of the corporation ever being in a position to pay any dividends or having any assets of determinable value. The continued existence of the corporation is questionable. Bankruptcy may result at any time.

(ii) Anyone considering purchase of this security must be prepared for immediate and total loss.

(iii) No representation is made that the possibility exists that the corporation can continue to exist.

(iv) No representation is made in this statement that the President or Secretary of the company have any capability that can benefit the corporation in any way.

(v) In view of the above unfavorable factors, and other unfavorable factors in every part of this offering circular, it would appear that it is self-evident that any prospective purchaser of [the stock of this company] should be prepared for immediate total loss.[44]

The potential investors, the SEC presumably thought, had been told too little to make an informed choice.

But does the notion of an uninformed assumption of risk make any sense? It presupposes that there is a difference between well-informed and poorly informed risk takers. But wherein lies the difference? It would seem as though every poorly informed risk taker could be recharacterized as a well-informed risk taker of a slightly larger risk encompassing the facts the ignorance of which made us call him poorly informed. Conversely, it would seem as though every well-informed risk taker could be recharacterized as a poorly informed risk taker of a slightly smaller risk. In other words, the purchaser of a stock about which next-to-nothing has been disclosed can be viewed as the well-informed investor of a very uncertain, open-ended venture. Otherwise, there is nothing to prevent someone from viewing the purchaser of a lottery ticket as an inadequately informed consumer, because he doesn't know whether his is the winning ticket. Or in other words: the uninformed assumption of a small risk is equivalent to the well-informed assumption of a big risk—a risk including uncertainty of the facts about which the decision maker was uninformed.

But there lurks behind this objection a valid intuition that somehow the uninformed decision maker's choices don't merely become riskier but also less rational. I will try to refine that intuition into a coherent claim. Experimental psychologists have, of course, compiled an amusingly long list of the cognitive foibles to which decision makers under risk are subject, and I have no wish to recapitulate those. I believe that the lack of information causes irrationality in a much more fundamental way than is suggested by these experiments, and that even those who are relatively immune to the psychologists' pet howlers cannot escape this kind of irrationality. To see this requires a little digression. Or maybe I should say a big digression, because, although short, it will at first glance not seem to have anything to do with the assumption of risk.

THERE IS A notorious form of argument which lawyers run into all the time and are never quite certain how to cope with, and for that very reason often try to use on others the "slippery slope" argument. Here is a typical instance of this argument as it might be used on behalf of a criminal defendant. The lawyer wants to persuade the jury that what his client has done has not reached the level of a criminal attempt, that what he did never went beyond "mere preparation." His basic argumentative strategy will be simple. He will divide what the defendant has done into a million little steps. The first few steps will clearly not amount to an attempt, and every additional step will be so small that we will find it difficult to say that *that* step should make the difference between guilt and innocence. We will find it difficult because when we compare our moral aversion toward the person who has actually bought his gun to our aversion toward the person who has also bought the binoculars he will need for this venture, the two seem indistinguishable in intensity. It would, therefore, seem that *moral* sentiment does not furnish us with a reason for treating the two cases differently. But since the route between merely thinking about murder and actually firing one's gun can be crossed by taking a large enough number of such steps, it is easy to maneuver us into concluding that there is no moral difference between the person who has merely thought about murder and the person who fired the gun. But where did we go wrong? Which of those steps were we not entitled to take?

I would argue that we made a mistake each step of the way. The mistake was in thinking that sufficiently small differences are imperceptible and, therefore, irrelevant. In fact, many cases deemed indistinguishable—whether along moral or any other grounds—are quite distinguishable if only one looks at them in the right way. What I have in mind is this: imagine that we had to rank by length 10,000 sticks which vary between one meter and two meters. The smallest of these is one meter long, the longest two meters, others being evenly distributed between them. In other words, each stick differs from its neighbor by about a tenth of a millimeter. A tenth of a millimeter is an imperceptibly small distance—so small that when two sticks differing by that much are placed side by side, the human eye is incapable of determining which is longer. Suppose that a millimeter is the smallest perceptible length-difference. Given that the differences between each stick and eighteen of its neighbors generally will be imperceptible, it would seem impossible to rank these sticks by length. First appearances notwithstanding, however, it can be done.

One simple method would be to take two sticks that seem indistinguishable and check to see if there is a stick that is distinguishable from the one but not the other. There will be at least one such stick: a stick that is one millimeter longer than the shorter of the two sticks will be indistinguishable from the longer and easily distinguishable from the shorter of the two. Use this trick often enough and you will achieve a perfect ranking of all sticks.

The lesson that can be drawn from this example is that what is indistinguishable on direct inspection may be quite distinguishable indirectly. Thus, our moral aversion to the would-be murderer who has bought the gun and to the would-be murderer who has bought gun *and* binoculars may be indistinguishable on direct inspection but perhaps not on a three-way comparison. Suppose we compare (1) the gun purchaser, (2) the gun-and-binocular purchaser, and (3) the gun-and-binocular-purchaser-who-has-also-rented-a-car-in-which-to-carry-out-his-plan. Cases (1) and (2) seem indistinguishable, (2) and (3) seem indistinguishable. But (1) and (3), on the other hand, seem distinguishable. One could conclude, therefore, that there is an important perceptible difference between (1) and (2), albeit one that is only indirectly perceptible: they differ in their degree of similarity to a third case. If (1) and (2) were genuine equals on the scale of moral aversion, this could not happen.

Could we always use this trick when two alternatives we are considering seem too close to directly distinguish—that is, find a third alternative which is distinguishable from the one but not the other? Unfortunately, the trick won't always work. It will often lead to inconsistency. The reason is instructive, and it takes us back to the question with which we began this section: the inherent irrationality of uninformed risk assumption.

Suppose someone were asked which of the following two bets he preferred: a 55 percent chance of getting $1, or getting 50 cents straight out. He might find it hard to decide. But he is not sure whether that is because he is genuinely indifferent or because he simply cannot distinguish his feelings about items that are very close together on the preference scale. He decides to use the above method. He notices that he would prefer a 60 percent chance of winning $1 to a 55 percent chance of winning $1, but that between a 60 percent chance of winning $1 and a sure 50 cents he would still be uncertain. He concludes that the sure 50 cents alternative must be slightly higher on the preference scale than the 55 percent–$1 combination (since 55 percent–$1 is clearly inferior to 60 percent–$1, whereas 50 cents-for-sure is not).

But if he so concludes, he is going to get trapped in self-contradiction. For if he were to engage in a bit more introspection, he would find that he was indifferent between a 55 percent shot at $1 and a sure 51 cents. But since 50 cents is clearly inferior to 51 cents, whereas a 55 percent shot at $1 is not, this would by the above logic imply that he likes the 55 percent shot at $1 better than the sure 50 cents— exactly the reverse of what he concluded in the previous paragraph.

W HY DOES THE method that worked so well for sticks fail us for bets? The reason will become obvious if we imagine that some of those sticks had their sizes written on them, and that in discriminating between sticks we failed to pay attention to whether we were doing it on the basis of coded sizes or on the basis of our perceptions. We might then conclude that a stick marked 1.0005 meters is longer than an unmarked stick of length 1.0007 meters because only the 1.0005-meter stick is easily distinguishable from the (marked) 1.0000-meter stick. That is, our method fails to work when some sticks are more easily comparable—or, in the language of ethics, more *commensurable*—than others. It will then lead us to confuse small but clear differences with large but less clear differences. Something like this probably explains the sense behind the proverb that a little knowledge is a danger-ous thing. More important, however, it explains our inconsistent ranking of risks. Our ability to distinguish 51 cents from 50 cents and our inability to distinguish either from a 55 percent shot at $1 does not mean that the 55 percent–$1 combina-tion lies between the two, but only that 50 cents and 51 cents are more commensu-rable than 50 cents and a 55 percent shot at $1.

Anytime incommensurability makes its way into someone's decision making, his decision ceases to be very meaningful. To see this clearly, imagine someone who is asked to choose between buying a Toyota and buying a Honda. Suppose he is indifferent. What if we were to toss an extra option for the Toyota into the balance: a passenger-side airbag at no extra cost. Would that necessarily decide the buyer in favor of the Toyota? It need not. If he is like most of us, he might well continue to feel indifferent, even with that extra factor in favor of the Toyota. The reason for this odd state of affairs is incommensurability. He is indifferent when it comes to choosing between the Honda and either of the Toyotas, not because he is in equipoise but because he finds them somewhat incommensurable. He is not indifferent of course about the merits of the regular Toyota and the Toyota with the extra airbag. These he finds highly commensurable: he prefers the extra airbag, since it's at no extra cost. The result is that if he is asked to choose between a regular Toyota and a Honda he might well choose the Toyota (since he is indifferent about the advantages of each). If asked to choose between the regular Toyota and the Toyota with extra airbag, he would of course choose the one with the airbag; but if asked to choose between the Toyota with airbag and the Honda, he might well choose the Honda (since he is indifferent). This kind of intransitive behavior many would consider the hallmark of irrationality. Anyone who exhibits it in the course of making up his mind about certain alternatives has not made a very meaningful choice.

Whenever people are asked to choose between very uncertain prospects, incommensurability is likely to figure very prominently in their decision. If people are asked to choose, for instance, between what's behind Curtain A and what's behind Curtain B—without having been told anything much about what might be behind those curtains—they are likely to behave like my car buyer. They will be indifferent between A and B and they will not be decisively moved in the direction of A even if they are offered some special goody along with whatever is behind A. With so little known about A or B, the two alternatives are deeply incommensurable, and A-plus-that-goody will continue to be incommensurable with B. Therefore a choice between the three alternatives is apt to exhibit intransitivity and thus to seem quite suspect.

One might thus argue that the reason the assumption of risk argument fails with insider trading is that investors are just too uninformed to make consistent choices. The problem with this explanation is that people often make decisions in a state of profound uncertainty, replete with numerous incommensurable alternatives, and we hold them to those decisions. So the problem with insider trading has to lie elsewhere.[45]

Another Red Herring:
The Hidden Victims of Insider Trading
(Also Optional)

Perhaps, though, the reason the assumption of risk argument fails with insider trading has to do with the peculiar relationship between the insider and the eventual victim of his trading. Remember that the person who suffers the loss is generally not the person who was selling the stock the insider bought but the person who would have bought the stock if the insider had not traded, that is, the person who never actually got to buy the stock. If the assumption of risk argument depends on the fact that the corporation announced to its potential shareholders that it was going to allow its insiders to engage in trading and that by buying the company's stock they consented to that, then how can victims who never actually owned the company's stock be said to have assumed the risk? In other words, for the assumption of risk argument to justify insider trading, the victim of insider trading must have had some interaction with the perpetrator that can be read to constitute an assumption of risk. The injury of insider trading, however, seems to befall someone who never had such an interaction with the insider.

Alas, I think in the final analysis this feature of insider trading is a red herring too and will not really explain what is wrong with it. To begin with, this argument only applies if it is the company that adopts a rule permitting insider trading. It does not apply if it is the stock market that adopts such a rule. For in that case presumably anyone deciding to trade on that stock market has assented to the rules by which it is run, and this holds for the people who did not get to purchase the stock the seller was making available. And yet we have a strong aversion to allowing a stock market to adopt such a rule, even if it were proven to be (as some economists have contended) highly efficient.

There is a second point. We could imagine away this peculiar "causal" feature of insider trading and yet we still would not allow insider trading. Let's suppose for instance that in every case it is really the activity of the insider that induces the seller to sell. Now the victim clearly is the person who sells the stock, the person who has assumed the risk by investing in the company whose stock he is selling. Nevertheless, we feel averse to allowing such a rule to be adopted.

Finally, the entire argument is built on the idea that the person who would have bought the stock if the insider had not been trading is the victim of his activities. It is perfectly true that that person is the only person who would be better off if the insider had not traded. But does that mean we should refer to him as the victim? Is everyone who is adversely affected by some wrongdoing of ours our victim? Suppose I run an illegal gambling operation. If I do this over a prolonged period, it is a statistical certainty that some of the people visiting the premises are going to have traffic accidents on the way to or from my premises. I have clearly engaged in wrongdoing by running the gambling operation, and the victims of those traffic accidents would clearly not have been injured if I had not engaged in this wrongdoing. But can they be described as the victims of my wrongdoing? I should think not. It would seem as though the relationship between the insider and the potential buyers of stock the insider bought is if anything more tenuous than this.

So what is wrong with insider trading?

THE REAL PROBLEM WITH INSIDER TRADING: FIRST VERSION OF THE ARGUMENT

Here are the steps of my moral argument against insider trading. I develop it with the help of some studiously ridiculous examples. Their ridiculousness stems from their emphatically schematic nature. Their clarity is intended to make up what they lack in natural grace and realism.

Step 1

Hanno's favorite hobby is the piano. Indeed, it is one of his chief joys in life. One day Hanno has a traffic accident. As he is pulled from the rubble, he cannot immediately tell what is wrong with him, but something does feel wrong. What he first notices, to his great alarm, is that the mobility of his hands is somewhat impaired. He has himself delivered to the next emergency room. There is precisely one physician, Marie, in attendance at the emergency room. Fortunately, there is no other patient around, and Marie will be able to devote herself to Hanno immediately. Alas, as Marie is about to examine Hanno's hands, a second patient, Ernest, is brought in. Ernest has suffered an injury to his left leg and is in such a condition that unless immediately attended to he will lose the use of that leg. Marie explains to Hanno that Ernest presents a more compelling case for her services and that he will have to wait. Hanno asks why. Marie is astonished.

"Surely, a case in which someone is about to lose the use of a leg is more pressing than one in which at worst someone will lose a little manual dexterity and thus perhaps not be able to play the piano as fluently as before."

"You don't understand," Hanno replies, "My piano playing is very important to me. If I am unable, or even just much less able, to play it, that will really take much of the joy out of my life. By contrast look at Ernest over there. I happen to know him. He is always depressed. With or without the use of that leg he is not going to be a happy person. You would do more for humanity by attending to my problem first."

"Ridiculous," says Marie, "the loss of a leg is a graver matter than the loss of some manual dexterity. And that's true whether you place some special value on your manual dexterity or not, and whether this depressed patient will be made much happier by my helping him or not. Preserving a leg is more important than preserving full manual dexterity, and, therefore, Ernest has more of a claim to my assistance than do you."

Marie is about to act accordingly, but then something else happens. Hanno notices that he has some injuries that neither he nor Marie have noticed so far. To be precise, he notices that he has some serious problems moving his legs, which so far he paid no attention to out of his great concern for his hands.

"Look here," he says, "I seem to have some real difficulty moving my legs." Marie looks over in Hanno's direction, and clearly he is right. Indeed, Marie immediately realizes that the problem Hanno is experiencing in both of his legs is identical to the problem Ernest is experiencing in his one injured leg. In other words, Marie realizes that if he is not immediately attended to he might lose the use of both of his legs, whereas Ernest, if not attended to, only risks losing the use of one of his legs.

"All right," Marie says, "I suppose I really should take care of your legs before I attend to Ernest."

As she is about to do so, Hanno makes a special request.

"Frankly, while I would be gravely disappointed if I were to lose the use of my legs, I would be even more disappointed if I were to loose some manual dexterity. I would much prefer it if rather than taking care of my legs you first took care of my hands."

Question: What should the doctor do?

Answer: I have contrived this example so that she has precisely three alternatives: treat Ernest's leg first, treat Hanno's two legs first, or treat Hanno's hands first. (Let's assume that treating one of Hanno's legs and then treating Ernest's leg is not an option. You could imagine all sorts of reasons why that might be so.) Each alternative, however, will on closer inspection turn out to have significant drawbacks. Each will seem pretty unpalatable. Let's examine why.

The most obviously unpalatable alternative is treating Ernest first. It is unpalatable because it seems unfair to save his one leg when the same amount of effort could save Hanno's two legs. Saving two legs is better than saving one.

The second alternative, treating Hanno's legs first, seems pretty unappealing as well. After all, he is pleading with the doctor to do his hands. It is his body. Why shouldn't he be able to decide which part of it gets saved? If he gets more pleasure out of having his hands saved than his legs, then, assuming we believe that he knows what he is doing, shouldn't we respect that?

So what is wrong with the third alternative, treating Hanno's hands first, just as he is requesting. Well, if the doctor does do that, Ernest is going to protest: "How can you judge Hanno's manual dexterity more important than my ability to walk?"

T HE DOCTOR of course could try to reply: "I don't really put his manual dexterity above your ability to walk. I simply let him trade in his right to get his legs treated first for the right to get his hands treated first."

To this, however, Ernest can now reply by marshaling some of the examples we encountered in the course of solving the punishment puzzle earlier. He asks the doctor to think about the case of the friend who might ask him for financial assistance so she can deal with a bothersome medical problem and after having been assured on that score calls him back to see if she can use the money for a cruise instead. He also makes the analogy to governmental assistance to the poor, which we grant in kind not because we are paternalistic and think we know better what is good for the poor than do they, but rather because we believe that they only have a claim on our providing them the particular things usually granted as part of aid-in-kind: medical care, food stamps, and the like. Ernest then points out to Marie that letting Hanno trade in his right to have his legs treated for the right to have his hands treated first is like letting the friend trade in a $2,000 medical subsidy for a $2,000 contribution to her bank account, or like letting a poor man trade his aid-in-kind for something else he would like better. Just as the friend only has a claim on another friend for medical assistance, not for a contribution to his wealth, just as the poor only have a claim on the rest of society for certain aid-in-kind (like food and medical care and education) and not for other kinds of goodies (like stereos or cruises), so Hanno only has a claim on the doctor's attention for treating his legs first, not for treating his hands first.

If this last argument is persuasive—and I find it so—it renders the last alternative unacceptable, and takes the wind out of our objections to the second alternative. Thus the moral course for the doctor is to treat Hanno's legs first.

Step 2

Consider a boxing match. Before going into specifics, let me make the following assumptions: (1) assaulting someone—that is, hitting him—is a crime, provided it is done either intentionally or recklessly; (2) boxing is *not* a crime, even though it consists of what would ordinarily count as assaults, provided it has been preceded by appropriate consents (waivers) from the participants.

Bertram and Cuthbert are both hobby boxers. One day Bertram, who has never yet fought Cuthbert, asks him for a match. Cuthbert being the stronger and more expert fighter is somewhat reluctant. He is worried about injuring Bertram. He is especially worried because no referee is around, and he fears that in the throes of a fight he might not notice it if the reeling Bertram should signal him to stop. He tells Bertram about his concerns. Bertram, a lawyer, quickly draws up a waiver formally stating that Bertram would be taking his chances. To be precise, the agreement says that Bertram would shoulder the risk of Cuthbert inadvertently, indeed even recklessly, continuing to hit him even after Bertram has tried to tell him to stop. But just to make sure that, notwithstanding this waiver, Cuthbert will still make a good faith effort to watch his step, the agreement adds that Cuthbert would in the event of a mistake (if it should have injurious consequences) be liable to Bertram for a specified sum of damages, let us say $1,000. Notice that this waiver is a little bit different from the usual waiver given in a boxing match, in which each party simply agrees to let the other try to get in as many hits as he can for the duration of the match.

The match begins. Just a few minutes into it, having received some fairly heavy blows from Cuthbert, Bertram indicates that he wants to stop. Cuthbert thinks to himself: "It looks like he wants to stop. But I'm not sure. I'd say there is a 70 percent chance he is indicating he wants to stop and a 30 percent chance that I am misreading his signals. Since I have that signed waiver from him, 30 percent seems like a good enough probability for me to proceed. If worse comes to worst, I'll have to pay him $1,000 in damages." And so he inflicts another heavy, and as it turns out very injurious, blow on Bertram.

Question: Is Cuthbert guilty of (reckless) assault, or should Bertram's waiver bar a conviction?

Answer: I believe the waiver in this case should be ineffective, because this case is analytically equivalent to the preceding one. We can make as much of an argument for requiring Cuthbert to ignore the waiver as we can for requiring the doctor to ignore Hanno's pleas to treat his hands rather than his legs.

Bertram has a claim against the state for protection against reckless and intentional assaults. He wants to trade in that right, much as Hanno wants to trade in his right for treatment of his legs for treatment of his hands, and as your friend wants to turn in his "right" to medical support from you for a right to some money, and as the poor might want to trade in their right to food stamps for a right to a CD. But since Bertram's claim on the government is not one for a certain amount of utility, and since your friend's claim upon you is not for a certain amount of generic support, and since the poor's claim upon society is not for a certain amount of pleasure, those claims are not exchangeable.[46]

Step 3

Leave everything the same in the above example but replace assault with some other form of wrongdoing, say, fraud. Nothing about the analysis, you will find, materially changes.

Bertram and Cuthbert are both entrepreneurs. One day Bertram, who has not yet done any business with Cuthbert, asks to invest in a company Cuthbert happens to be running. Cuthbert is a bit reluctant to let him. The reason, he explains to Bertram, is that he is often seized by the urge to purchase additional stock in his own company from other investors, but he is apt not to tell them certain material facts that have triggered such an impulse in him (like the discovery of an oil field), facts that would probably affect their decision to sell. In other words, he is worried that he might go so far as to buy stock from Bertram, which the latter if he had knowledge of all the facts would not consent to sell to him. He, Cuthbert, would then be guilty of defrauding someone to whom he owes a fiduciary obligation. Bertram declares that he is willing to shoulder that risk. Cuthbert is skeptical, but Bertram repeatedly reassures him. Finally, Cuthbert makes a proposal. It provides that in case Cuthbert should recklessly purchase stock from Bertram without disclosing a material fact, the latter waives his right to complain about fraud. Nevertheless, just to make sure that Cuthbert still makes a good faith effort to watch his step, he shall in such cases be liable to Bertram for a specified sum of damages, let us say $1,000.

Bertram invests with Cuthbert. One evening they have dinner at Cuthbert's apartment, where a friend of Cuthbert's also happens to be in attendance. In the course of dinner, Bertram mentions that he would like to sell Cuthbert some of his stock and asks him if he knows of anything that should make him hesitate to do so. Cuthbert says no. Cuthbert's friend in fact knows about a few things in Cuthbert's ken that he thinks material, things that he believes might well affect Bertram's decision to sell. While he is helping Cuthbert clear the table, he tells him so. Cuthbert replies: "You may be right. I would say there is a 70 percent chance that you are correct and that Bertram would in fact not be willing to sell if he knew those things. I would also, however, say that there is a 30 percent chance that you are wrong and that he would consent. Since I have that signed waiver from him, 30 percent seems good enough for me to take a chance on. If worse comes to worst, I'll have to pay him $1,000 in damages." And so Cuthbert purchases Bertram's stock, which in fact the latter would not have done had Cuthbert disclosed to him what he knew.

Bertram presses charges for fraud and for withholding of material information, namely, the information Cuthbert thought had a 70 percent chance of changing Bertram's mind about the sale.

I believe the waiver in this case would be ineffective, because this case is analytically equivalent to cases 2 and 3 above. We can make as much of an argument here for requiring Cuthbert to ignore the waiver as we can for requiring the doctor to ignore Hanno's pleas to treat his hands rather than his legs and Bertram's assault waiver before the boxing match.

Step 4

Typically of course the insider does not sit down with his victim for dinner. Typically he does not promise a fixed fee for every instance of retrospectively "nonconsensual" trading. But those are immaterial differences. Replace the dinner table with the stock exchange and the $3,000 fee with the pecuniary advantages that flow from investing in a company that allows insider trading and you have the canonical case.

THE REAL PROBLEM WITH INSIDER TRADING: SECOND VERSION OF THE ARGUMENT

Now for a different way of getting to the same result.

Step 1

All members of a small society get together one day to consider revising their criminal laws. Not too long into the proceeding, a fellow gets up to make this statement: "As everyone knows, there are some rare occasions where the interests of the community would be served by punishing an innocent. When for instance a rabble threatens to burn down the town and cause innumerable deaths unless a suspect, whom the authorities may well know to be innocent, is summarily executed. Under those circumstances I would like to give the authorities permission to appease the rabble by executing him." No one likes the idea of executing an innocent. But no one likes the idea of being killed by a rabble either. Since the odds of the former are clearly smaller than the odds of the latter, everyone agrees to the proposed reform.

Shortly thereafter a woman gets up. "As everyone knows, many people are killed and maimed each year by drunk drivers. So far we have only convicted drunk drivers of manslaughter and jailed them for but a few years—and that only if they have actually run someone over. I propose to occasionally impose the death penalty for drunk driving and to do so regardless of whether the driver has actually run someone over. On balance, this ought to result in a significant saving of lives at the slight cost of an occasional execution of a drunk driver. Even if you yourself had no control over whether you were going to be a drunk driver or not (which of course you do), on balance you are still better off with such a regime because your chances of dying as a victim of another drunk driver have been reduced much more than your chances of being executed as a result of drunk driving have been increased." No one likes the idea of executing a drunk driver. But no one likes the idea of being run over by a drunk driver either. The odds of the former being clearly smaller than the odds of the latter, everyone agrees to the proposed reform.

Shortly thereafter another fellow gets up: "We all know of cases where punishment is pretty pointless. Just think of the case of the robber-rapist who has inherited a fortune and has had an accident that makes it impossible for him ever again to feel any sexual impulse. Nothing is achieved in the way of prevention or deterrence by keeping him in jail, and it costs a lot of money to do so. I propose that in such cases we waive punishment." No one really likes the idea of not punishing deserving thugs, but no one likes the idea of paying hefty sums to keep them in jail either. The latter being a tangible cost, and the former being nothing more than a vague ideal, everyone agrees to the proposed reform.

Soon another woman gets up: "Negligent wrongdoing has cost this town much more than intentional wrongdoing. I therefore propose that we increase the punishment for negligent wrongdoing and lower the punishment for intentional wrongdoing." No one really likes the idea of punishing intentional wrongdoers less than negligent wrongdoers, but no one is happy with the losses currently suffered as a result of negligence. Seeing that the overall losses are going to be reduced by increasing punishment for the one and decreasing punishment for the other, everyone agrees to the proposed reform.

Now a young man speaks: "I have noticed that in this town many lives are lost when bad samaritans fail to come to the aid of people whose lives they could easily save, whereas intentional killings are exceedingly rare. I propose to increase the punishment for letting someone die to the level we currently reserve for actual killings and to reduce the punishment of active killers to that we currently have for bad samaritans: general disapproval but no actual jail time." No one likes the idea of letting killers go free and punishing severely bad samaritans who don't really leave the world any worse than they found it. But they also realize that they are far more likely to stay alive under a regime which punishes omissions and does not bother with actions, and thus everyone agrees to the proposed reform.

Another woman says: "Many of us value our property far more than our bodies. It should be an option for those who do to officially register their preference and in return be able to use deadly force to defend their property but only nondeadly force to protect their bodies." This too meets with general assent.

Says a man: "I just have a small matter to raise. Remember the case we had the other day involving someone who operated a trolley on which the brakes suddenly failed. He let the trolley run into five people, and when they were mortally injured and needed organ transplants, he killed the person on the other track whom he could have killed in the first place if he had turned the trolley, and used his organs to save the other five. We said that was impermissible. Well, I would say, we should allow whatever it is that maximizes the number of lives saved. And just as you would be willing to allow him to turn the trolley because that maximizes the number of lives saved, you should allow him to do what he did." Although everyone feels uncomfortable acquitting someone who did what this man did, they all realize that they are far more likely to survive under such a regime, and so everyone agrees to the proposed reform.

Another woman gets up: "I have conducted a study and found that con artists make the best corporate executives. We are depriving ourselves of great talents by locking them up just because they have committed one or another scam. I propose to eliminate the punishment for major frauds. On the other hand, corporate negligence costs us a lot of money and I propose to increase the punishment for it." This reform too meets with general assent.

What about these proposals? Are they permissible? Is it moral to punish someone consistent with these reforms? I think not, because that would result in graver punishment than people deserve. But doesn't consent change desert? Aren't these Pareto-optimal bargains? They are admittedly pareto optimal, but they do not change desert. Desert cannot be changed by contrast. We actually saw this already when we were talking about positive as opposed to penal desert. Just remember those contracts between the two mathematicians de l'Hospital and Bernoulli, or the agreement between John F. Kennedy and his alleged ghostwriters, or the agreement between Siegfried and Gunther. Here it was obvious that desert could not be contracted away. (Although of course it could be alienated in more devious ways, such as the one I imagined the first microscope maker and user Leuwenhook as resorting to in order to help his son! Namely, making the equipment available to him exclusively.) Now we are extending this lesson: Merit generally, whether positive or negative, cannot be contracted away. Consent to give up merit does not succeed in transferring it. To be sure, the incentive will always be there to do so. But that's irrelevant to the issue of its morality.[47]

Step 2

This kind of argument ought to be least surprising to someone already skeptical of plea bargaining. And the arguments against plea bargaining are quite formidable, some contrary argumentation notwithstanding. Let me restate them briefly in the form of a hypothetical based on the movie *The Morning After*.

A woman wakes up next to a dead man and a gun with her fingerprints on it. She was severely drunk the previous night and has no recollection of what happened. Given the situation she wakes up in, she has every reason to think that she killed him. She is arrested and charged with the man's murder. The prosecutor is delighted: the woman has been implicated in a number of fatal "accidents" in the past, but there never was adequate proof for a conviction. At last, it seems, he will be able to take her out of circulation. But shortly before the trial, the prosecutor learns of some surprise evidence: a film of the events on the night of the murder that has, somehow or other, come to rest in a certain safe deposit box. The film will settle, once and for all, whether the defendant or someone else is to blame for the murder. The prosecutor is less than pleased fearing that this evidence perhaps could exonerate the defendant whom he has for so long tried to lock up.

He tells the defendant about the new evidence. He also tells her that he doesn't know yet whether it will be exculpatory or inculpatory. The defendant is as uncertain as he. Both are simultaneously hopeful and fearful. The prosecutor then suggests a plea bargain—a significantly more lenient sentence than the one that would result from a murder conviction, but a heavy sentence nonetheless. The defendant accepts his offer.

Should we permit this plea bargain to go through? It is a bargain both sides desperately want to strike: neither side wants to be exposed to the not insignificant risk that the evidence might not turn out "well." Nevertheless, I suspect, in this case, even those who ordinarily have no problem with plea bargains must have qualms: after all, whatever the evidence finally reveals, we are 100 percent certain to regret our present decision to let the plea bargain go through. We are certain to regret it because if the evidence proves the defendant guilty, we will have let her off too lightly, and if it proves her innocent, we will have been too harsh. A decision we are certain to regret a moment from now should presumably not be made.[48]

Because plea bargains are so plainly morally problematic, they can help us understand why the reform proposals in Step 1 are also problematic. The two are problematic for the same reason: both involve contracting out of one's just deserts. In fact, the reform proposals can be thought of as nothing more than very fanciful kinds of plea bargains.

To see this, imagine that the agreement in my *Morning After* hypothetical is struck not *after* the death has occurred, but before. In other words, it is set up as an agreement among all citizens that *if* someone should ever find himself in the position of the woman and *if* someone else should ever find himself in the position of the prosecutor and *if* the lay of the evidence should be what it is in this case, they would all agree right now to do what the parties in this case are in fact crying out to do: settle on a moderate sentence. This kind of agreement already starts to look a lot like the reform proposals in Step 1. To close the loop, imagine next that the parties to the agreement extend its scope by having it apply to drunk driving cases: they agree that evidence of drunkenness will henceforth be considered the equivalent of evidence to kill. And the plea bargain we have now arrived at is one of the original reform proposals.

Step 3

We can extract an argument about insider trading from all this without too much further ado, since insider trading is just a special case of fraud, and we have already shown it to be morally impermissible to contract out of the rule against fraud. That's what the woman who had discovered that con artists make great corporate executives was proposing be done.

BLACKMAIL, INSIDER TRADING,
AND AMARTYA SEN'S LIBERTARIAN PARADOX
(STRICTLY OPTIONAL)

It may render many of the claims I made in previous sections less paradoxical, if I show you how they are related to a certain well-known paradox of long standing, to wit, Amartya Sen's so-called Libertarian Paradox. It will also serve to render that famous, but ill-understood, paradox less paradoxical.

Amartya Sen has argued that there is a deep, irreconcilable tension between believing that people have rights and believing in the freedom of contract. Those two things being what most libertarians typically profess, Sen's claim that they are irreconcilable is startling indeed, startling enough to qualify as a Paradox. Sen's argument runs as follows. To believe that people have rights is to think that every person has some protected sphere within which he can do as he pleases regardless of what other people think, or more broadly even, that it is usually all right to do as one pleases so long as one doesn't harm someone else. This would mean, for instance, that if Mr. Lewd enjoys reading and rereading *Lady Chatterly's Lover* and Mr. Prude does not, then Lewd is free to read it, regardless of how much this offends Prude, and Prude is free to avoid it, regardless of how much such prudishness irks Lewd. The paradox arises, says Sen, if we flesh these facts out a bit further. Let us suppose that Lewd is really anxious to loosen old Prude up a bit, so anxious that he would gladly give up his own copy of the book, indeed would give up his very right to read any copy of the book, if he could persuade Prude thereby to expose himself to its contents: he would happily promise never again to read the book if in exchange Prude would promise him to read it himself. Let us further suppose that just as Lewd is anxious to loosen up Prude, Prude is anxious to reform Lewd, so anxious that he would actually be willing to expose himself to the book's contents, if he could thus avert Lewd's spending time with it. Under these circumstances, Sen points out, freedom of contract dictates that the two be allowed to strike a bargain in which Lewd commits himself not to read the book and Prude commits himself to read it. But once they have struck that bargain, once we have given freedom of contract its sway, we have then done away with each person's protected sphere, each person's right to determine what he shall read and not read regardless of what someone else thinks. The only way to preserve those rights would be to limit freedom of contract—to prohibit Prude and Lewd from striking the bargain they both want to strike.

Many commentators have shown themselves utterly befuddled by Sen's argument, and they have in turn charged Sen with being befuddled. They refuse to recognize anything paradoxical in what Sen is pointing to. They say that Sen is simply confused about what it means for people to have rights, and that once that confusion is cleared away no tension between rights and freedom of contract remains. When someone has a right to do something, Sen's critics say, then one way of using that right is to sell it. Lewd and Prude are each making use of their right to determine what they read by selling it to the other. They are in this way enjoying their rights (their protected sphere) as well as full freedom of contract. Where is there a paradox?

With the help of what I said about blackmail and insider trading, we will, I think, be able to see just exactly what the point of Sen's paradox is, and how his critics are missing it. Let's take a closer look at the Lewd-Prude situation. Specifically, let's examine more thoroughly than we have so far what the world is like before they strike their bargain and what it will be like after. To begin with, ask yourself what would happen if, prior to making their bargain, either of the two parties quite simply tried to get his way against the other's will—if, for instance, Prude tried to just tear Lewd's copy away from him, or if Lewd tried to shove an amply illustrated copy in front of Prude's nose. If either of them tried to invade the other's rights in this way, the victim would of course be able to summon the police, to have the aggressor stopped in his tracks and duly punished.

Next ask yourself what would happen if, after entering into their agreement, either of the two parties tried to get his way against the other's will. "Getting one's way against the other's will" of course means something slightly different after the agreement than before: Lewd, for instance, might try to welsh on his promise by xeroxing the book before turning it over to Prude and then reading it anyway. Prude, in turn, might just sit on the book after Lewd has turned it over to him, refusing to open it. If either of them tried to invade the other's rights in this way, would the victim again be able to summon the police, to have the aggressor stopped in his tracks and duly punished? No, of course not. He can sue for breach of contract and seek damages, but he can't get the police to treat the breach like a crime and have them punish the offender accordingly.

But why exactly is that? Why are we not willing to take freedom of contract so far as to treat noncompliance with the terms of an agreement as being the kind of rights-invasion which one can call on the police to stop, and which one can have the perpetrator thrown into prison for committing? The situation is actually quite analogous to a set of examples we have encountered repeatedly by now: their most notable representative was the case of the friend who calls you up for help with her medical problems and later wants to put the cash you offered her to some other use. Lewd and Prude here occupy the position of your friend and the state occupies your position. It's as though Lewd had first said to the police: "Are you prepared to help me if Prude should try to medle with my right to read my book?" (Just as your friend asked: "Are you prepared to help me with my medical problems?") The police reply: "Of course. You have a deep and inviolable right to read what you want." (Just as you replied: "Of course. You have a deep claim on me as a friend to help you with your medical needs.") A little later Lewd calls back: "I changed my mind. I decided I would rather give up my right to read *Lady Chatterly* in exchange for the right to make Prude read it. He agreed to that. Will you help me if Prude should try to meddle with my right by not doing as he promised?" (Just as your friend called you back and asked: "I would really rather use the money for a cruise. It will make me happier than to see my medical problems relieved. Will you still help me?") To which the police reply: "Forget it. Protection against physical intrusion is one thing. Protection of your contract rights another. We aren't available for that." (Just as you replied: "Forget it. Help with your medical needs is one thing, help with a cruise is another. I'm not available for that.") It's not that you doubt that your friend would be made happier by a cruise than by the medical treatment; it's not that the police doubt that you will benefit more from contract enforcement than protection from physical intrusion. It's just that you have a stronger claim for their assistance with one than with the other.

But why exactly do the police think that you have more of a claim to be protected against physical intrusion than against breach of contract? The observations made earlier in our discussion of the punishment puzzle apply: an act is worse than an omission; an interference with your body is worse than an interference with mere extensions of your body—like your property. In fact this is the essence of what a libertarian believes. One cannot be a libertarian without taking the act-omission distinction very seriously, without believing, that is, that causing harm to someone by an act is far worse than harm one causes by not coming to his assistance. Which by the above logic then leads to some serious limitations on one's freedom of contract.

I have tried in the last few pages to illuminate Sen's Libertarian Paradox by looking at it as just a version of the blackmail and insider trading paradoxes. In the next few paragraphs I will try to do the reverse: to illuminate blackmail and insider trading by looking at them as just versions of Sen's Libertarian Paradox.

Each of the bargains described in my second version of the argument against insider trading is exactly like the Lewd-Prude deal and could be analyzed in precisely the same terms. In particular, the bargain exchanging your right to be protected against fraud (specifically your right to be fully informed by your fiduciary of all he knows before he buys your stock from you) in return for a higher rate of return is like that. If after having signed such a waiver you still insist on not being cheated by your fiduciary, that's like insisting on Prude's not interfering with your reading of the xerox you kept of *Lady Chatterly*. You are entitled to insist on such noninterference notwithstanding your contractual waiver. Prude may not physically interfere with your reading of the xerox. The most he can do is to seek contract damages from you. Similarly, the corporate fiduciary who had you sign a fraud waiver cannot use it to prevent you from insisting that he heed his obligations as a fiduciary and tell you everything a fiduciary has to tell his client. At most he can seek some sort of contractual recovery from you, like the recovery of whatever he gave or promised you in exchange for the waiver.

What about blackmail? How is that a special case of Sen's paradox? You have a claim to be subjected to no more than severe disapproval when you reveal a husband's infidelity to his wife, at least when you do so out of something other than kindly concern for her. You have a claim to be subjected to nothing more severe than a tort judgment when you behave with noncriminal negligence. The blackmailer, who is threatening to tell the wife about her husband's infidelity, or to drive by his victim's house twenty times everyday with noncriminal negligence, is offering to exchange these claims for something else, a claim for money typically. The blackmail doctrine makes the blackmailer as unable to exchange those claims for money as your friend is to exchange his claim on your kind help with medical bills for help with a cruise.

THE SHORT ANSWER
Blackmail

Were I to put my argument about blackmail into the tiniest of nutshells, it would go like this: the essence of blackmail resides in a strange, anomalous-looking fact. The defendant manages to leverage the threat of a mild wrong into a substantial advantage, and this leveraging is deemed by us a very major wrong. The so-called punishment puzzle—involving an eccentric homeowner who prefers taking a beating to losing a valuable heirloom—shows why this fact is not so strange and anomalous after all. It is a natural, but somewhat counterintuitive, consequence of the fact that blameworthiness is a function not merely of how much the victim hates the wrong being done to him but also a function of other attributes of the wrong, such as mens rea, actus reus, and so on. The fact that blameworthiness depends on these other attributes implies that situations will arise in which the victim will prefer to be subjected to a greater rather than a lesser wrong; which, in turn, implies that the victim's judgment cannot be trusted to rank wrongs; which, in turn, implies that a defendant who persuades his victim to accept a larger wrong in lieu of a smaller wrong should in fact be deemed guilty of the larger wrong. This is exactly what the blackmail doctrine does.

Insider Trading

In discussing my solution to the insider trading puzzle with others, I elicited the following objection: "What your argument comes down to is this. You say that one cannot consent to a wrong. Insider trading is a wrong. Therefore one cannot consent to it. But we've known all along that one cannot consent to a wrong. What we haven't known is whether insider trading is a wrong. You assume the latter and prove the former. But the former needs no proof. It's obvious. And the latter you leave as puzzling as ever."

Here is my response: "Few people have trouble accepting the idea that insider trading absent consent is wrong. And even as to those who do not accept that, there is nothing mysterious about the reasons that make them hesitate: Should silence ever count as fraud? Is the relationship between investor and company manager the sort that should suspend caveat emptor? What is genuinely mysterious is how it is possible to continue to treat insider trading as wrong even though there has been consent to practice it. We generally think that you can consent to a wrong and that it no longer is a wrong when you do. If you consent to a theft, it becomes a gift. If you consent to a rape, it becomes lovemaking. If you consent to a knifing, it becomes surgery. My argument is meant to show why consenting to insider trading is different."

Earlier in this book I noted that it is impossible to consent to the alienation of fame. I also noted that someone bent on alienating fame can in fact accomplish that end if he is willing to be sufficiently roundabout. I offered the example of Antony Leeuwenhoek, whose great talent as a lensmaker enabled him to make some major microbiological discoveries. Had Leeuwenhoek wanted to alienate his fame to his son, we saw, it would not have sufficed for him to "consent" for his son to receive part of the glory that would otherwise accrue to him. But what he could have done, had he wanted to, would have been to give his son exclusive access to his precious lenses and thus to put him in a unique position to make similar discoveries. In other words, while the first way of consenting to the alienation of fame does not work, the second one does. Consenting to intercourse (or a taking or a tackling) I claim to be like the second way; consenting to insider trading is like the first way.

PART THREE

The Misappropriation of Glory

THE PROBLEM

THE MILITARY HISTORIAN Richard Holmes writes about the research leading up to his book *Acts of War:* "[W]hatever men might say in public about
decorations, in private they were eager to discuss them at length, and my notes on
decorations eventually came to fill more index cards than those for any other single
subject."[1] The sociologist Robert Merton comments in the same vein:

> I have arrived at [this] rule-of-thumb . . . : whenever the biography or auto-
> biography of a scientist announces that he had little or no concern with pri-
> ority, there is a reasonably good chance that, not many pages later in the
> book, we shall find him deeply embroiled in one or another battle over pri-
> ority. A few cases here must stand for many. . . . Harvey Cushing writes of
> the brilliant Halsted that he was "overmodest about his work, indifferent to
> matters of priority . . ." Alerted by our rule-of-thumb, we find some 20
> pages later in the book where this is cited, a letter by Halsted about his
> work on cocaine: "I anticipated all of Schleich's work by about six years (or
> five) . . . [In Vienna], I showed Woelfler how to use cocaine. He had de-
> clared that it was useless in surgery. But before I left Vienna he published an
> enthusiastic article in one of the daily papers on the subject. It did not, how-
> ever, occur to him to mention my name." . . . Ernest Jones [writes] in his
> comprehensive biography that "Although Freud was never interested in ques-
> tions of priority, which he found merely boring, he was fond of exploring
> the source of what appeared to be original ideas, particularly his own" . . .
> In point of fact, . . . Freud expressed an interest in priority on more than
> 150 occasions. With characteristic self-awareness, he reports that he even
> dreamt about priority and the due allocation of credit for accomplishments
> in science.[2]

"Strange thing, this recognition," muses the mathematician Mark Kac,

> I recall my father telling me about a teacher of mathematics he had had in a
> school in Odessa which he attended briefly. The teacher, V. F. Kagan, was

internationally known for having given a simplified solution of one of Hilbert's famous problems and for many other important contributions to geometry. He applied to the University of Odessa, a miserable provincial school of no distinction at all, for a Doctor's degree,. . . . As part of the requirement Kagan had to defend a dissertation and on the day of the examination he met my father. . . . ."Why do I seek their recognition?" [he wondered out loud,] "There is no one on the committee who can possibly understand what I have written?" This is an extreme example but it does make one stop and think as to what it is all about. The fact is that when recognition comes, whatever the source, it brings with it pleasure. And when it fails to come, a degree of bitterness may be generated that can be destructive. That is the way we are and there is no use pretending that it is otherwise.[3]

Such intense feelings need not be in one's own behalf. Witness Ralph Waldo Emerson's ill-tempered (and in fact unjustified) outburst over the fact that America is not named for its true discoverer: "Strange . . . that broad America must wear the name of a thief. Amerigo Vespucci, the pickle-dealer at Seville . . . whose highest naval rank was boatswain's mate in an expedition that never sailed, managed in this lying world to supplant Columbus and baptize half the earth with his own dishonest name."[4] (Truth be told Amerigo had nothing to do with this misnomer. The fault lies with some confused early mapmakers who attached a peculiar significance to the fact that Amerigo, who really did travel to the New World, was the first to recognize that it was a separate continent.)[5]

Of course, when pleading their own case, most people will try to artfully disguise their thirst for glory as something else altogether. The craving was one that Ludwig Wittgenstein, for instance, would never deign to admit. Yet he fell prey to a painful bout of it when a contemporary, Rudolf Carnap, published a book containing several ideas that Wittgenstein considered his own. Although Carnap acknowledged Wittgenstein's help with the book, the latter was not appeased. "He did not mind a small boy's stealing his apples [he said], but did mind his saying that the owner had given them to him," and he never talked to Carnap thereafter.[6]

Lee Iacocca covers his desire for credit with a patina of good-humored indifference: "I'm generally seen as the father of the Mustang, although, as with any success, there were plenty of people willing to take the credit. A stranger asking around Dearborn for people who were connected with the Edsel would be like old Diogenes with his lantern searching for an honest man. On the other hand, so many people have claimed to be the father of the Mustang that I wouldn't want to be seen in public with the mother!"[7]

But some glory seekers approach the subject with refreshing forthrightness. Galileo adopts this disarming stance in the preface to *The Assayer,* in which he thunders openly at those who have

> attempted to rob me of that glory which was mine by pretending not to have seen my writings and trying to represent themselves as the original discoverers of these impressive marvels. I say nothing of certain unpublished private discussions, demonstrations and propositions of mine which . . . have sometimes been stumbled upon by other men who with admirable dexterity have exerted themselves to appropriate these as inventions of their own ingenuity. Of such usurpers I might name not a few. I shall pass over the first offenders in silence, as they customarily receive less severe punishment than repeaters. But I shall no longer hold my peace about one of the latter, who has too boldly tried once more to do the very same thing he did many years ago when he appropriated the invention of my geometric compass, after I had shown it to and discussed it with many gentlemen years before, and had finally published a book about it. May I be pardoned if on this occasion—against my nature, my custom and my present purpose—I show resentment and protest (perhaps too bitterly) about something I have kept to myself all these years. I speak of Simon Mayr of Guntzenhausen. . . . Publishing under the title of *The World of Jupiter,* he had the gall to claim that he had observed the Medicean planets which revolve about Jupiter before I had. . . . But note his sly way of attempting to establish his priority. I had written of making my first observation on the seventh of January, 1610. Along comes Mayr, and, appropriating my very observations, he prints on the title page of his book (as well as the opening pages) that he had made his observations in the year 1609. But he neglects to warn the reader that he is a Protestant, and hence had not accepted the Gregorian calendar. Now the seventh day of January, 1610, for us Catholics, is the same as the twenty-eighth day of December, 1609, for those heretics. . . . [S]o much for his pretended priority of observation.[8]

But few glory seekers can top the unabashed petulance with which the Polar explorer Roald Amundsen lashed out at Umberto Nobile, who had been the pilot in the Amundsen-Ellsworth expedition's flight across the North Pole. Amundsen spent the better part of a one-volume memoir puncturing Nobile's pretension to having played a major part in that expedition and vindicating his own, dominant role. "[That] strutting dreamer," he expostulated in a typical paragraph about Nobile, "[that] epaulleted Italian, who six months before had no more thought of Arctic exploration than he had of superseding Mussolini as the Chief of State, . . . shall not be permitted to usurp honors that do not belong to him. This record is written to prevent it."[9]

The preceding I should hope would convince you, if convincing you needed, that the theft of glory, however quaint a preoccupation it may seem at first, is no small beer. Alexander Pope may have given that preoccupation its most memorable form in his long poem "The Temple of Fame," whose closing lines hold this pious plea:

> [And] if no basis bear my rising name,
> But the fall'n ruins of another's fame;
> Then teach me, heav'n! to scorn the guilty bays,
> Drive from my breast that wretched lust of praise,
> Unblemish'd let me live, or die unknown;
> Oh grant an honest fame, or grant me none!

This then sets the stage for our problem. The question, which the last line of Pope's poem is meant to spark in you, and for which the preceding examples were meant to provide the kindling, is, *What exactly constitutes an honest fame, what a dishonest fame?* What are the rules, criteria, precepts, principles, if there be any, by which we decide whom to accord how much glory for what achievement, and by which we decide who has laid claim to fame that isn't his? Are there such rules, and do they span the full range of moral, scientific, and artistic accomplishments for which glory is bestowed?

It may seem very unlikely that there are rules of such wide applicability. After all, even just the category of moral achievement is a rather broad one. It encompasses, as the philosopher J. O. Urmson noted, the achievements of both saints and of heroes, which he observed are rather different. In general, he points out, a saint is someone who endures temptations to which most us yield, a hero someone who endures risks which most of us flee. And intellectual achievement is of an even more varied kind, in turn giving rise to sundry kinds of glory: As the writer C. P. Snow remarked to the mathematician G. H. Hardy, "Even if we grant that Archimedes will be remembered when Aeschylus is forgotten, . . . mathematical fame [is rather more] 'anonymous.' . . . We could form a fairly coherent picture of the personality of Aeschylus (still more, of course, of Shakespeare or Tolstoi) from their works alone, while Archimedes and Eudoxus would remain mere names." (To which Hardy replied that if Snow thought that the Shakespearean kind of fame was better than the Archimedean, he was mistaken. "If I had a statue on a column in London, would I prefer the column to be so high that the statue was invisible, or low enough for the features to be recognizable? I would choose the first alternative [even if Dr. Snow would choose the second].")[10] How could there possibly be rules that hold for such a wide and varied terrain?

Let me advance a slightly bizarre-sounding suggestion: one not unnatural place to look for such rules is the criminal law, consisting as it does of the rules we use to blame people. It isn't unnatural to think that those rules might have some relationship to the rules by which we praise them. The heart of the criminal law is made up of something commonly referred to as the "General Part," which refers to a set of rules that have relevance regardless of the specific crime with which someone is charged. They are the rules that define the meaning of a voluntary act, the distinction between an act and an omission, the meaning of the various mental states with which a crime can be committed (for example, intention, knowledge, recklessness, and negligence), as well as settling various other matters having to do with causation, complicity, criminal attempts, and the most general of defenses such as self-defense, insanity, necessity, and duress. The question we thus need to answer is how those rules, which were designed after all for the apportionment of blame, might help us with the apportionment of praise. The following conjecture suggests itself: since the very notions of praise and blame sound like mirror images of each other, could it be that the rules governing their apportionment are mirror images of each other as well, that the rules of praise are somehow symmetrical with those of blame, symmetrical enough anyway, so that we could derive a systematic statement of them just from our study of the criminal law's "General Part"?

To test out this conjecture, let's compare the sorts of things the criminal law would have us say about a group of criminals committing some killings, and the sorts of things the rules of praise would lead us to say about a group of soldiers killing for a just cause. What the principles of blaming, that is, the principles of the criminal law, would tell us about the group of criminals is this: those criminals who kill intentionally are more blameworthy than those who kill unintentionally, even if recklessly or negligently. Those criminals who kill by an act are more blameworthy than those who kill by an omission—for instance, by not coming to the dying victim's assistance. Those criminals who precipitate such a death directly (in more technical lingo, those who constitute the proximate cause of the death) are more blameworthy than those who precipitate such a death indirectly (that is, are its "remote" rather than its proximate cause). Those criminals who actually carry out the killing are more blameworthy than those who merely help, assist, are complicitous in it. Those criminals who actually bring off the killing are more blameworthy than those who try but fail (meaning, who merely engage in the attempt). Those criminals who act of their own free will are more blameworthy than those who are subject to some kind of compulsion (like the threat that they in turn will be harmed unless they commit this killing).

Now consider what we would say about the soldiers fighting for a just cause. We would say that among these soldiers, those who kill intentionally deserve more credit, glory, fame—in short, are more praiseworthy—than those who merely kill inadvertently or semi-advertently. Those soldiers who kill by an act are more praiseworthy than those who kill by an omission, that is, by not preventing their comrades from killing an enemy soldier. Those soldiers who precipitate the enemy's death directly, that is, are its proximate cause, are more praiseworthy than those who precipitate it indirectly, that is, are its remote, not its proximate cause. Those soldiers who actually carry out a killing are more praiseworthy than those who merely help, assist, or are only complicitous in one. Those soldiers who actually bring off the killing are more praiseworthy than those who merely try but don't succeed. Those soldiers who act of their own free will are more praiseworthy than those who are subject to some kind of compulsion (like the threat that they in turn will be harmed unless they commit this killing). It really does look as though the principles of praise are a spitting image of the principles of blame.

Although what I have said about the soldiers killing for a just cause is hardly controversial, I still derive some mild reassurance from certain corroborating findings by social psychologists. The findings come out of a series of experiments, in which psychologists have tried to get a fix on the factors that determine how grateful the recipient of a favor feels to his donor, and how strong an impulse he will have to reciprocate. The experiments show, among other things, that recipients tend "to reciprocate more when the benefit received was intentionally given by the donor than when it was chance-produced" and that they are "more likely to return a benefit when the donor's assistance was voluntary than when it was compulsory." Which is of course just what my soldier example would lead one to expect.[11]

How much further can we press the symmetry between praise and blame? How many of the features of the rules of blame have a looking-glass counterpart among the rules of praise? Well, here is a further and very significant one, though it will take more than a few words to get it laid out. A central feature of the criminal law, one which we explored in some detail earlier in this book, is the constraint it puts on the severity of punishment. We noted that even where a net saving of lives might result, it is not permissible to inflict the death penalty on drunk drivers. We do not care that at the expense of executing a few drunks many more innocents would be saved. Drunk driving just doesn't seem blameworthy enough for that severe a punishment. I am merely reminding you here of what I have noted before, that the criminal law is at bottom not a utilitarian enterprise. Its rules do not seem designed to minimize the amount of harm done. In this it is quite distinct from the tort law which covers largely the same conduct as the criminal law but sanctions it with damages. The tort law does seem like a far more utilitarian enterprise, principally designed to minimize the amount of harm done. Its "punishments," the damages imposed, correspond precisely to the harm someone does and take next to no account of the amount of fault he exhibited in bringing about such harm. This punishment is by criminal law standards generally too harsh or too lenient. From a utilitarian point of view, though, it makes good sense, as the economic analysis of tort law has so effectively shown.

What I have just described seems to have a mirror image in the sphere of praise. The rules of praise too seem to put a tight cap on the amount of praise that we can lavish on someone which may be quite out of keeping with what utilitarian considerations might call for. The discovery of penicillin might be more beneficial for the human race than Shakespeare's plays or Picasso's paintings. We nevertheless bestow greater esteem on Shakespeare and Picasso than on Alexander Fleming. Their achievements seem greater ones. But just as the nonutilitarian criminal law has a utilitarian twin in the tort law, the rules of praise also seem to have a utilitarian twin: the law of intellectual property. Unlike the rules of praise which govern who gets what award for which kind of achievement, the law of patents and copyright governs the award of royalties. Its stated aim is the "encouragement" of the arts and sciences. Its rules, like those of the tort law, seem designed mostly with that purpose in mind. The rewards it bestows on an author or discoverer do not correspond to the impressiveness of his accomplishment but to the profits that can be extracted from it.

THE NONUTILITARIAN CHARACTER of the rules of praise is worth drawing out a bit more because it helps account for things that have for some time puzzled scholars thinking about the norms of science. The economist George Stigler, for instance, has complained that originality is celebrated far more than is optimal for the progress of science, more at least than has been optimal for the science of economics. Too much originality, he notes, hampers rather than promotes progress:

> A new idea does not come forth in its mature scientific form. It contains logical ambiguities or errors; the evidence on which it rests is incomplete or indecisive; and its domain of application is exaggerated in certain directions and overlooked in others. These deficiencies are gradually diminished by a peculiar scientific ageing process, which consists of having the theory "worked over" from many directions by many men. This process of scientific fermentation can be speeded up, and it has speeded up in the modern age of innumerable economists. But even today it takes a considerable amount of time, and when the rate of output of original work gets too large, theories are not properly aged. They are rejected without extracting their residue of truth, or they are accepted before their content is tidied up and their range of applicability ascertained with tolerable correctness. A cumulative slovenliness results, and is not likely to be eliminated until a more quiescent period allows a full resumption of the ageing process.[12]

Once one realizes that the rules of praise, unlike patent and copyright law, are not designed to maximize the praiseworthy, the excessive promotion of originality is not to be wondered at.

What is true of originality in science is probably also true of valor on the battlefield. It too is praised in a manner that a utilitarian military man will often regret. Many a general has been upset when his staff officers plunged into the thick of battle, impervious to the fact that safely staying behind the lines would enable them to make far more of a contribution to eventual victory. But although it would make more of a contribution, it would not lead to a commensurate amount of honor. The medals that count are won in battle. Eisenhower's homily that those also serve who stand and wait is just the military version of George Stigler's exhortation for economists to be useful rather than original.

There is still a further fact that might help to convince one of the similarly nonutilitarian character of the rules of praise and the rules of blame. Although we habitually list promoting discoveries as the purpose of praise and deterring crime as the purpose of blame, we have only qualified admiration for the person who achieves out of a pure greed for glory, and we are uneasy about the person who conforms only out of fear of punishment. We don't like discoverers who tailor their pursuits too closely to the available prizes, and we like even less criminals who tailor their conduct too closely to the chance of being caught.

All of this so far suggests a simple and straightforward answer to the problem of what is an honest and what a dishonest fame. An honest fame is a fame that accords with the rules of praise. And the rules of praise are just a looking-glass version of the rules of blame, the General Part of the criminal law.

Would that it were that simple! So far we have only looked for examples to support the thesis that the praise-side mirrors the blame-side. Unfortunately, once we start looking for counterexamples, for cases in which the symmetry breaks down, there seems to be no dearth of them. Adam Smith dwells at length on one such asymmetry in his *Theory of Moral Sentiments:* Undeserved praise does not give the good man much pleasure, he notes, but undeserved blame still gives him much pain:

> The most sincere praise can give little pleasure when it cannot be considered as some sort of proof of praise-worthiness. It is by no means sufficient that, from ignorance or mistake, esteem and admiration should, in some way or other, be bestowed upon us. If we are conscious that we do not deserve to be so favourably thought of, and that if the truth were known, we should be regarded with very different sentiments, our satisfaction is far from being complete. The man who applauds us either for actions which we did not perform, or for motives which had no sort of influence upon our conduct, applauds not us, but another person. We can derive no sort of satisfaction from his praises. . . . They are the most frivolous and superficial of mankind only who can be much delighted with that praise which they themselves know to be altogether unmerited. Unmerited reproach, however, is frequently capable of mortifying very severely even men of more than ordinary constancy. Men of the most ordinary constancy, indeed, easily learn to despise those foolish tales which are so frequently circulated in society, and which, from their own absurdity and falsehood, never fail to die away in the course of a few weeks, or of a few days. But an innocent man, though of a more than ordinary constancy, is often, not only shocked, but most severely mortified by the serious, though false, imputation of crime; especially when that imputation happens unfortunately to be supported by some circumstances which give it an air of probability. He is humbled to find that any

body should think so meanly of his character as to suppose him capable of being guilty of it. Though perfectly conscious of his own innocence, the very imputation seems often, even in his own imagination to throw a shadow of disgrace and dishonour upon his character.[13]

This I find to be a striking asymmetry indeed. Not just striking, but puzzling. Why should one's inner compass prevent one from thrilling to false compliments but not from wincing at false accusations?

Less striking, but well worthy of note, are two others, the unequal roles *effort* and *risk* play on the praise- and on the blame-side. A soldier fighting for a good cause reaps more praise for a killing the greater the risk and the effort required. A murderer on the other hand does not reap more blame the greater the risk and the effort required. Although the point is obvious and indisputable enough once stated, it is counterintuitive at the level of subliminal perception. Subliminally, this is an asymmetry we don't expect. Indeed it almost offends us. Here lies the origin, I believe, of our hard-to-articulate bafflement at the "banality of evil" phenomenon Adolf Eichmann is said to exemplify. A hero is someone who makes superhuman exertions for the good; *therefore,* a great evildoer is someone who makes superhuman exertions for the bad. Or so our false subliminal sense of symmetry leads us to subliminally expect.

Unfortunately, then, we shall have to back away from the simple suggestion I initially made for answering the question of which rules determine how praise is properly apportioned. Praise is not totally symmetrical with blame. Still, the suggestion is far from useless. Although imperfect, the symmetry between praise and blame is clearly extensive. Asymmetries wouldn't engender the surprise they do if they didn't occur against the background of so much symmetry. So for purposes of laying bare the rules that govern the apportionment of praise, a detailed examination of the rules of blame looks in fact quite promising. And that is precisely what I shall undertake next: a leisurely trek through the General Part of the criminal law, in the course of which I shall take up its principal doctrines and see what they yield when we try to look for their mirror image on the praise-side. In the course of this trek, I shall not be shy about picking up whatever incidental insights it should afford about various collateral issues, not strictly relating the rules of praise. It seems likely, for instance, that looking at the rules of blame side by side with the rules of praise will tell us something new not just about praise but also about blame. Nor will I be shy about raising but leaving unanswered all manner of questions that will suggest themselves along the way. One question in particular will hover unanswered over much of the ensuing discussion: Why does the symmetry sometimes hold and sometimes fail? "Why do mirrors reverse left and right and not up and down?" a famous philosophical conundrum asks. That conundrum is about to gain a lot of siblings.

A brief road map of what lies immediately ahead: the criminal law conceives of each crime as consisting of two parts, one physical, the other mental, the *actus reus* and the *mens rea,* the "bad act" and the "guilty mind," in the case of murder the act of killing and the intent to kill. The section immediately following shall deal with various rules relating to the *actus reus* of a crime, and the corresponding *actus reus* of doing good; the section thereafter shall deal with various rules relating to the *mens rea* of a crime and the corresponding *mens rea* of doing good. The sections following deal with other standard clusters of rules of the General Part, relating to such topics as causation, attempts, complicity, various defenses, and miscellaneous other stuff. (I have subdivided the sections into subsections, each of which deals with a different rule, aspect, precept, element, or distinction relating to the section's general heading.) Now, then, put on your hiking boots and let's begin our trek through the General Part of the criminal law and its looking-glass counterpart in the world of praise.*

*Praise and blame usually being referred to in one breath, one might think that the symmetry between the rules used to ascribe them has been thoroughly investigated. Alas, it has not, although there have been some seminal forays into it, for instance Elizabeth L. Beardsley's "Moral Worth and Moral Credit," *Philosophical Review* 66:304–28, and Susan Wolf's "Asymmetrical Freedom," *Journal of Philosophy,* 77:151–166. The most extensive and explicit treatment, however, I have found in Michael Zimmerman's superb *Essay on Moral Responsibility* (Totowa, N.J., Rowman & Littlefield, 1987). His discussion takes many different turns and reaches many different conclusions from mine, but on the fundamental symmetry, what I say fully echoes him—although I only found that out after I had written a draft of Part III. Another seminal book in this area to which I want to draw special attention is Franz Stuhlhofer's *Lohn und Strafe in der Wissenschaft* [*Reward and Punishment in Science*], (Wien, Böhlau Verlag, 1987). Despite its title, the book is not concerned with the symmetries of praise and blame, but almost exclusively with praise. (The "punishment" in the title refers to the denial of praise.) Stuhlhofer's book proved an invaluable source of examples against which to test out my claims.

THE ACTUS REUS OF DOING GOOD
Omissions

One is liable for acts but not for omissions—so runs one of the most basic rules of the criminal law. Killing is bad, letting die is all right. What happens to the act-omission distinction if we look at the rules of praise? It seems to apply with, if anything, greater force than in the realm of blame. Those who merely stand by and do not prevent important work from going forward, though they could if they were determined to, are felt to deserve significantly less glory than those who actually carry out the mission or the discovery. Indeed the notion of an award would become meaningless if all noninterferors, all "omitters," were viewed as on a par with the "actor."

But there are some apparent counterexamples that we need to attend to. The first concerns the German physicist Werner Heisenberg, whom Thomas Power, author of the book *Heisenberg's War,* praises for the moral achievement of denying Hitler the atom bomb by not inventing it for him. Heisenberg, Power argues, had privately derived much of the theory needed to build a bomb but withheld it from his superiors. When asked about the prospects of building a bomb, he would consistently emphasize its uncertainty, cost, and far-off time horizon. He also made some efforts to give notice of German developments to physicists in the Allied camp, albeit with the objective of getting them to agree to do as he did in Germany, nip all bomb research in the bud. After the war, Heisenberg was reticent to talk about these facts. He feared his countrymen would denounce him as a traitor and that others would not believe him anyway and take him to be an opportunistic liar. What credit does Heisenberg deserve for his role? Thomas Powers thinks a considerable amount. But it is revealing that in summarizing Heisenberg's activities during the war, he goes to considerable rhetorical lengths to try to describe Heisenberg's *failure* to produce the bomb as an act and no mere omission: "Zeal was needed [to give the German bomb project a chance]; its absence was lethal, like a poison that leaves no trace." Or: "Heisenberg did not simply withhold himself, stand aside, let the project die. He killed it." "Heisenberg guide[d] the German atomic research effort into a broom closet, where scientists tinkered until the war ended." Powell here seems implicitly to concede that Heisenberg's credit critically depends on his achievement's being in the nature of an act, not an omission.[14]

Let us assume that Heisenberg's withholding all he knew or all he could discover involved some risk, though that is quite unclear. Should we still care, then, whether his contribution was by way of an omission or an act? The puzzle can be sharpened by comparing the following two cases:

Case I: *Terrorist* threatens to kill *Defendant* unless *Defendant* kills *Victim*. *Defendant* knows that it is far from certain that *Terrorist* will make good on his threat, but he might. *Defendant* in fact refuses to shoot; and luckily for him *Terrorist* does not kill him.

Case II: *Terrorist* threatens to kill *Victim*. *Defendant* can prevent *Terrorist* from doing so, but he knows that if he tries to do that, *Terrorist* just might shoot him in the resulting struggle. *Defendant* is not certain that this will happen, but it might. *Defendant* in fact tries to prevent *Terrorist* from killing *Victim;* and luckily for him *Terrorist* does not kill him.

How does the behavior of *Defendant* in both cases compare as to praiseworthiness? Case II is pretty clear. *Defendant* has behaved valiantly, heroically, in risking his own life to save that of *Victim*. Case I, however, is murky. If *Defendant* had actually fired the shot he would have behaved in a highly blameworthy, indeed downright criminal, fashion. But how can it be that the mere failure to behave in a very blameworthy, downright criminal fashion should count as heroism? If there was risk in what Heisenberg did, his position was really more like *Defendant*'s in Case I than Case II, and we are left correspondingly doubtful about his merits.

A second apparent counterexample to the act-omission distinction on the praise-side is the battle of Tannenberg, fought at the outset of the First World War in which a vastly outnumbered German army crushed its Russian opponent. Close to a hundred thousand Russians were taken prisoner, sixty trainloads of weaponry were seized, and the humiliated Russian commander, General Samsonov, took refuge in suicide. In later years, the battle gave rise to a historical controversy on how the credit should be apportioned between the German officers in charge of the German army—to be precise, between three men: the nominal commander of the German forces at Tannenberg, Hindenburg, his chief of staff Ludendorff, and his chief of operations, Colonel Max Hoffman. A not uncommon description of what happened was that Hoffman had formulated the basic plan to encircle and isolate the Russian army in East Prussia, Ludendorff had launched its practical implementation, and Hindenburg had let Ludendorff be and "steadied his nerves" at certain critical moments. In his own memoirs, Hindenburg sought considerable credit for "giving free reign to the brilliant inspirations and never-flagging energy of my chief-of-staff." The relationship between him and Ludendorff, he said, was that of a "happy marriage" in which the "words of the one usually express perfectly the thoughts and feelings of the other." Ludendorff and Hoffman, however, thought that Hindenburg was getting more than his due. When many years later Hoffman, then chief of staff on Hitler's Eastern Front, took visitors over the field of Tannenberg, he told them with undisguised sarcasm: "This is where the Field Marshall slept before the battle; here is where he slept after the battle; here is where he slept during the battle."[15] Nevertheless, the modern historian Gordon A. Craig, on these very facts, is willing to credit the battle to the "complementary talents of Hindenburg, Ludendorff, and Hoffman," Hindenburg's talent presumably being that of having the guts and the insight to let a risky, tricky, but ultimately good thing take its course.[16]

The act-omission distinction also is at issue in a controversy surrounding the apportionment of credit among the various contending discoverers of insulin at the University of Toronto around 1920. Frederick Banting, popularly known as "the" discoverer of insulin, was infuriated when in 1923 he was made to share his Nobel Prize in medicine with James McLeod, the professor of physiology at the University of Toronto, in whose laboratory Banting had worked. And in certain utterances since then the Nobel committee has indicated that it too thinks a mistake was made in giving MacLeod the prize. The facts behind this controversy, very briefly put, were as follows: when McLeod was approached in 1920 by Banting—who was a small-town surgeon with hardly any research experience but with an idea for some diabetes-related experiments—he had the generosity and, as it turned out, good sense to permit Banting to use his laboratory. He even made a medical student, Charles Best, available for research assistance. Over the first few months of experimenting Banting and Best managed to derive an insulin-containing extract that had the potential of relieving diabetes, provided (and the proviso was a big and hard-to-meet one) they could somehow purge the extract of its various toxic elements. Unbeknownst to Banting and Best, others had independently already gotten to that stage and had actually published their results, a fact Banting and Best had somehow overlooked. It was at this point in their research that McLeod made some further contributions to their work by giving them advice which, along with the assistance of a chemist by the name of J. R. Collip, allowed them to detoxify their extract and produce insulin as we know it. Other than this advice, McLeod really played no role in the experiments, except to continue to make laboratory space and research animals available. Indeed he was out of the country when the initial round of experiments were conducted.[17]

Did all of this entitle McLeod to a share in the Nobel Prize? While I do not hope to settle that question, the facts of this controversy can help us to deepen our understanding of the act-omission distinction in the award of praise. Suppose that McLeod's actual advice at the tail end of the insulin research were not grounds enough for awarding him the prize. Then what about the fact that he presided over the laboratory and kept reasonably close tabs over and actively supported the work of Banting and Best? Let us construe the evidence in the best possible light for McLeod. Let us suppose that he not only had a refined understanding of what Banting and Best were doing, but that he had far more penetrating insight into the likely direction and outcome of their research than they did themselves (there is a good deal in the actual facts to support this) and that he let them continue in what they were doing precisely because he understood the promise of the line of research on which they had, somewhat blindly, embarked. In other words, let us suppose his insight, and perhaps even his analytical effort, actually exceeded that of the people performing the manual work on the experiments. Nevertheless let us suppose further that his contribution to what they were doing was very much by way of omission. He simply let them continue where others might have cut them off. Would he then be entitled to share in the prize honoring the outcome of their research? Oddly enough, I think he would not be. After all, we can imagine various other people, the janitor, for example, who might have learned of their research, realized its promise, and, therefore, desisted from doing anything he otherwise might have (out of spite, for instance) to interfere with it. We would not think that the janitor is due any significant credit by reason of that omission. The same goes for McLeod.

Conditions and Passive States

A man named Speck was charged with the act of gross indecency with a child. Speck had been sitting in a chair when a little girl approached him, fondled his genitals, and elicited an erection. Speck endured all this with great pleasure and complete immobility. The court had great trouble convicting, and many think its decision to convict a bad one, because it collided heavily with another aspect of the criminal law's act requirement: we are not just reluctant to punish omissions but feel similarly about mere conditions, passive states, and status offenses, what one might call quasi-omissions.[18] (Unlike straight omissions, such quasi-omissions don't allow us to say that if the defendant did not exist things would have happened pretty much as they did; but they do allow us to say something analogous. Had Speck had a fatal heart attack before the girl approached him, things would still have happened pretty much as they did. In other words, Speck's presence played a very peripheral part in the offense.)

This aspect of the act requirement also has its counterpart in the praise-sphere. We don't much honor passive achievements. Two examples will make the point. Commenting on beauty contests, Michael Walzer has observed that the organizers of such events "seem to have a dim and embarrassed sense that the winner would not be [truly] honored were she chosen merely for her natural endowments, for they have introduced a variety of 'talent' criteria. Honor is (for us) the recognition for an *action;* and displaying one's physical beauty or, for that matter, announcing one's noble birth and blood does not qualify as an action in the proper sense. It is necessary to use one's endowments in some socially valued way."[19] Tom Wolfe makes a similar observation about the Mercury Seven, the astronauts inhabiting our first space capsules. They were worried and annoyed at being mere "lab rats," passive endurers of risk, doing little more than a monkey could do, sitting through the flight, twiddling the occasional knob, and being heroic by merely surviving. Their less celebrated colleagues, the ordinary test pilots from whose ranks the Mercury Seven had been plucked, reminded them of it every chance they got; they also tried to tell the press but to no avail.[20]

Mere Thoughts

Perhaps the most puzzling aspect of the act requirement is the fact that a mere thought, a mere sinful intention, which the defendant has done nothing to translate into action, does not qualify for punishment. Finding a suitable explanation for this aspect of the act requirement actually has some practical significance. It will influence our approach to the *actus reus* requirement for attempts. If, for instance, we dispensed with the requirement altogether, if we were content to punish someone as soon as we had reliable evidence (through his diary, say) of a firm intention to commit a crime, then the entire, long-standing controversy about where to draw the line between preparation and attempt would become pointless. We should simply punish anyone who has manifested a sufficiently firm and reliable intention to commit a crime. If, on the other hand, we believed that this aspect of the act requirement had some substance, the controversy would continue to retain importance. But does it have substance? Why do we insist on a physical act rather than a mere sinful thought?

Looking at the praise-side of the question here can be genuinely revealing. What sorts of cases would be the praise counterpart to the act problem? They would have to be cases in which a defendant somehow mistakenly imagines himself to be performing heroic deeds, to be standing up to menacing thugs, to be making momentous discoveries, to be breaking Olympic records, to be scaling remote mountain peaks, but he isn't really doing any of that. He is just hallucinating. Our intuition here is strong that no credit is due for that sort of imaginary achievement, however genuinely felt. What's more, we are in a pretty good position to explain the basis of our intuition. That basis we already established when we considered (in Part I) our aversion to entering Robert Nozick's Experience Machine, to buying fake life insurance for our family, to not listening to made-up baseball games, to not reading fabricated memoirs. It is the intrinsic value we place on the "reality-connection." What then is more natural to suppose than that this very phenomenon accounts for the act requirement in criminal law as well.

THE MENS REA OF DOING GOOD

A crime can be committed intentionally, knowingly, recklessly, or negligently. A good deal of case law and commentary is devoted to unwrapping those notions. Not all of them have clear counterparts in the praise-sphere, but many do. I shall be focusing on some of those next.

Transferred Intent

A shoots at B, but misses him and ends up shooting C instead. This is a notoriously vexing case for the criminal law. Under the so-called transferred intent doctrine, most Anglo-American jurisdictions take the position that this amounts to an intentional killing, since A meant to kill a human being and did in fact kill a human being. Other countries, most notably the German-speaking world, take the view that since A did not intend to kill C, there is nothing more here than an attempt to kill B, and the inadvertent, at most reckless, killing of C.

How does this case look in the praise-sphere? Imagine A intends to rescue B but ends up rescuing C instead, altogether inadvertently. Would C feel great gratitude vis-à-vis A? Would we be inclined to award A the same kind of honor and recognition in the way of civic medals and such as we would if he had rescued B? I think not.

Back to the criminal law. Consider this familiar variation on the problem with which we began: A means to kill B, but mistaking C for B shoots him instead. Here the analysis in every jurisdiction in the world seems to be pretty much the same. Since A meant to kill that particular human being over there whom he mistook for C, he intentionally killed a human being and is guilty of murder.

This time around the corresponding praise-sphere counterpart looks puzzlingly different. *A* means to rescue *B*, but mistaking *C* for *B* rescues him instead. More concretely: I see someone I mistake for my sister drowning and jump into the stormy sea to rescue her. Then I see that the person I have pulled out of the water only looks like her. I would never have made the risky plunge for that stranger's sake. Surely I should not earn much gratitude from the person I rescued and not much in the way of civic recognition either. Although we are willing to say that a person deserves praise for incurring risk and effort to rescue another human being, we are not, interestingly enough, willing to see that norm met if the person I rescue is someone other than who I thought I was rescuing.

Unreasonable Hopes

There is an odd fact about the concept of intention that has been unjustly neglected. Consider the case of a defendant who takes aim at his mortal enemy, even though that enemy is standing very far away and the defendant is a rotten shot and has no reasonable expectation of hitting his mark. He hopes against hope, fires his gun, and, miracle of miracles, kills his prey. We have no problem holding him liable for intentional murder, even though success was so very improbable. All of this seems to readily carry over into the praise-sphere. A soldier (fighting for a just cause), at great risk and with great effort, takes aim at an enemy much too far away for him to have a reasonable hope of hitting him, hits him all the same; we have no problem crediting that soldier for his miraculous success.

We can use this aspect of intentions to illuminate some puzzling facts about the way we award credit in the sciences. There is the already mentioned issue of why we admire Copernicus as much as we do. When he proposed his heliocentric model of the universe, it was in many ways more complicated than Ptolemy's and no more accurate in predicting observed astronomic events. (Copernicus made next to no astronomical observations of his own, relying almost completely on the faulty records of the ancients.) Perhaps most important of all, it was inconsistent with then well-accepted principles of physics. Copernicus had no answer for questions such as: If the solar system really is a swiftly moving Copernican merry-go-round, how do we avoid being thrown overboard? Why do birds flying near the equator not get left behind? Why don't balls dropped somewhere near the equator follow a curvy path to the ground? It took all the ingenuity of a Galileo to find the answers to these compelling objections. It's not that there wasn't a good deal to be said *for*

Copernicus, most notably perhaps Copernicus's demonstration that all those loop-ing retrogressions the various planets engaged in vis-à-vis the earth disappeared, as it were, once one thought of the planets as circling the sun. Under the Ptolemaic scheme that fact simply had to be dismissed as a geometrically interesting coinci-dence.[21] Still, on balance one might easily conclude that it was not quite rational to embrace the Copernican view in light of all the objections arrayed against it. Why then do we praise Copernicus for doing the irrational thing, for persevering in what was at least initially an unjustified departure from orthodoxy? How can we admire such irrationality?

Heinrich Schliemann, the discoverer of Troy, is another case in point. Contem-porary archeologists had good reasons for thinking that if Troy existed at all it lay beneath the village of Bunarbashi. Schliemann, who took his Homer more literally than a sane person should, thought otherwise. An excerpt from his memoirs will give a fair example of his reasoning:

> [I] walked aside the Bunarbashi hill . . . , following constantly westward the
> same route which Achilles must have necessarily passed in order to meet
> Hector before the Scaen gate. . . . After a strenuous one-hour march I
> reached a precipitous slope. . . . There the two heroes would have had to
> descend in order to get to the Scamander [river] and to round the city. I left
> my guide and the horse on the hill, climbed down the precipice [so steep]
> that I was forced to crawl on all fours. I needed almost a quarter of an hour
> to get to the bottom. I then became fully convinced that no mortal, not
> even a goat, would have been able to descend in a speedy trot . . . and that
> Homer, who is so meticulous in his topographic details, could never have
> entertained the thought that Hector and Achilles in their race around the
> city had run three times down this slope—which is an absolute impossi-
> bility. . . .[22]

Guided largely by considerations like these, Schliemann dismisses Bunarbashi and digs elsewhere, in a village called Hissarlik, and finds Troy. Why do we consider him more than a lucky fool, as irrational and as lucky as, say, Copernicus?

Alfred Wegener is celebrated for first seriously proposing, sometime around the turn of the century, the theory of Continental Drift. What led Wegener to adopt the theory was the snug topographical fit between the opposing American and African coastlines and various more particular geological and biological affinities between corresponding points on the two coastlines. It is just as if we put together the ragged edges of a torn newspaper, he said, then discovered that the lines of print run evenly across. That was the gist of his argument. But the theory was vulnerable to significant, indeed crippling, criticisms. Wegener had offered no mechanism for the continents to move. Besides, it was known that the rocks beneath the continents were softer than those beneath the oceans. How could such soft rock have pushed through the hard rock? As for the perfection of the fit, one geologist showed how it was possible to neatly fit Australia and New Guinea into the Arabian Sea, though no one of course thought that they had ever been located there. With the passage of the decades those objections crumbled. Mechanisms for continental movement were found; the perfection of the coastline fit was enriched by a mountain of supporting detail. But if the eminent geologists who had initially objected to Wegener's theories as foolish and unpersuasive were not themselves foolish in doing so, was not Wegener foolish in championing it so zealously? So why do we celebrate this lucky fool?[23]

What would happen to the reputation of Erich von Daeniken, the Swiss hotelkeeper and much ridiculed author of *Chariots of the Gods,* if he turned out to be right after all? If the earth really was once visited by astronauts from other planets, if it really was they who built the pyramids, if they really did use the ark of the covenant as an intercom to communicate with Moses, if they really were the original models for the giant statues at Tula, if they really did inspire our religions just as our World War II pilots inspired those in previously secluded islands? He would receive prizes, have biographies written about him, be congratulated on his perseverance, yet the initial adoption of his views would not have been proved one whit more rational than it was. Right now most scientists think of him as a fool. So if he proved right, could he be more than a lucky fool? And do lucky fools merit prizes and adulatory biographies?

Our admiration for the tenacity and naivete of Copernicus, Schliemann, Wegener, and maybe one day von Daeniken should seem less puzzling once we juxtapose it with its criminal law mirror image. Are they not very much like the defendant who takes aim at his mortal enemy, even though the intended victim is standing far away and the defendant is a rotten shot and has no reasonable expectation of hitting his mark? If against all odds he does succeed, we blame him for an intentional killing. Copernicus, Schliemann, and Wegener were in an analogous position. They hoped against hope, irrationally in fact, that their theories were right, and against all odds they turned out to be right. If the murderer deserves blame, even though no reasonable person should have expected him to succeed, then it seems only natural to say that Copernicus, Schliemann, and Wegener deserve praise—*even though no reasonable person should have expected them to succeed either.*

Roundabout Wish-Fulfillments

A shoots at *B,* intending to kill him, misses, but his shot stampedes a herd of wild pigs which trample *B* to death. Although *A* intended to kill *B,* and although *A* in fact caused *B*'s death, we would not say that *A* intentionally killed *B*. The death did not occur in the manner intended and, therefore, *A* will receive much less of the blame for it.

This seems to carry over pretty easily to the praise-sphere. *A* tries to rescue *B,* fails, but in the process somehow inadvertently sets into motion a Rube Goldberg sequence of events by which *B* ends up being saved anyway. We would credit *A* with no more than the attempt to rescue *B*. There are some real-life examples of this in the history of science. I already made mention of Frederick Banting who is generally credited as the principal discoverer of insulin. Over time Banting's fame for his discovery has in fact taken quite a beating, as numerous errors have been discovered in his work. None of those errors changed the bottomline: errors or not, Banting had really been the first to produce usable insulin, only the road to that end result was littered with blunders, which in one way or another turned out to correct each other and to keep him on the right path. So, for instance, in one of the intermediate experiments leading up to the isolation of insulin, Banting used what was an early approximation of the insulin extract in treating diabetic dogs. He examined the dogs and found them all to have improved. In reality only a few had, and it was, in good part, this egregious misdiagnosis that caused Banting to persist along the line he was traveling. Similar mishaps occurred during the most crucial stage of the experiment in which the insulin was actually isolated. In the end, as I noted earlier, Banting achieved his breakthrough in spite of a "wrongly conceived, wrongly conducted and wrongly interpreted series of experiments"; his discovery "proved to have resulted from a stumble into the right road where it crossed the course laid down by faulty conception."

Poor Banting is not alone. Similar findings have chipped away at the reputation of Johannes Kepler. Concluding his story of the discovery of Kepler's Second Law, Arthur Koestler writes:

yet the last step which had got [Kepler] out of the labyrinth had once again been a faulty step. For it is not permissible to equate an area with the sum of an infinite number of neighboring lines, as Kepler did. Moreover, he knew this well, and explained at length why it was not permissible. He added that he had also committed a second error, by assuming the orbit to be circular. And he concluded: "But these two errors—it is like a miracle—cancel out in the most precise manner, as I shall prove further down."

The correct result is even more miraculous than Kepler realized, for his explanation of the reasons *why* his errors cancel out was once again mistaken, and he got, in fact, so hopelessly confused the argument is practically impossible to follow—as he himself admitted. And yet, by three incorrect steps and their even more incorrect defense, Kepler stumbled on the correct law. It is perhaps the most amazing sleepwalking performance in the history of science—except for the manner in which he found the First Law.[24]

But why does any of this matter? Faulty logic or not, Banting really did find insulin, and Kepler really did find the formulas for the planetary paths. We give credit not for brains per se but for achievement. A dull scientist who achieves a breakthrough gets more credit than a brilliant one who doesn't. So even if Banting's and Kepler's fortuitously self-correcting mistakes impugn their intellect, why do they impugn their achievement? *Because they show that their breakthrough occurred in a manner so different from the one intended and so different from the one they thought they were engaged in, as to put them in the position of that killer who kills by triggering a stampede.*

CAUSING GOOD
Luck

Perhaps the feature of the criminal law most upsetting to criminal law scholars and laymen alike is the role it accords to luck. An assassin fires a shot at his victim. If he kills him, he is guilty of murder. If he misses, he is guilty only of attempted murder and punished far more lightly. A driver recklessly hurtles through a busy and narrow alleyway. If he kills someone, he is guilty of manslaughter. If he doesn't, he is at most guilty of reckless endangerment, which is punished far more lightly if at all. This greatly disturbs many, who observe that it is really only external circumstances that distinguish the "successful" from the "unsuccessful" wrongdoer. Isn't it a fundamental precept of morality, and shouldn't it be a fundamental precept of the criminal law, that the extent of someone's blameworthiness and the severity of his punishment should not hinge on such incidental, external circumstances? Doesn't it make blameworthiness and punishment mere matters of luck?

We should be very wary of this kind of juxtaposition argument. There are numerous instances where it quite clearly leads us astray. A murderer well-schooled in sophistry might mount this kind of juxtaposition argument: "Look here, if I had killed my victim in just the manner I did, but without meaning to, I would not be guilty of murder. Therefore, what distinguishes me from the accidental killer are only my thoughts. But a fundamental precept of the criminal law says that no one should be punished for his thoughts." We may not be able to say just why the argument is wrong, but that it is wrong we will not hesitate to say.

Consider a juxtaposition argument even closer to the original one. A murderer argues: "Look here, in my anger at my wife, I shot her. If at the very moment that my anger started to get the better of me, I had had an asthma attack, I quite clearly would not have shot her, my anger would have had time to evaporate, and that would have been the end of the matter. In other words, I invite you to compare me to the hypothetical would-be killer who had such an asthma attack at just the right time, whom you would let go free. Isn't it a fundamental precept of morality, and shouldn't it be a fundamental precept of the criminal law, that the extent of someone's blameworthiness and the severity of his punishment should not hinge on such incidental, external circumstances. Doesn't it make blameworthiness and punishment mere matters of luck?"

Not everyone will consider this last argument patently fallacious. Many people are worried by such things as Stanley Milgram's experiment about blind obedience to authority and conclude that anyone who obeyed Milgram's instruction to inflict electric shocks on the putative student in that experiment would be willing to obey the orders of a German concentration camp commander to torture camp inmates. What that means, they say, is that most of us but for the grace of God would have been brutal concentration camp guards, and in a perfectly moral world should be treated as though we had been. (As an aside, I should note that it has always puzzled me why people put such a grim face on the Milgram experiment. Wouldn't the same blind obedience, that led subjects to commit out-of-character atrocities on a psychologist's say-so, enable them to commit similarly out-of-character acts of heroism on a commanding officer's say-so? Thus why not regard every compliant Milgram subject as a hero *manqué* rather than a war criminal *manqué?*)

But even those who occasionally pay lip service to such a view don't really swallow it. It is interesting to note, for instance, that one of the most moralistic of modern playwrights, the German Rudolf Hochhuth, has no trouble acknowledging the "Here-but-for-the-grace-of-God-go-I" point while condemning those who, lacking that grace, committed atrocities. The dramatis personae of his most famous play *The Deputy*—assessing the pope's role during the Second World War—lists its characters in several clusters. One cluster contains the pope and a German weapons manufacturer, another cluster contains Adolf Eichmann and a prisoner of the Gestapo, a third contains a Catholic priest, an SS corporal, and a Jewish kapo. Each cluster, Hochhuth requests in his casting instructions, should be played by the same actor: "[I]n the age of the draft, it is not necessarily to one's credit or one's shame, or even a sign of one's character, that one ended up in this uniform rather than that, on the side of the hangman rather than that of the victim."[25] This may suggest that Hochhuth is willing to accept the argument of my sophistical murderer. Yet in fact Hochhuth's play is thoroughly judgmental. He quite clearly does condemn those who did wrong, however contingent the circumstances that caused them to do so.

What role does luck play on the praise-side? How does its role compare with that on the blame-side? Can anything at all be learned from the praise-side that could explain the role of luck on the blame-side?

To begin with, luck clearly plays an ample and probably even larger role with praise than with blame. "[T]hough the intentions of any person should be ever so proper and beneficent," Adam Smith wrote, "yet, if they fail in producing their effects, his merit seems imperfect. . . . The man who solicits an office for another, without obtaining it, is regarded as his friend, and seems to deserve his love and affection. But the man who not only solicits, but procures it, is more peculiarly considered his patron and benefactor, and is entitled to his respect and gratitude." Smith went on:

> Even the merit of talents and abilities which some accident has hindered
> from producing their effects, seems in some measure imperfect, even to
> those who are fully convinced of their capacity to produce them. The gen-
> eral who has been hindered by the envy of ministers from gaining some
> great advantage over the enemies of his country, regrets the loss of the op-
> portunity for ever after. Nor is it only upon account of the public that he re-
> grets it. He laments that he was hindered from performing an action which
> would have added a new lustre to his character in his own eyes, as well as in
> those of every other person. It satisfies neither himself nor others to reflect
> that the plan itself was all that depended on him: that no greater capacity

was required to execute it than what was necessary to concert it . . . and that had he been permitted to go on, success was infallible.[26]

Nothing but this sort of view can explain the furious controversy that still surrounds Admiral Robert Peary's quest for the North Pole in the early part of this century. Peary had spent the bulk of his professional life preparing himself for the assault on the Pole; he had by all accounts the will and the ability to get there; most would have said he "deserved" success. But he rightly realized that none of that would save him from ignominy in the end unless he could claim to actually have set foot on the Pole. It was quite clear to Peary that however great his exertions, however splendid the design of his expedition, there would be no monuments, no pensions, no medals, no eager audience for his memoirs unless the world believed he had really rubbed his heels against that mathematically sacred spot. As bad luck would have it, he had by miscalculation probably narrowly missed it. And that he knew made all the difference in the world. Which is why to his dying day he lied about it.[27]

Some Nobel awards have come to be viewed as complete or partial "errors," because the research on which they were based has turned out to have been in complete or partial error. The entries into this category make desert's dependence on luck especially salient. They usually involve researchers whose work was neither fraudulent nor sloppy but, on the contrary, generally so brilliantly conceived and executed as to falsely persuade most contemporaries that it was right. Sometimes, to paraphrase Albert Einstein, the good Lord misses an opportunity to make the real world as elegant as a brilliant scientist imagines it to be. An example is the work of Johannes Fibiger who is "regarded after the fact as one of the least meritorious of laureates because his work on the propagation of malignant tumors was altogether mistaken. The Nobel Committee for Medicine was so embarrassed by this episode that, drawing a dubious inference, it declined to give a prize for cancer research for almost forty years." Another example is the chemist H. O. Wieland "who got his prize for deducing the structure for the sterol skeleton in 1927," which was later found to be in need of drastic revision. The error is said to have been mitigated by the fact that Wieland himself (with others) provided that revision. Yet another example is Enrico Fermi who "received his award in 1938 in part for having 'demonstrated the existence of new radioactive elements produced by neutron irradiation.' . . . [In fact] fission was what Fermi and his group had observed, but they did not know it at the time." Here the committee is said to have been saved from complete "error" by the fact that they also cited some other, unre-futed work. Finally, there is the case of Theodor Svedberg

> who received the prize in Chemistry in 1926, primarily for studies in
> Brownian motion. . . . Svedberg claimed he had demonstrated the correct-
> ness of Einstein's theory of Brownian motion and, in fact, that he had em-
> barked on his experiments before having read Einstein's work. Einstein,
> however, rejected Svedberg's claim and later it was decisively challenged by
> Jean Perrin who, ironically, would win the prize in physics the same year
> Svedberg won his award. . . . The Chemistry Committee made a mis-
> take. . . . Svedberg did not even mention the Brownian motion research in
> his Nobel address.[28]

Nobel observers and the Nobel committee itself have refused to take the position that brilliant research leading to conclusions justified in light of available evidence at the time of publication deserves acclamation regardless of its ultimate fate. In other words, there is no Nobel version of the malpractice defendant's state-of-the-art defense.

What's remarkable is that even when we ostensibly honor the sacrifice someone makes rather than an end he has attained, luck looms very large. We only give the Purple Heart to those soldiers who were injured, not those who took equal risks but survived unscathed. We honor the martyrs, who actually suffered, far more than those who stood ready but somehow were spared. The Church canonizes those who died defending the faith, not those who took great risk defending the faith and then died in some other way. To fully appreciate the role that luck plays in our honoring of martyrdom, consider the cases of those who performed some great and risky deed, subsequently took ill, perhaps even died, but left us uncertain as to the causal connection between their illness and their heroism. Galileo went blind late in life, and it is thought but of course not certain that this was because of his experiments peering at the sun through his telescope. Marie Curie died of cancer, and it is thought but of course not certain that this was because of her exposure to radioactive materials during her experiments. We judge their martyr-dom rather differently depending on the fortuitous fact of whether there actually was a causal link. John F. Kennedy made clever use of this when during his presidential campaign he tried to attribute signs of the Addison's disease he suffered from to his heroic actions in the Pacific. The illness itself would have no bearing on the heroism of his actions, but nevertheless the voters would only overlook it if, as luck would have it, it was in fact attributable to that act.

The strangest and most extreme manifestation of luck in the award of credit is what I will, for reasons that will quickly become apparent, call the OTSOG principle. "If I have seen farther than others," Newton famously said, "it is because I have stood on the shoulders of giants." (OTSOG!) He said it because he felt a good deal of credit was due those giants. However self-evident this proposition may seem, it should start to seem more than a little puzzling if we juxtapose it with the corresponding proposition on the blame-side, which nearly everyone would reject out of hand. We are not generally willing to say that the person who has committed a bad deed, let's say a killing, which then leads to some further deaths the perpetrator could not foresee, should be punished for those further repercussions. Newton however is saying that the person who has committed a good deed for science, which then leads to some further discoveries this person could not possibly foresee, deserves credit for those further repercussions. However odd the proposition may now start to sound, it really does seem to describe what we do. Jacques Hadamard writes in his classic *Psychological Invention in the Mathematical Field*: "When the discoverer of a certain fact hears that another scholar has found a notable consequence of it, if this improvement has required some effort, the former will consider it not a failure but a success: he has the right to claim his part in the new discovery."[29]

A striking illustration of this principle is the career of Alexander Fleming and the discovery of penicillin. Fleming discovered penicillin's ability to kill bacteria in 1928. He did not then think to turn it into a treatment for infected humans, partly because of some general considerations that made this an unpromising prospect—he knew penicillin took a long time to kill bacteria but only stayed in the blood a short time—and partly because of a general prejudice throughout his lab against chemical forms of treatment. It remained for Ernest Chain and H. V. Florey to discover its miraculous medical potential. Fleming's breakthrough, however important it was already thought when he first made it, gained immensely in credit when Chain and Florey were able to put it to such extraordinary practical use—*even though Fleming did not think this possible*. Fleming ended up sharing a Nobel Prize with Chain and Florey (he receiving half, they splitting the remainder) which would almost certainly not have happened without Chain and Florey's work. Already after discovering penicillin, but before the Chain-Florey breakthrough, Fleming had applied for membership in the Royal Society and had twice been refused. Not until *after* the Chain-Florey breakthrough was he elected.[30]

Incidentally, Newton himself must share credit for stating the OTSOG principle with certain forerunners on whose formulations of the principle he was improving—as shown in Robert Merton's classic history of the phrase. Merton tracks its origins back all the way to a pronouncement by a "gloomy cleric" named Goodman who said that "we are like dwarfes set upon the shoulders of Gyants, discerning little of our selves but supposing the learning and ground-works of the Ancients, we see much further than they . . ." and further back yet to one Bernard of Chartres who created it as a result of *mis*translating a Latin writer named Priscian.[31]

Adam Smith at various times suggests we are mistaken in according luck such a role in either blame or praise. "That the world judges by the event, and not by the design, has been in all ages the complaint, and is the great discouragement of virtue. Every body agrees to the general maxim, that as the event does not depend on the agent, it ought to have no influence on our sentiments, with regard to the merit or propriety of his conduct."[32]

Smith is wrong, and looking at luck on the praise-side rather than at the blame-side will make it easier to see why, though in the end the argument does, I believe, apply to both sides. Once more the analogy with Robert Nozick's Experience Machine will stand us in good stead. Once more it will help to remind us of our aversion to entering that machine or doing various real-life analogues like buying fake life insurance for our family, listening to made-up baseball games, or reading fabricated memoirs. It is the intrinsic value we place on the "reality-connection" that willy-nilly leads us to give a leading role to luck, because the presence of that reality-connection is by assumption a matter of luck. And there is (as I already noted when discussing the act requirement) no reason why this argument should only hold for the good things in life. Just as we will feel disappointed if on leaving the Experience Machine we discover that we haven't really won the Nobel Prize we hallucinated winning, or that we didn't really lead the playboy life we hallucinated leading, so we will feel elated that we didn't really neglect our family as we thought we did in the course of working toward the prize, or that we didn't really rob the bank as we thought we did in order to support a playboy lifestyle. It only stands to reason that those who don't admire us for only imagining we won the Nobel Prize should also not blame us for only imagining we were neglecting our family; and that those who don't envy us our imagined millions should also not condemn us for our imagined bank robbery.

Factual Causation

Certain problems of factual causation produce as much unease on the praise-side as they do on the blame-side. By and large, we say that if A killed B, it's no defense that seconds later B's independently fired bullet entered the dead victim's body and would have killed him if A's bullet hadn't already done the job. Preemption is still adequate factual causation. By and large, glory goes to the first one to find something, even though in some sense his contribution is rather insignificant, since shortly thereafter someone else was about to provide humanity with the same insight. Hence all those priority disputes. Nevertheless, I say "by and large," because it does matter to us somewhat. Kenneth Arrow takes less credit for his work on general equilibrium theory than some other work he did, because several people were about to publish similar results when his paper came out.[33] Darwin took less pride in his discovery once he learned of Wallace's independent rediscovery of natural selection. Similarly, defendants do keep raising preemption arguments in criminal cases, expecting at least a jury to be sympathetic, even if the law is not.

Proximate Causation

We already know that not every intentional act designed to bring about death counts as murder. If Mabel climbs to the window ledge and threatens to jump unless Gus stays with her, and if Gus abandons her nevertheless, perhaps even silently hoping that she will jump (no more alimony payments), we know he is not guilty of murder. For murder, the death must have been brought about *proximately,* which here it was not. Mabel's decision to jump breaks the chain of causation.

Something analogous has to be true on the praise-side, as anyone who has ever tried to compose the acknowledgments to a book will know. The critic Joseph Epstein seems to know it better than anyone else, as shown by his keen observations on the subject:

> Not least among the problems presented by acknowledgments is to decide how far down one ought to dip in the well of debts incurred when ladling out thanks. One can easily enough imagine acknowledging one's parents—if not precisely for help on the book in question, then certainly for one's intellectual development generally. But what about the man who made it all possible to begin with—one's mother's obstetrician, "without whose steady hands and grace under pressure this book might never have been written"?

And while at it, "I should also like to thank the dentist of my early years, Dr. Joseph Chulock, whose program of sound dental hygiene made possible the dazzling smile I display on the back of this dust-jacket. My janitor, Tony Ardecelli, in the midst of a serious energy crisis, kept the heat coming into my apartment, making it possible for me to work on this book through the exceptionally severe winters of 1978 and 1979. My postman, Lester Goodman . . ."[34]

The principles on the blame-side are reasonably clear. In the criminal law, two kinds of events break the chain of proximate causation: first, cases like that of Gus and Mabel, namely, cases involving a voluntary intervention by a third party; and second, cases involving abnormal intervening events like a tree collapsing on top of the ambulance that is carrying the defendant's victim to the hospital. What about the praise-side? The first principle seems to have a reasonably straightforward counterpart here. Someone who intentionally causes someone else to commit a creative or courageous act still will not be credited with that act. If Armand Hammer has a brilliant inspiration about whom to hire to work on a particular project, and the people he recruits have a brilliant inspiration about how to get the project done, he may get rich, but he won't get the prize. Father Mersenne was a seventeenth-century cleric who functioned as a sort of scientific clearinghouse for a far-flung, often mutually hostile network of scientists: he transmitted the unpublished results of Galileo to interested parties in France; he needled Descartes into finally committing his ideas to paper. He is referred to by Robert Merton as "that great evoker of excellence."[35] He may well have been more crucial to seventeenth-century science than most scientists in his network, but he still deserves less glory than they. Movie directors have occasionally rebelled against this principle and tried to reap credit not only for their own creative work but for the creative work they bring out in others. It is a view made fashionable by Francois Truffaut under the highflown label *auteurism*. It didn't much catch on. As the screenplay writer William Goldman sarcastically noted, there has really only been one director who could legitimately be called the author of his movies, only "[o]ne man who thinks up his own stories, and produces his pictures and directs them too. And also serves as his own cinematographer. Not to mention that he also does his own editing. All of this is connected with an intensely personal and unique vision of the world. . . . Russ Meyer [the adult-movie maker]. I can't wait for Truffaut's book about *him*."[36] If God said, "Let Newton be and all was light," then God gets credit for creating Newton but not for discovering the laws of gravity.

226

What about the second principle of proximate causation, that abnormal events cut off the causal chain? Does it have a counterpart? Something like it seems to hold true on the praise-side, but it is very hard to get it stated right. It is quite clear that accidents do tend to break the causal chain; but it isn't easy to spell out exactly when and how. The ancient Greeks deemed it necessary for a mathematician to know beforehand the conjectures he was seeking to prove rather than to stumble across them, if he wanted any glory for his achievement. They held that a proper theorem, for which credit was due, was only something "which is proposed with a view to the demonstration of the very thing proposed. . . . [They] did not think much of propositions which they happened to hit upon in the deductive direction without having previously guessed them. They called them *porisms,* corollaries, incidental results springing from the proof of a theorem on the solution of a problem, results not directly sought but appearing, as it were, by chance, without any additional labor, and constitution, . . . a sort of windfall or bonus."[37]

Indeed Galileo tried to take this Greek view so far as to argue (albeit not very successfully) that he deserved more credit for *re*-discovering the telescope after merely hearing that someone else had come up with such a thing than did the original discoverer. This is because "solving a specified problem requires far more ingenuity than stumbling across the solution of an undefined problem, one whose solution no one had even been searching for, since in the latter case accident plays a far greater role, whereas in the former case we have a genuine achievement of Reason. We all know that the original inventor of the telescope was a simple lens-maker, who worked with lenses of all kinds and once happened to look through two of them at once, a concave and a convex one at varying distances. . . . In this manner he noticed its effects and discovered the instrument. I, on the other hand, through said news, discovered the very same thing through the careful use of Reason."[38] (The evidence indicates that Galileo, contrary to his claimed reliance on the "theory of optics," really just engaged in a lot of tinkering until he had the thing in hand.) I tend to think, though, that the Greek view here overstates the blocking effect accident can have on glory.

I am not at all sure what to make of the role accident played in a case recounted by the mathematician Littlewood. He tells the story behind something known as *Bloch's theorem,*

> [It is] [o]ne of the queerest things in mathematics, and some might judge
> that only a madman could do it. [Bloch] was aiming at an "elementary"
> proof of Picard's theorem, an impudently "damn fool idea." With this as a

start it is just a reasonable stroke of insight to *conjecture* Bloch's theorem.
The result once conjectured (and being true), a proof was, of course, bound
to emerge sooner or later.[39]

The power of accident to rob a person of the glory for his achievement comes
out nicely in the kinds of legends with which authors and inventors like to surround
their proudest creations, legends that are meant to disguise the part that trial and
error had in what they did. When Samuel Taylor Coleridge published his poem
"Kubla Khan: Or a vision in a Dream," he insisted both by its title and an accompanying preface that the whole thing had come to him in his sleep,

> during which time he ha[d] the most vivid confidence, that he could not
> have composed less than from two to three hundred lines; if that indeed can
> be called composition in which all the images rose up before him as *things,*
> with a parallel production of the correspondent expressions, without any
> sensation or consciousness of effort. On awakening he appeared to himself
> to have a distinct recollection of the whole, and taking his pen, ink, and
> paper, instantly and eagerly wrote down the lines that are here preserved.
> At this moment he was unfortunately called out by a person on business for
> Porlock, and detained by him above an hour, and on his return to his room,
> found, to his no small surprise and mortification, that though he still re-
> tained some vague and dim recollection of the general purport of the vi-
> sion, yet, with the exception of some eight to ten scattered lines and im-
> ages, all the rest had passed away.[40]

Coleridge's account is now known to be a fabrication, because an earlier draft of
the poem has been found. Coleridge, it turns out, would habitually invent false
pedigrees for his work. He subtitled a 400-line poem called "Religious Musings" a
"Desultory Poem, Written on the Christmas Eve of 1794," but drafts of it go back
for at least two years.[41] Presumably Coleridge lied because he deemed it more
impressive to have composed the poem in a "species of fine frenzy—an ecstatic
intuition" rather than a drawn-out process of trial and error. He just didn't want it
to look like the accidental product of a series of lucky stumbles.

Edgar Allan Poe chose a different route to the same end in his account of the
origins of "The Raven." "It is my design," he explains in his essay "The Philosophy
of Composition," "to render it manifest that no one point in [The Raven's] composition is referable either to accident or intuition—that the work proceeded, step by
step, to its completion with the precision and rigid consequence of a mathematical

problem." He goes on to explain how he systematically "solved for" each of the important variables of the poem: its length, its tone, and its one-word refrain. Here in his explanation of how he "deduced" that that word just had to be "Nevermore":

The question now arose as to the character of the word. Having made up my mind to a *refrain,* the division of the poem into stanzas was, of course, a corollary, the *refrain* forming the close of each stanza. That such a close, to have force, must be sonorous and susceptible of protracted emphasis, admitted no doubt, and these considerations inevitably led me to the long *o* as the most sonorous vowel in connection with *r* as the most producible consonant.

The sound of the *refrain* being thus determined, it became necessary to select a word embodying this sound, and at the same time in the fullest possible keeping with that melancholy which I had predetermined as the tone of the poem. In such a search it would have been absolutely impossible to overlook the word "Nevermore." . . .

The next *desideratum* was a pretext for the continuous use of the one word "Nevermore." In observing the difficulty which I at once found in inventing a sufficiently plausible reason for its repetition, I did not fail to perceive that this difficulty arose solely from the pre-assumption that the word was to be so continuously and monotonosuly spoken by a *human* being—I did not fail to perceive, in short, that the difficulty lay in the reconciliation of this monotony with the exercise of reason on the part of the creature repeating the word. Here, then, immediately arose the idea of a *non-*reasoning creature capable of speech; and very naturally a parrot, in the first instance, suggested itself, but was superseded forthwith by a Raven, as equally capable of speech, and infinitely more in keeping with the intended *tone.*[42]

Poe here tries to do Coleridge one better. He didn't merely conceive "The Raven" in a moment of divine inspiration, in a "species of fine frenzy—an ecstatic intuition," which still to him smacked too much of an accident or too transparent a lie. Rather he derived it systematically, methodically, logically, without the least help from providence or accident, in the course of, say, an afternoon's worth of reflection, in just the way his detective Auguste Dupont derives the solution to that mystery in the Rue Morgue.

Of course Poe, like Coleridge, is lying. Like most poetry, "The Raven" involved a lot of trial-and-error over a period of years, chance encounters, and inspired borrowings from materials near at hand. Drafts of the poem go back several years. Poe's interest in ravens appears to have been awakened when he was reviewing Charles Dickens's *Barnaby Rudge,* which contains the raven Grip, on which the review lavishes some special attention. The phrase "Nevermore" echoes several memorable lines from poems of Poe's contemporary Thomas Holly Chivers: "No nevermore!" as it occurs in his poem "Lament on the Death of My Mother" and "there to rest forevermore" as it occurs in his "To Allegra Heaven."

All of this shows that under certain circumstances, accidents do rupture the causal chain between the glory seeker's actions and their results, but that still leaves us woefully uncertain, I admit, as to exactly what those circumstances are.

Special Forms of Causation

Many offenses entail some further, rather special causal requirements. The various theft offenses, as we already had occasion to see, are distinguished by the differing routes by which the thief appropriates another's belongings: Does he take it furtively (larceny)? Does he take it by force (robbery)? Does he keep something entrusted to him (embezzlement)? Does he take it by trickery (fraud), etc.? The various degrees of murder are partly distinguished by the route through which the killer causes death: a killing is considered more severe if it occurs by means of an ambush or poison, and if it goes against someone with whom one has a special relationship, one's parents, siblings, or even close friends.

What is the significance of these causal attributes when the killing or the theft is for a good cause? If there were symmetry, killings by means of ambush or poison and killings directed against one's family or friends would have to be especially praiseworthy. Likewise for thefts that involve force rather than mere furtiveness (that is, robberies, as opposed to larcenies). Some would say that there is no symmetry here. That even in behalf of a good cause, an open killing is nobler than a sneaky one, the killing of a stranger nobler than the killing of a trusting friend, the furtive removal of property nobler than its exaction by force. Others would see the matter more the way Plutarch did when he assessed the morality of Caesar's murder by Brutus. Plutarch acknowledges, "The greatest thing charged on Brutus is that he, being saved by Caesar's kindness, having saved all the friends whom he chose to ask for, he moreover accounted a friend, and preferred above many, did yet lay violent hands upon his preserver." But according to Plutarch they are mistaken: "Does not, however, the matter turn the other way? For the chief glory of [Brutus] was [his] hatred of tyranny, and abhorrence of wickedness . . . [which in

Brutus was] unmixed and sincere . . . for he had no private quarrel with Caesar, but went into the risk singly for the liberty of his country."[43] In other words, does it not enhance Brutus's heroism that for the sake of democracy he was willing not merely to commit a killing but to commit a treacherous killing, an ambush against a trusting friend?

Most praiseworthy accomplishments are not of course simply "crimes" committed for a good cause. Those other accomplishments usually carry with them their own peculiar causal requirements. Take bullfighting. It is not enough to cause the death of the bull, it must be done in a risk-maximizing way. Anyone can manage the "riskless assassination" of a bull, writes Hemingway in *Death in the Afternoon*,

> by slipp[ing] the sword into an unprotected and vulnerable spot. The reason the man is required to kill the bull high up between the shoulders is because the bull is able to defend that place and will only uncover it and make it vulnerable if the man brings his body within range of the horn. . . . To kill a bull in his neck or his flank, which he cannot defend is assassination. To kill him high up between the shoulders demands risk by the man and studied ability.[44]

The causal role of risk in bullfighting is relatively clear: cause death via a riskier route and your feat is more praiseworthy. It is more mysterious with other kinds of risky feats—like Polar exploration. I became acutely aware of this in reading Roland Huntford's book about the race for the South Pole between (the Norwegian) Roald Amundsen and (the Englishman) Robert Scott. Scott and his team not only failed to get there first but died on the way back to their ship. Huntford concludes the acknowledgments of his book with an intriguing, half-hearted apology to Robert Scott's son Peter, who furnished him with some of the papers he relied on for his account:

> Sir Peter Scott, son of the late Captain Scott, has requested me to make it clear to all readers that the thanks I have expressed to him in the list of acknowledgments for material which he made available to me under no circumstances be interpreted as approval of anything in the book, from which he totally disassociates himself and which he did not moreover see before printing. His view is that in order to make a comparative study of Amundsen and Scott, it was not necessary to denigrate Scott. . . . I do not accept that this is what I have done but I greatly regret any distress that my treatment of the subject has caused to Sir Peter or others.[45]

Aside from being a riveting read, Huntford's book is indeed an all-out assault on Scott's reputation. It is Huntford's relentlessly pressed thesis that Scott was a bumbler who deserved to lose and Amundsen a virtuoso just then at the top of his form. The book is studded with examples of Scott's alleged bumbling: his aversion to dogs and skiing; his fondness for man-hauling his sleds; his eagerness to pile sacrifice upon unnecessary sacrifice by wintering in the ice just prior to a major expedition; his perennial tendency to run close to the edge of his supplies; his enthusiasm for last minute improvising; his sentimental refusal to permit dogs to be eaten; his squeamish reluctance to allow the dogs to feed on excrement, a nutritious and efficient way to clean up a campsite; his arrogant disregard of Eskimo know-how; his foolish optimism about the weather; his ridiculous idea to bring ponies and new-fangled motor sledges to the Antarctic. Had Scott not died on the way back, says Huntford, he might have been court-martialed for his incompetence. As for Amundsen: all you need do is negate each of the above criticisms and you have a list of his virtues, as seen through Huntford's eyes.

But I am not convinced. Huntford, it seems, just has a different view than Scott of the role risk should play in an enterprise such as this one. It is pretty clear from Scott's letters, diary entries, and books, that his alleged follies were the result of ethical choices. Getting to the Pole he recognized to be in the nature of an athletic challenge, virtually devoid of scientific significance. As such, it was ennobled by every extra obstacle the athlete managed to brave in the course of accomplishing it. Scott thus naturally thought it nobler to reach the Pole by man-hauling than by using dogs and skis; nobler to extend the challenge a bit by wintering in the ice just prior to making the run for the Pole; nobler to react to the moment and take some risks with weather and supplies; nobler not to permit such unseemly things as the consumption of dogmeat by humans or of excrement by dogs; nobler to construct one's own equipment rather than ask the Eskimos how it's done. To be sure, he vacillated on occasion, which is what led him to bring along the ponies. He was not too unhappy when they failed him and he had to fall back on man-hauling. Bringing along the motor sleds (which also failed him) by contrast seems quite consistent with his penchant for risk-taking. It was a new piece of equipment, and he wanted to see how it worked under extreme conditions. Why should any of this be viewed as negligence or grounds for a court-martial? Or so one would argue if one assigned risk in Polar expeditions the same role as in bullfights. Huntford never explains what would be wrong with that view.

Creative feats too have their own peculiar causal requirements. To be praiseworthy, the creator must do more than proximately bring about a new creation; he must do so in the right way. It is remarkably easy to overlook this point, which is well illustrated by the praise erroneously lavished some years ago on an allegedly creative computer program capable of generating innovative proofs of elementary geometrical theorems. What specifically first caught people's attention was the program's unusual proof of the theorem which holds that the two angles of an isosceles triangle are equal.[46]

There is a familiar and clumsy way of proving it, presented in most high school texts, that goes like this: imagine a plain old isosceles triangle, with its left side equal to its right side, resting on a base of no particular length, and forming an angle at its apex of no particular size. Now drop an imaginary line from the apex to the base that cuts the apex angle exactly in half. We now have divided the original triangle into two adjacent smaller triangles. These two triangles we know to be congruent because we know that two of their sides are equal (the one in which they abut and the two legs of the isosceles triangle), and they are equal as to the angles which those two sides form (since by assumption the line cut the apex angle in half). Therefore, the two triangles are congruent, and, therefore, the two base angles are equal.

The computer program came up with a more original, simpler way of proving the same result. It boiled down to this: again start by imagining a plain old isosceles triangle, just like before. But now also imagine that it is covered completely by a second, identical triangle. In other words, think of two triangular pieces of paper, one covering the other. Next, imagine lifting the topmost triangle up, flipping it around till its backside becomes its frontside and its frontside becomes its backside, and putting it back down until it matches up again with the original triangle. We know that this is possible to do because the left and right side of the triangles are equal. But if it is in fact possible to do this, then the formerly left-hand angle of the top triangle must fit on top of the right-hand angle of the bottom triangle, and the formerly right-hand angle of the top triangle must fit on top the left-hand angle of the bottom triangle. And so the right-hand and left-hand angles of the two triangles must also be equal to each other. Presenting the proof in clumsy prose, without some helpful pictures and notation along the way, can probably only convey a whiff of its elegance, but that will do.

When the program first generated this proof, it seemed like indisputable demonstration of the enormous creative capacities of such programs: the proof is in fact identical to one produced several centuries ago by a Greek mathematician named Pappus and has long been celebrated for its ingenuity. Much later, however, it was pointed out that initial appearances notwithstanding there was actually nothing creative about what the computer program had done. Not because Pappus had already come up with the proof: that is of purely historical relevance. Not because computers don't have minds: we could easily deal with that by having a human being perform each of the operations the computer here performed. Not because the creator of the program is really the author of the proof: after all, he had no idea that his procedures would give rise to this elegant proof. The reason the computer program could not be described as creative was rather this: what makes us celebrate Pappus was his ingenious idea of thinking about a triangle as really being two triangles stacked on top of each other and then imagining one being lifted up and twisted around. The computer program itself contained absolutely no geometric representations. Instead, it translated every geometric figure into letters, manipulated the letters according to suitable rules to arrive at the desired theorem, and the proof was completed. When others subsequently examined what the computer had done, they would "read" Pappus's proof into it. The computer itself (or for that matter a human following its procedures) had never visualized anything at all, least of all two triangles stacked on top of each other. Does that mean that the person "reading" Pappus's proof into the computer's record is being creative? No, because anyone examining the computer's output would have "read" the same thing into it. The fact of the matter is that one can arrive at startling results in creative and noncreative ways. And the computer arrived at Pappus's method by a noncreative route.

However artificial in every sense of the word this example may look, it has some real-life counterparts. Several decades ago the statistician-biologist R. A. Fisher re-analyzed the plant experiments by which Gregor Mendel purported to have discovered the basic laws of genetics (most fundamentally the fact that inheritance is not a "blending" process but a mixing of particulates, genes). Fisher's analysis of Mendel's data suggested that Mendel had tampered with it; the data seemed too good to be true. Fisher, however, did not think that this served to reduce Mendel's stature. Quite the contrary. While it might detract from his integrity, it enhanced his originality. Mendel's laws are really a hidden implication of Darwin's theory of natural selection. Unless something very much like Mendelian inheritance is posited, natural selection will not work. If, for instance, inheritance worked the way many of Darwin's contemporaries envisioned it, as a sort of blending between the mother's and the father's characteristics, much as one might mix up two cans of color, populations would grow ever more uniform over time, and there would not be enough variety within it for natural selection to do its work. Mendel, so Fisher thought, had the brilliant intuition to see this when no one else did. The most convenient way to convince the rest of the world, however, was to do the experiments, at which point it was tempting to manipulate his data to yield up the results he had already intuited to be the right ones. The sort of honor we bestow on Mendel should clearly hinge on which route he used to get at his results. The experiments are much more akin to what the computer did; what Fisher suspected is much closer to what Pappus did.[47]

This suggests to me, incidentally, that committees doling out prizes probably do too little in the way of ferreting out the intellectual processes by which the recipient made his contribution.

ASSISTING WITH THE GOOD

Think back to my hypothetical comparing the actions of a group of criminals and those of a group of soldiers fighting for a good cause. There seemed to be a perfect symmetry in the way we treated complicity in those two contexts. As to the criminals, we are able to say that those who actually perpetrate the crime are more blameworthy than those who merely aid, assist, help, or support it—the principals of a bad deed are worse than its accomplices. Symmetrically, we are able to say about the soldiers that those who actually perpetrate the valiant act are more praiseworthy than those who merely aid, assist, help, or support it—the principals of a good deed are better than its accomplices.

Because our sense of symmetry concerning issues of complicity is so pronounced, various writers and advocates have occasionally been able to exploit it to make palatable views that at first glance seem quite repellent. The German-Jewish writer and Auschwitz survivor Jean Amery, for instance, wanted to argue for the morality of collective responsibility, by which he meant something more far-reaching than ordinary accomplice liability. He meant to hold future German generations responsible for the sins of their forefathers. His argument was a simple but ingenious appeal to symmetry. *If Germans want to take credit for Goethe and Mozart, he reasoned, they must take the blame for Hitler and Himmler.*[48]

Although collective responsibility of precisely the sort Amery envisioned is not a part of the criminal law, something like it is. And it should, therefore, not surprise us that when prosecutors try to make this sweeping and repellent-looking doctrine palatable to juries they use exactly Amery's strategy of appealing to our sense of symmetry. The doctrine I have in mind is known as the *Pinkerton* rule. It says that a member of a conspiracy is liable for any and all crimes of a coconspirator even if he had no inkling what his coconspirator was up to. To convince reluctant jurors to go along with this sweeping rule, prosecutors like to remind them that "*[i]f Michael Jordan scores, the whole team wins.*"[49] But the more appropriate lesson to draw from Amery's example would seem to be that yet again the symmetry between blame and praise is breaking down, admittedly for reasons that are somewhat mysterious.

Other aspects of complicity law, however, seem to exhibit valid symmetries, which as it happens also serve to cast new light on some puzzling features of the criminal law and the rules of blame it embodies.

The Difference One Makes

The most puzzling aspect of the concept of complicity on the blame-side is this basic question: What kind of contribution does it take to become an accomplice? The problem is neatly posed by the case of *Wilcox v. Jeffery*.[50] In 1949 a man named Coleman Hawkins, described by the court as a "celebrated professor of the saxophone," arrived in London to give a jazz concert at the Prince Theater.[51] He did so without having a work permit, which was generally known. Among the people greeting him at the airport was one Herbert Wilcox, the owner of a magazine called *Jazz Illustrated*. Wilcox attended the concert and gave it an enthusiastic review. Then, no doubt to his great surprise, he found himself being charged with aiding and abetting Hawkins in the crime of working without a work permit. Affirming his conviction, the court of appeals calmly explained:

> [Wilcox] paid to go to the concert and he went there because he wanted to report it. He must, therefore, be held to have been present, taking part, concurring or encouraging, whichever word you like to use for expressing this conception. It was an illegal act on the part of Hawkins to play the saxophone or any other instrument at this concert. [Wilcox] clearly knew that it was an unlawful act for him to play. He had gone there to hear him, and his presence and his payment to go there was an encouragement. He went there to make use of the performance, . . . he went there . . . to get "copy" for his newspaper. It might have been entirely different . . . if he had gone there and protested, saying: "[T]he musicians' union do not like you foreigners coming here and playing and you ought to get off the stage." If he had

booed, it might have been some evidence that he was not aiding and abetting. If he had gone as a member of a claque to try to drown the noise of the
saxophone, he might very likely be found not guilty of aiding and abetting.
In this case it seems clear that he was there, not only to approve and encourage what was done, but to take advantage of it by getting "copy" for his paper. [Thus we can say that] he aided and abetted.[52]

It is to be noted that according to the court's logic all of the other applauding
spectators were probably guilty as well. Is this a sensible outcome? Many think it
is not. Surely, they say, a more substantial contribution is needed to make one an
accomplice than something as insignificant as attending and applauding. But in the
aggregate, replies the other side, the various spectators did make a substantial
contribution, one without which Hawkins's performance would not have taken
place.

How common is this sort of problem? This is where looking at the mirror image
of the problem, its counterpart on the praise-side, proves of some use, because
the praise-side version of the problem is exceedingly familiar. It is a well-known
phenomenon in economics that when you add up the marginal contributions of
every worker in some enterprise (the amount of the total product that would not
have been produced if that worker were absent) these contributions frequently do
not add up to the enterprise's total output. After all, every corporation would
pretty much run on as it does if any one of its employees were to be cut. That
employee's absence would subtract a smidgeon at most from the corporation's total
output. Add up the smidgeons of all employees and their sum is still less than the
total product the corporation turns out. This is just a special manifestation of the
principle of diminishing marginal returns, which should perhaps more revealingly
be called the principle of increasing marginal redundancy: in group activities everyone is more or less redundant and becomes increasingly so as the size of the
group increases. Therefore, adding up the amounts that would not have been
achieved but for any individual's presence will generally fall short of the actual
total.

With this in mind, it's pretty easy to think of lots of cases that are like *Wilcox v.
Jeffery.* Imagine that *A, B, C,* and *D* jointly issue some stock. As the law requires,
they prepare a prospectus describing the stock to be given to every potential purchaser. A number of people buy. Then it turns out that the prospectus contained
four egregious misrepresentations, falsehoods deliberately inserted to boost the

value of the stock. When the truth comes out, the stock price falls. Some injured shareholders sue *A, B, C,* and *D.* The trial reveals that each of the four defendants contributed one of the misrepresentations. A study is performed to assess the damages, and it determines them to be $1,111. The study also determines that had there been only one misrepresentation, damages would have been $1,000, had there been two they would have been $1,100, and had there been three they would have been $1,110. In other words, each liar caused a mere $1 in harm; but together they caused $1,111 worth.

It's also easier now to understand the purpose of the law of complicity. Under traditional, noncomplicity doctrines, everyone is only liable if but for him some substantial harm would not have happened. Under that approach most members of a vicious group would be let off. Like the lying stock issuers, they would get off by reason of redundancy.

Once one has decided that it is possible to be an accomplice both to good and to bad deeds without actually making a difference, and certainly without making a substantial difference, one confronts a further problem. How is one going to distinguish bona fide accomplices from everyone else who didn't make a difference to the outcome either? If I shout encouragement at a would-be assassin, I am an accomplice, even though the assassin was already determined to go ahead without my encouragement. If I shout encouragement at a deaf assassin, or at the television set carrying live coverage of an ongoing assassination (as when Jack Ruby shot Oswald), I am *not* an accomplice. Yet in both cases I shouted encouragement which made no difference. Why in the former case am I an accomplice and not in the latter?

Again, thinking about the praise-side helps in clarifying matters on the blame-side. Darwin, Wallace, and Disraeli were all superfluous to the discovery of natural selection. So why are Darwin and Wallace credited with its discovery and Disraeli is not? Presumably because the reasons for Darwin's and Wallace's superfluousness are different from the reasons for Disraeli's superfluousness. Darwin and Wallace were each superfluous by reason of redundancy. Disraeli was superfluous because he wasn't working on the problem. As to Darwin and Wallace, we are able to say that if we subtracted either of them from the scene, the other's contribution would no longer be superfluous. Not so with Disraeli. The same is true on the blame-side. If I shout encouragement at a determined assassin I am superfluous to the outcome by reason of redundancy. If I shout encouragement at a deaf assassin or at the television set carrying the assassination live, I am superfluous because my voice never reaches the principal's ear.

Ignorant Intermediaries

A second rather basic problem concerning complicity on the blame-side is exemplified by the case of Mrs. Richards, whose marriage had been deteriorating and who resolved upon a somewhat peculiar strategy to regain her husband's affections. She arranged to have him badly beaten up so that he would have to spend a month in the hospital, which would then give her the opportunity to care for him solicitously. She paid two thugs five pounds each to inflict the beating. Both she and her two henchmen were subsequently charged with the felony of "wounding with intent to inflict grievous bodily harm" and the misdemeanor of "wounding without intent to inflict grievous bodily harm." The jury convicted the two thugs only of the misdemeanor and Mrs. Richards of the felony, evidently believing the two thugs intended to wound only slightly, whereas Mrs. Richards intended them to wound grievously. That seems like a perfectly plausible view of the matter. But there is another perfectly plausible view of the matter as well, which the appeals court took and as a result of which it overturned the conviction. It reasoned: the accomplice "cannot be guilty of a graver crime than the crime of which the two [henchmen] were guilty. There was only one offense that was committed, committed by the [two henchmen]," namely, the misdemeanor of wounding without intent to wound grievously. Hence Mrs. Richards could not be guilty of assisting in anything graver.[53]

For the looking-glass counterpart of this problem on the praise-side: when Andy Warhol exhibits his Brillo boxes in a museum, or Duchamp his grooming comb, bottle rack, bicycle wheel, or urinal, ought they to be able to reap more credit for doing so than the original designers of those products? In a sense, Warhol and Duchamp here stand in the shoes of Mrs. Richards, whereas the original designers of the exhibited objects stand in the shoes of her henchmen. Just as Mrs. Richards's henchmen only possessed a fairly low level of blameworthiness, these designers possessed only a low level of originality, that is, praiseworthiness. As with her, we are plagued by ambivalence. Can it really be a significant artistic achievement to procure the exhibition of something which itself is not a significant artistic achievement? Then again, if those objects, looked at in the Warholian spirit, indeed reveal unsuspected depths, perhaps their exhibitors really do deserve to be credited with bringing those depths to our attention—after all, isn't that what every artwork does? We vacillate as we do about the case of Mrs. Richards.[54]

ATTEMPTING THE GOOD
Failure

Neither in tort law nor in the law of intellectual property do unsuccessful attempts pay any dividends. In criminal law and under the rules of praise, they do. Robert Scott earned much glory for his valiant, fruitless, and eventually fatal attempt to be the first man at the South Pole. Not the glory of the winner, but something quite significant nonetheless. ("In February 1913 the cables flash tidings to the homeland; an astonished and admiring world reads his last letters and the extracts from his diary; the King joins in the tribute to his memory by attending the memorial service in St. Paul's Cathedral." So writes Stefan Zweig, in his 1927 bestseller *Tides of Fortune,* a collection of "famous moments" in history, in which he includes Scott's, but not Amundsen's story.)[55] Pedro Sarmiento "almost" discovered Australia in 1568. He proposed, but never succeeded in getting command of, an expedition that would have taken him straight to Australia, and he has earned some modest fame for that proposal. (An expedition was sent under someone else's command but failed to follow Sarmiento's recommended path and found little.)[56] James Cook courageously searched for the mythically large continent on the southern part of the globe and later on for the Northwest Passage. Though he found neither, he did find glory.

But other failed attempts have done much less for the reputations of their protagonists. Historians of science have pointed out that one of Ampère's experiments put him within striking distance of discovering how moving magnetic fields induce electrical currents. Instead, the discovery fell to Faraday who performed the same experiment soon thereafter and immediately understood its significance.[57] The modern French mathematician Jacques Hadamard thought Pascal was only a hop, skip, and a jump away from discovering non-Euclidean geometry, if only he had paid attention to the immediate implications of certain observations in his notes. Others have suggested that it was nearly a miracle that Henri Poincaré did not discover the theory of relativity before Einstein, considering how closely it followed from certain things he did discover. None of these near-misses, however, earned their protagonists much credit. How come? Why do the near-misses of Ampère, Pascal, and Poincaré count for less than the near-miss of Scott, and the not-so-near misses of Sarmiento and Cook?

Again looking at the mirror image of this problem on the blame-side proves suggestive. Criminal attempts aren't mere fragments of completed crimes. The completed crime may require a mental state other than intention, but the attempt to commit that very crime requires such an intention. Scott, Sarmiento, and Cook, all were aiming for a particular, identifiable objective. Ampère, Pascal and Poincaré unintentionally, "recklessly" one might say, got within close proximity of a breakthrough in the course of aiming for other things. Just as unintentionally getting close to, creating a high probability of, a crime gets little blame, doing the same with respect to a discovery, gets little credit.

The Intent Requirement

There is a rule in the law of criminal attempts that has puzzled scholars for a long time. Let us suppose that I aim to kill the queen and that in order to do so I plant a bomb in her coach. I firmly expect, but sincerely regret, that the bomb will kill not only the queen but also her coachman. Now suppose further that my attempt is stopped in time: the bomb is noticed and removed and I am in due course arrested and tried. What will I be guilty of? The attempted murder of the queen, that part is easy. But what about the coachman? Am I guilty of the attempted murder of the coachman? I put him in as much danger as the queen. I firmly expected him to die. Nevertheless, under the law of criminal attempt, I will not be found guilty of attempting to kill the coachman, because I did not intend the coachman to die, I merely expected him to die. The queen by contrast I not merely expected but intended to die, which is why I am guilty of an attempt as to her.

Does this make sense? It might make sense under a purely linguistic interpretation of the concept of an attempt. It is hard to say of someone that he is attempting, or trying, to bring about a certain result if he doesn't really want that result to happen. But that doesn't resolve the moral question whether I should not be found guilty of something morally equivalent to an attempt, or whether we shouldn't stretch the legal concept of an attempt a little beyond its linguistic boundaries to cover conduct like mine. Is there really an important moral difference between my actions vis-à-vis the queen and the coachman so as to justify punishing me severely for what I did vis-à-vis the queen and not punishing me at all, or hardly at all, for what I did vis-à-vis the coachman? Scholars have long been critical of this aspect of the law of attempt. Nonetheless, it has pretty much remained in place.

By looking at the mirror-image of the criminal law, we can, I think, account for that. It is not, however, the direct counterpart of this facet of the attempt rule to which I want to draw your attention. (To be sure, the direct counterpart displays the symmetrical oddity: I surely earn far more credit if I arduously try to rescue someone than if I happen to be going about an arduous task for some other purpose but think that in the course of it I will have the opportunity to rescue someone.) As it happens, we can get more illumination by rummaging among some others of the principles on the praise-side.

The principle that will prove most illuminating here is one we already encountered when discussing the notion of intention. We then noticed that intentions, both on the praise- and on the blame-side, have this peculiar property: if I intend to bring about a bad consequence by my actions, then even though my actions may not be very promising, even though they have only a low probability of successfully implementing my intentions, if they do succeed, I shall be deemed to have brought them about intentionally and to be blamed accordingly. (If I shoot at my victim from far away, then however unlikely I am to kill him, if I do kill him, I have killed him intentionally.) Pari passu for praise: if I intend to bring about a good consequence by my actions, then even though my actions may not be very promising, even though they have only a low probability of successfully implementing my intentions, if they do succeed I shall be deemed to have brought them about intentionally and to be praised accordingly. (Which is why Copernicus and Schliemann reap so much praise despite the arguable irrationality of their intentions.) Now return to my example of planting a bomb in the queen's coach. By planting that bomb, I sincerely hope to kill her, and I equally sincerely hope that by some miracle the coachman escapes unscathed. *But then if he does escape unscathed, either because the bomb was found in time, or because miraculously it only killed the queen, then I can be said to have intentionally spared him and should be credited with that accordingly. And what can it mean to credit me for sparing the coachman, if not that I should not be punished for the attempt to kill him?*

Abandonment

When toward the end of his life Copernicus finally brought himself to publish his *Book of Revolutions,* he agreed that a theologian named Andreas Osiander should provide it with a preface. That preface consisted of an astonishing list of disclaimers, easily rivaling the most cautious securities prospectus. I will quote Arthur Koestler's summary thereof:

> The preface was addressed TO THE READER, CONCERNING THE HYPOTHESES OF THIS WORK. It started out by explaining that the ideas

of the book need not be taken too seriously: "For these hypotheses need not be true or even probable"; it is sufficient that they should save the appearances. The preface then went on to demonstrate the improbability "of the hypotheses contained in this work" by pointing out that the orbit ascribed to Venus would make that planet appear sixteen times as large when closest to the earth as when farthest away—"which is contradicted by the experience of all ages." The book, furthermore, contained "no less important absurdities, which there is no need to set forth at the moment." On the other hand, these new hypotheses deserved to become known "together with the ancient hypotheses which are no more probable," because they are "admirable and also simple, and bring with them a huge treasure of very skilful observations." But by their very nature, "so far as hypotheses are concerned, let no one expect anything certain from astronomy, which cannot furnish it, lest he accept as the truth ideas conceived for another purpose [i.e. as mere calculating aids], and depart from this study a greater fool than when he entered it. Farewell."[58]

There has been much debate over what part Copernicus had in the writing of this preface, whether he approved of it, and if he did whether he did so only to appease the Church. All the while, there has also been much puzzlement as to whether Copernicus's relationship to the preface really matters. After all, Copernicus's contributions to science are to be found in the text proper, which are not altered by the contents of the preface. The most the preface reveals to us is Copernicus's attitude toward his lifetime work as he was about to die. Why should that be relevant to his scientific reputation?

The criminal law's abandonment defense helps us make sense of our ambivalent reactions to the preface. Abandonment is a defense only for attempts, not for completed crimes. Because of the abandonment defense, the bank robber who decides to turn around at the last minute, leaving the money in the already-opened safe untouched, is not guilty of attempted bank robbery. But the defense does not exculpate the bank robber who decides to return money he secretly removed just yesterday. Giving back the money will mitigate his punishment but not change the fundamental fact of liability. If we are unsure what significance to attach to the Osiander preface, that is probably because we are unsure whether to regard Copernicus's book as an attempted or a completed deed. Both views seem possible. We might view it as an attempt to describe the solar system, that was only "completed" when eventually substantiated by more extensive observational data than Copernicus possessed. In that case, the last-minute abandonment understandably diminishes Copernicus's credit greatly. We might also view Copernicus's book as a completed discovery. In that case, the preface becomes irrelevant.[59]

Impossibility

What happens when someone attempts to do the impossible? He reaches into a pocket that is in fact empty. Or he engages in intercourse with a twenty-year-old female while entertaining the mistaken belief that sex with anyone less than twenty-one constitutes statutory rape. Are the defendants in these cases guilty of attempted theft and attempted statutory rape?

For each of these cases the criminal law has created a separate doctrine, and each of these doctrines has a direct counterpart on the praise-side. The first case—that of the empty pocket—the criminal law refers to as one of "factual impossibility." The attempt was impossible because some fact was different from what the defendant thought. Mere factual impossibility does not serve to get a defendant off the hook. An attempt that fails merely because the defendant made some factual mistake, absent which he would have been successful, is still a criminal attempt. The would-be pickpocket is guilty of attempted theft. His praise counterpart would be someone embarking on a rescue mission in behalf of one who, unbeknownst to him, is already dead. The would-be rescuer would presumably glean a lot of credit for his valiant attempt. Thus a factually impossible attempt to do bad remains bad and a factually impossible attempt to do good remains good notwithstanding the impossibility.

Things are different in the second kind of case, intercourse with a woman whom the defendant mistakenly believes to be underage because he thinks anything less than twenty-one is underage. This is a case the criminal law refers to as one of "legal impossibility." The attempt was impossible because some law was different from what the defendant thought. Legal impossibility does indeed serve to get a defendant off the hook. An attempt that fails because the defendant made some legal mistake, absent which he would have been guilty, is not a criminal attempt. You cannot be punished merely because you imagined there is a law punishing what you do. This too holds up on the praise-side: an attempt that fails because what the defendant believes to be highly praiseworthy really is not, does not thereby become a praiseworthy attempt. I may think that saving mice from being devoured by cats is a very noble act, and I may work strenuously at the task. That doesn't mean I will earn the credit of having attempted a very noble act.

Looking at the mirror image of legally impossible attempts has some important fringe benefits. Cases in which the defendant attempts the legally impossible are part of a larger category of cases in which the defendant makes some sort of mistake about the law governing his conduct. But whereas in cases of legal impossibility the mistake leads him to think that something which is legal is really forbidden, in other cases his mistake leads him to think that something which is illegal is perfectly all right. The latter kind of case is one we usually refer to under the heading of "ignorance of law." Ignorance of law we usually declare is no defense, and the defendant who makes such a mistake should nevertheless be punished. That principle, as I have noted earlier in this book, has come in for a lot of criticism, has been judged by many to be too harsh and really inconsistent with morality. Looking at cases of legal mistake from the perspective of the praise-side, however, makes the criminal law's treatment both of ignorance of law and of legally impossible attempts quite persuasive. That's because on the praise-side we have no trouble at all putting aside the defendant's mistaken beliefs about the legal or moral status of what he was doing when we evaluate his conduct. We have no trouble hailing Oscar Schindler, the Righteous Gentile who saved more than a thousand Jews, even though he thought he had done little more than ordinary decency required; or Ronald Coase, the economist who helped give birth to a new academic discipline, the economic analysis of law, even though he thought he was engaged in little more than some conceptual housecleaning; or P. G. Wodehouse, even though he thought that what he wrote was no more than skillful lowbrow entertainment. (If this sounds familiar, it's because I made the same point in Part I, using some other examples, when first discussing the ignorance of law principle and its connection with legal uncertainty and indeterminacy.) That said, what the criminal law does seems a lot more defensible.

DEFENSES AND DETRACTIONS

When a crime is committed in a fit of madness, under the spell of hypnosis, in the thrall of compulsion, in the frenzy of anger, in the shock of hypoglycemia, or in the innocence of one's infancy, we are inclined to excuse it, maybe not always, and maybe not altogether, but by and large. And here we have a signal asymmetry: it hardly seems to diminish, the glory we bestow for a great artwork, for a scientific breakthrough, or for a heroic feat, that it was accomplished in a fit of madness, under the spell of hypnosis, or in the thrall of compulsion. We forgive Samuel Johnson, who suffered from Tourette's syndrome, his many lapses of decorum, his goofy, irksome tics, and other "mis-demeanors," but we do not hesitate to celebrate him for the startling wit that same ailment produced in him. Mad geniuses and child prodigies earn more rather than less glory for their good deeds by dint of their madness and immaturity. Were things symmetrical, mad thugs and wicked children should earn more rather than less blame for their bad deeds; yet the reverse is true. *Excuses generally diminish blame but not praise, they are a defense but not a detraction.* (I say generally because in a few narrow cases they seem to be both: if I save you from mortal danger because my delusions have blinded me to the risk I am taking, that certainly will reduce the glory I reap, just as if I kill you under certain delusions, that will reduce the blame I elicit.)

Justifications (such as self-defense) are different. They seem to work more symmetrically than excuses. They can serve to defend against blame and detract from praise. If I shoot you in self-defense, that reduces my blameworthiness. If I rescue you because you are the only possible donor of a compatible kidney for me—again, as it were, in self-defense—that reduces my praiseworthiness, though not perhaps by as much. Plutarch makes a telling observation in point when he explains why in certain crucial ways he believes that as between Theseus and Romulus, the founding figures of Greece and Rome, Theseus is the more praiseworthy. "Theseus," he remarks, "out of his own free-will, without any compulsion, when he might have reigned in security at Troezen in the enjoyment of no inglorious empire, of his own motion affected great actions, whereas [Romulus], to escape present servitude and a punishment that threatened him . . . , grew valiant purely out of fear, and dreading the extremest inflictions, attempted great enterprises out of mere necessity."[60]

There is a special problem surrounding most defenses in the criminal law. Two illustrations will show most clearly what I have in mind:

1. The defendant imbibes large quantities of alcohol, deliberately renders himself intoxicated, hoping that he will thus acquire the necessary courage to kill his enemy *and also hoping that his mind will be so clouded in the process that the killing cannot now be classified as an intentional homicide but reckless manslaughter at worst.*

2. Rather than killing his enemy outright, the defendant decides to tease him mercilessly until he has goaded him into making a physical attack on the defendant, whereupon the defendant kills him in self-defense. (This is a variation of the case dealt with in Part I.)

As we saw in Part I, it is a long-standing issue in the criminal law whether a defendant who has created conditions that are meant to make it easy for him to commit a criminal act still retains the defenses to which those conditions would ordinarily entitle him. If the defendant deliberately clouded his senses so he could "manslaughter" rather than murder his victim, or if the defendant deliberately goaded his victim into attacking him so he could kill him in self-defense rather than outright, does he retain the defense of intoxication or self-defense?

The counterpart problem to the self-intoxicating killer on the praise-side is the self-intoxicating soldier fighting for a just cause. Is his heroism diminished if he renders himself "chemically valiant," that is, if he increases his tolerance for risk and pain with suitable drugs? What about those ferocious Arabic warriors battling the Crusaders, known as *hashshashin* because they steeled their nerves with hashish before an attack (hence our word "assassin")? Or those Asian tribes who discovered a mushroom with a powerful analgesic effect, which they enhanced further by "feeding the mushroom to reindeer and gathering their urine," resulting in a concentrated extract of the compound: "Apparently, men who took the drug became almost totally immune to pain and at the same time became capable of great feats of physical strength and endurance. Warriors were able to carry heavy loads great distances and had greater physical strength and stamina in battle. What is most interesting is that the drug apparently did not reduce the mental awareness of the soldiers and, like a natural amphetamine, might well have enhanced it for a short period of time. Equally important, the soldiers were able to sleep normally."[61] Do powerful intoxicants like this negate claims of heroism?

The counterpart to the killer who goads his enemy into attacking him (so he can kill him in self-defense) is the soldier who puts himself in situations where doing the valiant thing is the only way to stay alive. The classic example here is Cortés burning his ships to prevent his troops from retreating. In that case one has an even stronger sense, that if Cortés's soldiers advanced as courageously as they did because this was their only hope of survival, then what they did could no longer be considered all that courageous.

But perhaps there is a simple way out. One could say that although there is no heroism in battling, when you have steeled your nerves with drugs or cut off your own retreat, nevertheless there is heroism in creating those conditions. When you decide to take the drugs and to cut off your own retreat you embrace danger, and you do so while you are not yet under the influence or without a possible retreat. *That* is the moment at which you act heroically. That's certainly how the nineteenth-century historian William Prescott judges the matter, when in his *Conquest of Mexico* he describes this moment as being the most "remarkable . . . in the life of this remarkable man." But I think it far from obvious that he is right. In *Death in the Afternoon,* Ernest Hemingway describes a very nervous bullfighter named Domingo Hernandorena. "His feet were obviously not under his personal control and his effort to be statuesque while his feet jittered him away out of danger was very funny to the crowd. . . . The bull stood against the barrier watching him. Hernandorena could not trust his legs to carry him slowly toward the bull. He knew there was only one way he could stay in one place in the ring. He ran out toward the bull, and ten yards in front of him dropped to both knees on the sand." This being the only way in which he could keep himself from running away from the bull, he then remained on his knees, "spread the red cloth with his sword and jerked himself forward on his knees toward the bull." In the end he flubbed the encounter anyway, was injured and had to be carried out of the ring. But he got no sympathy from the crowd. Not because he flubbed the killing, says Hemingway, but "[b]ecause he was a coward . . . The knees are for cowards." Why are they for cowards? Presumably not because they diminish the risk of being killed, but because they make it easier to put up with the risk by making it harder to flee. And is the crowd wrong to think this? I simply don't know.

SOME QUESTIONS OF PROCEDURE

So far I have only looked for symmetries in the rules that assign responsibility for good and bad deeds. Yet it doesn't seem illogical to also look for such symmetries among the procedures that control the application of those rules.

Double Jeopardy and Double-Dipping

It had been Roald Amundsen's original ambition to be the first to reach the North Pole. He gave up his venture when he heard that Admiral Robert Peary had already gotten there. Instead, he turned his attention to the South Pole, and this time he got there first. He brought off another great feat a few years later, the first flight over the North Pole. Amundsen, as we have already seen, was not shy about claiming credit, but nowhere was his aggressiveness about claiming credit as much in evidence as when he tried to describe these *two* major feats as really amounting to *three* major feats. He pointed out that he enjoyed the further distinction of being the first to have been at both Poles. At first I thought he was cheating by double-counting. But then I thought of multistage athletic events, bicycle races extending over several days, and decathlons.

When a racer comes in second every day in a ten-day race, he will never earn more than that day's silver medal. Yet his consistent silver-medal performance may result in the best overall time. It doesn't seem to amount to any double-counting to award him a separate gold medal for his overall performance in addition to the ten silver medals he already garnered for each of his daily performances. By the same token, a competitor in a decathlon may not receive the top score in any single event but may rack up the most points overall. Again, it doesn't seem to be double-counting if in addition to the modest honor we bestow on him for his merely "good" performance in the individual events we grant him a separate honor for his truly extraordinary overall performance. Which is exactly what Amundsen is claiming. To further dramatize the rightness of Amundsen's claim, imagine that he had in fact been only the fifth person to get to the North Pole, fifth to get to the South Pole, fifth to climb Mount Everest, and fifth to perform a number of other such feats. We would not think that even the accumulation of all the smallish honors due someone who is only fifth to do those things would award him his just deserts. More is due him than that.

A corresponding problem has arisen on the blame-side. Many states punish repeat offenders more severely than first-time offenders. In addition, the federal government punishes more severely those whose crimes form a "pattern of racketeering," those who, as the inspired title of one law review article has it, are guilty of "The Crime of Being a Criminal."[62] Critics have objected to these kinds of provisions on the ground that they involve double-counting, that they really amount to a kind of double jeopardy. "It is hard to see how a string of prior burglary convictions could increase the wrongdoing of the current burglary charged in the indictment."[63] That is where the analogy with relay races and decathlons proves useful. Now it is no longer hard to see. Just as the individual silver medals do not recognize the consistently good performance of the racer with the best overall time, the modest punishments meted out for the individual burglaries do not recognize the consistency of the bad performance of the repeat offender. The premium added for recidivism or for a "pattern of racketeering offenses" takes care of that. (This does not of course settle the question whether the size of the premium currently given is not perhaps excessive.)

Standards of Proof

Although it may appear as though it were the special pain and iniquity of sending an innocent to the dungeon that causes the standard of proof to be as high as it is in criminal law, in fact the standard of proof for the award of honors tends to be equally or nearly as high. A mere preponderance of the evidence will not satisfy the Catholic church that someone deserves to be canonized. Lengthy investigations, briefs pro and con, and review at various levels all are meant to prove to a certainty that the would-be saint merits such recognition—proof to a near-certainty that he died defending the faith, that he produced miracles, and so forth. The Nobel committee similarly would not be content with the level of proof that would lead a court to find in favor of someone claiming a patent.

Forward- and Backward-Looking Remedies

Let us ponder the following two possibilities:

1. There is a fairly high probability that a certain person will at some point in the future commit a serious crime or make an important discovery.

2. There is a fairly high probability that a certain person has at some point in the past committed a serious crime or made an important discovery.

As far as compensation goes—if we assume the crime also amounts to a tort and the discovery happens to be patentable—both (1) and (2) merit it equally. In fact many have advocated, without getting more than practical kinds of objections, that compensation should be granted to persons who have been exposed to dangerous chemicals, even if they have not yet developed any disease but simply have a heightened probability of developing such a disease. Similarly, it is of course common to pay someone upfront for any discoveries he might make in the course of his employment over the next two years, even if he does not yet have an inkling as to what those discoveries might be.

It is not acceptable, by contrast, to bestow either punishment or prizes in advance—even where it might make a lot of utilitarian sense, for instance, because we are unlikely to catch the criminal if we wait for him to commit his crime, or because we are unlikely to give out the award in time for the beneficiary to still be able to enjoy it, if we wait for him to make his discovery. Our reluctance, however, has nothing to do with uncertainty, since uncertainty about past events makes us— as (1) and (2) show—far less reluctant about bestowing blame or praise. In other words, as far as punishment and rewards go, we distinguish strictly between (1) and (2). Of course, since punishment and tort judgments, royalties and prizes, aren't always so distinct, our attitudes about the one are likely to be infected by our attitudes about the other.

Vanity and Contrition

Immodesty impairs the credit we give for an achievement. No bragging, please! Affecting an air of high dudgeon, the historian Frantisek Link complains:

The present nomenclature of lunar formations we owe to Riccioli and Gri-
maldi, who gave to lunar craters the names of famous astronomers, mathematicians and philosophers. In the course of this, they managed to smuggle
their own names onto the moon as well.[64]

Outrageous!

Why is immodesty so harmful to a discoverer's reputation? Because it is a character flaw? In that case, one would expect immodesty in general to diminish the
credit we give. But immodesty about one's appearance, or even about achievements
other than the one under investigation, does not diminish the credit we give for
this achievement. The immodesty has to pertain to *this* achievement to have its
deleterious impact. The significance of immodesty starts to seem a little less mysterious if we cast about for a criminal law counterpart. Such a counterpart is to be
found in the role of regret, remorse, repentance. Just as the vain discoverer accords
to himself the admiration, which by rights the public ought to give him, the re-
morseful criminal subjects himself to the disapprobation which by rights the public
ought to administer. Having given to himself a good deal of what the public generally bestows, further public intervention seems superfluous. A similar logic may
underlie our reluctance to be too admiring of the vain discoverer.

The Matching Requirement

In summarizing her interviews with Nobel laureates in the sciences, the sociologist
Harriet Zuckerman notes that "[n]early half of the laureates who were interviewed,
although conceding the scientific significance of their [Prize-winning] research,
were convinced that it was not their best scientific work."[65]

It is not uncommon for a Pulitzer Prize or an Oscar to be given for some recent
work that doesn't really merit it to make up for the fact that the author or actor
did not get it for some earlier works that really did deserve it.

The foregoing raises this problem: if the Nobel committee or the Motion Picture Academy erred *not* in awarding the prize to a given person but rather in their
selection of the achievement for which they gave it, has a significant injustice been
done? Suppose *X* is unjustly imprisoned for a crime he did not commit. Thereafter
he commits a crime of the same caliber, but before he can be punished he dies. Are
we entitled to say: "What a good thing we punished him falsely for that other crime,
since we didn't get to inflict the punishment owing him for the crime he really
committed"? Occasionally we do say that. Lev Kopelev, the Russian dissident who

spent many years imprisoned in the GULAG, writes: "I came to understand that my fate, which had seemed so senselessly, so undeservedly cruel, was actually fortunate and just. It was just because I did deserve to be punished—for the many years I had zealously participated in plundering the peasants, worshipping Stalin, lying and deceiving myself in the name of 'historical necessity,' teaching others to believe in lies and to bow before scoundrels."[66] But in general, Kopelev is wrong. We are not entitled to reason as he does, because that would mean that had X lived, we would not have been entitled to punish him in light of the sentence he already served.

This would suggest that if someone achieves a breakthrough which does not merit the Nobel but for which he is erroneously given one anyway, then other Nobel-worthy achievements of his cannot be used to rationalize that award but should, on the contrary, be the basis for further awards—regardless of whether the error with the first award is ever admitted. After all punishment for the second crime is merited, regardless of whether the error with respect to the first crime is ever admitted.

The Competency Requirement

We encountered earlier in this book a somewhat peculiar rule of criminal procedure: a defendant cannot be tried or punished or executed if he is not fully competent, if he is not able to appreciate what is being said and done to him. Something like this seems also to be true on the praise-side. We are of course prepared to honor people posthumously, and that seems to conflict with the competency requirement. But a version of the requirement crops up in our thinking about gratitude. Social psychologists have conducted experiments asking subjects the following question: "If you were indebted to someone, how indebted would you still feel if you repaid the help-giver but he/she was unaware that you were the one who had helped them." Responses showed that "despite having repaid the benefit, the fact that the donor believed the debt still remained was sufficient to cause a substantial number of subjects to feel that they continued to be indebted to the donor."[67]

Compromises, Settlements, and Plea Bargains

There is a mystery concerning settlements and plea bargains that the mirror-image approach helps us resolve. According to conventional wisdom, the settlement of a tort case is a wonderful thing, devoutly to be desired, nearly always better than actually litigating a case through. But although nearly everyone agrees that settlements are very desirable, the same cannot be said for plea bargains. Plea bargains are something which many, perhaps most scholars, find morally repellent, at best a necessary evil, at worst an intolerable one. Yet a plea bargain is nothing more than the settlement of a criminal case. Why such applause for settlements and such disdain for plea bargains?[68]

To heighten the mystery, let me remind you of the hypothetical I used to convince you of the moral difficulties with plea bargains.

> A woman wakes up next to a dead man and a gun with her fingerprints on it. She was severely drunk the previous night and has no recollection of what happened. Given the look of things, she has every reason to think that she killed him. She is arrested and charged with the man's murder. The prosecutor is delighted: the woman has been implicated in a number of fatal "accidents" in the past, but there never was adequate proof for conviction. At last, it seems, he will be able to take her out of circulation. But shortly before the trial, the prosecutor learns of some surprise evidence: a film of the events of the night of the murder that has, somehow or other, come to rest in a certain safe deposit box. The film will determine, once and for all, whether the defendant or someone else is to blame for the murder. The prosecutor is less than pleased—what if this evidence should exonerate the defendant whom he has for so long tried to lock up?
>
> He tells the defendant about the new evidence. He also tells her that he doesn't know yet whether it will be exculpatory or inculpatory. The defendant is as uncertain as he. Both are simultaneously hopeful and fearful. The prosecutor then suggests a plea bargain—a significantly more lenient sentence than the one that would result from a murder conviction, but a heavy sentence nonetheless. The defendant feels the same way and accepts his offer.

I then asked whether we should permit this plea bargain to go through. It is a bargain both sides desperately want to strike: neither side wants to be exposed to the not insignificant risk that the evidence might not turn out "well." It also does not look like the usual kind of case in which we meddle with freedom of contract: there is no obvious way in which a third party is being injured by this contract. Society's interest in adequate deterrence certainly isn't affected: the probability of apprehension and conviction for criminals remains unaltered. Nevertheless, I said, one cannot but have qualms about this bargain, since we know *that whatever the evidence finally reveals, we are 100 percent certain to regret our present decision to let the plea bargain go through.* Why are we certain to regret it? Well, if the evidence proves the defendant guilty, we will have let her off too lightly; if not, we will have been too harsh. A decision we are certain to regret a moment from now should, presumably, never be rendered. What's worse, this isn't even a case where plea bargaining saves us money, since waiting for the evidence doesn't cost us anything. Nor is this a case where waiting takes an excessive emotional toll on the parties to the contract, since the evidence could be obtained almost instantly. The only reason for the plea bargain is the risk-aversion of its participants.

But suppose the same suit were a civil one—a wrongful death action. Replace the prosecutor with a private plaintiff, who offers a settlement as soon as the existence of that telltale film is revealed. The plaintiff is eager to avoid the possibility of recovering nothing; the defendant is eager to avoid the possibility of horrendous liability, and they settle on an intermediate amount. Why do we applaud this settlement when we disapprove the corresponding plea bargain? It seems we are able to register the same objection to this settlement that we made against the plea bargain. Either the evidence proves the defendant guilty and we will have let her off too lightly, if not we will have been too harsh.

Take a look, though, at the mirror-image on the praise-side of plea bargains and settlements and the mystery disappears. What is the mirror-image of a plea bargain? The settlement of a disputed claim of glory of course. And the counterpart of a settlement of a tort claim is just the settlement of a patent or copyright claim. We do in fact abhor the settlement of disputed claims of glory, but we have no problem with the settlement of patent and copyright claims. And why should that be so?

To settle a disputed claim of glory would be to agree, for instance, not to take issue with someone's authorship of a novel or a scientific idea or with his claim to have performed some heroic deed, and to let him collect whatever prizes accrue to such authors and heroes. A particularly striking example of such an agreement is one that at least one historian of science has argued accounts for Mendel's recognition as the founder of genetics. Mendel, this historian contended, actually was no Mendelian properly speaking. His "discovery was attributed to him by biologists who gave new meaning to his work in a new context at the turn of the century. Mendel's rediscovery, [the historian] has argued, has to be understood in terms of a priority dispute among De Vries, Correns and Tshermak. The labeling of the discovery as Mendel's laws was a strategy to neutralize the dispute. This is perhaps

the single most important fact in the reification of Mendel as the founder of genetics."[69]

We disallow the settlement of disputed claims of glory because we disallow the
alienation of claims of glory. We saw earlier that it is morally impermissible for
Bernoulli to surrender credit for a mathematical theorem to de l'Hospital, or Sorensen and Schlesinger to surrender credit for *Profiles in Courage* to John F. Kennedy,
or Siegfried to surrender credit for defeating Brunhilde to Gunther. If we think
that the desires of the parties are irrelevant in deciding who deserves glory for an
achievement, it would seem odd to pay attention to those desires if there happens
to be some factual dispute about who deserves such glory.

We don't run into the same roadblock when dealing with settlements of disputed patent and copyright claims. Since patents and copyrights themselves are
readily alienable, the alienability of disputed patent and copyright claims seems to
follow presently.

So there we have our explanation of the plea bargain–settlement dichotomy.
Just as you may not alienate the credit you deserve, you may not alienate the blame
you deserve. We do not allow you to contract with someone to serve your jail term
in your behalf or even to pay your criminal fine in your behalf. (No insurance for
crimes allowed!) It follows naturally that you cannot alienate disputed desert claims
either. Not so with settlements. Since you are entitled to contract with someone
to pay your tort judgment (that's what liability insurance does), it follows naturally
that you can alienate disputed tort judgments as well.

The Value of a Thing

In 1912, the stockholders of the American Tobacco Company almost unanimously
adopted a new incentive compensation formula for their managers, hoping to spur
them on to ever greater productivity. Essentially, the formula awarded key managers an annual bonus consisting of a certain percentage of the company's profits.
The formula achieved its intended goal: the company flourished. So much so that
over the years the incentive compensation formula generated bonuses of munifi-
cent size. Some stockholders decided the managers were really being paid too
much, more than a fair assessment of their contributions to the company's fortunes
justified. They brought suit, asking that the managers be forced to return some of
their excess earnings. The judge in this case did what most judges in such cases
have done; he refused. His explanation differed from that customarily given only

in being more elaborate and purplish in its prose than customary. "Yes," he acknowledged, "the Court possesses the power to prune these payments." But what, he asked, would be a "rational or just gauge for revising these figures. . . . No blueprints are furnished. The elements to be weighed are incalculable; the imponderables manifold. . . . If comparisons are to be made, with whose compensation are they to be made—executives? Those connected with the motion picture industry? Radio artists? Justices of the Supreme Court of the United States? The President of the United States?" Later he added, "Many instances of underpayment will come to mind, just as instances of apparent rank overpayment abound. Haplessly, intrinsic worth is not always the criterion. A classic might perhaps produce trifling compensation for its author, whereas a popular novel might yield a titanic fortune. Merit is not always commensurately rewarded, whilst mediocrity sometimes unjustly brings incredibly lavish returns. Nothing is so divergent and contentious and inexplicable as values."[70]

It has happened of course time and again that people who willingly entered into a bargain have gone on to complain to courts that the price they were required to pay was excessive, unfair, unconconscionable, extortionate, usurious, gouging, and should be revised retrospectively. Courts have generally declined with sentiments much like those of the judge just quoted, by asserting slightly inconsistently (a) that there is no way to tell what price would be a just one, other than the price the buyer declared at the time he was willing to pay; and (b) that life is unfair. Sentiment (a) is best captured in an eighteenth century couplet still fondly quoted by lawyers:

> The value of a thing
> Is exactly what 'twill bring

Sentiment (b) is best expressed in the advertising slogan of Kasson's Negotiation Seminar: "In business you don't get what you deserve, you get what you negotiate." But (b) seems more in the nature of an afterthought. What mostly seems to disturb the courts is that there appears to be no sensible standard by which the fairness of the terms of an exchange can be judged. This is perfectly in line with the attitude economists in general strike vis-à-vis the medieval notion of a "just price." The economist suspects that the people who invoke such notions or try to conform their behavior to them are talking incoherently and behaving irrationally. And for a long time this is exactly how I thought. But thinking about glory has made me quite uncertain on that score.

Let us consider a variation of the above case, involving not a business enterprise but a university, specifically, involving the fairness not of a manager's but a professor's compensation. For reasons that will quickly become evident, I have named each of the characters in my little scenario for a certain character in that episode from the Nibelungen saga I described earlier. A young assistant professor named Dr. Gunther approaches his dean and asks for a promotion and a raise. He tells the dean that he is sitting on top of a path-breaking paper that will permit radical advances in cancer treatment. A good deal of what is in the paper, he explains, is probably patentable, but in the public interest he wants to just publish it and make the benefits of his findings available free of charge, provided the university will honor and pay him accordingly. The dean, one Professor Brunhild, is perfectly amenable, but she is curious to know how Gunther made his discovery. Now imagine several possible replies:

Case I. Gunther says: "My brother Siegfried actually discovered it. In fact, he is still in the process of completing his research on it. It has been clear to me from the first moment he explained it to me that he was onto something very important, and I have kept him company during all this time, by not moving out of his house, even though his suicidal nature is quite hard to take. Had I not stayed around, he would probably have killed himself and taken his discovery to the grave with him. In fact, unless you promise to give me the promotion and the raise I am requesting, I will move out of the house today, and the unpleasant consequences of which I spoke would come to pass." Whereupon Brunhild says: "That's outrageous. I can't give you a raise and a promotion under these circumstances." Asks Gunther: "Why not?" Replies Brunhild: "Because you don't deserve it. Basically, you failed to interfere with an important discovery. You didn't actually *do* anything great. That doesn't deserve a raise and a promotion."

Counters Gunther: "In business you don't get what you deserve, you get what you negotiate. If you want me to publish those findings, you'll have to give me what I want." "But this isn't business. As a practical matter you may be able to force me to give you what you want. But that's really blackmail." "Well, I don't see it that way." And there we may leave them.

Case II. In response to Brunhild's question about how he made the discovery, Gunther says: "Actually, I came upon my discovery in the following haphazard fashion. . . . [He then tells a story that is a more extreme version of the story of Frederick Banting and insulin.] Admittedly, I was more lucky than smart, but unless you award me that raise and promotion, you shall never see what I found, at least not without paying the royalties a patent would exact from you." Whereupon Brunhild says: "That's outrageous. I can't give you a raise and a promotion under these circumstances." Asks Gunther: "Why not?" Replies Brunhild: "Because you don't deserve it. You were sort of like the fellow who aimed to shoot someone, missed but caused a herd of animals to stampede out of the closet and kill his victim. Your story kind of reminds me of Chauncy Gardner in Jerzy Kozinski's novel *Being There*. I won't deny that you deserve some credit for what happened to you, but you don't deserve the raise and the promotion."

Counters Gunther: "In business you don't get what you deserve, you get what you negotiate. If you want me to publish those findings, you'll have to give me what I want." "But this isn't business. As a practical matter you may be able to force me to give you want you want. But that's really blackmail." "Well, I don't see it that way."

Case III. In response to Brunhild's question, Gunther replies: "I actually don't yet have the discovery, but I can quickly get it. The discovery was made by a very young publicity-shy Soviet dissident, whom I helped support over the last decade, while he undertook his research. I am the only one to know his identity and location. I am prepared to smuggle him out of the country with his discovery, provided you promise me the raise and promotion." Whereupon Brunhild says: "That's outrageous. I can't give you a raise and a promotion under these circumstances." Asks Gunther: "Why not?" Replies Brunhild: "Because you don't deserve it. I will admit that your actions caused the discovery to be made. And we are all grateful for that. But not everyone who stands in a causal relationship to a discovery deserves to be honored as a discoverer. The relationship must be a more proximate one than that, which yours is not."

Counters Gunther: "In business you don't get what you deserve, you get what you negotiate. If you want me to publish those findings, you'll have to give me what I want." Brunhild: "But this isn't business. As a practical matter you may be able to force me to give you what you want. But that's really blackmail." Gunther: "Well, I don't see it that way."

Why couldn't one have the same kind of conversation with the executives of the American Tobacco Company? Why wouldn't the same principles of responsibility that allow us to decide on the appropriateness of prizes, promotions, and salary raises in a university context be applicable in the corporate context? Because—the answer goes—executive compensation is not in the nature of prizes and if it were treated as such enormous economic inefficiencies would result.

That reply strikes me as valid but not devoid of difficulties. To take the last point first, there would indeed be an unspeakable loss of economic efficiency if managerial compensation were subjected to such fairness constraints. But is that objection any different from the utilitarian's criticism of criminal punishments as being inefficiently light? If we feel bound to respect the constraints of proportionality, of just retribution, in the criminal law, why should we not feel equally constrained here?

What then about the other point, that salaries are different from prizes, that criteria suited to awarding prizes are not suited to setting salaries. But how different are salaries from prizes? In the university context, the difference seems really hard to make out. It also proved hard to make out for the IRS some years ago when the tax law still treated prizes as not constituting (taxable) income. Courts then had to somehow settle tricky questions such as whether the $25,000 awarded the person who manages to catch a marked rock fish should be deemed income or a prize, or what to do about the Mustang awarded the "Most Popular Dodger" by a devoted local car dealer, or the bejeweled S. Rae Hickock Belt given the outstanding athlete of the year.

Business enterprises setting salaries in fact often feel uncomfortable making too much of the salary-prize distinction. They proceed as though they thought that the "just desert" ideas behind the award of prizes ought to also control the setting of salaries. The sociologist Karol Solton has described this process in great detail in his book *The Causal Theory of Justice*.[71] Large organizations set wages by means of elaborate, formulaic job evaluation schemes. Relying sometimes on a point system, sometimes on a simple ranking procedure, sometimes on statistical "factor analysis," these schemes classify every job according to what it requires in the way of skills (measured in terms of the subcategories "education, experience, initiative"), effort (typical subcategories: "physical effort, mental/visual effort"), and responsibility (typical subcategories: "working conditions, unavoidable hazards"). The classification schemes are not particularly responsive to market conditions, except in the broadest sense. Although the overall wage level is influenced by the market, the relative compensation of the people in various job categories is not. Only acute shortages will cause someone in a "lower" job category to be paid more than someone in a "higher" job category. Everyone's perception of these schemes—"everyone" being the management, the employees, and the consulting firms who design them—is that they are governed by "fairness," not "market" considerations. Most especially, that's how arbitrators see the scheme when called upon to adjudicate disputes to which they give rise. "In some ways," writes Karol Soltan, "these model systems are more like normative theories in ethics than like organizational rule systems. They specify what some large set of organizations should do and what wage systems they should adopt."[72]

The prize-like character of wages becomes especially clear if one asks about the attributes of the most coveted and admired jobs (ignoring, for the moment, how well they pay). The typical wish list which research into this question has generated includes "skill variety," "task significance" (a job with "substantial impact on the lives or work of other people"), "autonomy" (a job that "provides substantial freedom, independence and discretion"), "task identity" (a job that "requires completion of a whole and identifiable piece of work"), and "feedback" (a job that "results in the individual's obtaining direct and clear information . . . about his performance"). What is striking about this list is that it is nearly identical with the attributes that characterize the best-paid jobs in the job evaluation schema. Unless one recognizes the prize aspect of wages, it is hard to figure out this coincidence.

> It may seem paradoxical [writes Soltan] that the performance of the more intrinsically rewarding tasks is held to deserve higher pay. If people would do them anyway, why should we pay more to have them done? Is not the intrinsic reward, reward enough? Yet my claim is precisely this: the more important and difficult jobs are more intrinsically rewarding *and* are held to deserve greater pay. Indeed, these are simply two alternative ways to express the same hierarchy of value. This apparent paradox can be understood properly only if we see it in context: the same paradox holds for all (or almost all) deserving of benefits. An outstanding performance of an actor in a theater or a student on a test deserves greater reward than a poor performance. It is also more intrinsically rewarding.[73]

We now understand why it sounds so outrageous to our ears for an employer to say to his employee: "I am willing to grant you a promotion from secretary to editorial assistant, which as you know involves more interesting and prestigious work, and for which by virtue of your extensive education [skills], tenacity [effort], and ability to manage subordinates [responsibility] you are especially suited. *However,* this will entail a salary cut, which you will presumably not mind, given the greater nonpecuniary rewards of the job I am offering you." This sort of bargain offends against the perceived prize-like character of wages.

In fact when economists seek to defend the justice of the current distribution of income, they do so by implicitly looking at salaries like prizes and asking whether the income is deserved under the norms that control the award of prizes. They are able to answer in the affirmative because they are usually unaware of all the norms that control the award of prizes. The only one they are clearly aware of is the causal requirement—the recipient of a reward must have conferred a benefit commensurate with the reward he is receiving. The fact that wages in a competitive system correspond to the value of someone's marginal product, therefore, seems to support the idea that an employee is paid what according to the norms of prizes he deserves. But that also means that the wages bear no relationship to whether the contribution is made by an act or an omission, with the appropriate mental state, by remote or proximate causation, and in conformity with all the other criteria that determine the justice of a prize award. In his *Foundations of Economic Analysis,* Paul Samuelson makes a somewhat cryptic quip which I think is really meant to get at this fact. "Perhaps the bourgeois penchant for laissez-faire is the only case on record where a substantial number of individuals have made idols of partial derivatives, i.e. imputed marginal productivities," he writes.[74]

Yet for all that, I think the distinction between prizes and salaries is valid and sensible, and I would not have us impose on commercial exchanges the norms that control the award of prizes. The relationship between wages and prizes I think is rather like that between tort judgments and criminal punishments. Constraints of proportionality that are appropriate for criminal punishments are not so for the kind of utilitarian enterprise the tort law represents. Yet there are many cases where we hesitate whether to characterize something as a tort or criminal proceeding, which is reflected in the long-standing legal debates over whether the procedural protections of a criminal trial are due in deportation hearings, disciplinary hearings, or legal proceedings in which only civil penalties are at stake. Sometimes even a regular tort trial has so taken on the color of a moral crusade that we are tempted to subject it to the proportionality constraints that are really meant for a criminal trial. It is this kind of confusion I believe besets organizations, when they feel obliged to observe norms of fairness in setting salaries, and economists, when they try to justify salaries by arguing the justice of paying someone his marginal contribution.

THE SHORT ANSWER

The problem of Part III, if amidst the proliferation of detail you still remember it, was to determine the principles that separate an honest from a dishonest fame, the just from the unjust award of glory, in short, the rules of praise. Those rules turned out to be something of a mirror-image of the rules of blame, provided we count fun-house mirrors as mirrors.

Despite that not inconsiderable "fun-house" distortion, the juxtaposition of the rules of praise and blame proved to hold some useful lessons. Many a phenomenon that looked puzzling on the praise-side ceased to be so once we examined its counterpart on the blame-side, so long as we had a sufficiently strong intuition that some sort of symmetry between the two should exist. Celebrating Copernicus even though he may have been irrationally precipitate in his beliefs is easier once we have seen the notion of intention at work in the criminal law. Appreciating the significance of Copernicus's recantatory-sounding preface to his treatise is easier once we have thought about abandonment in the criminal law. Denying Heisenberg too much credit for not inventing the atom bomb is easier once we have considered the role of omissions in the criminal law.

Conversely, many a phenomenon that looked puzzling on the blame-side ceased to be so once we examined its counterpart on the praise-side (again, so long as we had a sufficiently strong intuition that some sort of symmetry between the two should exist). Punishing ignorance of the law is easier once we have seen how ignorance of moral rules is treated on the praise-side. Punishing recidivists more harshly than first-time offenders is easier once we have thought about decathlons and other multistage competitions. Punishing for bad luck is easier once we have contemplated entering an Experience Machine.

Sometimes of course juxtaposing the corresponding rules of praise and blame simply led us to be puzzled by the evident asymmetry they displayed: for instance, that strict liability should be so intolerable on the blame-side and so natural on the praise-side, that insanity should be so exculpatory on the blame-side and so unimportant on the praise-side.

A more general lesson of the rules of praise was to give the lie to the oft-uttered cliche that there are no yardsticks of fairness in exchanges, which is not to say however that it would be well for us to observe those yardsticks.

Denouement

Some years ago I read a letter to Ann Landers written by the annoyed parents of two adult children. They complained that whereas their married daughter dutifully brought her husband and family to spend Thanksgiving and Christmas with them, their son chose to spend the holidays with his in-laws instead. Why couldn't sons be as dutiful as daughters! That there was a bit of a logical difficulty here, that it would be difficult for every married son and every married daughter to make their families spend the holidays with their parents rather than their in-laws, did not dawn on me until Ann Landers with her usual relish asked them what they thought their dutiful daughter's in-laws were saying about *their* son.

In a way, each of the three parts of this book is built around a logical difficulty of just this type. In each of the three parts I exploit a different feature of the basic rules by which we apportion blame for wrongdoing. Certain things that a casual observer will think can be demanded simultaneously of a sensible system of responsibility turn out to be incompatible in nearly as straightforward a way as the things that Ann Landers's correspondents were demanding. Our basic rules of responsibility tell us the degree of blameworthiness that attaches to various actions, and tell us in particular that, roughly speaking, blameworthiness is determined by the mental state with which a harm was brought about, by whether that harm was brought about through an act or an omission, by the causal relationship between the act and the harm, and by the size of the harm. From this simple statement follows a bit more than we are at first inclined to think. If every daughter makes her family spend the holidays with her parents, we know that means necessarily that sons cannot be spending the holidays with *their* parents. If more than just harm determines how blameworthy an action is, if the way in which the harm is brought about also affects its blameworthiness—well, then by rearranging the route by which a harm is effectuated one can affect one's blameworthiness. But "route" is just another term for "form," and rearranging is just another term for avoision. This realization is the essential idea behind Part I's defense of a lot of what gets denounced as evasion.

If more than just harm determines how blameworthy an action is, something else follows as well. Since preferences and consent affect at most this one element of blameworthiness, harm, but leave the others unchanged, their capacity for cleansing a transaction of criminal taint is bound to be in some way limited. The blackmail law and related restrictions on jointly desired bargains are the law's expression of that limitation. This is the essential idea behind Part Two.

Finally, if more than just harm determines how blameworthy an action is, this suggests still something else. The factors other than harm that determine blameworthiness, the mental state, the presence of an act, the causal nexus, sound like they are really about responsibility, not blameworthiness. When something bad happens, they become relevant to blameworthiness only because they help us decide who among a variety of candidates is in fact to be held responsible for that bad result. But suppose something good happens. Then too it makes sense to see if anyone can be held responsible. And what principles are we to use to make *that* determination? It is not unnatural to suppose that the same principles that tell us how to assign responsibility for the bad also tell us how to assign responsibility for the good. At least my example comparing a group of criminals with a group of soldiers fighting for a just cause suggested as much.

If that is even partly true, then various other things follow: that just as blame is not given out in a utilitarian fashion, praise is probably not given out in a utilitarian fashion either. In other words, just as the rules of blame aren't designed so as to minimize the amount of blameworthy conduct (that is, to maximize deterrence), so the rules of praise aren't designed to maximize the amount of praiseworthy conduct (that is, maximize encouragement of science, art, and virtue). Something else too would seem to follow: just as every criminal offense merits a certain amount of disapproval and punishment (often at variance with what deterrence calls for), so every praiseworthy act merits a certain amount of applause and reward (often at variance with what an encouragement view, or the market, calls for). Note that this gives the long-dead medieval notion of a "just price" a new lease on life. It vindicates the intuition many people have that even in a market transaction the value of a thing is not just what 'twill bring (even though we would often do well to proceed as though it were). This is the essential idea behind Part Three.

Samuel Johnson, who did not think much of Jonathan Swift, said about *Gulliver's Travels* that once you had the idea about little people and big people everything else readily followed. So I shouldn't object if you said the same about this book: keeping in mind the above three ideas, everything else readily follows.

Acknowledgments

"I fairly confess that I have served myself all I could by reading, that I made use of the judgment of authors dead and living; that I omitted no means in my power to be informed of my errors, both by my friends and enemies." Alexander Pope was a generous man, but I will content myself with footnoting the authors dead and living of whom I made use and enumerating the friends on whom I relied to inform me of my errors; I'll skip the enemies.

Never shy to point out error, find fault, take issue, or be cantankerous was my friend and longtime office neighbor at the University of Michigan Rick Pildes. Less cantankerous help I got from other readers of the manuscript: Michael Moore, Stephen Morse, Guyora Binder, Bill Miller, Seth Kreimer, Jim Lindgren, Larry Alexander, Heidi Hurd, Jacqueline Ross, Avery Katz, Eric Posner, Jacques de Lisle, Kent Syverud, Heidi Feldman, Joe Vining, Joel Seligman, Jana Katz, and Friedrich Katz. Guyora Binder also tried, alas unsuccessfully, to teach me the rudiments of baseball, which would have been helpful for Part Three of this book.

Elizabeth Warren first told me about the wonderful problem of exemption planning.

My three tax scholar friends—Jeff Lehman, David Shakow and Reed Schuldiner—all took issue with my tax analysis.

Legal advice on various subjects was also rendered by Bruce Mann (trusts and estates), Stephen Burbank and Leo Levin (procedure), and Becky Eisenberg (intellectual property). For sociological advice I went to Kim Scheppele.

Frequent sparring partners on this or that argument in this book were Ed Rock, Louis Feldman, Howard Lesnick, Jeff Lange, and Skip Bean.

Several classes in my course in Law and Morality at the Universities of Michigan and Pennsylvania, as well as several workshop audiences at the Universities of Oklahoma City, Virginia, Northwestern, Southern Illinois at Edwardsville, and Buffalo opened their hearts, minds and pocketbooks to portions of the manuscript.

Debórah Dwork's magic pen traveled down every line of Part One of this book, in search of the clumsy, the wordy, the sexist, or the perniciously cute. Debórah, to whom this book is dedicated, thought the world of it even before it was written. Of course, if everyone had had her sagacity, there would have been no point in writing it.

Philadelphia
Fall 1994

Notes

INTRODUCTION

1. Quoted in Alexander Kohn, *Fortune or Failure: Missed Opportunities and Chance Discoveries in Science* (Cambridge, Mass.: Basil Blackwell, 1989), 156.

2. Howard Margolis, *Patterns, Thinking, and Cognition: A Theory of Judgment* (Chicago: University of Chicago Press, 1987), 6.

PART ONE

1. This is a much embellished version of a passing suggestion made by Gunther Jakobs in "Noetigung durch Drohung als Freiheitsdelikt," in *Einheit und Vielfalt des Strafrechts: Festschrift fuer Karl Petters,* vol. 69, ed. Juergen Baumann and Klaus Tiedemann (1974).

2. *The Threepenny Opera,* text by Bertolt Brecht, music by Kurt Weill, English adaptation by Marc Blitzstein (Vienna: Universal Edition, 1954).

3. See Borris Bittker and Lawrence Lokken, *Federal Taxation of Income, Estate and Gifts,* 2d ed., vol. 3 (Boston: Warren, Gorham and Lamont, 1991). See generally chap. 75, "Assignments of Income," and specifically sec. 75.3.5, "Gift-Leasebacks of Income-Producing Property."

4. T. Alexander Aleinikoff and David A. Martin, *Immigration: Process and Policy,* 2d ed. (St. Paul: West Publishing Co., 1991), 777–779.

5. W. D. Macdonald, *Fraud on the Widow's Share* (Ann Arbor: University of Michigan Law School, 1960).

6. *United States v. Stewart,* 336 F.Supp. 299, 301 (E.D.Pa., 1971).

7. See generally Douglas G. Baird, *The Elements of Bankruptcy* (Westbury, N.Y.: Foundation Press, 1923), 24–54.

8. *Time,* November 9, 1992:60.

9. *Roccograndi v. Unemployment Comp. Bd. of Review,* 178 A.2d 786 (Pa.Super., 1962), reprinted in Robert Hamilton's *Corporations* casebook, from whence it came to my attention.

10. RGSt [Entscheidungen des Reichsgerichts in Strafsachen] 27: 307.

11. Alfred Bergmann, *Das Unrecht der Noetigung* (Berlin: Duncker and Humblot, 1983), 142–147.

12. Joseph Isenbergh, "Musings on Form and Substance in Tax Law," *University of Chicago Law Review* 49 (1982): 859, 865.

13. The example is Mark Kelman's. See Kelman, "Personal Deductions Revisited: Why They Fit Poorly in an Ideal Income Tax and Why They Fit Worse in a Far from Ideal World," *Stanford Law Review* 31 (1979): 831; and his "Consumption Theory, Production Theory, and Ideology in the Coase Theorem," *Southern California Law Review* 52 (1979): 669. See also Paul B. Stephan, "Federal Income Taxation and Human Capital," *Virginia Law Review* 70 (1984): 1357.

14. Lloyd Jensen, "Predicting International Events," *Peace Research Reviews* 4, no. 6 (1971).

15. Robyn Dawes, "The Robust Beauty of Improper Linear Models in Decision Making," in *Judgment under Uncertainty: Heuristics and Biases,* ed. Daniel Kahneman, Paul Slovic, and Amos Tversky (Cambridge: Cambridge University Press, 1982), 391–407.

16. Joern Kalkbrenner, *Urteil ohne Prozess: Margot Honecker gegen Ossietzky-Schueler* (Berlin: Dietz Verlag, 1990).

17. Martin Dewhirst and Robert Farrel, eds., *The Soviet Censorship* (Metuchen, N.J.: Scarecrow Press, 1973), 135.

18. Galileo, *Dialogue Concerning the Two Chief World Systems,* trans. Stilman Drake, 2d ed. (Berkeley: University of California Press, 1967), 5–7.

19. Ernest Jones, *The Life and Times of Sigmund Freud,* vol. 3 (New York: Basic Books, 1957), 226.

20. Bob Woodward and Carl Bernstein, *All the President's Men* (New York: Simon and Schuster, 1974), 180.

21. Id., 173.

22. Philip Roth, *Goodbye Columbus* (New York: Modern Library, 1966), 130.

23. Id., 134.

24. George Ticknor, *Life of William Hickling Prescott* (Philadelphia: J. B. Lippincott and Co., 1882), 17–18.

25. Christopher Browning, *Ordinary Men* (New York: Harper Collins, 1992), 73.

26. Charles Mackay, *Extraordinary Popular Delusions and the Madness of Crowds* (New York: Harmony Books, 1980 [1841]), xix.

27. Richard P. Feynman, *Surely You're Joking, Mr. Feynman* (New York: W. W. Norton, 1985), 260.

28. Id.

29. Jacob Katz, *The Shabbes-Goy,* trans. Yoel Lerner (Philadelphia: Jewish Publications Society, 1989).

30. Blaise Pascal, *The Provincial Letters,* trans. A. J. Krailshaimer (Baltimore: Penguin Books, 1967), 145.

31. Id., 106.

32. Id., 186.

33. Id.

34. Id., 120–121.

35. Id., 121.

36. Id., 122.

37. Id., 140.

38. Id., 76.

39. Thomas N. Tentler, *Sin and Confession on the Eve of the Reformation* (Princeton: Princeton University Press, 1977), 6.

40. See Paul H. Robinson, "Causing the Conditions of One's Own Defense," *Virginia Law Review* 71 (1985): 1; and Joachim Hruschka, *Strafrecht nach logisch-analytischer Methode,* 2d ed. (Berlin: Walter de Gruyter, 1987), 353.

41. Christopher Boorse and Roy Sorensen, "Ducking Harm," *Journal of Philosophy* 85 (1988): 115.

42. Program on KERA-TV, Philadelphia, March 1, 1992, transcript XKERA-101. A coproduction for PBS by KERA Dallas/Fort Worth, J March Group and Video Publishing House, Inc. Transcript produced by Journal Graphics, Inc., "Street Smarts: How to Avoid Being a Victim—with Detective J. J. Bittenbinder." Copyright 1992.

43. Id.

44. The seminal article that first uncovered this phenomenon is Mark Grady, "Why Are People Negligent? Technology, Nondurable Precautions, and the Medical Malpractice Explosion," *Northwestern Law Review* 82 (1988): 293.

45. *D.P.P. v. Smith* [1960] A.C. 290.

46. *R. v. Serné,* 16 Cox Crim. Cas. 311 (1887).

47. Jacob Katz, *The Shabbes-Goy,* 20–21.

48. Albert Speer, *Inside the Third Reich,* trans. Richard and Clara Winston (New York: Macmillan Co., 1970), 18–19.

49. Id., 112–113.

50. Id., 375–376.

51. Matthias Schmidt, *Albert Speer: The End of a Myth,* trans. Joachim Neugroschel (New York: St. Martin's Press, 1984), 195.

52. Jon Elster, *Sour Grapes* (Cambridge: Cambridge University Press, 1983), 149.

53. Paul Veyne, *Did the Greeks Believe in Their Myths?* trans. from the French by Paul Wissing (Chicago: University of Chicago Press, 1988), xi.

54. Elster, *Sour Grapes,* 152.

55. Id.

56. Kendall L. Walton, *Mimesis as Make-Believe* (Cambridge, Mass.: Harvard University Press, 1990), 175.

57. Id., 142.

58. New York Times, August 1, 1981, 16, quoted in Stephen Gillers, *Regulation of Lawyers: Problems of Law and Ethics,* 3d ed. (Boston: Little, Brown and Co., 1992), 338.

59. Model Penal Code Sec.5.01(4).

60. Roy Sorensen, *Blindspots* (Oxford: Oxford University Press, 1987), 37.

61. Edmund Wilson, *Patriotic Gore* (New York: Oxford University Press, 1962), 101.

62. Clifford Browder, *The Money Game in Old New York: Daniel Drew and His Times* (Lexington: University Press of Kentucky, 1986), 117.

63. The hard case here would be that of Martin Guerre, the protagonist of the old French legend-turned-movie *The Return of Martin Guerre*. Is the man pretending to be Martin Guerre, Madame Guerre's long-lost husband, guilty of raping her?

64. Kurtz, Discussion on Questionable Positions, 32 Tax Lawyer 13, quoted in Bernard Wolfman and James P. Holden, *Ethical Problems in Federal Income Taxation,* 2d ed. (Charlottesville, Va.: Michie Co., 1985), 62–63.

65. Judith Jarvis Thomson, "The Trolley Problem," in *Rights, Restitution and Risk* (Cambridge, Mass.: Harvard University Press, 1986), 94–116.

66. Jonathan Glover, *Causing Death and Saving Lives* (Harmondsworth: Penguin, 1977), 102.

67. Michael S. Moore, "Torture and the Choice of Evils," 23 *Israel Law Review* 23 (1991): 280, 290. The template for this argument was first introduced in Robert Nozick's *Anarchy, State and Utopia* (New York: Basic Books, 1974), chap. 3, and is explored at length by Samuel Scheffler in *The Rejection of Consequentialism* (Oxford: Oxford University Press, 1982).

68. Bertolt Brecht, *The Measure Taken.* I am quoting the translation by Martin Esslin, in *Brecht: The Man and His Work* (New York: Doubleday and Co., 1960), 157.

69. It also bears pointing out that the deontological case is greatly aided by the sheer number of examples presented throughout Part I, for which the deontological approach can most readily account.

70. William Riker, *The Art of Political Manipulation* (New Haven: Yale University Press, 1986), chap. 7.

71. Id., chap. 2.

72. Sun Tzu, *The Art of War,* trans. Samuel B. Griffin (Oxford: Oxford University Press, 1963), 60.

73. Michael E. Levine and Charles R. Plott, "Agenda Influence and Its Implications," *Virginia Law Review* 63 (1977): 561.

74. Bob Woodward and Scott Armstrong, *The Brethren* (New York: Avon Books, 1981), 202.

75. H. W. Perry, *Deciding to Decide* (Cambridge, Mass.: Harvard University Press, 1991), 199.

76. Id., 200.

77. Adam Morton, *Disasters and Dilemmas* (Oxford: Basil Blackwell, 1991), 25–26.

78. R. A. Duff, *Trials and Punishments* (Cambridge: Cambridge University Press, 1986), explores the insanity paradox in depth.

79. Judith Jarvis Thomson, "Liability and Individualized Evidence," in *Rights, Restitution and Risk,* 224–250.

80. Nozick, *Anarchy, State and Utopia,* 42.

81. James Griffin, *Well-Being* (Oxford: Clarendon Press, 1986), 9.

82. Peter Unger, *Identity, Consciousness and Value* (New York: Oxford University Press, 1990), 301–302.

83. Richard S. Schwartz, "Mood Brighteners, Affect, Tolerance, and the Blues," *Psychiatry* 54:398. See also Peter D. Kramer, *Listening to Prozac* (New York: Viking Press, 1993), 250–300.

84. Francis Sparshott, "The Disappointed Art Lover," in *The Forger's Art,* ed. Denis Dutton (Berkeley: University of California Press, 1983), 246–263.

85. Unger, *Identity, Consciousness and Value,* 315–318.

86. Piers Paul Read, *The Train Robbers* (New York: Avon, 1979), xiv.

87. Id., 352.

88. Martha Gellhorn, "Guerre de Plume," *Paris Review* 23, no. 79 (Spring 1981): 286.

89. Wright, *Lillian Hellman* (New York: Ballantine Books, 1986), 396–397.

90. Id., 392.

91. Id., 15.

92. *The Nibelungenlied,* trans. A. T. Hatto (Baltimore: Penguin Books, 1965), 66.

93. Id., 66.

94. Moritz Cantor, *Vorlesungen ueber die Geschichte der Mathematik,* 2d ed. (Leipzig: B. G. Teubner, 1921), 222–226.

95. *New York Times,* November 15, 1989: sec. C, p. 17, col. 1, late ed.

96. Paul de Kruif, *Microbe Hunters* (New York: Harcourt, Brace, Jovanovich, 1926), 15.

97. You may be wondering, What about the president who is also a principal shareholder? Isn't his connection with the enterprise as direct as that of a partner in a partnership whom we do think it fair to subject to liability to the enterprise's tort victims? Because of the constraints that corporate formalities impose even on a president who is also a principal shareholder, his situation is rather like that of an engineer who rides along in a largely computer-operated locomotive to take care of problems as they arise. By contrast, the situation of the partner is rather like that of a driver.

98. See Unger, *Identity, Consciousness and Value,* chap. 5.

99. Adam Robinson and John Katzman, *Cracking the System: The SAT* (New York: Villard Books, 1991), 9. See also David Owen, *None of the Above* (Boston: Houghton Mifflin Co., 1985).

100. Robinson and Katzman, *Cracking the System,* 28.

101. Id., 72–73.

102. Kathy Crafts and Brenda Hauther, *How to Beat the System* (New York: Grove Press, 1981), 79–81.

103. Id., 133–135.

104. James M. Eagan, *A Speeder's Guide to Avoiding Tickets* (New York: Avon Books, 1991).

105. Crafts and Hauther, *How to Beat the System,* 191.

106. Robert Cialdini, *Influence: The New Psychology of Persuasion* (New York: William Morrow, 1984).

107. For a survey of this problem, see Stanley S. Surrey and Paul R. McDaniel, *Tax Expenditures* (Cambridge, Mass.: Harvard University Press, 1985).

108. Guido Calabresi, *Ideals, Beliefs, Attitudes and the Law* (Syracuse: Syracuse University Press, 1988), 1.

109. *United States v. Girard,* 601 F.2d 69 (2d Cir., 1969).

110. *United States v. Bottone,* 365 F.2d 389 (2d Cir. 1966).

111. *McNally v. United States,* 107 S.Ct. 2875 (1987).

112. Gregory, Kalven, Epstein, *Torts,* 3d ed. (Boston: Little, Brown and Co., 1976), 659.

113. Cialdini, *Influence,* 28.

114. Amos Tversky and Daniel Kahneman, "The Framing of Decisions and the Psychology of Choice," *Science* 211, January 30, 1981:453.

115. Thomas Mann, *Confessions of Felix Krull, Confidence Man* (New York: Alfred A. Knopf, 1955), 21–30.

116. In his book *Metamagical Themas* (New York: Basic Books, 1985), Douglas Hofstadter remarks: "What if someone said to you, 'The ultimate basis of this brick's solidity is that it is composed of a stupendous number of eensy-weensy brick-like objects that themselves are rock-solid'? You might be interested to learn that bricks are composed of micro-bricks, but the initial question—'What accounts for the solidity?'—has been thoroughly begged. What we ultimately want is for solidity to vanish, to dissolve, to disintegrate into some totally different kind of phenomenon" (475).

117. Giovanni Boccaccio, *The Decameron,* trans. G. H. McWilliam (Penguin Books, 1972), 87–89.

118. Gotthold Ephraim Lessing, *Nathan the Wise,* trans. Bayard Quincy Morgan (New York: Frederick Unger Publishing Co., 1955), 75–78.

119. See Gary Lawson, "Proving the Law," *Northwestern Law Review* 86 (1992): 859.

120. This equivalence argument is based on Roy Sorensen, *Blindspots* (Oxford: Oxford University Press, 1987).

121. *People v. Marrero,* 507 N.E.2d 1068 (N.Y.Ct. of Appeals, 1987).

122. *Lambert v. California,* 355 U.S. 225 (1957).

123. Michael Holroyd, *Bernard Shaw,* vol. 1 (New York: Random House, 1988), 409.

124. Robert Caro, *Means of Ascent: The Years of Lyndon Johnson* (New York: Alfred A. Knopf, 1990), chap. 3.

125. Thomas Reeves, *A Question of Character* (New York: Free Press, 1991), 68.

PART TWO

1. 357 U.S. 513, 540–541.

2. The *locus classicus* for the distinction between threats and offers is Robert Nozick, "Coercion," in *Philosophy, Science and Method: Essays in Honor of Ernest Nagel,* ed. Sydney Morgenbesser et al. (1969), 440.

3. See generally Alan Wertheimer, *Coercion* (Princeton: Princeton University Press, 1987).

4. Restatement (Second) of Torts, Paragraph 496E, illus. 5 (1965).

5. Note that this problem would not disappear if the contractor had thrown in some token consideration for a higher price. It doesn't exonerate the robber any that he offered to exchange his empty wallet for the victim's full one. See Wertheimer, *Coercion,* at 95–103. Wertheimer's book neatly lays out how the underlying logical structure of the Restatement and of cases dealing with coercive contracts, illegal searches, and plea bargains is in fact identical. My illustrations in the first half of this subsection, and my interpretation of those illustrations, borrow heavily from his book.

6. Robert Nozick, *Anarchy, State and Utopia,* 57.

7. As an aside, I alert the reader to the fact that there is a real puzzle surrounding peace treaties. Since they are frequently signed at the point of a gun, whence do they derive their moral force? More concretely yet, what about the army that purports to surrender by waving a white flag, and as the other side approaches, already off its guard, launches a new attack? Clearly the surrender was coerced. So whence its moral force?

8. What follows is not intended as an exhaustive presentation of all extant notable theories of blackmail, but only a smattering of those that try to assimilate it to traditional notions of coercion. For a superb discussion of most of the competing approaches prior to 1984—I say "most" because the Germans have invented a few more variations—see James Lindgren, "Unraveling the Paradox of Blackmail," *Columbia Law Review* 84 (1984): 670, 680–701. For more recent work, see the 1993 Blackmail symposium Lindgren and I edited in the *University of Pennsylvania Law Review.*

9. Richard Epstein, "Blackmail, Inc.," *University of Chicago Law Review* 50 (1983): 553, 562–563.

10. Id., 564.

11. See Hans von Hentig, *Die Erpressung* (Tübingen: J. C. B. Mohr (Paul Siebeck), 1959), 197–198.

12. Nozick, *Anarchy, State and Utopia*, 84.

13. Id., 85.

14. Joel Feinberg, *The Moral Limits of the Criminal Law*, vol. 3, *Harmless Wrongdoing*, Oxford: Oxford University Press (1990), 238–274. This is only one of two theories of blackmail Feinberg advances. The other is based on exploitation.

15. Feinberg acknowledges this objection. It just doesn't move him.

16. James Lindgren, "Unraveling the Paradox of Blackmail," *Columbia Law Review.*

17. See Guido Calabresi, "The Beliefs of a Reasonable Person," in *Ideals, Beliefs, Attitudes, and the Law,* 45.

18. See for instance *Payne v. Tennessee,* 111 S.Ct. 2597, 2609 (1991) (holding that the Eight Amendment did not erect a per se bar prohibiting a capital sentencing jury from considering victim impact evidence).

19. See H. L. A. Hart, *Punishment and Responsibility* (New York: Clarendon Press, 1968), 231–237.

20. Michael S. Moore, *Law and Psychiatry* (1984) 241–243. See also his essay "The Moral Worth of Retribution," in *Responsibility, Character, and the Emotions,* ed. Ferdinand Schoeman, 1987), 179.

21. Nozick, *Anarchy, State and Utopia,* 61–62.

22. See Peter Spierenburg, *The Spectacle of Suffering* (Cambridge: Cambridge University Press, 1984), 73–74.

23. See Thorsten Sellin and Marvin E. Wolfgang, *The Measurement of Delinquency* (New York: John Wiley and Sons, 1964): 268. See also George A. Gescheider, *Psychophysics,* 2d ed. (Hillsdale, N.J.: Lawrence Erlbaum Associates, 1985), 227–267.

24. Gescheider, *Psychophysics,* 254.

25. In addition to being discussed in Gescheider's *Psychophysics* textbook, this finding is the subject of an original paper by Gescheider, E. C. Catlin, and A. M. Fontana, "Psychophysical Measurement of the Judged Seriousness of Crimes and Severity of Punishments" *Bulletin of the Psychonomic Society* 82 (1982): 275.

26. How dependent is my analysis on the rightness of retributivism? Although a retributivist view greatly facilitates it, most of what I say can readily be adapted to alternative views. That's most obvious if you subscribe to a certain version of the mixed view. That is, suppose that you think that punishment serves both deterrent and retributive purposes, but that most punishments are as low as they are because retributivism keeps them down: We don't impose the death penalty for drunk driving because retributivism forbids it, *not* because it wouldn't have a huge deterrent impact and save more lives than it would cost. Your view is then really equivalent to retributivism within the relevant punishment range. My analysis also straightforwardly holds for at least one kind of utilitarian, the kind Bernard Williams has called the "government house utilitarian," namely, the person who believes that utilitarian ends are best achieved if we all adopt a nonutilitarian frame of mind. But I

suspect that even if you are a utilitarian of a more ruthless or antidiluvian hue, a version of the analysis I offer can be carried over.

27. We are now, incidentally, better able to see what it means to criminalize an area of misconduct. It means not so much replacing private suits with public ones and damage awards with the assessment of fines as it means keying the penalty structure to fault: to make it sensitive to the presence of intention as opposed to mere recklessness, to make it encompass not just completed offenses but also attempts; and to make it distinguish between degrees of complicity, between being a principal and being an accessory. Note that when the gap between penal desert and tort damages becomes too large, we often become queasy and seek to "criminalize" the tort law by introducing punitive damages.

28. Steven Kelman makes this very point in "A Case for In-Kind Transfers," *Economics and Philosophy* 2:55–72.

29. Thomas Scanlon, "Preference and Urgency," *Journal of Philosophy* 7 (1975): 655, 659–660.

30. See Ronald Dworkin, "What is Equality? Part I: Equality of Welfare," *Philosophy and Public Affairs* 10 (1981): 185; see also Thomas Nagel, *The View from Nowhere* (1986), 171n.1.

31. Robert Nozick and Jeffrie Murphy have wondered whether it would really constitute blackmail for a newspaper to suppress an embarrassing story if the victim promises to reimburse them for the lost profits. Although traditional blackmail law would probably count this as blackmail, many people's intuitions are with Nozick and Murphy in discounting this as blackmail. The explanation for our ambivalence would appear to be that running the story nonretaliatorily does not seem like a wrong. Hence, to make money out of its suppression is not to make money out of a threatened wrong. On the other hand, some would view even the printing of such a story on a nonretaliatorily basis as a wrong—especially if it constitutes an invasion of privacy—and so would want to deem the exchange of money for its suppression as blackmail.

32. One could for instance imagine the case of someone who was ready to tell your spouse about your infidelities but lets you know that he is corruptible, that for a suitable fee he will suppress his friendship instinct and not tell on you. If that is really his frame of mind, I would not treat that as blackmail. To be sure, most courts would, but only because they haven't thought the issue through adequately.

Admittedly things get harder if the blackmailer threatens to report a crime. Shall we say about him that he is threatening to report the crime in retaliation for not being paid, or that he is simply telling his victim that he is willing to suppress his good citizenship instincts for a suitable fee? Generally, I suspect the former will be a better description of his frame of mind than the latter.

Now you might object to making the blackmail status of a threat dependent on whether it will be carried out for retaliatory reasons. No doubt the notion of "retaliatory reasons" *is* a bit murky, but it is a murky concept of which the law avails itself all the time, and it is in fact quite similar in operation to a doctrine that is solidly at home in the criminal law: the doctrine of abandonment, which calls for assessments of motive very much like those required in thinking about "retaliatory reasons." Anyone who has embarked on a criminal attempt, say a bank robbery, can escape punishment if he *voluntarily* abandons the crime prior to completion: for instance, if he closes the open safe door without removing the money and leaves. It is voluntary only if it occurs for the right kind of reason. If he abandons because he sees the police coming, or because the safe is too hard to crack, or because the money he finds inside is too little to be worth bothering with—those are not good enough reasons. One does not get an abandonment defense if the abandonment is (in the words of the Model Penal Code) "motivated in whole or in part, by circumstances, not present or apparent at the inception of the actor's course of conduct, which increase the probability of detection or apprehension, or which make more difficult the accomplishment of the criminal purpose." Application of this doctrine will involve lots of tricky judgment calls. A would-be rapist—in the 1966 case of *Le Barron v. State,* 145 N.W.2d 79 (Wis.S.Ct.)—decided to desist when he discovered his victim was pregnant. Are his qualms to be counted as pangs of conscience, or are they more like a burglar's discovery that the contents of the safe are not attractive enough to be worth bothering with? The Nazi plenipotentiary Werner Best first asked for Hitler's permission to round up all Danish Jews, and later on he helped them flee to Sweden when he discovered that the deportations would render Denmark's population so rebellious as to be ungovernable. Is that an abandonment for the "right" kind of reason?

Answering the question whether the motives behind someone's threatened conduct are bad enough to render it a serious wrong (which is what my theory requires for it to be blackmail) seems no harder than determining whether they were too ignoble for his abandonment to count as voluntary.

33. Well, perhaps not quite. There is this minor difference: the sincere robber stood ready to commit a worse act than the sincere blackmailer. The robber, in addition to being guilty of a theft, is also guilty of something akin to an attempted assault, or even attempted murder. The blackmailer, in addition to being guilty of a theft, is guilty only of an attempted noncriminal immorality. And that makes him marginally better.

34. From the vantage point of my proposed solution, it should prove illuminating to look back at other solutions, to see more clearly both why they appealed and why they didn't completely persuade.

We can certainly now better understand both the attractions and the shortcomings of Lindgren's theory of blackmail: the argument that blackmail involves playing with someone else's bargaining chips. For Busybody to actually reveal Philanderer's infidelity to his wife to settle a score with Philanderer is swinish; it uses the wife's feelings as a mere tool to get back at her husband for not paying up. Leveraging the threat to engage in such swinishness into a substantial gain is as blameworthy as the flat-out misappropriation of that gain. What is usually described as playing with someone else's bargaining chips will invariably turn out to involve the threat to commit some such swinishness unless one is paid off, and that sort of leveraging we know to be wrong for the now familiar reasons. It is thus that anything that passes Lindgren's bargaining chip test will turn out to be blackmail. Which explains why Lindgren's test, unlike so many of the others, is not overinclusive.

On the other hand, not all threats to commit some kind of swinishness pass the bargaining chip test. Threatening to encourage someone's son to volunteer for combat duty in Vietnam is an example of one that doesn't. Using that threat for leverage would under my theory be blackmail. Which explains why Lindgren's test is sometimes underinclusive.

The virtues and defects of Feinberg's theory also become more apparent now. To the extent that Feinberg declares proposals that are rooted in the threat of noncriminally wrongful conduct to be blackmail, we are now able to account for that as a straightforward consequence of the fact that blameworthiness is only partially a function of harm. To the extent that Feinberg declares proposals that are rooted in the promise of noncriminally wrongful conduct to be blackmail, we are now able to see where he is correct and where he is not. He is incorrect about such cases as the proposal to carry out a killing-for-hire, because the threatened defendant "misconduct," "retaliatory nonkilling," is not really any kind of misconduct at all. Feinberg is correct about such cases as the proposal to withhold damaging information from the IRS, because a retaliatory reporting of such information to the IRS, that is, the reporting of such information *not to help the government but to settle a score* strikes us as quite immoral—not immoral at the level of criminality or tortiousness but immoral all the same. Leveraging such immoral conduct into a substantial gain then becomes blameworthy at the level of the theft.

Also we can see now why Nozick's test for distinguishing blackmail from other contracts works somewhat but not quite. His test was to ask whether the victim would be better off if the defendant didn't exist. In the case of an ordinary contract, the victim would be sorry not to have the defendant around for a mutually beneficial exchange. In the case of blackmail, he would wish for the defendant not to be around. Nozick's "existence" test is actually a test for whether the defendant is threatening to engage in an act or an omission. The test for distinguishing acts from omissions is this very one: Would the victim have fared any differently if the defendant didn't exist? Because most contracts involve the threat of an omission ("I won't sell you X if you don't pay me Y"), and most immoral conduct involves acts, a test simply distinguishing acts from omissions is a pretty good proxy for figuring out whether we are dealing with blackmail or not.

Epstein's theory deems it crucial that blackmail involves the disclosure of damaging information. Clearly most blackmail, the archtypical kind of blackmail, does involve the threat of embarrassing disclosures. Now we can see why. Most immoral misconduct at the noncriminal level is of an informational nature. If the misconduct is more tangible than that it probably is a crime. If it is less tangible than that it falls below the threshhold of serious immorality.

35. I owe this joke, like 90 percent of my Jewish jokes, to the late Hans Zeisel. For an inventory of the punchlines to the best of Hans's jokes see Harry Kalven, "Hans," *University of Chicago Law Review* 41 (1974): 209, 211–12.

36. Roy Sorensen, *Blindspots,* 251–252. Some of you may be thinking, "Doesn't this have something to do with chaos theory?" Yes, insofar as radical discontinuities are the bread-and-butter of what gets grouped under that heading.

37. Richard Rhodes, *The Making of the Atomic Bomb* (1986), 8 (quoting Emilio Segré).

38. See Michael Thompson, *Rubbish Theory: The Creation and Destruction of Value* (1979).

39. See Leo Katz, *Bad Acts and Guilty Minds* (Chicago: University of Chicago Press, 1987), chap. 3, 292.

40. For especially illuminating discussions of discontinuity in connection with judgments of identity, see part 1 of Robert Nozick's *Philosophical Explanations* (Cambridge, Mass.: Harvard University Press, 1981); and nearly all of Unger's *Identity, Consciousness and Value* (Oxford: Oxford University Press, 1991).

41. Sidney W. DeLong, "Blackmailers, Bribe Takers, and the Second Paradox," *University of Pennsylvania Law Review* 141 (1993): 1663–1693.

42. A more realistic version of this is the journalist who gathers embarrassing information, makes sure the target hears about what he has found, and then, rather than approaching the target with a blackmail proposition, waits for the target to approach him and ask for nonpublication in return for a suitable fee.

43. If you are familiar with Scott Turow's *Presumed Innocent,* you might remember that a Mildred-like trick constitutes a central device. Sandy Stern, the protagonist's defense attorney, puts in place a mechanism whereby the presiding judge's embarrassing past is inevitably going to be revealed as part of his client's defense unless the judge finds a way to dismiss the case. Stern makes clear to the judge the looming danger simply by the direction of his questions to various witnesses, but he never actually threatens the judge, never says, for example, "Dismiss the case or all this bad stuff will come out."

44. *Holmes v. Carey,* 234 F.Supp.23, 24 (N.D.Ga. 1964).

45. Although I first came by the idea of incommensurability by following up on some idea of Nelson Goodman, *The Structure of Appearance,* 3d ed. (Dordrecht: D. Reidel Publishing Co., 1977), chaps. 9 and 10, in fact, incommensurability receives a very explicit and deep discussion in Joseph Raz, *The Morality of Freedom* (Oxford: Clarendon Press, 1986), chap. 13, and in Griffin, *Well-Being,* chap. 5, albeit along somewhat different lines than I give it here.

46. But what about the ordinary consent by which a participant in a boxing match makes what would otherwise be an assault noncriminal? That kind of consent is perfectly

valid, because it is subtly but importantly different from my own special case. In the ordinary case, the victim is consenting to the possibility of being hit at the moment at which the assailant is making the decision to hit him. Not so in my special case. I admit it seems strange that so much of moral significance should turn on so small a distinction. It's just another example of those moral discontinuities I discussed in the section on the "kreplach problem."

47. In criticizing consensual theories of punishment and defending retributivism, Larry Alexander has made precisely this point: "The consensual theory of punishment, though a paradigmatically liberal theory, has implications so draconian that liberals should surely pause before embracing it." Larry Alexander, "Consent, Punishment and Proportionality," *Philosophy and Public Affairs* 15 (1986): 178–182.

48. In discussing waivers of constitutional rights, Seth Kreimer gives a very succinct statement of this point: "Even where there are no effects on third parties, it may be that we have constitutional preferences regarding their distribution of the right in question. If our conception of democracy requires that voting power be distributed equally, or if our view of justice requires that punishment be imposed according to guilt, the opportunity to exchange the power to vote or the freedom from punishment for government favors will result in deviation from those norms. The rights will then be distributed according to which right-holders have particular need of the government favors in question. This will violate the appropriate distribution of the right." See also the articles cited in n.76 of part 3 of Seth Kreimer, "Allocational Sanctions: The Problem of Negative Rights in a Positive State," *University of Pennsylvania Law Review* 132 (1984): 1293, 1390.

PART THREE

1. Richard Holmes, *Acts of War: The Behavior of Men in Battle* (New York: Free Press, 1985), 355.

2. Robert Merton, "The Ambivalence of Scientists," in *Sociological Ambivalence* (New York: Free Press, 1976), 37–38.

3. Mark Kac, *Enigmas of Chance* (Berkeley: University of California Press, 1985), 146.

4. Quoted in Daniel J. Boorstin, *The Discoverers* (New York: Random House, 1983), 244–245.

5. Stefan Zweig, *Amerigo: Die Geschichte eines historischen Irrtums* (Stockholm, 1944).

6. A. J. Ayer, *Parts of My Life: Memoirs of a Philosopher* (New York: Harcourt Brace Jovanovich, 1977), 130.

7. Lee Iacocca, *Iacocca: An Autobiography* (New York: Bantam Books, 1984), 81.

8. Galileo, *The Assayer*, in *Discoveries and Opinions of Galileo*, trans. Stillman Drake (Garden City, N.Y.: Doubleday Anchor Books, 1957), 232–233.

9. Roald Amundsen, *My Life as an Explorer* (Garden City, N.Y.: Doubleday, Dovan, 1928).

10. G. H. Hardy, *A Mathematician's Apology* (Cambridge: Cambridge University Press, 1967 [1940], 153). With a preface by C. P. Snow in 1967 ed.

11. Martin S. Greenberg, "A Theory of Indebtedness," in *Social Exchange,* ed. Kenneth Gergen, Martin S. Greenberg, and Richard H. Willis (New York: Plenum Press, 1980), 3.

12. George Stigler, "The Nature and Role of Originality in Scientific Progress," in *Essays in Economic History* (Chicago: University of Chicago Press, 1965 [1987 Midway reprint]), 14.

13. Adam Smith, *The Theory of Moral Sentiments* [1759]. I am using the Liberty Classics edition (published in Indianapolis, copyrights 1969 and 1976), 209–216.

14. Thomas Powers, *Heisenberg's War* (New York: Alfred A. Knopf, 1993), 479–480.

15. Barbara Tuchman, *The Guns of August* (New York: Macmillan, 1962), 345.

16. I rely for a survey of the discussion on Wolf Schneider, *Die Sieger: Wodurch Genies, Phantasten und Verbrecher beruehmt geworden sind* (Sternbuch, Gruner und Jahr, 1994), 36–37.

17. Michael Bliss, *The Discovery of Insulin* (Toronto: McClelland and Steward, 1982).

18. *R v. Speck,* 2 All ER 859 (Court of Appeal, 1977).

19. Michael Walzer, *Spheres of Justice* (New York: Basic Books (1983), 180.

20. Tom Wolfe, *The Right Stuff* (New York: Farrar, Straus and Giroux, 1979; Bantam Books, 1980), 90–107.

21. See Arthur Koestler, *The Sleepwalkers* (London: Hutchinson, 1959), 119–219; Margolis, *Patterns, Thinking and Cognition,* chaps. 11–13.

22. *Memoirs of Heinrich Schliemann,* ed. Leo Deuel (New York: Harper and Row, 1977). See also C. W. Ceram, *Gods, Graves and Scholars* (New York: Alfred A. Knopf, 1951), 30–47.

23. H. E. LeGrand, *Drifting Continents and Shifting Theories* (Cambridge: Cambridge University Press, 1988).

24. Koestler, *The Sleepwalkers,* 328.

25. Rolf Hochhuth, *Der Stellvertreter* (Rowohlt, 1963), 14.

26. Adam Smith, *The Theory of Moral Sentiments,* 183–186.

27. Wally Herbert, *The Noose of Laurels* (New York: Atheneum, 1989).

28. Harriet Zuckerman, *Scientific Elite: Nobel Laureates in the United States* (New York: Free Press, 1977), 213.

29. Jacques Hadamard, *Psychological Invention in the Mathematical Field* (New York: Dover Publications, 1954), 53–54.

30. Gwyn McFarlane, *Alexander Fleming: The Man and the Myth* (Cambridge, Mass., Harvard University Press, 1984).

31. Robert K. Merton, *On the Shoulders of Giants* (New York: Free Press, 1965).

32. Adam Smith, *Theory of Moral Sentiments,* 194.

33. William Breit and Roger W. Spencer, eds., *Lives of the Laureates: Seven Nobel Economists* (Cambridge, Mass.: MIT Press, 1986), 53–54 (see essay by Kenneth Arrow).

34. Joseph Epstein, *The Middle of My Tether* (New York: W. W. Norton and Co., 1983), 16.

35. Robert Merton, *The Sociology of Science* (Chicago: University of Chicago Press, 1973), 430.

36. William Goldman, *Adventures in the Screen Trade* (New York: Warner Books, 1983), 105.

37. Imre Lakatos, *Proofs and Refutations,* ed. John Worrall and Elie Zahar (Cambridge, Cambridge University Press, 1976), 9 n.1.

38. Albrecht Foelsing, *Galileo Galilei: Prozess ohne Ende* (Muenchen: Piper, 1989), 189–190.

39. *Littlewood's Miscellany,* ed. Ben Bollobas (Cambridge, Cambridge University Press, 1986), 145.

40. D. N. Perkins, *The Mind's Best Work* (Cambridge, Mass.: Harvard University Press, 1981), 10.

41. Id., 14–15.

42. Id., 15–18.

43. *Plutarch's Lives,* trans. John Dryden (New York: Random House, Modern Library, 1220).

44. Ernest Hemingway, *Death in the Afternoon* (New York: Charles Scribner and Sons, 1932), 246.

45. Roland Huntford, *Scott and Amundsen* (New York: G. P. Putnam's Sons, 1980), xii.

46. Margaret Boden, *The Creative Mind: Myths and Mechanisms* (New York: Basic Books, 1990), 104.

47. Jan Snapp, *Where the Truth Lies: Franz Moewus and the Origins of Molecular Biology* (Cambridge: Cambridge University Press, 1990), 103–115. See also Richard Dawkins, *The Blind Watchmaker* (New York: W. W. Norton and Co., 1986), 114–115.

48. Jean Amery, *At the Mind's Limits: Contemplation by a Survivor on Auschwitz and Its Realities,* trans. Sydney Rosenfeld and Stell P. Rosenfeld (Bloomington: Indiana University Press, 1980).

49. I owe this example to Jacqueline Ross.

50. *Wilcox v. Jeffery* [1951] 1 All E.R. 464. Reproduced in Kadish and Schulhofer, *Criminal Law,* 5th ed. (Boston: Little, Brown and Co., 1989), 705–707.

51. Id.

52. Id.

53. *Regina v. Richards,* [1974] Q.B. 776, reproduced in Kadish and Schulhofer, *Criminal Law and Its Processes* (Boston: Little, Brown and Co., 1995).

54. The particular examples are taken from Arthur Danto, *The Transfiguration of the Commonplace* (Cambridge, Mass.: Harvard University Press, 1981).

55. Stefan Zweig, *Tides of Fortune* (New York: Viking Press, 1940), 246.

56. Franz Stuhlhofer, *Lohn und Strafe in der Wissenschaft* (Vienna: Böhlau Verlag, 1987), 190.

57. N. R. Hansen, *Patterns of Discovery: An Inquiry into the Conceptual Foundations of Science* (Cambridge: Cambridge University Press, 1958).

58. Koestler, *The Sleepwalkers,* 166–167.

59. But what if, as seems not unlikely, Copernicus abandoned because he felt coerced by the church? In the analogous case on the blame side—abandoning a crime because the police are around the corner—the defense would not exculpate. It is not clear whether coercion on the praise-side operates in the same way. A failure in courage arguably *should* deprive Copernicus of the glory for his views.

60. Plutarch, 46.

61. Richard A. Gabriel, *No More Heroes: Madness and Psychiatry in War* (New York: Hill and Wang, 1987), 138.

62. Gerard Lynch, "RICO: The Crime of Being a Criminal," *Columbia Law Review* 87 (1987).

63. George Fletcher, *Rethinking Criminal Law,* (Boston: Little, Brown and Co., 1978), 462.

64. Stuhlhofer, *Lohn und Strafe in der Wissenschaft,* 102.

65. Zuckerman, *Scientific Elite,* 210.

66. Lev Kopelev, *To Be Preserved Forever* (Philadelphia: J. B. Lippincott Co., 1977), 260–261.

67. Greenberg, "A Theory of Indebtedness," in *Social Exchange,* ed. Kenneth Gergen, Martin S. Greenberg, and Richard H. Willis, 11.

68. For a classic examination of the arguments for and against plea bargaining, see Albert W. Alschuler, "The Changing Plea-Bargaining Debate," *University of California Law Review* 69 (1981): 652. Second thoughts about settlements (and second thoughts about second thoughts) are the subject of Jules R. Coleman and Charles Silver, "Justice in Settlements," *Social Philosophy and Policy* 4 (1986): 103. Frank Easterbrook takes issue with both pieces in "Justice and Contract in Consent Judgments," *University of Chicago Legal Forum* (1987): 19.

69. *Where the Truth Lies,* 29–30, summarizing A. Brannigan, "The Reification of Gregor Mendel," *Social Studies of Science* 9:432–454.

70. *Heller v. Boylan,* 26 N.Y.S.2d 653 (1941).

71. Karol Soltan, *The Causal Theory of Justice* (Berkeley: University of California, 1987).

72. Id., 113.

73. Id., 190.

74. Paul Samuelson, *Foundations of Economic Analysis* (Cambridge, Mass.: Harvard University Press, 1947), 225.

Index